T0332060

"Capital allocation is not always considered as an equal to business, operational, and people strategies even though it represents at least as much sustained economic opportunity. David Giroux takes his experiences as one of the best investors in the market and converts those insights into a veritable owner's manual to value creation through capital. By doing so, he provides a simple road map for management and boards to test the efficacy of their capital strategies—and deliver best-in-class returns for their stakeholders."

—Jeff Yabuki,
Former CEO, Fiserv, Inc.

"*Capital Allocation* brings new important insights to management teams and boards of directors. A thoroughly researched and insightful book that gives practical frameworks on how a business can navigate making appropriate capital allocation decisions. David Giroux's deep credibility makes this book an invaluable resource."

—Marc N. Casper,
Chairman, President, and CEO, Thermo Fisher Scientific

"David Giroux is an astute investor focused on understanding management's strategic vision and assessing their ability to turn words into action. His deep investment experience, spanning decades of alpha generation, and his passion for rigorous analysis underpin his work. His book provides valuable insights and guidance for both investors and business leaders."

—Dan Glaser,
President and CEO, Marsh McLennan

"David Giroux, a leading portfolio manager with longstanding best-in-class performance, delivers again with an impactful work on capital allocation. By pairing clear concepts and connected real-world case studies, Giroux aims to fill the void that exists between academic theories and business press headlines. He challenges some conventional notions and provides a comprehensive framework for companies and boards to think about capital allocation. All of it, but in particular his chapters on acquisitions, should be required reading for boards, management teams, investment professionals, and students of business."

—Daniel Comas,
Former CFO, Danaher Corporation; Adjunct Professor,
Georgetown University

"Most important decisions boards and CEOs make to deliver long-term value are: right CEO selection and talent, capital allocation, risk management, and ensuring the right culture. This is the best book I have read on all aspects of capital allocation with real-life examples as well as actionable recommendations, including how to measure the impact of decisions. I certainly learned a great deal and highly recommend *Capital Allocation* to both private and public company CEOs and boards."

—Raj Gupta,
Chairman Aptiv PLC and Avantor Inc.; former CEO of
Rohm and Haas Company, and former Board member of
Vanguard Group, DuPont, HP, and Tyco

"One of the leading investors of his generation, David Giroux highlights the critical role of capital allocation to corporate success. His readable and insightful stories about real companies will help you understand why some companies thrive and others falter. This is a high ROI book!"

—William J. Stromberg,
CEO and Chairman, T. Rowe Price

CAPITAL ALLOCATION

CAPITAL ALLOCATION

PRINCIPLES, STRATEGIES, AND
PROCESSES FOR CREATING LONG-TERM
SHAREHOLDER VALUE

DAVID R. GIROUX

CHIEF INVESTMENT OFFICER FOR EQUITY & MULTI-ASSET
T. ROWE PRICE

New York Chicago San Francisco Athens London Madrid
Mexico City Milan New Delhi Singapore Sydney Toronto

2 3 4 5 6 7 8 9   LCR   27 26 25 24

ISBN   978-1-264-27006-4
MHID   1-264-27006-2

e-ISBN   978-1-264-27007-1
e-MHID   1-264-27007-0

This publication is designed to provide accurate and authoritative information in regard to the subject matter covered. It is sold with the understanding that neither the author nor the publisher is engaged in rendering legal, accounting, securities trading, or other professional services. If legal advice or other expert assistance is required, the services of a competent professional person should be sought.
> —*From a Declaration of Principles Jointly Adopted by a Committee of the American Bar Association and a Committee of Publishers and Associations*

Library of Congress Cataloging-in-Publication Data

Names: Giroux, David, author.
Title: Capital allocation / David Giroux.
Description: New York : McGraw Hill Education, [2021] | Includes bibliographical references and index.
Identifiers: LCCN 2021018184 (print) | LCCN 2021018185 (ebook) | ISBN 9781264270064 (hardcover) | ISBN 9781264270071 (ebook)
Subjects: LCSH: Capital investments. | Corporations—Finance. | Corporate divestiture.
Classification: LCC HG4028.C4 G57 2021 (print) | LCC HG4028.C4 (ebook) | DDC 338.4/3—dc23
LC record available at https://lccn.loc.gov/2021018184
LC ebook record available at https://lccn.loc.gov/2021018185

McGraw Hill books are available at special quantity discounts to use as premiums and sales promotions or for use in corporate training programs. To contact a representative, please visit the Contact Us pages at www.mhprofessional.com.

Disclosure: Views expressed are the author's, are subject to change without notice, and may differ from those of other T. Rowe Price associates. Information and opinions are derived from sources deemed reliable; their accuracy is not guaranteed. This material does not constitute a distribution, offer, invitation, recommendation, or solicitation to sell or buy any securities; it does not constitute investment advice and should not be relied upon as such. Investors should seek independent legal and financial advice before making investment decisions. ***Past performance cannot guarantee future results***. All investments involve risk. The charts and tables are shown for illustrative purposes only.

Dedicated to Ann
My wife and best friend

CONTENTS

Acknowledgments ix

CHAPTER 1   The Power of Capital Allocation 1

CHAPTER 2   Capital Allocation in a Slow-Growth World 13

CHAPTER 3   Optimizing the Capital Structure: Advantages of an
             Alternatives-Based Capital Allocation Framework 29

CHAPTER 4   Five Stress Test Rules for Downturns 53

CHAPTER 5   Capital Spending 67

CHAPTER 6   Dividends and the Case for Returning Excess Capital
             to Shareholders 83

CHAPTER 7   The "Regular-Special" Dividend: A New Way to Allocate
             Excess Capital 97

CHAPTER 8   The (Alleged) Seven Deadly Sins of Share Repurchase 115

CHAPTER 9   How Should Management Teams and Boards Think
             About Share Repurchase? 139

CHAPTER 10   AutoZone: The Power of Intelligent Share Repurchase 147

CHAPTER 11   Acquisitions 155

CHAPTER 12   Complex Transactions 181

CHAPTER 13   Superior Businesses with Lower Valuations 191

CHAPTER 14   Private Deals **205**

CHAPTER 15   Distressed Sellers **217**

CHAPTER 16   Non-Core Divestitures **225**

CHAPTER 17   Short-Term Challenges, Long-Term Benefits **235**

CHAPTER 18   The Rise and Fall of the General Electric Empire **259**

CHAPTER 19   Inferior Businesses with Higher Valuations **295**

CHAPTER 20   Low-Return, Strategic Acquisitions: A Cautionary Tale **305**

CHAPTER 21   Supply/Demand Imbalance **319**

CHAPTER 22   Short-Term Plug Deal **341**

CHAPTER 23   Spin-Offs **349**

CHAPTER 24   Restructuring **361**

CHAPTER 25   Secular Challenges **371**

CHAPTER 26   Best Board Practices: The 14-Point Strategic Plan **389**

CHAPTER 27   Capital Allocation: Establishing a Long-Term Focus
               and Good Corporate Citizenship **399**

CHAPTER 28   Conclusions **409**

               Appendix: The 14-Point Strategic Plan Checklist **413**

               List of Abbreviations **415**

               References **417**

               Notes **431**

               Index **447**

ACKNOWLEDGMENTS

I have been interested in capital allocation ever since becoming an industrials analyst in 2000. During my time as an analyst, I saw firsthand the power of capital allocation to create long-term shareholder value—and destroy it. As a portfolio manager since 2006, I attribute much of my long-term success to filling my portfolio with stocks run by management teams and boards that deploy capital exceedingly well.

I started to explore the possibility of writing this book in 2015 during my family's summer vacation. Much of the book outline was put together then. Unfortunately, my job managing the T. Rowe Price Capital Appreciation Fund and being a husband and father meant that I had little time to write it. Running an $80 billion strategy across multiple asset classes with very demanding client objectives is an all-consuming responsibility that has always limited the amount of time I have to pursue personal interests. In the years that followed I would be named one of T. Rowe Price's Chief Investment Officers and its Head of Investment Strategy, which further limited the free time I had.

However, in early 2019, my wife decided she wanted to take our two children to Europe for the first time for an extended vacation. I knew it was now or never for this book and I wrote the majority of it over the course of that summer.

There are a number of people who deserve credit for the book you are about to read.

First and foremost are my wife Ann and two children Katherine and Abigail, who have been very understanding throughout this process even when it meant my limited time with them was curtailed further. Ann, who is my best friend and the best wife imaginable, in particular was very understanding, helpful, and supportive throughout this process. Ann is a distinguished architectural historian and author, and her experience and advice were invaluable.

The first person to read the draft was my good friend Farris Shuggi. Farris's commentary and insights were extremely helpful and pushed me to explore some additional topics that made the book much better.

In addition, my former associate portfolio manager, Steven Krichbaum, was kind enough to read through the manuscript and provide valuable feedback.

My Capital Appreciation teammate Ira Carnahan was the last person to read the manuscript and went through it with a fine-tooth comb. He pointed out areas that might be confusing to the lay reader as well as areas where I needed to support my thesis better. His assistance made this a better book and a much better read.

There were a number of people at T. Rowe Price, who upon finding out that I had written a book, volunteered to provide their considerable expertise in areas where I had no experience. These are people with full-time, important positions in the organization, who took an interest in this project and provided invaluable assistance in areas such as legal, marketing, and public relations. They include Sylvia Toense, Ed Giltenan, and Bill Benintende from public relations and brand management. From legal Swabi Uus and John Zevitas were great resources. In addition, Michelle Renaud, Gavin Daly, Dan Middleton, Chris Dillion, Chris Newman, George Riedel, and Dee Sawyer all helped as well. A special thanks goes to Laura Parsons from the public relations team, who coordinated all of this assistance at T. Rowe Price.

I would also like to thank Eric Veiel, the Director of Equities at T. Rowe Price, who gave me the green light to embark on this project in 2019.

I was very lucky to work with Keri White over much of 2020. Keri is a gifted copy editor who not only improved the book but as a non-finance person, helped make sure this was a book that a non-finance person could read, appreciate, and understand.

Keri also introduced me to Stephanie Scherer in the middle of 2020. Stephanie is a graduate student at the University of Pennsylvania who helped make sure all the citations were done correctly, helped with the editing process, and created the work-cited part of the book. She was an absolute pleasure to work with.

My friend Sebastien Page is the head of T. Rowe Price's Multi-Asset division and someone I worked with very closely when I served as the Co-Chairman of T. Rowe's Asset Allocation Committee. Sebastien, who just published the wonderful book: *Beyond Diversification: What Every Investor Needs to Know About Asset Allocation,* was kind enough to introduce me to Stephen Isaacs at McGraw-Hill.

As this was the first book I had published, I was a little concerned how the process would go once I turned over the manuscript to McGraw-Hill. However, my concerns were misplaced as the team of editors at McGraw-Hill has not only improved the book, but allowed it to remain true to the vision I had back in the summer of 2015. Stephen Isaacs, Judith Newlin, Kevin Commins, Joseph Kurtz, Allison Schwartz, Scott Sewell, and Steve Straus have been a pleasure to work with.

I also want to thank all of the executives who were willing to endorse this book. These individuals either run or serve as board members of large public companies. Not only did they take time to read and review the book, but many provided feedback that strengthened it.

Finally, I want to express a special thanks to my former professor at Hillsdale College, Howard Morris. Howard is a gifted investor who took me under his wing during my last two years in college. He mentored me for the CFA exam, introduced me to Berkshire Hathaway's annual report letters, gave me a job grading tests, and ultimately helped me get a job at T. Rowe Price. Right at the time I was just beginning to learn about investing, his tutelage and encouragement helped spark a love for investing that continues to this day.

CHAPTER 1

The Power of Capital Allocation

O ne of the great mysteries of my 23-year career working in the investing and finance arena is how little time, attention, and focus is directed toward the topic of capital allocation. While there are hundreds, if not thousands, of business books on such wide-ranging topics as marketing, the secrets of managerial success, operational excellence, and how to grow your business, there are few books that address the topic of capital allocation.

Capital allocation warrants far more time and attention than it receives. It rarely makes headlines, except in the case of megamergers. Even in these situations, the media focus is on the size of the newly combined company, how the companies' share prices reacted to the news, and the strategic rationale behind the deal. No one focuses on the anticipated cash-on-cash returns associated with the transaction. No one asks whether this capital deployment was the highest return and best use of capital for long-term shareholders among all the other alternatives. In addition, despite the critical importance of strong board oversight on management teams' capital allocation decisions, there are relatively few capital allocation experts on the boards of directors of the largest publicly traded companies in the United States.

Even the ways in which investors have chosen to define success for capital allocation are fundamentally misguided. Professional investors measure capital allocation success rather crudely. Their assessment is often based on how accretive to earnings per share (EPS) the acquisition, share repurchase program, or internal investment is anticipated to be. For management teams and boards, capital allocation is deemed successful when returns are above the firm's theoretical weighted average cost of capital. Both of these are flawed metrics that fail to take into account the embedded opportunity cost of the capital deployment, or more precisely, how the cash-on-cash returns compare to the various alternatives available to the firm at the time.

One of the challenges associated with capital allocation is that firms have limited resources, so they have to make choices. This book will examine the choices and inherent trade-offs that firms make with regard to the deployment of capital. It is my sincere hope that readers of this book will emerge with a far greater understanding of the following:

- How to analyze the returns associated with capital allocation
- How the right capital allocation decision differs greatly depending on the specific characteristics of a firm
- How to create a framework, strategy, and process that best positions a firm to make intelligent capital allocation decisions to drive long-term shareholder value

Throughout this book, I attempt to shine a bright light on the power and importance of intelligent capital allocation. I explore the stories of firms that have created significant shareholder value through sound capital allocation. I share the untold story of how consistently poor capital allocation led to the titanic fall of General Electric. More importantly, I examine the *processes* these firms used to make their capital allocation decisions. In addition, I summarize the academic evidence on the various alternatives that a firm has for deploying capital, much of which contradicts the prevailing views on the subject. Finally, I promulgate a thesis that management teams and boards of directors should aim to deploy capital toward investments that generate the highest intermediate-term and long-term returns on capital among all the various alternatives they have. Management teams that adopt this guiding framework are likely to create long-term, sustainable shareholder value for their investors.

WHAT IS CAPITAL ALLOCATION?

Capital allocation is defined as the process by which management teams and boards deploy their firm's financial resources both internally and externally. Examples of capital allocation include:

- Building a new plant
- Expanding into a new market or geographic region
- Increasing or decreasing the R&D budget
- Making an acquisition
- Paying a dividend
- Repurchasing shares
- Buying new enterprise software

All of these capital allocation examples involve an outlay of cash or shares (i.e., the investment) and should be expected to generate an attractive return for shareholders on the investment over a reasonable time period.

However, there frequently will be a lag between when the investment is made and when the return is generated. Building a new plant might cost $5 million up front and generate mid-single-digit returns in the first year, high-single-digit returns in year two, and then strong double-digit returns in year three as volumes increase and productivity improves.

The same thing might be true with an acquisition in which returns are modest during the early years of the deal but ramp up in future years as sales grow and margins expand. This lag period between the investment and the return highlights the importance of judging the attractiveness of the investment over the intermediate term.

This leads to an important question: **What is the objective of good capital allocation?**

Unfortunately, the debate surrounding this question often centers around two very different extremes:

1. **Maximize short-term returns.** Maximizing short-term returns can generate higher earnings growth and immediate stock price appreciation. Leveraging up the balance sheet to take on excessive debt to buy back stock or make acquisitions can generate strong earnings accretion in a world of low interest rates, even if the ultimate return on that capital deployed is subpar. Cutting R&D or advertising, excessive head count reductions, or large cuts in capital spending can generate higher free cash flow (FCF) in the short term, but at the expense of long-term returns. There are powerful forces in the equity market (activists, short-term-focused investors) that put pressure on management teams and boards to take such actions.

2. **Be willing to accept low returns.** At the other extreme, some boards and management teams are willing to accept low returns on investments for "strategic" reasons, diversification, or because the company's core business is under pressure.

Both of these extremes are flawed.

In place of these extremes, this book will promulgate a thesis that boards and management teams should strive to deploy capital at the highest possible returns on a risk-adjusted basis to maximize returns for long-term shareholders. Deploying excess capital at attractive rates of returns can create compelling value for long-term investors, even with only modest, GDP-like underlying organic growth.

IMPLICATIONS OF STRUCTURALLY SLOWER GROWTH FOR CAPITAL ALLOCATION

The importance of making sound capital allocation decisions is particularly important in the current economic environment in which a variety of megatrends are creating more excess capital for boards to deploy.

Structurally slower GDP growth has increasingly become a macroeconomic fact of life for much, if not all, of the developed world. In a world of slower growth with much lower interest rates, effective capital allocation has become increasingly critical.

As shown in Table 1.1, for the 17 years between 2001 and 2018, US real GDP grew at around 2%. This is 1.7 points slower than the real GDP growth rate of the preceding 17 years (1983–2000). Contrary to what many politicians on both sides of the aisle might argue, there is nothing nefarious behind these declining growth rates. There are essentially two key drivers of this reduction in economic growth rates:

- Slower population growth
- An aging population that results in a lower percentage of people working

These trends are not unique to the United States; they have resulted in structurally slower growth across Western Europe and Japan as well. In many respects, based on demographics alone, growth rates are more likely to decelerate than accelerate over the next 17 years.

TABLE 1.1

Decelerating Nominal US GDP Growth (compounded annual growth rates)[2]

	Nominal GDP	Real GDP	CPI
1983–2000	6.3%	3.7%	2.6%
2001–2018	4.0%	2.0%	2.0%

At a very basic level, the amount of capital a firm has available to deploy is principally driven by the amount of FCF it produces. FCF is defined as the amount of operating cash flow a firm generates minus its capital spending. There are two cash calls on a firm that typically result in its FCF being less than its net income or profits. The first is capital spending (cash expense), which is typically greater than depreciation (income statement expense). The spread between capital spending and depreciation normally results in FCF that is lower than net income. In addition, as a firm grows, it needs to invest in net working capital (i.e., inventory + receivables − payables) to support this growth. If net working capital equals 20% of sales, the firm will need to invest $0.20 in net working capital to support every $1 of growth.

In a world with nominal GDP growth at 4% or less (like 2001–2018), the amount of capital spending and net working capital investment a firm needs to support its growth is materially less than is required in a world of 6.3% GDP growth (like 1983–2000). Lower levels of capital spending and investment in net working capital result in more FCF in absolute terms and a structurally higher FCF to net income conversion ratio. Essentially, in a slower growth world, firms have significantly more excess FCF to deploy as a percentage of their net income.

This structural trend toward firms having more excess FCF to deploy even after investing to support and grow their businesses is augmented by a variety of other factors:

Embracing Lean Manufacturing

More and more companies across a variety of industries are using lean manufacturing principles to organically create the manufacturing capacity required to support the growth of their businesses. If a widget manufacturer is growing in line with nominal GDP, the company can either spend capital to add a new building and/or production line, or better yet, work to become more efficient within its existing footprint. The latter option would involve improving its manufacturing processes to accommodate growth without the need for additional capital spending, or at a minimum, to grow capital spending at a slower rate than sales growth. This trend puts downward pressure on capital spending and increases the amount of FCF available for capital deployment.

China

One of the reasons that inflation has come down so materially over the last 20 years is that China and many developing nations have effectively exported deflation to the developed world, especially with regard to goods. In most years, the goods component of the consumer price index actually deflates, whereas the service component rises. The combination of these factors has tended to put a lid on inflation in the United States at around 2%[†] and driven even lower levels of inflation in other developed markets. Structurally lower inflation results in lower nominal GDP growth, diminished organic growth for the average firm, and lower required levels of net working capital investments.

Structurally Low Interest Rates

Low interest rates allow firms to safely support more debt in their capital structures without incurring excessive interest expense payments or risking financial ruin in an economic downturn. In an environment of higher inflation and interest rates (like 1983–2000), the optimized level of debt to EBITDA may very well have been 1.5x.

Today, in a world of structurally lower interest rates, the optimized balance sheet might very well be 2–3x debt to EBITDA. The level of debt in a firm's capital structure should be directly related to

---

† The United States is likely to experience higher than trendline inflation in 2021 due to the economic recovery post the COVID pandemic, the Biden administration's large stimulus package, easy inflation comparisons from 2020, and COVID-induced supply chain challenges. However, none of these events are likely to cause a material change in longer-term inflation. Despite higher near-term inflation, long-term interest rates are still well below 2017–2019 levels as of May of 2021. Throughout this book, in all of the various examples and analyses, I assume interest rates rise to levels more consistent with pre-pandemic levels.

the underlying volatility and sustainability of its cash flows in an economic or industry-focused downturn (see Chapter 4). This increased level of debt in a firm's capital structure allows firms to safely add more debt as they grow their EBITDA and provides even more excess capital for management teams and boards to deploy wisely.

All of these megatrends result in management teams and boards having more excess capital left over to deploy, even after investing in their businesses.

NO EASY ANSWERS

There are no easy answers when it comes to capital allocation. If you were expecting me to rank order capital allocation from best to worst in this book, you will surely be disappointed.

There is no silver bullet, no magic pill, but there are many ways to optimize capital allocation. The right framework depends on a variety of factors, including:

- The valuation/multiple of your company's stock
- The valuation/multiple your company pays for acquisitions
- The supply/demand environment for acquisitions within your sector
- The magnitude of the synergies you can extract from an acquisition
- Your company's ability to successfully integrate acquisitions (deliver synergies, not negatively impact culture or the acquirer's top-line growth rate)
- The returns your company can generate from greenfield and brownfield capital spending
- The expectations of investors in the sector for a certain level of dividend payout ratio
- Return potential from modernizing plants and distribution networks and incremental capital spending projects
- The volatility of your firm's cash flows

BOARD COMPOSITION

I reviewed the board composition of the 25 largest publicly traded companies in 2018. The results are displayed in Table 1.2.

Surprisingly, most of the board members from these large firms do not have much experience with capital allocation, nor have they spent a lot of time throughout their careers focused on it. Only about 1 in 7 of the 288 board members examined had been chief financial officers or were professional investors.

While many CEOs will concentrate more on capital allocation decisions after they become CEO, it is generally a new area of focus for them, coming late in their careers. Moreover, their capital allocation vision and expertise were almost never a primary reason they earned the top job. CEOs are typically chosen to run a company based on leadership, operational, manufacturing, and/or marketing skills. Many ran one or more large divisions within the company prior to becoming CEO. However, successfully deploying excess FCF was rarely an important job requirement for the role of CEO.

TABLE 1.2

Level of Capital Allocation Expertise (high to low)[3]

High	CFOs, CEO/CFOs, Investors	15.6%
	CEOs	43.8%
	Divisional Head, Nonprofit CEO, Consultant	25.0%
Low	Government, Academia, Economist, Lawyer, Other	15.6%

Note: CEO/CFOs are former CEOs who were also at one time CFOs.

Boards of directors fulfill many important roles, including serving as advocates for the shareholders who elect them. These roles include:

- Management oversight and selection
- Strategic counsel

- Oversight and auditing of financial statements
- R&D, legal, innovation, tax, and governmental insight

All of these functions are of critical importance. A healthcare company should be expected to have multiple healthcare professionals with deep scientific experience on its board. A defense company is likely to have multiple board members with governmental and geopolitical experience. The board of a technology company is likely to include innovation experts and venture capital investors to make sure the company is constantly aware of new competitive risks and opportunities.

In a world where capital allocation is of increasing importance, I do not necessarily believe the answer is for boards to radically alter their composition by recruiting more CFOs and professional investors.

A far better outcome that balances all of the responsibilities of the board (including capital allocation) would be to simply educate board members about capital allocation theory and enable them to provide more informed counsel on this increasingly important topic.

This is exactly what this book hopes to achieve. The following chapters will focus on the various alternatives for capital allocation: dividends, special dividends, acquisitions, share repurchase, capital spending, spin-offs, and more. In addition, I highlight academic research pertinent to this topic and provide examples of good and bad capital allocation processes.

WORKING WITH IMPERFECT INFORMATION: A DISCLAIMER

When it comes to analyzing capital allocation, especially with regard to mergers, acquisitions, and divestitures, it can be difficult or impossible to access the full spectrum of relevant data. Public companies rarely disclose exactly how an acquisition performed after the fact. Once an acquisition is completed, it is often consumed within an operating segment, which makes it impossible to tell how the business performed relative to the existing business within the segment.

While analysts can monitor the purchase price of most medium-size and large acquisitions and divestitures, many small acquisitions and divestitures are not announced via press releases. When a press release is issued, the purchase price or the sale price is often missing. Even in the statement of cash flows where there is a discrete line for the acquisition cash costs, the amount of debt that may have come along with the acquisition is omitted.

For example, based on everything publicly available about GE's water acquisitions, there were four large acquisitions that totaled an aggregate purchase price of around $3.9 billion, and GE sold these businesses for $3.1 billion in 2017. Did GE make a series of small bolt-on acquisitions in addition to the four large water deals, and should the aggregate purchase price really have been closer to $4.2 billion? Or did GE actually sell down some noncore product lines between 2002 and 2017, resulting in an actual net purchase price (net of divestitures) of $3.7 billion? The truth of the matter is that we don't know for sure.

Retrospective analyses of capital allocation decisions, like those outlined in this book, will never be 100% accurate, because we are working with less than perfect information. However, my calculations are based on thorough research into all publicly available information in order to ensure the highest level of accuracy possible.

In addition, over my 23 years as an associate analyst, investment analyst, portfolio manager, and now chief investment officer and head of investment strategy, I have had thousands of interactions with management teams, and the topic of capital allocation has frequently come up; however, none of my personal discussions with management teams on capital allocation will be reported or cited in this book. All of the analyses and conclusions presented in this book, while informed by my extensive career experience, are my own and informed exclusively by data and statistics accessible to the public and cited throughout the chapters.

CHAPTER 2

Capital Allocation in a Slow-Growth World

I n a world of structurally lower growth rates, capital allocation decisions are particularly vital to generating value for long-term shareholders. In this chapter, I'll demonstrate the practical implications of the lower economic growth and other megatrends described in Chapter 1 and their effects on capital allocation. I'll also examine the importance of developing a sound process in making capital allocation decisions.

Let's look at two companies that grow revenues at nominal GDP. As displayed in Table 2.1, Firm A grows revenues at a level consistent with nominal GDP during the 1983–2000 period, and Firm B grows at a rate consistent with nominal GDP in the 2001–2018 period.

TABLE 2.1

Same Firm, Different Economic Environments

	Firm A	Firm B
	1983–2000	2001–2018
Organic Sales Growth	6.3%	4%
Operating Margin	15%	15%
Capital Spending/Depreciation	1.35	1.15
Working Capital/Sales	20%	20%
Interest Expense (millions)	$250	$250
Sales (millions)	$10,000	$10,000
Dividend Payout Ratio	30%	30%
Use of FCF After Dividend	Buyback	Buyback

The two firms are identical with the exception of the organic growth rates and the ratio of capital spending to depreciation. Tables 2.2, 2.3, and 2.4 demonstrate how these factors impacted the generation of FCF and shareholder returns.

TABLE 2.2

Firm A Growing at Nominal US GDP 1983–2000

	Year 0	Year 1	Growth
Sales	10,000	10,630	6.3%
EBIT	1,500	1,595	6.3%
EBIT Margin	15%	15%	
Interest Exp	(250)	(250)	
Pretax Profit	1,250	1,345	7.6%
Taxes	(313)	(336)	7.6%
Tax Rate	25%	25%	
Net Income	938	1,008	7.6%
Average Shares	100	97	−2.8%
EPS	9.38	10.38	10.7%

(continued)

Firm A Growing at Nominal US GDP 1983–2000 *(continued)*

	Year 0	Year 1	Growth
Net Income		1,008	
Depreciation	400	425	
W/C		−126	
OCF		1,308	
Cap Ex		574	
FCF		734	
FCF/Net Income		72.7%	
Dividends		303	

Note: Rounded all numbers to nearest million.

TABLE 2.3

Firm B Growing at Nominal US GDP 2001–2018

	Year 0	Year 1	Growth
Sales	10,000	10,400	4%
EBIT	1,500	1,560	4%
EBIT Margin	15%	15%	
Interest Exp	(250)	(250)	
Pretax Profit	1,250	1,310	4.8%
Taxes	(313)	(328)	4.8%
Tax Rate	25%	25%	
Net Income	938	983	4.8%
Average Shares	100	96	−3.6%
EPS	9.38	10.19	8.7%
Net Income		983	
Depreciation		416	
W/C		−80	
OCF		1,319	

(continued)

Firm B Growing at Nominal US GDP 2001–2018 *(continued)*

	Year 0	Year 1	Growth
Cap Ex		478	
FCF		840	
FCF/Net Income		85.5%	
Dividends		295	

Note: Rounded all numbers to nearest million.

TABLE 2.4

Sources of Total Shareholder Return (TSR)

	Firm A	Firm B
	1983–2000	2001–2018
Sales	6.3%	4.0%
Leveraging Interest Expense	1.3%	0.8%
Organic EPS Growth	7.6%	4.8%
Benefit from Buyback	3.1%	3.9%
EPS Growth	10.7%	8.7%
Dividend Yield	2.0%	2.0%
Total Shareholder Return Algo	12.7%	10.7%
% of TSR from Organic Growth	59.8%	44.9%
% of TSR from Capital Deployment	40.2%	55.1%

Key Takeaways
- While Firm A grew earnings per share (EPS) at a faster rate than Firm B, Firm A's FCF conversion rate was only 73%, versus 86% for Firm B.
- Firm B generated $106 million more FCF than Firm A, even though it had lower profits.
- Firm B had significantly more excess FCF left over, even after investing in its business.

- For Firm B, a majority of the total shareholder return came from capital deployment (dividends + buybacks), as opposed to only 40% for Firm A.
- In many respects, this is a microcosm of what is happening across the equity markets as firms have more excess capital to deploy in a slower-growth world.

If you were to add in the incremental debt capacity created by the growth in EBITDA for both firms, you will see that Firm B's capital deployment potential is even greater, as demonstrated in Tables 2.5, 2.6, and 2.7.[†]

TABLE 2.5

Firm A Incremental Debt Capacity

	Year 0	Year 1
EBITDA	1,900	2,020
EBITDA Growth		120
Leverage Level		1.5
Incremental Debt Capacity		180

TABLE 2.6

Firm B Incremental Debt Capacity

	Year 0	Year 1
EBITDA	1,900	1,976
EBITDA Growth		76
Leverage Level		3
Incremental Debt Capacity		228

---

† This was a simplistic example to isolate the impact of organic growth, capital spending, and working capital investment on FCF generation and debt capacity. In reality, both firms would not have the same depreciation level from the start, and if firm A was truly operating in the 1983–2000 era its interest expense would be higher, reflecting higher interest rates at the time. However, changing those assumptions would not change the outcome materially.

TABLE 2.7

Total Deployable Capital

	Firm A	Firm B
FCF	734	840
Incremental Debt Capacity	180	228
Total Capital to Deploy	914	1,068
Dividends	303	295
Total Capital to Deploy After Dividends	611	773

This example uses the repurchase of stock and paying dividends. However, the math is similar when excess FCF is deployed on acquisitions, additional capital spending, dividends, or special dividends, assuming they generated similar cash-on-cash returns.

This highlights the increasing importance of good capital allocation in a world with structurally slower growth rates.

THE POWER OF RETURNS

Now that I have demonstrated that mature firms have more FCF to deploy than in the past and that capital allocation is an increasingly important driver of total shareholder returns, let's focus our attention on the importance of generating attractive returns on capital deployment.

Table 2.8 quantifies and contrasts the impact on earnings per share (EPS) growth rates for capital that is deployed wisely versus poorly for a company with similar organic operating fundamentals.

TABLE 2.8

With Organic Profit Growth of 4%, What Is EPS Growth Potential?

Returns on Excess Capital		FCF Conversion		
Year 1	Year 5	60%	85%	100%
0%	−4%	2.3%	1.3%	0.8%
0%	0%	4.0%	4.0%	4.0%
0%	4%	5.7%	6.5%	7.0%
2%	6%	6.5%	7.7%	8.4%
3%	7%	6.9%	8.3%	9.2%
4%	8%	7.3%	8.9%	9.9%
5%	10%	8.1%	10.1%	11.2%
6%	12%	8.9%	11.3%	12.7%
7%	15%	10.1%	12.9%	14.5%

This example utilizes a mature company that is able to grow its profits organically by 4% per year and has to spend 10% of its FCF to offset employee stock grants to hold its share count flat. This company does not pay dividends.

This table also illustrates the importance of FCF. A firm that can convert its profits into high-quality FCF will have more capital to deploy and therefore a faster growth rate in EPS, all else being equal.

The compounding power of generating strong returns on excess capital and a strong FCF conversion rate (FCF divided by net income) cannot be overstated.

A company that grows its profits at 4% organically but is able to earn 10% returns on excess capital deployment by year five and convert 100% of its net income into high-quality FCF can grow EPS at an impressive 11.2% per year. Another company with a similar organic growth profile that is only able to generate 6% returns on excess capital deployment and converts its net income into FCF at a 60% conversion rate will only grow at 6.5% per year.

To illustrate the compounding effect of these deltas, let's look at three companies with $5 billion in profits and $75 billion market capitalizations with the same organic profit growth, shown in Table 2.9 and Figures 2.1, 2.2, and 2.3.

- Company One converts net income into FCF at a 60% rate and achieves 6% ROIC on its excess capital by year five.
- Company Two converts net income into FCF at an 85% rate and achieves an 8% ROIC on its excess capital by year five.
- Company Three converts at a 100% level and achieves a 10% ROIC on its excess capital by year five.

TABLE 2.9

FCF Conversions Rates and Returns on Excess Capital

	FCF Conversion	Year 5 Return on Excess Capital	Description
Company One	60%	6%	Poor returns/FCF conversion
Company Two	85%	8%	Average returns/FCF conversion
Company Three	100%	10%	Strong returns/FCF conversion

FIGURE 2.1

Net Income in Year 10

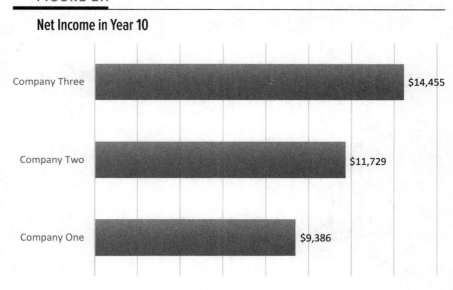

FIGURE 2.2

Cumulative 10-Year FCF Generation

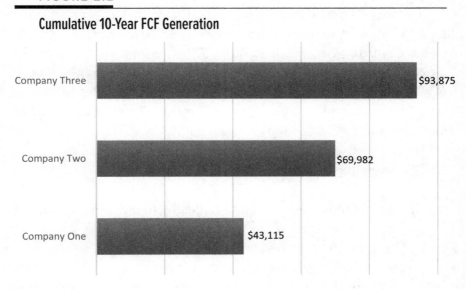

FIGURE 2.3

Anticipated Year 10 Market Capitalization

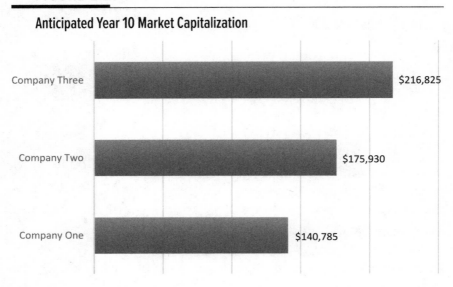

Company Three (Strong Returns/FCF Conversion) is able to create $76 billion in additional shareholder wealth over a decade relative to the Company One (Poor Returns/FCF Conversion), even though its core underlying profit growth is exactly the same: In addition, this likely understates the level of incremental shareholder value creation. Investors are likely to award Company Three with a higher valuation multiple reflecting its faster EPS growth trajectory and its strong FCF conversion ratio.

These examples demonstrate:

1. There is more excess capital to deploy today in a structurally slower growth world.
2. For many mature companies, the returns they are able to generate on the deployment of excess capital can be an important source of differentiation in EPS growth rates and total shareholder returns.

3. Increasing the FCF conversion rate of a firm has the potential to increase its EPS growth rate and improve total shareholder returns.
4. Capital allocation is one of the most important responsibilities of a management team and a board of directors.

THE IMPORTANCE OF PROCESS

We live in a world that is almost completely fixated on outcomes over process. We all unconsciously exercise hindsight bias. The quality of the decisions we make in life, in business, or investing are too often defined by the outcome as opposed to the quality of the decision-making process.

Imagine it is the bottom of the ninth inning in game seven of the World Series. The game is tied with the bases loaded and two outs. Next up for the home team is the pitcher and, not surprisingly, the manager decides to bring in a pinch hitter. All they need is someone to reach first base via a hit, walk, or being hit by a pitch.

The manager is faced with a seemingly difficult decision. He has two possible pinch hitters left on his bench. The first is a 35-year-old veteran first baseman who has played in multiple playoff games throughout his career. The second is a 24-year-old outfielder who has no playoff experience besides this year. The manager taps the 35-year-old veteran. On the second pitch, the veteran hits a walk-off home run into the left field bleachers and wins the World Series for his team.

The manager is a hero and is celebrated in the press for his astute decision to send up the experienced veteran who came through in the clutch. In playoff baseball, experience matters, and the home run proved it.

But was it really the right decision?

- What if I told you the veteran first baseman had an on-base average of only .290 during the year?

- What if I told you the young outfielder had an on-base average of .360 during the year?
- What if I told you that playoff experience does not matter?

According to renowned baseball expert Russell A. Carleton:

There is no evidence that postseason experience (and I attempted five different definitions of "experience") has any effect on players in the postseason over and above their previously established talent levels. The idea that postseason experience confers some sort of advantage on a player or team is not supported by the data.[1]

While the outcome of the decision to pinch-hit the veteran was great, the decision and the thought process behind the decision were flawed. By choosing the veteran over the younger player, the manager reduced the chance that his team would win the game. Essentially, the manager got lucky and this overcame a poor decision. However, if you run this scenario 100 times or 1,000 times, the element of luck vanishes, and the expected outcome and the actual outcome converge. A manager who systematically makes decisions like this over the course of his career will cost his team runs, wins, and maybe even a championship.

The same outcome bias seen in sports is also prevalent with regard to capital allocation.

Newspaper articles written during and after the Great Financial Crisis (GFC) criticized companies that bought back stock in 2006 and 2007 at prices well below where they were trading in 2008–2009. Two informative examples include Floyd Norris's and John Waggoner's comments in articles published, respectively, in the *New York Times* and *USA Today*:

Home Depot spent more than $10 billion in the third quarter of 2007 buying back stock. That buying might have slowed the drop in its stock price as the housing market collapsed, but the result was that the company spent an average price *of $37 a share. Early this year, when Home Depot was no longer a buyer, the price fell to under $18.*[2]

You would think that a corporation would know when its stock was a real value, and therefore worth buying. You'd be wrong. For example, General Electric bought 160.4 million shares of its own stock in the third quarter of 2007 at an average price of $39.40 a share, according to InsiderScore. GE closed Thursday at $22.28 a share.[3]

However, this hindsight bias ignores the potential outcomes of alternative uses of capital. If these companies had built a new plant or made an acquisition in 2006 or 2007 instead of buying back stock, would the results have been any better? Given the decline in aggregate demand during the global recession, it is exceedingly likely that the new plant would not have been needed from a capacity standpoint and its returns on capital would have been very poor. Numerous acquisitions executed during 2006–2007 also generated subpar returns on capital as the cash flows from many of those businesses declined materially during the crisis.

This hindsight bias also fails to reflect the fact that a financial crisis and a recession of the magnitude of the GFC tend to be quite rare. Low probability, low frequency events like a financial crisis should not be (and were not at the time) a reasonable baseline economic assumption on which to judge the quality of a capital allocation decision. Many, but not all, of the companies that deployed capital in 2006–2007 were partially unlucky from a timing perspective as a low probability event played out. The only sound capital allocation decision from a purely outcome perspective was to do nothing.

GILEAD BUYS PHARMASSET

Within the pharmaceutical space, this same outcome bias presents itself in the case of Gilead Science's 2012 acquisition of Pharmasset, Inc. (VRUS).

This is generally viewed as one of the best pharmaceutical acquisitions in recent history. Gilead paid $11 billion for VRUS. At the time, VRUS had three phase 3 trials underway for a drug that could potentially cure hepatitis C; the drug had already performed well in earlier phase 2 trials. By 2015, Gilead was generating more than $19 billion in sales annually from this drug as it was able to enjoy monopoly pricing power with a stunning price tag of $1,000 per pill. At its peak, before new competition entered the hepatitis C space, Gilead was likely generating close to a 100% return on capital from its acquisition of VRUS.[4] This was an amazing outcome in an industry where many acquisitions are value destructive.

While the outcome was great, was it a good capital allocation decision from a process standpoint? Let's look at the facts:

First, Gilead paid an 89% premium to acquire VRUS. With a premium of that magnitude, it made a big bet that a reasonably efficient stock market was dramatically undervaluing VRUS.

Second, while the phase 2 data at the time looked good, there are hundreds, if not thousands of examples within the pharmaceutical industry in which drugs appear efficacious in smaller phase 2 studies only to fail later in larger phase 3 studies. There was no guarantee this drug would work.

Third, VRUS had multiple competitors also working on drugs to cure hepatitis C. Bristol-Myers announced the acquisition of Inhibitex for $2.5 billion in January of 2012. Inhibitex's lead drug, INX-189, was also focused on curing hepatitis C.

However, in August of 2012, Bristol announced it was suspending its hepatitis C drug program due to cardiovascular side effects. This news came out after Gilead had already agreed to purchase VRUS. This failure assured Gilead that it would have a monopoly on the hepatitis C market for a period of time, assuming the VRUS drug actually worked.

This new monopoly status for the VRUS drug would enable it to command a much higher market share and a much higher price. When competition did emerge a few years later, Gilead's pricing on the drug and market share both declined materially.

Fourth, over time, large pharmaceutical companies have struggled to replenish their revenues and pipelines organically as their drugs face patent cliffs. This has led to a situation in which small and mid-cap biotech companies with promising drugs are often acquired for large premiums to their market capitalization. The fact that four other pharmaceutical companies that were invited to bid on VRUS were all unwilling to pay $11 billion for it suggests that they thought VRUS was worth less, as did investors at the time.

While the acquisition outcome created significant near-term shareholder wealth, it is far less clear whether it was a great decision from a process standpoint. If you went back in time and looked at every acquisition in the history of the pharmaceutical industry in which the acquirer paid a significant premium to its public market value, there were multiple bidders for the asset, phase 3 data was not yet available, and a competitive product was likely coming to market as well, the odds of creating significant shareholder value would likely be quite low.

Like the baseball manager who tapped the veteran to pinch-hit, luck most likely compensated for a poor decision.

STRONG OUTCOME, WEAK PROCESS

Focus on sustainable, repeatable processes. It would be very easy for me to fill this book with examples of acquisitions that have created significant shareholder value. The problem is that in many of those cases, like GILD/VRUS, luck may have played a key role in the success of the acquisition.

You cannot learn from luck. Trying to learn from luck leads to flawed processes and bad outcomes that will outnumber good outcomes.

The baseball manager who watches the opposing manager send up the veteran with two outs and internalizes the outcome becomes a worse manager over time. The pharmaceutical CEO who is now more willing to pay an 89% premium to the market price for an acquisition as a result of what happened to Gilead's stock is far more likely to destroy shareholder value.

Throughout this book, I will focus on capital allocation process as opposed to outcomes in evaluating acquisitions, share repurchase, capital spending programs, and dividends. I examine the facts and circumstances surrounding the capital allocation decisions at the time they were made. This analysis demonstrates that a disciplined, strategic capital allocation process will create a high percentage of good outcomes. Hindsight bias will find no home in these pages.

Optimizing the Capital Structure: Advantages of an Alternatives-Based Capital Allocation Framework

Before delving into the pros and cons of the various capital allocation options available to a firm, it is essential to first explore the question of how to optimize a firm's capital structure. A capital structure refers to the mix of equity and debt that is used to finance the enterprise. This process also plays an important part in determining how much actual capital the firm has to deploy on an annual basis. Optimizing a firm's capital structure is critical to balancing growth and returns with risk and volatility of cash flow.

There is a group of firms that will likely not benefit from this chapter. In many regulated industries, the entities responsible for providing oversight often set limits on leverage.

- **Regulated utilities.** As part of its rate-making process, the state utility commission will set a predetermined equity level that is usually around 50% of total book capital.
- **Regulated financials.** The same holds true for many balance-sheet-intensive financials such as banks, investment banks, and insurance companies. These firms' regulators all use complex risk-based capital metrics to calculate the minimum levels of equity that a firm needs to maintain. In addition, since the Great Financial Crisis (GFC), large banks and investment banks have been required to undergo extensive annual stress test examinations to make sure that they maintain a minimum level of equity and would remain solvent if another GFC-like event were to occur.

There is also a group of firms in which the decision concerning the balance sheet is fairly obvious.

- **Small firms that are bleeding cash.** A venture-backed startup firm or an emerging biotech company that is bleeding cash would almost surely look to fund itself with equity as opposed to debt, especially as the cost of the debt would be very high given the risk inherent in the business. Many of these firms measure their monthly or quarterly cash burn rate and are continually raising additional equity to offset it.
- **Balance sheet strength is central to the customer decision-making process.** If a customer is making a long-term commitment to a small firm with an outsourcing contract or critical software application, she might take into consideration the strength of the firm's balance sheet as a sign that the firm will be around for the long term to fulfill the contract's obligations.

However, for the vast majority of publicly traded firms that generate positive FCF, and especially for more mature businesses, identifying the optimal capital structure is a very worthwhile exercise.

If you were to ask the CFO of most publicly traded companies about the firm's capital structure, she would almost surely tell you they set up the capital structure to achieve the optimal weighted average cost of capital (WACC).

In almost all cases, this is the wrong answer.

Finance theory suggests that the WACC is calculated by looking at the mix of a firm's cost of equity capital and its after-tax cost of debt capital. A firm with a 50/50 equity and debt split with a 9% cost of equity and 4% after-tax cost of debt would have a 6.5% WACC. The mix of equity and debt that goes into the calculation is typically based on the market-derived trading value of a firm's stock and debt. While calculating the after-tax cost of debt is fairly simple, determining the cost of equity involves calculating the risk-free rate (three-month Treasury bills), beta, and the expected market return. An investor should theoretically demand a higher return (and thus a higher cost of equity capital) for a higher beta stock than for a lower beta stock.

PROBLEMS WITH WACC

The idea is that firms create value by making investments that generate returns above their cost of capital (WACC). The greater the spread between returns and a firm's WACC, the greater the economic value creation. Thus, achieving the lowest WACC seems like a sound objective. This all seems very logical, right?

However, there are numerous problems with WACC that render it less than useful:

Problem 1: Optimizing the WACC Is Not Paramount

In the developed world, where the after-tax cost of debt capital is quite low, one could make the argument that firms should have materially more debt in their capital structures if the minimization of their WACC were their sole objective.

The challenge with this objective is that it could put the firm and its long-term shareholders at risk during an economic or industry-specific downturn. Minimizing WACC might be the right decision 80–90% of the time, but having too much debt the other 10–20% of the time can be value destructive for long-term shareholders. Having too much debt in the capital structure at the wrong point in the cycle can lead to dividend cuts, expensive debt financing, dilutive equity raises, reducing internal investments to maximize cash generation, and in a worst-case scenario, bankruptcy.

The mix of equity and debt capital should be optimized not to minimize the WACC, but to a level that balances long-term growth rates of FCF and protects the firm and its long-term shareholders during periods of economic stress.

Problem 2: WACC Ignores the True Cost of Equity Capital

Shouldn't the valuation of a company's shares be an important input in determining an economic cost of equity? Shouldn't a firm be more willing to issue shares at an elevated valuation than a cheap valuation?

If my firm is going to purchase a manufacturing facility by raising additional equity and debt, the valuation multiple of that equity (and the interest rate on debt) play an important role in determining how much value I will create for my existing shareholders. While this makes intuitive sense, looking at this purely through a WACC lens could lead to value-destructive conclusions.

A very simple one-year forward model proves this point. In this example, let's assume that a firm decides to purchase a manufacturing facility for $200 million and that it expects to generate a year one 6.5% return on capital from it. What are the implications if the shares it issues are trading at 10x FCF or 20x FCF multiple, as shown in Table 3.1?

From a WACC perspective, almost paradoxically, when the shares are trading at 10x FCF, the firm's cost of capital might be lower because the market-derived mix of equity becomes a smaller part of the capital structure.

TABLE 3.1

Firm Purchases Plant for $200 Million and Expects Year One Return of 6.5%

	Balance Sheet	10x FCF	20x FCF
Shareholder Equity	$500	$750	$1,500
Debt	$500	$500	$500
Market Value of Equity/ Book Value of Equity		1.5	3
Mix of Equity	50%	60%	75%
Mix of Debt	50%	40%	25%
Cost of Equity		8%	8%
Cost of Debt		3%	3%
WACC		6.00%	6.75%

In looking through a purely WACC lens, the company should issue shares and debt to fund the purchase of the facility when its shares are trading at 10x FCF (6.5% return vs. 6% WACC), but not when its shares are trading at 20x FCF (6.5% return vs. 6.75% WACC). The lower the valuation placed on the shares by the market, under a WACC framework, the more willing a company should be to issue them. This does not make sense.

However, from a shareholder perspective, as demonstrated in Tables 3.2 and 3.3, issuing shares and debt to pay for the facility when its shares are trading at 10x FCF is value destructive, and issuing shares and debt to pay for the facility when its shares are trading at 20x is value accretive.

TABLE 3.2

Issuing Equity at 10x FCF and Debt at 3% to Purchase the Facility

Firm Before Facility + Equity Offering	
FCF	100
Shares Outstanding	10
FCF/Share	$10.00
Issue 1.2 million Shares at 10x FCF	
New Share Count	11.2
Existing FCF	100
Issue $80 million of Debt at 3%	−2.4
FCF from Facility	13
New FCF	110.6
FCF/Share	$9.88
Change in FCF/Share	−1.3%

TABLE 3.3

Issuing Equity at 20x FCF to Purchase the Facility

Firm Before Facility + Equity Offering	
FCF	100
Shares Outstanding	10
FCF/Share	$10.00
Issue 750k Shares at 20x FCF	
New Share Count	10.75
Existing FCF	100
Issue $50 million of Debt at 3%	−1.5
FCF from Facility	13
New FCF	111.5
FCF/Share	$10.37
Change in FCF/Share	3.7%

Remember, under a WACC cost of equity framework, it is the beta of the stock that differentiates one firm's cost of equity from another firm's rather than its growth prospects or valuation multiple. Most of us would naturally assume that a company trading at a higher valuation with a better business model and stronger growth would have a lower cost of capital—but that often is not the case with WACC. As we will see later in this chapter, some of the highest-valued companies in the stock market with the best growth prospects and strongest balance sheets have some of the highest WACC-derived costs of capital, even though their true economic cost of capital is quite low.

In addition, while the beta of a company's stock tends not to move that much over the course of a year (beta is typically calculated looking at the stock's relative volatility over the last five years), the valuation multiple awarded to the company can vary dramatically based on near-term fundamentals and market sentiment. A company could easily to trade between 13x and 17x forward FCF over the course of a year even if its underlying beta does not change materially. A company's decision whether to issue equity to fund an acquisition or capital investment should be heavily influenced by how cheaply or expensively its shares are being valued by a rather fickle and manic equity market. Issuing shares to fund an investment when shares are cheap (13x) may be value destructive to existing shareholders, while issuing shares when they are expensive (17x) may be value accretive. A WACC-based cost of equity ignores this important reality.

In reality, the true economic cost of incremental equity capital is the inverse of the firm's forward FCF yield and the organic growth of that FCF.

Table 3.4 highlights a firm's economic cost of equity at different points in time and at different valuation levels. In reality, a firm trading for 33x FCF would likely have a materially faster growth rate than a firm trading at 10x FCF, and the economic cost of equity spread between these firms would compress over time.

TABLE 3.4

Calculating a Firm's True Economic Cost of Incremental Equity Capital

Forward FCF Yield on Firm's Equity	Year 1	Year 2	Year 3	Year 4	Year 5
3% (33x FCF)	3%	3.1%	3.2%	3.4%	3.5%
5% (20x FCF)	5%	5.2%	5.4%	5.6%	5.8%
7% (14.3x FCF)	7%	7.3%	7.6%	7.9%	8.2%
10% (10x FCF)	10%	10.4%	10.8%	11.2%	11.7%

Note: Assumes 4% growth rate in organic FCF.

Another way to conceptualize this framework is to examine a firm that is trading at 20x forward FCF. If this firm chooses to repurchase its shares, it can expect to generate a 5% return in year one and a 5.8% return in year five for its remaining shareholders, who now own a slightly larger piece of the enterprise. If, instead, the company sold additional shares to fund an investment, in order to create value, the firm would need to be able to reinvest the proceeds at a higher rate than 5% in year one and 5.8% in year five. In this latter scenario, the shareholders are essentially diluting their interest in the cash flows of the existing enterprise for a share of the future cash flows from the investment.

In other words, if I had to dilute my existing shareholders by issuing additional equity, would the cash-on-cash returns from the investment be superior to the cash-on-cash returns of buying back those shares, or would I be better served by simply holding onto those shares and forgoing the investment?

Now let's alter our example to highlight this concept of the true economic cost of incremental equity capital to remove any debt from the capital structure of our company. In addition, let's increase the expected return from 6.5% to 8.5% in year one and look at this from the perspective of the return on capital and economic cost of equity.

FIGURE 3.1

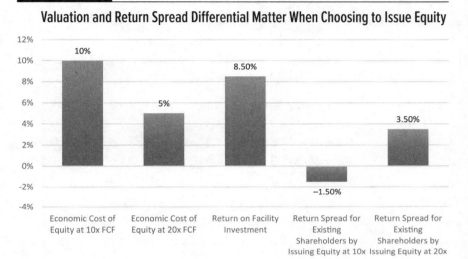

Valuation and Return Spread Differential Matter When Choosing to Issue Equity

In this example, for simplicity's sake, the returns from the investment, the cost of equity, and the return spread differential were examined on a one-year forward basis. However, the return characteristics of investments and the cost of equity should be examined more on an intermediate-term basis (over four to six years) as opposed to on a short-term basis. This more fully takes into account the return potential from the investment as well as the intermediate-term economic cost of equity issuance.

Let's assume that the purchase of the facility generates a 10% return on capital employed in year five, as shown in Tables 3.5 and 3.6. We can then determine where the transaction would be value accretive to existing shareholders by looking at the current valuation of the firm and its expected organic FCF growth rate.

TABLE 3.5

Year Five Economic Cost of Equity Capital

		Organic growth in FCF				
		2%	4%	6%	8%	10%
Forward	10x FCF	10.8%	11.7%	12.6%	13.6%	14.6%
Year FCF	12x FCF	9.0%	9.7%	10.5%	11.3%	12.2%
Multiple	14x FCF	7.7%	8.4%	9.0%	9.7%	10.5%
	16x FCF	6.8%	7.3%	7.9%	8.5%	9.2%
	18x FCF	6.0%	6.5%	7.0%	7.6%	8.1%
	20x FCF	5.4%	5.8%	6.3%	6.8%	7.3%

TABLE 3.6

Year Five Return Spread

		Organic growth in FCF				
		2%	4%	6%	8%	10%
Forward	10x FCF	−0.8%	−1.7%	−2.6%	−3.6%	−4.6%
Year FCF	12x FCF	**1.0%**	**0.3%**	−0.5%	−1.3%	−2.2%
Multiple	14x FCF	**2.3%**	**1.6%**	**1.0%**	**0.3%**	−0.5%
	16x FCF	**3.2%**	**2.7%**	**2.1%**	**1.5%**	**0.8%**
	18x FCF	**4.0%**	**3.5%**	**3.0%**	**2.4%**	**1.9%**
	20x FCF	**4.6%**	**4.2%**	**3.7%**	**3.2%**	**2.7%**

Note: This spread is the difference between the expected 10% return on the investment in year five and a firm's true economic cost of equity capital as shown in Table 3.5. A positive spread (bolded) implies value accretion for existing shareholders, whereas a negative spread implies value destruction for existing shareholders.

Issuing equity between 16 and 20x forward FCF would be value accretive to existing shareholders in this example, whereas issuing shares at 10x forward FCF would be value destructive. The decision to issue shares between 12 and 14x forward free cash flow would depend heavily on the expected organic growth rate in the firm's existing FCF over the next five years.

Problem 3: Do Investors Really Demand Higher Returns for Higher Risk?

The reality of the last 50 years is that investors have not been compensated with higher returns for taking on additional risk within equities.[1] Low beta stocks have systematically outperformed high beta stocks. This is not consistent with financial theory. There are numerous possible explanations for this inconsistency, including the secular decline in interest rates that has increased demand for lower volatility, higher dividend stocks.

However, I believe the most important reasons are that most investors systematically:

- Overestimate growth rates for higher-risk or higher-beta companies
- Undervalue the attractiveness of steadier, low-risk firms
- Undervalue the predictability and stability of the portion of total shareholder return (TSR) that comes from dividends relative to stock price appreciation
- Paradoxically favor volatility, as many portfolio managers are compensated on absolute returns as opposed to risk-adjusted returns and, in theory, highly volatile stocks have more upside optionality in the short term

Highly volatile stocks can act like lottery tickets. At an individual stock level, they offer the potential and promise for significant upside, but investing in a broad portfolio of high-volatility stocks is value destructive over time, especially on a risk-adjusted basis.

The point here is not to settle this argument, but to demonstrate that the last 50 years of financial reality are inconsistent with a central tenet of the WACC calculation.

Problem 4: WACC Ignores Opportunity Cost of Capital

In my 20-plus years of investing, I have never attempted to calculate a cost of equity or WACC for any company that I have invested in, and I don't plan to start. A firm's weighted average cost of capital is not only difficult to calculate accurately, but from a capital allocation perspective, it is irrelevant.

What really matters is the opportunity cost of capital!

An intelligent management team and board should not look at a single capital allocation decision in isolation. For example, if you make an acquisition, you can expect to generate a 7% return on capital, and that is above our 6% cost of capital.

In many ways, the cost of capital calculation has become a crutch that management teams and boards can lean on while they claim to create shareholder value by delivering returns above this threshold. However, what if there are multiple options for deploying capital that can generate returns greater than the isolated option they have chosen to pursue?

A management team should examine the returns on all the various capital allocation alternatives available relative to the return the firm is expected to generate on any one specific capital allocation option. These alternatives may include internal investment, share repurchase, dividends, acquisitions, and special dividends.

Let's return to our example of the firm that is exploring an acquisition with a 7% expected return in year five and a theoretical cost of capital of 6%, shown in Table 3.7.

In this case, there are three options for deploying capital that generate returns greater than the firm's cost of capital by year five and one option (share repurchase) that generates higher returns than the firm's cost of capital in the very first year.

Instead of focusing on some flawed theoretical cost of capital calculation, a firm should examine all of the various capital allocation alternatives and choose the one—or more accurately the mix—that generates the highest cash-on-cash returns for shareholders. A firm that embarks on this strategy is far more likely to systematically deploy capital with attractive returns.

TABLE 3.7

Capital Allocation Alternatives: Cash-on-Cash Returns

	Year 1	Year 2	Year 3	Year 4	Year 5
Acquisition	4.5%	5.5%	6.2%	6.7%	7.0%
Alternatives to Acquisition					
Internal Investments	5.0%	5.5%	6.1%	6.7%	7.3%
Share Repurchase	7.0%	7.4%	7.7%	8.1%	8.5%
Dividends/Special Dividends	5.0%	5.2%	5.4%	5.6%	5.8%

Throughout this book, I will provide you with the tools and framework for estimating the returns on growth capital spending and acquisitions, as well as the less intuitive returns from buying back shares or paying regular dividends or special dividends. In addition, I have already highlighted a way to determine the economic cost of equity for firms that may use equity financing to fund their capital deployment.

This makes the cost of capital analysis far less irrelevant. If a company is generating excess capital, it needs to do something with that capital or risk diluting returns. This is not to suggest that a firm needs to deploy 100% of its excess capital immediately. However, over an intermediate-term period, a firm should not systematically hold a significant amount of excess capital. This is especially true for a more mature firm.

Looking at the world through a WACC lens, a firm should return excess capital to shareholders once all of the investments the firm can make above the firm's WACC have been exhausted. The far superior alternatives-based approach allows for the possibility that returning capital to shareholders may produce the best returns, as opposed to being the default option only after all internal investments have been prioritized. This approach also allows for the possibility that internal investments that don't meet a flawed theoretical cost of capital threshold should be funded as long as the returns are greater than the returns from returning capital to shareholders.

A Real-Life Example: Tesla

To provide a more real-life example here, think about a high growth and highly valued company like Tesla. Given the high beta nature of its stock and its almost exclusive equity-based capital structure (98.1% on market-derived-basis), its theoretical cost of capital was 13.7% as of March 5, 2021, according to Bloomberg. In fact, its Bloomberg-derived cost of capital has more than doubled since the end of 2019 when it was only around 6%.

However, the auto business is a very capital-intensive business that typically does not produce strong FCF returns on capital. It is possible that Tesla's cash-on-cash returns from making additional investments could fall below its more recent, elevated cost of capital.

If the board were strictly focused on making investments that generated returns above its new materially higher cost of capital, Tesla would stop building new plants and start paying dividends to shareholders or even worse start buying back shares. But that would be a disastrous decision for Tesla and its board. Its market capitalization would likely drop by hundreds of billions of dollars, as its shareholders would react very poorly as they are clearly focused on growth above all else.

Instead, Tesla and its board have correctly taken advantage of a highly valued share price to issue shares to fund growth at an extremely low near-to-intermediate-term true incremental cost of equity capital. This dynamic is in no way unique to Tesla. Many higher-valued and higher beta companies with equity-heavy capital structures will have a massive spread between their theoretical cost of capital and their true incremental cost of equity capital even looking out five or more years.

Take a software company growing 12% per year and trading for 35x FCF. Like most software companies, it has cash and no debt on its balance sheet. Given the short-term investment time horizon of its investor base and the high volatility of technology stocks, it is quite possible this firm might have an elevated beta and a cost of capital of 12%. That is despite the fact that its underlying business is far less volatile than the overall market, with a high level of recurring revenue growth and a rock-solid balance sheet.

Assume the management team brings the board of directors a proposal to acquire a smaller software company with an adjacent software offering. Both firms are expected to grow 12% per year. After taking into account the synergies, the firm can buy the smaller firm for only 30x FCF.

From an economic perspective, this makes a lot of sense. The company will issue shares to acquire this firm at a lower valuation than its own and, in the process, increase the FCF per share for existing shareholders without sacrificing the growth rate of the firm. In addition, strategically it allows the firm to enter an attractive adjacency. However, looking at this through a WACC lens, the return on this acquisition in year 1 will only be 3.3% relative to the firm's 12% cost of capital. The acquiring firm will not generate a return above its cost of capital until year 13, even assuming the 12% growth rate is sustainable for that many years. Yet, the board should still clearly approve the deal given the cash flow accretion and strategic benefits even though the deal looks horrible through a WACC lens.

Given the numerous challenges with the WACC calculation, the alternatives-based approach for deploying excess capital is a far more logical framework for boards and management teams to adopt.

RISK-ADJUSTED RETURNS, CORRELATIONS, AND ROTS (RETURN ON TIME SPENT)

Unfortunately for boards and management teams, devising the correct capital allocation strategy is not always as simple as choosing the options with the highest expected returns. There are three other factors that management teams and boards need to consider prior to choosing the right capital allocation plan:

Risk-Adjusted Returns

The risk profile of a series of capital allocation alternatives can be quite heterogeneous. An investment in an emerging market or frontier economy with higher rates of inflation, a less stable government, and increased currency volatility is inherently riskier than an investment in the United States or Europe, and thus should require a higher expected return. A consumer staples firm with an established business in sauces that intends to expand into salsa incurs less risk than if it wants to expand into cereal or muffins. An acquisition that involves the closing of multiple plants across three continents, integrating sales forces, and divesting large parts of the target's revenue base involves more risk than a small bolt-on acquisition within one of the business's subsidiaries.

Just because a capital deployment alternative is riskier does not mean that it should be avoided. A management team and board just need to make sure that the risk-adjusted returns are sufficient to justify the capital deployment option.

Considerations for assessing risk:

- **Execution risk.** How difficult will it be to integrate the acquisition, achieve the synergies, and merge the two firms' cultures? What are the risks of completing the new plant or new production line on time and on budget?
- **Geographic risk.** Emerging markets and frontier economies tend to be riskier for investment given currency volatility, higher inflation, and less stable governments and/or rule of law.
- **Knowledge risk.** While companies can perform due diligence on an acquisition, there is no way that they can know the business, employees, culture, and new product pipeline as well as

they know their own company. As a result, if the return on an acquisition is the same as on share repurchase, all else being equal, the management team should choose to execute a share repurchase program to compensate for the inherent knowledge risk and uncertainty associated with the acquired target.

- **End-market risk.** Entering new businesses, new industries, or new product categories in which your firm does not have an existing business is inherently riskier. An expansion into a business that is adjacent to an existing business is less risky than an expansion into a completely different end-market or product category.

Correlations

In order to reduce the risk profile on the aggregate level of capital deployment, to the extent possible, a firm should try to make investments that are not completely correlated to one factor, one geographic area, or one business. However, a company should not look to diversify its capital allocation bets for diversification reasons alone. Often, a company will have one or two growth businesses that generate significantly higher returns on incremental capital. These divisions will rightly receive a disproportionate amount of capital relative to other businesses.

However, when a firm has multiple divisions operating in various geographic regions, it makes sense to take advantage of diversification if:

- The correlations between the operating results among these divisions and geographies are relatively low.
- The returns on incremental capital deployment are similar.

This reduces the risk that the returns from excess capital deployment fall materially short of expectations because of a macro factor (e.g., unemployment rate), a business (e.g., the aerospace division), or geography (e.g., China) yielding a surprise to the downside.

ROTS (Return on Time Spent)

Management's time is not infinite, so management teams and boards need to factor this into their capital allocation decision frameworks. If there are two capital allocation alternatives with 10% expected returns by year five, but one requires 20% of management's time over the next two years and one requires less than 1% of management's time, the latter alternative is clearly superior, all else being equal.

A management team that is focused on integrating a large, complicated acquisition risks taking its eye off the day-to-day running of the business, spends less time on new product development and R&D, neglects customers, and fails to nurture internal talent.

I generally oppose hostile transactions due to the amount of time that management has to dedicate to them, combined with their relatively low completion rates.

In terms of maximizing ROTS, I would rank the options as follows, from lowest to highest:

1. Hostile acquisitions
2. Large, complicated acquisitions
3. Expansion into completely new business
4. Building a large, new facility
5. Expansion into adjacent business
6. Private, bolt-on acquisition
7. Small capital investments/R&D investments
8. Share repurchase/dividend/special dividends

Just as an aside, when a company becomes the target of an activist investor, a management team will need to spend considerable time conferring with its investors to defend itself, working with investment bankers, meeting with the activist, and potentially embarking on cost cutting, divestitures, and asset sales. In addition, existing board members might be replaced with more disruptive board members of the activist's choosing. Management's time and focus on running the business for the long term inevitably suffer.

The best defense against an activist: intelligent capital deployment!

OVERVIEW OF RATINGS/LEVERAGE

Before turning to a discussion of a more practical way to think about optimizing a capital structure that goes beyond WACC, it is necessary to dive deeper into the differences between the investment-grade and high-yield debt markets (see Table 3.8). Additionally, it is imperative to explore how the credit rating agencies apply ratings to debt instruments, and the trade-off between higher leverage and a higher cost of debt.

TABLE 3.8

Overview of Ratings, Leverage, and Credit Spreads[2]

Moody's Rating	S&P Equivalent	Moody's Debt/EBITDA Median	Avg. Spread 2001–2018	Standard Deviation of Spread 2001–2018
Aaa	AAA	1.9	82	62
Aa	AA	1.8	103	75
A	A	2.3	139	92
Baa	BBB	2.9	199	112
Ba	BB	3.7	378	178
B	B	5.2	532	243
Caa	CCC	8.1	936	447

In theory, the higher the rating, the lower the risk of default, and the lower the rating, the higher the risk of default. The risk of a default with a AAA issuer should be materially lower than with a CCC issuer.

In addition, looking at the average credit spread over time is instructive in helping inform an expected long-term cost of debt at various ratings. However, the volatility and upside risk to credit spreads is just as valuable when considering the cost of issuing or refinancing debt during periods of economic stress (see Figure 3.2).

FIGURE 3.2

Two-Standard Deviation Event Spread Risk

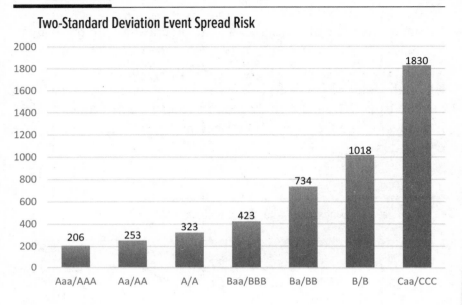

The absolute leverage a firm has relative to its EBITDA, FCF, and book equity plays an important role in determining the rating. However, based on my experience, there are two other factors that also play an important role in determining the credit rating a firm receives: the size of the company and the volatility of the firm's cash flows. For example, a large company with very stable and predictable cash flows, such as American Tower, can maintain an investment grade rating despite being leveraged 5x or more. However, a smaller company with more volatile cash flows, such as Korn Ferry, is a non–investment grade company despite being only leveraged 1x (at the top of a cycle). Investment grade and high-yield rating categories are shown in Table 3.9.

It also follows that if a company can reduce the volatility of its cash flows, it will be able to support a capital structure with more debt without sacrificing its credit rating or putting its shareholders at risk during an economic or industry-specific downturn. In addition, the introduction of more low-cost debt in the capital structure should support faster FCF per share growth over the long term.

TABLE 3.9

Investment Grade Versus High Yield

Investment Grade		High Yield	
Moody's	S&P	Moody's	S&P
Aaa	AAA	Ba	BB
Aa	AA	B	B
A	A	Caa	CCC
Baa	BBB		

For most mature companies, the investment-grade market tends to be a more attractive market for a variety of reasons:

- **Lower spread volatility and lower risk of being unable to issue or refinance debt.** Investment-grade spreads are less volatile than high-yield spreads. In addition, the risk of being unable to access the investment-grade market is much lower than the risk in the high-yield market during periods of market stress. If a firm has a bond that is maturing during a period of stress, the risk of being unable to refinance that debt instrument, needing to tap a bank line, being forced to pay an elevated rate to get the bond placed, issuing equity, or potentially defaulting is materially higher for a high-yield issuer than for an investment-grade issuer.
- **Longer duration, easier to spread out debt maturities.** Investment-grade companies can typically issue longer-dated bonds. It is rare to see high-yield companies issue 10- or 30-year debt. As a result, the high-yield market is a much shorter duration market than the investment-grade market. Consequently, the percentage of a high-yield firm's debt that will come due in any one year will typically comprise a much greater share of its outstanding debt, relative to that

of an investment-grade company. If credit spreads spike, the magnitude of the credit spread increase will be greater for the high-yield issuer, and the percentage of outstanding debt that it will need to refinance at the abnormal rate will be higher as well. This will increase interest costs over the life of the new bond and negatively impact FCF, returns, and growth.

Why in the World Would Any Firm Choose to Issue High-Yield Bonds?

Remember, the after-tax cost of debt capital, even for most high-yield issuers, is materially lower than the cost of equity capital. The more debt a firm can have in its capital structure, the faster its growth rate should be, all else being equal.

A firm with steady cash flows and a low degree of cyclicality may find that being leveraged at 5x debt/EBITDA is the optimal capital structure as the risks of a default, issuing equity, cutting the dividend, being downgraded, or losing financial flexibility are very low.

Some of the largest participants in the high-yield universe such as cable, telecom, restaurant franchisers, and insurance brokerage firms tend to have very steady cash flows, so becoming a high-yield issuer makes sense for them. Furthermore, many companies in the high-yield market are too small to be rated investment grade and thus don't have much choice.

There are also the so-called fallen angels. These firms were previously investment-grade issuers but were downgraded into the high-yield market as their leverage levels spiked, cash flows weakened, or risk profiles increased. In late 2015, when oil prices collapsed, many investment-grade energy companies with what appeared to be reasonable leverage metrics at $100 per barrel oil found they were too leveraged in a world of sub-$50 per barrel oil. Many of these firms were downgraded into the high-yield market.

Firms backed by private equity are also large participants in the high-yield market. Private equity firms will normally acquire a firm, increase leverage to 4–6x EBITDA, focus on improving the level of

EBITDA, pay down debt, and sell or IPO the company over a five- to eight-year period. By loading up debt, they can maximize returns on their equity investments.

While this private equity strategy can often generate mid-teens returns over time, the composition and risk profile of those returns might not be acceptable for most publicly traded companies. Moreover, most private equity investors don't own businesses for the long term; they are more like renters. Sometimes renters of businesses can take actions that maximize short-term profits and returns at the expense of the long-term health and competitiveness of the business.

For companies that choose (or are forced) to become high-yield issuers, I would make the following recommendations:

1. Spread out your debt maturities as best you can. The more spread out your maturities are, the lower your risk of having to refinance a large chunk of your debt at an inopportune time. The risk of a large dilutive equity raise is diminished, and the risk of default is lessened.
2. Most high-yield debt instruments have call features that allow the issuer to retire the debt prior to its stated maturity at a modest premium to par value. In addition, bank debt or leveraged loans that are syndicated to investors are almost always callable at par value. Smart high-yield firms will look to refinance their high-yield and leveraged loans one to two years prior to maturity in order to minimize the risk of being forced to issue new debt or loans during a period of market stress.
3. Maintain as large a revolving line of credit as possible. Paying banks for a line of credit that you are not using in most years does depress returns and cash flows, but it is a great insurance policy.
4. Credit market investors typically only care about financial covenants during periods of stress when covenants actually matter. Breaking through a financial covenant (typically debt/EBITDA) in a downturn could result in an immediate spike

in your cost of debt, or even force your firm into a default. It is worth paying a slightly higher initial interest rate to limit financial covenants and achieve maximum flexibility around whatever financial covenants remain in your revolver, leveraged loans, and high-yield bonds.

Regardless of whether an issuer is in the high-yield or investment grade category, when determining the optimal capital structure, the management team and board should consider the following factors and find the right balance between the two:

1. The capital structure that produces the fastest growth rate in FCF per share
2. The capital structure that protects the firm and its long-term shareholders during periods of economic or firm-specific challenges and maintains financial flexibility

The next chapter discusses the five rules that management teams and boards should strictly adhere to in order to protect the firm and its shareholders during periods of economic and firm-specific stress.

CHAPTER 4

Five Stress Test Rules for Downturns

To protect the firm and its long-term shareholders during periods of weakness, there are five stress test rules every management team and board should follow. **Breaking any of these rules in a downturn is a surefire way to destroy shareholder value.**

These are, in order of importance:

1. Don't go bankrupt.
2. Don't issue equity from a point of weakness.
3. Don't cut the dividend.
4. If you are an investment-grade firm, remain investment grade throughout the downturn.
5. Don't lose financial flexibility (i.e., maintain the ability to deploy capital opportunistically).

Taking into account the unique characteristics of each firm, a management team and board should employ as much leverage as possible to maximize growth in FCF per share while not risking any of the aforementioned five negative outcomes. Too little leverage or too much leverage can lead to suboptimal returns for shareholders. Finding the right balance is key.

Just like the Federal Reserve stress tests banks' balance sheets in a theoretical future downturn to make sure they will have enough equity to remain solvent, a CFO and board should stress test the firm's capital structure in order to make sure it won't violate any of the aforementioned rules in a future downturn.

While the Great Financial Crisis (GFC) was a very painful time for most Americans, at least one positive did emerge from it. The crisis serves as a useful starting point for analyzing how well or how poorly a firm's financials are likely to fare in a future downturn. This can be an effective baseline for a firm's stress test.

Stress test questions:

- How much would EBITDA, operating cash flow, and FCF decline (or increase)?
- Would FCF cover the dividend? If so, by how much?
- If we had to issue new debt and/or pay off maturing debt, what rate would we be forced to pay? How would this change if we had more or less debt in the capital structure?
- Would we be downgraded by the rating agencies? Would we remain investment grade? How much debt could we have in our capital structure prior to the downturn and still remain investment grade throughout the downturn?
- Is there a risk that we would have to raise equity in the downturn to pay down debt?
- Would we have the ability in the downturn to go on the offensive to buy back shares on the cheap or potentially make an acquisition of a distressed competitor at an attractive price?

As an aside, I would not recommend that firms maintain too much financial flexibility for an eventual downturn. The challenge is that, outside of a distressed situation, few companies will choose to sell at the bottom of a stock market and/or economic cycle. The idea that a firm should maintain a suboptimal or lazy balance sheet to take advantage of a situation that is unlikely to materialize can have adverse long-term consequences. This suboptimal balance sheet is likely to result in slower long-term growth in FCF and lower returns on capital, especially if the firm maintains an excessive level of low-return cash and marketable securities on its balance sheet. In addition, a suboptimal balance sheet is like catnip for activists. Financial flexibility really refers to the ability to buy back at least some stock in a downturn at distressed prices, execute a couple of bolt-on acquisitions, or in the case of a high-yield company, buy back debt well below par.

This annual stress test should accomplish the following:

- Allow the firm to optimize the capital structure to include as much low-cost debt as possible in order to maximize long-term growth rates in FCF per share.
- Minimize the risk of breaking any the five aforementioned stress test rules.
- Reduce the likelihood that the management team and board will panic in a downturn by husbanding too much cash at a time when long-term returns on capital deployment are likely at their zenith. The stress test analysis allows the management team and board to put together a collaborative strategic action plan prior to the downturn.

USING LEVERAGE TO MAXIMIZE GROWTH IN FCF PER SHARE

To illustrate this example, let's look at four companies with the same underlying organic growth rate, operating margin, and FCF/net income conversion ratio, shown in Table 4.1.

TABLE 4.1

Four Companies with Similar Underlying Fundamentals, but Different Capital Structures

Companies	Gross Debt to EBITDA	Expected Credit Rating
A	0	
B	2.3	A
C	2.9	BBB
D	5	B

Note: Company A is unlikely to have a credit rating.

Let's run all four companies through four simulations:

1. 10-year scenario with no downturn and firms use all available capital to make acquisitions at 8x forward EBITDA or 1.6x sales (Figure 4.1).
2. 10-year scenario with no downturn and firms use all available capital to make acquisitions at 10x forward EBITDA or 2.0x sales (Figure 4.2).
3. 10-year scenario with no downturn and firms use all available capital to make acquisitions at 12x forward EBITDA or 2.4x sales (Figure 4.3).
4. Downturn scenario for each company[†] (Table 4.3).

Assumptions:

1. 4% organic growth
2. 20% EBITDA margins
3. 90% FCF to net income conversion ratio
4. 30% dividend payout ratio
5. 1% dilution from stock grants
6. Risk-free US government debt at 2.25%

---

† Forward EBITDA denotes first-year EBITDA as part of the new company.

7. Credit spreads consistent with the long-term average of their rating

Anticipated 10-Year FCF/Share Growth Rates

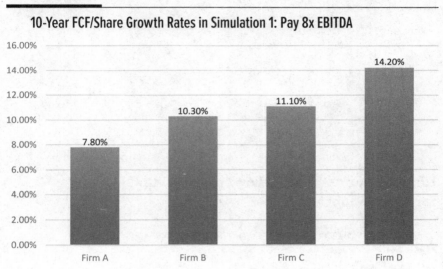

FIGURE 4.1

10-Year FCF/Share Growth Rates in Simulation 1: Pay 8x EBITDA

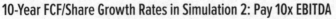

FIGURE 4.2

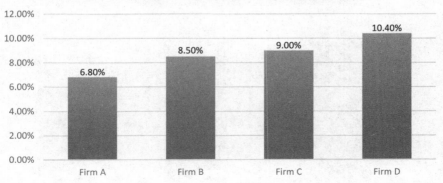

10-Year FCF/Share Growth Rates in Simulation 2: Pay 10x EBITDA

FIGURE 4.3

10-Year FCF/Share Growth Rates in Simulation 3: Pay 12x EBITDA

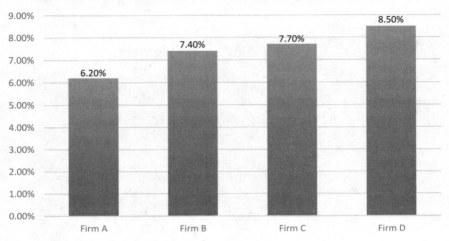

FIGURE 4.4

Higher Returns from Paying Lower Multiples for Acquisitions

Year Five Cash-on-Cash Returns from Acquisitions

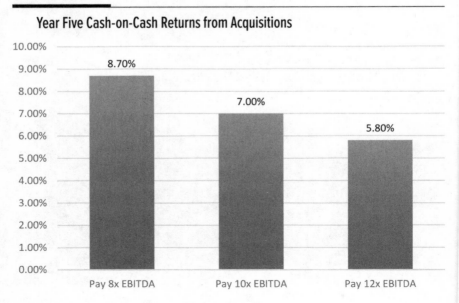

TABLE 4.2

Benefit from Leverage Amplified by Higher Returns on Capital Deployment

	Firm B	Firm C	Firm D
Simulation 1: Change in FCF/Share Growth per Change in Turn of Leverage	1.09%	1.14%	1.28%
Simulation 2: Change in FCF/Share Growth per Change in Turn of Leverage	0.74%	0.76%	0.72%
Simulation 3: Change in FCF/Share Growth per Change in Turn of Leverage	0.52%	0.52%	0.46%

The analysis displayed in Table 4.2 compares the growth rates for firms B–D relative to firm A (with no debt). For every turn in leverage (going from 1x to 2x, for example), how much faster will the firm's FCF per share growth be?

While adding debt to the capital structure to enhance growth rates is somewhat intuitive, this analysis also highlights that the benefits from additional leverage are amplified or curtailed by the levels of returns on capital deployment. For Firm C, every turn of incremental leverage relative to Firm A increased its FCF/share growth rate by 1.14% when returns were high (8.7%), but only by 0.52% when returns were low (5.8%). This spread was even more magnified for Firm D (1.28% vs. 0.46%).

What Do These Simulations Demonstrate?

1. Adding lower-cost debt to the capital structure allows a firm to grow FCF faster. The compounding benefit of this can be compelling for long-term shareholders.
2. The benefit to FCF growth from higher levels of debt is amplified (simulation 1, pay 8x EBITDA) or curtailed (simulation 3, pay 12x EBITDA) by the valuation multiple you have to pay for acquisitions. The higher the returns are on excess capital

deployment, the more FCF/share growth will benefit from additional debt in the capital structure.

3. The long-term impact of a lazy balance sheet manifests itself in meaningfully slower FCF growth rates.

How Would This Change If Interest Rates Increase?

If the after-tax risk-free rate of interest were to increase from 2.25% to 3.75%, it would reduce, but not eliminate, the benefit of having more debt in the capital structure when viewed in isolation. However, during a period of rising interest rates, it is very likely that stock market valuation multiples would decline and the returns from buying back stock, paying dividends, and making acquisitions would increase as a result. This may completely or partially offset the FCF/share growth headwind from higher interest costs.

A fear of higher interest rates should never be an excuse for not optimizing a firm's capital structure.

Downside Scenarios

TABLE 4.3

Organic EBITDA Falls by 20% and 50%

Company	Impact on Gross Leverage		
	Pre-Downturn Leverage	20% Downturn Leverage	50% Downturn Leverage
A	0	0	0
B	2.3	2.7	3.9
C	2.9	3.4	5
D	5	5.7	9.3

Note: Assumes firms use some or all of their FCF to pay down debt to minimize spike in leverage.

Table 4.3 shows that most of the firms can handle a 20% decline in organic EBITDA without violating any of the five stress test rules. Nevertheless, the degree of financial flexibility does drop for every company and gets very close to zero for Company D. A 20%

reduction in EBITDA means lower FCF, increased leverage levels, and a reduction in the amount of opportunistic capital that the company can deploy in the downturn. However, no one is at risk for bankruptcy, no one needs to raise equity to shore up the balance sheet, and no one is at risk of having their debt downgraded below investment grade (see Table 4.4). All of the companies can continue to pay their dividends out of their FCF.

TABLE 4.4

Violation of the Five Rules in 20% EBITDA Decline Scenario

	Firm A	Firm B	Firm C	Firm D
Don't go bankrupt	No	No	No	No
Don't issue equity	No	No	No	No
Don't cut dividend	No	No	No	No
Retain investment grade rating	No	No	No	N/A
Don't lose all financial flexibility	No	No	No	Maybe

Note: Firm D cannot be downgraded to high-yield as it is already a high-yield company.

However, in a 50% organic EBITDA decline environment shown in Table 4.5, Companies B, C, and D all violate one or more of the five rules. Company D may violate all of them depending on how much debt it has coming due in the year of the downturn.

TABLE 4.5

Violation of the Five Rules in 50% EBITDA Decline Scenario

	Firm A	Firm B	Firm C	Firm D
Don't go bankrupt	No	No	No	Maybe
Don't issue equity	No	No	No	If it can*
Don't cut dividend	No	Borderline	Yes	Yes
Retain investment grade rating	No	Maybe	Yes	N/A
Don't lose all financial flexibility	No	Yes	Yes	Yes

*Note: Firm D might consider raising equity, but, given that it would be levered at 9.3x, it may be unable to issue equity.

What Do These Simulations Tell Us About Leverage?

Most firms, even select high-yield firms, can survive a 20% decline in EBITDA without violating any of the five stress test rules. All of the firms will have less financial flexibility as FCF and incremental debt capacity fall in a downturn. If your firm's stress test suggests that your EBITDA will decline by 20% or less in a severe economic or industry downturn, you clearly have room for a reasonable amount of leverage in your capital structure. This is not to suggest that you should leverage your firm up to 5x, as there are clearly downsides to being a non–investment grade company. A leverage level between 2x and 3x EBITDA would be very reasonable and allow the firm to generate attractive EPS and FCF/share growth rates.

If your firm's stress test reveals that a 50% EBITDA decline is possible, the level of leverage in your capital structure should remain low. A leverage level of 0.5x–1.25x would be much more prudent. If a company's stress test reveals large negative cash outflows in a downturn, maintaining a balance sheet with a net cash position and a large undrawn revolver might be ideal to minimize the risk of issuing equity at distressed levels or filing for bankruptcy in a downturn.

Optimizing Capital Structure Conclusions
1. A management team and board of directors should perform an annual stress test of their capital structure.
2. A management team and board should put in a place a collaborative strategic plan as to what potential actions the company would pursue in a downturn to take advantage of dislocations in equity valuations, distressed competitors, and opportunistic asset/investment prospects.
3. A firm should maximize the amount of leverage within its capital structure to generate the fastest growth rate in FCF per share. This should be balanced by minimizing the risk of violating any of the five stress rules. **Don't break any of the five rules!**

4. For most mature companies, remaining an investment-grade issuer is preferable to being a high-yield issuer. A firm that decides to become a high-yield issuer to maximize long-term earnings and FCF growth per share should make sure that its EBITDA is relatively stable (not down more than 20%) even in a downturn. In addition, a management team and board should only choose to become a high-yield issuer if the returns on the firm's excess capital deployment are high enough to drive a materially faster FCF/share growth rate.

SUPPLEMENTAL DISCUSSION ON THE COVID-19 PANDEMIC

The global outbreak of the COVID-19 pandemic in 2020 raised a number of important questions with regard to how companies should approach their capital structures, liquidity management, the stress test process, and the five rules focused on in this chapter.

Should the COVID-19 Downside Case Become the Default Stress Test for Companies Instead of the GFC?

While every firm should create a stress test scenario that it is comfortable with, I would not advise most firms to use the COVID-19 downturn as their new default stress test scenario. This is especially true for firms and industries that have historically experienced modest to moderate levels of cyclicality in prior economic downturns but were far more impacted during the COVID-19 pandemic due to social distancing and mandatory store or facility closings.

The issue really comes down to whether one believes a pandemic that shuts down large swaths of the global economy for a period of time is a black swan event or a reasonable base case scenario for a future downturn. While no one can say for sure, history would suggest that although painful recessions such as the GFC are rare, global pandemics are far rarer. Prior to the COVID-19 pandemic, there had not been a global pandemic that materially disrupted the global economy in 100 years since the Spanish flu outbreak of 1918–1920.

Are There Important Principles That the COVID-19 Pandemic Should Reinforce?

Absolutely. Consider the following:

- Spread out debt maturities as far as possible to minimize the risk of a large tranche of debt coming due during a crisis. Issue as much longer-duration debt as you can, even if it means paying a modestly higher interest rate.
- Minimize or reduce maintenance covenants in newly issued debt instruments and leveraged loans during periods of market strength when most market participants are less focused on a potential future economic or industry-specific downturn.
- Maintain as large a line of credit/revolver capacity with your bank group as possible. This is a cheap insurance policy against a black swan event or a deep economic or industry-specific downturn.
- Minimize the amount of debt that is in the form of commercial paper for all but the most resilient business models.
- Have an optimal amount of debt in the capital structure that allows the firm to grow cash flows and earnings faster over time. The after-tax cost of debt capital in almost all cases is materially lower than the cost of equity capital. However, there is no need to push the envelope too far with regard to attaining the absolute lowest cost of debt possible. Issuing a lot of commercial paper and short-duration debt, having a few large debt instruments outstanding, and maintaining a small backup line of credit with your bank group will minimize your interest expenses and bank fees. However, it also increases the risk to the firm at exactly the wrong time in the business or industry cycle. In almost all cases, having a slightly higher all-in interest cost, especially on an after-tax basis, does not materially alter

the earnings growth or cash flow growth rate of a firm with an optimal capital structure. In addition, it materially reduces the risk associated with that optimized capital structure.

- The amount of debt in the capital structure should be directionally proportional to the volatility of the firm's cash flows and more specifically, to the level of cash flows a firm produces in a downturn.

How Should One Think About the Five Rules in a Black Swan Event?

In a black swan event, such as COVID-19, if your firm can get through the crisis without breaking any of the five rules, that is great. If that is the case, it might very well suggest that you have too little debt in your capital structure.

For companies that are most impacted by COVID-19, whether it be travel-related or energy firms, victory should be measured not necessarily by their ability to avoid violating any of the five rules, but instead merely to avoid bankruptcy and the need to issue equity from a position of weakness.

CHAPTER 5

Capital Spending

The years between 2001 and 2005 were the best of times for Hershey. Hershey's sales grew at 5% per year, which is quite impressive for a domestically focused consumer staple company in a rather mature industry. Even more impressive, Hershey's adjusted EPS grew at a 14% rate during this period as profit margins inflected higher. Not surprisingly, Hershey's stock price rose by 75% on a total return basis (inclusive of dividends), easily outpacing the S&P 500's and S&P Packaged Foods Index returns of 17% and 22%, respectively.

However, despite these strong results, the long-term health of the business was deteriorating beneath the surface. When Richard Lenny became CEO of Hershey in 2001, the company was spending $187 million on advertising or 4.5% of sales. Over the next six years, Hershey slashed advertising spending to $108 million or 2.2% of sales. The decline in advertising spending was a principal factor behind the margin expansion during this period.

Advertising spending is critical for both the maintenance and strengthening of consumer brands as well as the introduction of new products and innovation to drive consumer trial and adoption. However, advertising spending, like R&D, is an expense that when deferred, delayed, or reduced, can result in a relatively minor near-term impact on revenues and a temporary boost to operating profits as in the case of Hershey. Nevertheless, the long-term consequences can be disastrous.

In addition, Hershey attempted to diversify away from its mature confectionary business by aggressively expanding into what it perceived as adjacent snacking categories. In many ways, Hershey management took its eye off the ball of its core business just when some of its competitors were upping their game from an innovation perspective.

In 2006–2007, Hershey hit a wall. Sales growth slowed to 2.5% in 2006 and was basically flat in 2007. After gaining 70 basis points of market share in 2005, Hershey lost share in both 2006 and 2007 (Figure 5.1). Gross margins came under pressure from higher milk and cocoa prices. Adjusted EPS peaked in 2006 at $2.37 per share and then fell in both 2007 and 2008, hitting a low of $1.88 per share. Between 2005 and 2007, Hershey's stock fell by 26% on a total return basis while the S&P rose 22% and the S&P Packaged Foods Index rose 20%. CEO Richard Lenny resigned as CEO in 2007.

Hershey was in trouble, and there were no easy answers.

Management's initial plan to address this challenge was both unexpected and unconventional: invest an extra $278 million in capital expenditures and additional restructuring dollars to optimize its manufacturing footprint.

Hershey management realized that its global manufacturing footprint was suboptimal. It had 17 manufacturing plants and a low 42% capacity utilization rate. Most of its plants were located in the Northeastern United States, which resulted in its chocolate bars needing to travel long distances to reach many of its customers. By closing unproductive plants and building a new state-of-the-art plant in a different region, Hershey was poised to generate $180 million in annual savings.

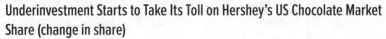

FIGURE 5.1

Underinvestment Starts to Take Its Toll on Hershey's US Chocolate Market Share (change in share)

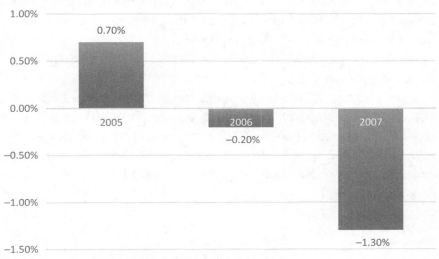

Source: The Hershey Company, 2005–2007 Annual Reports

Most importantly, these savings would give management the resources to aggressively increase advertising spending and put additional feet on the street in important channels, such as convenience stores, to reignite sales growth and regain market share.

A second phase of this program involved the closure of a century-old plant in Hershey, Pennsylvania, with a massive expansion of a newer plant that had been built in 1992 in the same city. This program required an additional $275 million of capital but promised to generate $60–$80 million in savings by the end of 2013.

Gross margins, which troughed at 35.4% (excluding charges) in 2007, expanded to 46% (excluding charges) in 2013. The two supply chain initiatives were important drivers of the expansion in the gross margin. In addition, management refocused its time and attention on innovative new confectionary products among its three strongest brands and put significant advertising resources behind both the new products and the core brands. Advertising spending that had troughed at $108 million (2.2% of sales) in 2006 rose to $582 million in 2013 (8.2% of sales). Sales growth accelerated to an impressive 7% growth rate between 2009 and 2013. Hershey regained the market share it had lost in 2006–2007 and took additional market share from its two largest competitors (Figure 5.2).

EPS rose to a record $2.82 per share in 2011, and by 2013, Hershey earned $3.72 per share. In addition, by 2013, the quality of Hershey's earnings was very strong; the company generated $837 million in FCF, or $3.68 per share for a free cash conversion ratio of 99%. On a total return basis, Hershey's stock price increased by 218% from the end of 2008 to the end of 2013 relative to a 128% return for the S&P 500 and a 132% return for the S&P 500 Packaged Foods Index.

FIGURE 5.2

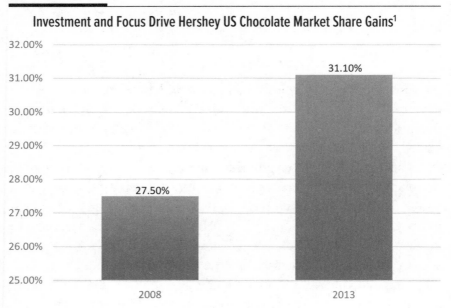

Investment and Focus Drive Hershey US Chocolate Market Share Gains[1]

I would be remiss if I failed to mention the returns Hershey generated from its supply chain initiative. After all, one of the most important roles of a management team and board of directors is to invest capital at the highest rates of return for long-term shareholders.

The two supply chain initiatives produced $163 million in annual, after-tax FCF. The total cash cost of the programs was $773 million. This equates to a very attractive 21% return on investment. This return also excludes any potential cash benefits associated with improved working capital from this program.

The returns on the first supply chain initiative were stronger than the second, but in aggregate the program generated very attractive returns on capital.

The supply chain optimization programs at Hershey exemplify a very intelligent use of shareholders' capital to deliver attractive returns and establish a sustainable flywheel for value creation.

The Hershey Flywheel
1. Supply chain optimization leads to higher gross margins and gross profit dollars.
2. Higher gross margins and gross profit dollars enable Hershey to increase advertising, increase consumer promotion, and fund sales force expansion while still delivering savings to the bottom line to improve underlying operating margins.
3. Higher advertising, higher consumer promotion, and sales force expansion lead to accelerating sales growth and market share gains.
4. Accelerating sales growth and market share gains drive margin expansion (through leveraging fixed costs) and allow for even more investment dollars to be deployed on new product development, advertising, consumer promotion, and sales force expansion.

While Hershey was led by an excellent CEO in Dale West and benefited from declining raw material inflation during this period of time, the Hershey Flywheel is something that any firm can and should attempt to replicate.

WHAT DOES THE ACADEMIC EVIDENCE ON CAPITAL SPENDING SUGGEST?

Capital spending is generally viewed very positively by just about everyone. Politicians often incentivize capital spending through accelerated write-offs such as bonus depreciation. They do this because they believe that higher capital spending drives stronger economic growth in the short term. Much of the current anger around stock repurchase programs stems from a view that these programs are diverting funds away from capital spending. However, for almost every publicly traded company I have ever come across, their capital allocation waterfall almost always begins with internal investment/ capital spending at the top of the list.

Unfortunately, and somewhat surprisingly, the academic evidence surrounding capital spending is quite clear: companies that increase capital spending the most underperform the market and their peers across multiple metrics.

As Jeffrey S. Abarbanell and Brian J. Bushee explain in "Abnormal Returns to a Fundamental Analysis Strategy:"

> *[T]he CAPX signal [change in cap ex relative to change in industry cap ex], which was constructed to test the notion that it is good news for future earnings when firm-specific capital expenditures outpace industry average capital expenditures, yields results directly opposite to what was hypothesized.*[2]

What is interesting about the CAPX signal is that it not only fore-shadowed weak relative near-term earnings growth, but also weak long-term earnings growth for companies that grew capital spending faster than their industry peers.

Further, Sheridan Titman, K.C. John Wei, and Feixue Xie, in their paper entitled "Capital Investments and Stock Returns," conclude that:

> *investors tend to underreact to the empire building implications of increased investment expenditures. Specifically, [they] find that firms that increase their investment expenditures the*

most tend to underperform their benchmarks over the following five years. . . . Moreover, this negative relation between increased capital expenditures and subsequent returns tends to be stronger for firms with greater investment discretion, i.e., firms with less debt or more cash flows.[3]

These two academic papers call attention to the fact that firms that choose to grow capital expenditures faster than peers experience weak relative stock price appreciation, and more important, that this underperformance has a long tail to it.

Louis K.C. Chan, Jason Karceski, Josef Lakonishok, and Theodore Sougiannis report similar findings in their working paper on "Balance Sheet Growth and the Predictability of Stock Returns." They assert that:

[f]irms ranked in the top quintile by changes in investment spending have average abnormal returns of −0.127 percent per month over the following year. . . . The poor price performance of firms increasing property, plant, and equipment is also eye-catching, regardless of the method of financing.[4]

In his dissertation entitled "The Implications of Capital Investments for Future Profitability and Stock Returns: An Overinvestment Perspective," Donglin Li emphasizes that high levels of capital spending foreshadow future margin degradation, and he highlights the reoccurring theme that firms that are flush with cash and/or have excessively strong balance sheets are more likely to engage in low or negative net present value capital spending.

Capital investments have a robust negative association with future profitability ratios. . . . Managers of firms with high free cash flow can act opportunistically and indulge in "value destroying activities" and to "over invest and misuse the funds" (Jensen 1986). Excessive free cash flow enables managers to invest in negative NPV projects after exhausting positive NPV projects (Blanchard et al. [1994], Richardson [2002]).[5]

CONCLUSIONS FROM ACADEMIC RESEARCH ON CAPITAL SPENDING

Clearly, the popular view that elevated capital spending is a panacea for long-term shareholders is mistaken.

- Firms that increase capital spending at a rate faster than their industry peers and broader market indexes will experience weaker than average short-term and long-term stock returns, slower earnings growth, as well as relative operating margin pressure.
- This phenomenon is even more pronounced in companies with significant cash flows and low debt levels. Companies with a significant amount of capital to deploy and a limited number of net present value (NPV) positive investment opportunities may make discretionary growth capital spending investments with low or negative returns.

Shouldn't a firm be able to earn at least 7–8% returns on growth capital spending? Can't firms find internal projects that generate higher returns than they can achieve by making acquisitions or buying back stock? This seems like a low bar. However, the academic evidence is clear: firms that accelerate capital spending or spend at higher rates than their industry peers underperform in the short, intermediate, and long term with regard to growth in earnings and stock returns. The only possible explanation for this is that the returns on "growth" capital spending often tend to be very low, and in some cases negative. Again, it seems illogical for management teams to sanction investments with low or negative returns.

Why is this?

Timing Challenges

In some cases, a large capital spending program may take years before it generates a return on capital while a plant, facility, or piece of machinery is built. This will depress cash flows and returns during the construction period. However, once the plant, facility, or piece of machinery is operating, returns and cash flows should improve. While this timing delay may partially explain some of the near-term earnings and stock price weakness noted in the academic research, it is inconsistent with the evidence suggesting that growth in capital spending impacts intermediate-term and long-term earnings, returns, and stock price performance.

A more likely explanation for this phenomenon is that an acceleration in capital spending occurs during a period when demand for goods is strong and the firm is generating strong cash flows. The firm decides to invest a portion of its improved cash flows into capital programs to grow the business and meet what appears to be robust demand. Often, by the time the new plant, facility, or machinery is completed, the demand environment may be less robust, and the firm (and potentially its competitors) has just added capacity that is not needed, thus leading to poor returns.

One of the challenges for any management team or board is that cash flows and business sentiment are typically the strongest in the mid-to-late part of the business cycle when there is no evidence that the cycle is nearing its end. As a result, companies open the purse strings on capital spending at precisely the wrong time. Trying to predict the end of a cycle is a loser's game, but ignoring the potential for a downturn when making capital spending decisions can be just as a dangerous.

Productivity of a Firm

Let's go back to the firm discussed earlier that is growing its top line by 4%. As the firm begins planning for the following year, it could simply increase its manufacturing capacity by 4% by adding new manufacturing lines, expanding the footprint of an existing plant, or even building a new plant. Those decisions result in higher capital spending and all else equal, weaker cash flows, but may be necessary to support top-line growth.

However, what if the firm's chief competitor were a leader in lean manufacturing focused on productivity, efficiency, and continuous improvement? Instead of looking to expand its manufacturing footprint at a level consistent with expected sales growth, it would look to use these lean manufacturing principles to drive efficiency on the manufacturing floor by reducing the steps in the manufacturing process, redesigning the manufacturing line, reducing rework, and/ or simplifying the number of SKUs produced to reduce changeover time. Both firms would be able to meet the increased demand for their goods, but the latter firm that is focused on lean manufacturing principles would be able to do so with a much smaller level of incremental investment. This firm would generate higher returns and have more cash flow left over to deploy in M&A, share repurchase, or dividends.

I believe at least some of the return discrepancy between high growth in capital spending firms and low growth in capital spending firms is actually tied to the adoption of lean manufacturing principles as a source of competitive advantage. The low-growth capital spending firm is simply creating capacity for growth through low-to-zero cash cost productivity improvements. The high-growth capital spending firm is creating capacity for growth through new, high cash cost capital expenditures.

Necessary Investments with Low Returns

Purely discretionary capital spending on a new headquarters is likely to generate very low returns for shareholders and should be executed only when absolutely necessary. However, there is a series of required investments that generate very low or zero returns. A company may need to spend aggressively to implement a new cyber security software solution to protect intellectual property and customer data. A major upgrade of an enterprise risk planning system might be necessary from a long-term business perspective even if the incremental return on that upgrade might generate low returns. In these examples, while the return might be low, the risk to the long-term health of the business would be even worse if the company failed to make the investment.

CAPITAL SPENDING QUESTIONS

A firm should undertake any capital spending program that has a high probability of generating cash-on-cash returns that are higher than those to be obtained by buying back shares, engaging in M&A, or paying dividends. If a management team and board of directors have a program that can generate strong returns, they should absolutely undertake such a program.

However, given the very strong and consistent academic research with regard to elevated levels of capital spending, before undertaking such a program, a board should ask the following questions:

1. What are the returns from such a program if the end market or economy were to weaken over the forecast period? If the "downside" returns are still good, that is a very positive sign.
2. Are we growing capacity (and is the industry growing capacity) at a rate faster than long-term demand growth?
3. Are the returns greater than the returns from other capital allocation options?
4. Can we create capacity through productivity and lean manufacturing as opposed to capital?
5. Are we growing capital spending faster than our competitors? Why or why not?
6. How have other similar capital spending programs we have implemented performed in recent years?
7. Have we established a robust system for monitoring the returns for these investments and holding management accountable if the returns fail to deliver?
8. Can we incorporate a return on invested capital metric as part of management's compensation to encourage a focus on generating strong returns on capital spending programs?
9. Instead of investing capital, can we outsource manufacturing of low-value or commodity components of the manufacturing process to improve returns and cash flows?

I would be especially concerned if a management team were to propose growing capital spending materially faster than the rate of sales growth or materially faster than the long-term end-market demand in the middle-to-late part of an economic expansion.

CONCLUSION

Based on the observations and evidence presented in this chapter, here are the five key capital spending priorities:

1. Quasi-Guaranteed Returns

In certain industries, there may be an opportunity to lock in very strong returns from capital spending. These investments should be prioritized, especially if the returns are significantly higher and/or materially less risky than other capital allocation alternatives.

A utility that has the ability to build a wind farm for $100 million, put this into their rate base with the blessing of the state public utility commission, and generate a return of 9–10% on that investment, should be very willing to undertake such a capital program. An industrial gas manufacturer that can sign a take-or-pay contract with a large refinery to build a hydrogen plant right next to the refinery to supply it with hydrogen for the next 15 years and generate low-teens return on capital should, in most circumstances, undertake such an investment. In this example, the firm would want to do a thorough analysis of the competitiveness and financial health of the refinery to make sure it would likely continue to operate and pay its bills over the course of the contract.

2. Hershey Playbook

The Hershey playbook described at the start of this chapter has been copied by other consumer staples firms in recent years. I am frankly surprised that more companies have not looked to overhaul their manufacturing footprint to drive higher gross margins that can produce increased profits and additional resources for investment in the business.

As the Hershey example demonstrated, the returns from this capital spending and restructuring program can yield exceptional returns relative to other capital allocation alternatives. I would encourage management teams and boards to regularly review their manufacturing footprint, capacity utilization levels, and supply chain efficiency to see if there are opportunities to deploy capital at very high rates of return.

3. Brownfield Versus Greenfield Expansion

Not all capacity expansion is created equal. A greenfield expansion refers to building an entirely new plant from scratch. A brownfield expansion refers to adding capacity to an existing facility and/or de-bottlenecking a facility to drive more throughput. A brownfield expansion generally has many advantages. First, it is typically much less expensive and less risky as the plant is already built. Second, the lag time between when capital is deployed and when the capital is generating a return is shorter. Third, returns on brownfield expansion are typically 2–3x that of greenfield expansions, based on my experience.

4. Maintenance Capital Spending

While the academic evidence strongly suggests that high levels of capital spending growth relative to peers have negative implications for returns, earnings, and future stock price performance, this should not be interpreted to suggest that a firm's capital spending should ever go beneath its maintenance capital spending level.

Maintenance capital spending refers to the level of capital spending required to continue to run the plants efficiently and safely for a certain level of production. Equipment and facilities wear out over time and need to be replaced. A firm that attempts to run equipment beyond its useful life will likely find that its manufacturing lines are frequently down and in need of repair. A restaurant that fails to upgrade its dining area over time will lose customers because it will look increasingly outdated relative to its competition. A waste management company that puts off buying a new waste hauler will find its maintenance and fuel costs rising, as well as having its customers upset if their trash is not picked up consistently due to frequent breakdowns.

While maintenance capital spending is unlikely to generate strong returns, milking a business for short-term cash by reducing maintenance capital spending is generally a horrible idea. The company is likely to suffer negative consequences in the short and long term, such as higher maintenance and repair costs, employee safety issues, customer loss, fuel/electrical inefficiency, and so on.

5. High-Return Capital Spending Projects

A management team and board should sanction capital spending programs that are expected to generate returns on capital that exceed the returns on all of the other capital allocation alternatives available to the company at the time. These expected returns should be based on mid-cycle industry economics.

Capital Spending vs. Research and Development (R&D) Spending

I made a decision in this book not to have a chapter dedicated to R&D spending. The most important reason is definitional. The intended outcome or return from allocating capital to R&D should be new, innovative products and services that delight customers, drive market share gains, and generate attractive cash-on-cash returns for long-term shareholders. For many firms, only some of the spending related to new product development flows into the R&D line on the income statement. While the bulk of a pharmaceutical company's spending on drug development will be classified as R&D, for an automotive company a large percentage of the spending to develop a new car may count as engineering expense. Service and digital companies may report very low levels of R&D relative to revenue, but at the same time spend significant resources developing new products and services. These definitional issues make it very difficult to compare firms on an apples-to-apples basis.

Nevertheless, there are a couple of important points on R&D spending, or more accurately any spending related to the development of new products and services, that need to be addressed.

R&D Spending Is at a Disadvantage on the Income Statement

For most businesses, R&D is expensed on the income statement as it is incurred. Capital expenditures, on the other hand, are depreciated on the income statement over their useful life. Thus, a firm that spends $10 million on R&D in a given year will bear the full income statement burden of those expenditures in the year they are spent. A firm that spends $10 million on capital expenditures will only burden its income statement with $500,000 or $1,000,000 of depreciation expense. While capital spending and R&D both involve an outlay of cash with the expectation of returns in future periods, they are treated very differently.

For a management team or board correctly focused on FCF as opposed to earnings, this accounting difference is irrelevant. The only thing that matters is the intermediate-term cash-on-cash returns from the investment, regardless of the income statement impact. But unfortunately, not all management teams have this mindset. The result is a bias toward capital spending over R&D.

R&D Has Greater Potential to Differentiate a Firm Relative to Capital Spending

For some unknown reason, capital spending has become a badge of honor for many firms. This is despite strong evidence that firms that spend the most on capital spending systematically underperform across multiple metrics. I believe the lifeblood of most firms and the most important driver of long-term market share gains is in fact the development of innovative new products and services. Investing R&D into the creation and enhancement of high-impact products and services can truly differentiate one firm from its competitors. New products and services can improve market share, drive stronger top-line growth, and increase gross profits that can be dropped to the bottom line or used to fund additional investments (as at Hershey) that keep the flywheel going. Spending on capital can increase the capacity of a firm and in some cases improve productivity. However, with some notable exceptions (such as the large IT cloud companies—Amazon, Microsoft, and Google), capital spending rarely creates a sustainable competitive advantage. If a firm has a choice between R&D and capital spending and the expected returns are similar, I would almost always choose R&D as this has a far greater likelihood of differentiating the firm from its competitors.

CHAPTER 6

Dividends and the Case for Returning Excess Capital to Shareholders

If you were to ask a CFO or CEO why she was not returning more capital to shareholders, you would likely get one or more of the following answers:

- We have significant opportunities to invest that will generate returns for shareholders well above our cost of capital.
- Returning excess capital to shareholders means that we as executives have failed to find enough attractive, high-return projects for investment. Investors and our board will view this negatively. It is a sign we are giving up.
- Returning excess capital to shareholders is a signal to the market that we are no longer a growth company. If we return excess capital to shareholders, our valuation multiple (P/E ratio) will fall and we will underperform as a result.

The first answer is very reasonable as long as the company can demonstrate that the returns on these investments (internal, acquisitions) are more attractive than the alternative, which involves the distribution of excess capital to shareholders in the form of dividends, special dividends, or share repurchases.

The second and third answers are far less reasonable and are not supported by the largely positive performance of firms that return excess capital to shareholders, or by the preponderance of academic evidence on the subject.

In reality, the vast majority of excess capital return is executed by mature firms that simply don't have enough incremental high-return projects to undertake relative to the amount of FCF they are generating.

The following chapters will highlight multiple firms that are growing faster than their end markets by investing aggressively to expand their businesses and making attractive bolt-on acquisitions, yet are still able to return significant excess capital to shareholders. Returning excess capital to shareholders and investing to grow your business are not mutually exclusive.

Returning excess capital to shareholders is not a new phenomenon. According to a 2011 article published by the consulting firm McKinsey & Company, over the last 50 years, publicly traded firms have returned 60% of earnings back to shareholders.[1]

In most cases, a shift in capital return policy to distribute more excess capital to shareholders is perceived as a positive rather than a negative signal by the market. Few investors would be disappointed in or critical of a management team that returned excess capital to shareholders instead of taking on low, or even negative, net present value capital projects. The majority of academic evidence on the subject also supports this conclusion. This will be a common theme in the chapters on dividends, special dividends, and share repurchase.

This chapter explores dividends as one avenue that firms can utilize to return excess capital to shareholders.

The performance of firms that pay dividends, especially those in the first two quintiles (top 40%) of payout ratio (dividends/earnings), is compelling over the last six decades.

Firms that pay out a reasonable amount of earnings in the form of dividends tend to outperform the market while exhibiting lower-than-average volatility. On the other hand, firms that don't pay dividends or that have low payout ratios generally underperform the market and have higher-than-average volatility.

Multiple academic and investment bank analyses show a linear relationship between the risk-adjusted returns of a firm and its dividend yield with one modest exception. A portion of the highest-dividend-yield firms in these analyses will not be able to sustain their current dividend payout ratio. Based on my experience, these future-cutters are likely to generate lower future returns and materially lower risk-adjusted returns. As a result, the best risk-adjusted returns are not found in the highest quintile of dividend yield, but in the second highest quintile. These firms are much less likely to need to cut their dividend in the future.

In addition, these compelling results tend to be fairly consistent across both US and international equity markets.[2]

Why do firms that fail to pay dividends so often and so consistently underperform the market and their dividend-paying peers?

First, I would hypothesize that investors are focused on two sources of return streams: capital appreciation and dividends. The combination of these return streams drives total shareholder returns. Investors tend to systematically overestimate the expected capital appreciation return stream and underappreciate the more stable and predictable dividend return stream. This inefficiency causes firms with zero-to-minimal dividend payouts to underperform and higher dividend stocks to outperform.

Second, management teams and boards of firms that are retaining all of their earnings must believe that the returns from investing this excess capital are greater than their cost of capital. Additionally, they consider this course of action superior to the returns implicit in returning excess capital to shareholders. As discussed in Chapter 5, this is often not the case.

While the case for dividends over the long term is compelling, I would be remiss if I failed to mention that over the last decade, high dividend stocks have trailed the performance of low or no dividend stocks.[3] From my perspective this has less to do with the dividend policy or capital allocation strategy of mature firms and is much more driven by the extraordinary and unprecedented outperformance of growth stocks over the last decade. Almost all of these disruptive technology companies have paid out little or no dividends to their shareholders and probably should not have, given where they were in their business's evolution. Firms such as Alphabet (Google) and Amazon and many other disruptive companies made the right capital allocation decision as the returns from their investments (acquisitions, R&D, and capital spending) were high, in most cases, and far superior to the returns their investors could have generated if these high-growth firms had been paying out large chunks of their earnings in the form of dividends. However, over the next decade and beyond, as many of these firms' revenue growth slows due to the law of large numbers, I fully expect dividend policy and, more broadly, capital return policy will play an increasingly important role in determining whether these firms can continue to outperform. Firms such as Apple and Microsoft have continued to outperform in part due to shareholder-friendly capital allocation strategies that balance dividends and share repurchase with capital spending, acquisitions, and internal investment.

ACADEMIC RESEARCH ON PAYING OUT DIVIDENDS AND RETURNING EXCESS CASH TO SHAREHOLDERS

Why would a firm engage in low or negative return internal projects?

Agency costs are the best explanation. Agency costs refer to the economic inefficiencies and conflicts of interest created when owners (shareholders) of a business hire a principal (management team) to make decisions on their behalf.

In "Agency Costs of Free Cash Flow, Corporate Finance, and Takeovers," Michael Jensen[†] suggests that there is a conflict between managers of firms whose incentive is to grow the company versus owners/shareholders who desire all excess capital to be returned after all projects above a firm's cost of capital have been undertaken. Jensen writes:

> *Managers have incentives to cause their firms to grow beyond optimal size. Growth increases managers' power by increasing the resources under their control. It is also associated with increases in managers' compensation, because changes in compensation are positively related to the growth in sales. . . . The problem is how to motivate managers to disgorge the cash rather than investing it below the cost of capital or wasting it on organization inefficiencies.[4]*

In this paper, Jensen argues that firms should take on additional debt (up to an optimal level) to buy back stock. He asserts that this will pressure the organization to avoid investing in low-return projects now that there is debt in the capital structure, and some inherent, long-term risk to the business if managed poorly. Jensen also notes that this strategy will limit the amount of cash flow that management can invest, because some of it is required for debt service.

Numerous papers have affirmed Jensen's thesis around agency theory. These include works by Arnott and Asness (2003); Allen, Bernando, and Welch (2000); and Zhou and Ruland (2006).[5] Researchers have found that both dividends and special dividends reduce the agency conflict between managers and shareholders by limiting the amount of cash flow available for investment. By reducing the amount of cash flow available for investment, managers are

---

† It should be noted that Michael Jensen's views on corporate governance, agency costs, and capital returns have changed and sometimes dramatically in the last 35+ years. My citation of his work here should not infer that he continues to hold these views.

forced to prioritize only those investments with the highest returns. Consequently, the risk of low return or negative investments is decreased.

Jensen's hypothesis is also supported by the academic research on capital spending cited in Chapter 5. Overall, firms that increased capital spending underperformed. But the firms that underperformed the most were those with increased capital spending, substantial FCF, and limited debt.

This is a logical explanation for why firms that don't pay out dividends tend to underperform. The lack of a dividend results in these firms having more capital available to deploy. As a result, much of this excess capital is invested at low or negative returns after all the high return projects have been funded.

THREE ADDITIONAL BENEFITS OF DIVIDENDS

In addition to the benefits described in academic literature, dividends provide organizations and shareholders with other advantages.

Dividends Attract a Yield-Oriented Investor

Dividends are very important to many different types of shareholders. Typically, dividends are taxed at a lower rate than interest income or wages. They can grow over time, whereas the interest payments on a bond will fail to grow and almost certainly decline in real terms after accounting for inflation.

As interest rates have fallen dramatically over the last couple of decades, the relative attractiveness of dividends has only increased, as shown in Table 6.1 and Figure 6.1. In fact, at the end of 2020, the average 10-year bond yield of the United States, Germany, Japan, and Switzerland combined was slightly negative in nominal terms and very negative in inflation-adjusted terms. At the same time, the payout ratio (dividends/earnings) has decreased in the United States, as many firms increasingly use share repurchase to return excess capital to shareholders. Moreover, demand for dividends is increasing as baby boomers retire and require additional income sources that can grow with or faster than inflation.

In reality, the attractiveness of dividends has increased relative to other income sources at exactly the same time that dividend payouts have decreased and demand from retirees has increased.

It is not surprising that investors would flock to a firm with a reasonable dividend payout ratio under these circumstances. Chapter 7 will discuss how the Chicago Mercantile Exchange (CME) increased its dividend materially, instituted a special dividend policy, and saw its earnings valuation multiple double over the next six years, even as its revenue growth decelerated.

TABLE 6.1

10-Year Bond Yields Versus Dividend Yields

	10-Year Bond Yields		Dividend Yields	
	Dec. 31, 2010	Dec. 31, 2020	Dec. 31, 2010	Dec. 31, 2020
Switzerland	1.57%	−0.49%	2.89%	2.75%
United States	3.29%	0.92%	1.76%	1.53%
Germany	2.97%	−0.58%	3.23%	2.64%
Japan	1.18%	0.02%	1.67%	1.48%
Average	2.25%	−0.03%	2.39%	2.10%

Note: Indexes used: US S&P 500, Germany DAX, Japan Nikkei 225, and FTSE Switzerland

Source: FactSet financial data and analytics, accessed February 13, 2021

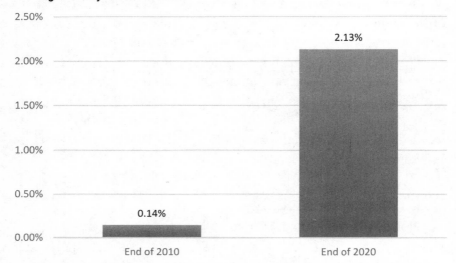

FIGURE 6.1

Dividend Yield Advantage Relative to 10-Year Bond Yields Has Expanded Significantly in Last 10 Years

Notes: Indexes used: US S&P 500, Germany DAX, Japan Nikkei 225, and FTSE Switzerland. This represents the dividend yield minus the 10-year bond yield average spread across the United States, Germany, Japan, and Switzerland.

Source: FactSet financial data and analytics, accessed February 13, 2021

Dividends Reduce Volatility

Earlier in the chapter, I referenced multiple dividend studies, which demonstrated that firms with reasonable dividend yields tend to have lower betas or less volatile stock prices.

Moreover, while this is more anecdotal, I often find that firms with stable, low cash flow volatility businesses and low payout ratios tend to have stocks that are much more volatile than their underlying cash flow volatility. In other words, even though the underlying cash flows of the firm are not that volatile, the stock price fluctuates much more than it should for firms with no/low dividend yields.

It should be pointed out that a high dividend stock with a payout ratio that is not sustainable is likely to have a materially higher beta as investors anticipate a potential future dividend cut or elimination.

Dividends Bring Forward Cash Flows and Lower Risk

The future is less certain than the present. There is more confidence in a dividend to be paid today than the promise of a dividend to be paid 10, 20, or 30 years in the future. If the value of a stock is the present value of its future cash flows, its inherent riskiness is lessened by having a reasonable proportion of those future cash flows paid to investors in the short-to-intermediate term relative to the long term.

Does this mean that all firms should massively increase their dividend payout ratios tomorrow? No, it does not.

A startup firm that is bleeding cash or a newly public biotech company with multiple drugs in development but no cash flows should not be paying dividends. However, the more mature a firm is and the stronger its FCF generation, the more important it is for the firm to pay dividends.

HOW SHOULD A FIRM SET ITS DIVIDEND?

Firms should consider a variety of factors in setting a dividend that will attract investors.

> **Minimum token dividend.** Every firm that has positive cash flow beyond maintenance capital spending should, at a minimum, pay a token dividend. By doing so, you open your firm to dividend-focused institutional investors who can now own your shares. While a token dividend alone is unlikely to attract a large number of these investors, it does allow them to own your stock. Without the dividend, in most cases, they would be unable to own your stock. While this dividend is unlikely to meaningfully reduce incentives to invest in the kind of low-return projects that Jensen discussed in his paper, it should help on the margin.

> **Set the dividend at a sustainable level.** The dividend should be set at a level that is sustainable through an economic, industry, or

company-specific downturn. Firms that cut dividends underperform by almost 4% over the three days following a dividend cut.[6] As Cesare Fracassi suggests in his academic paper on the subject, a dividend cut is a powerful signal that the firm is moving from a mature stage of its life cycle to a decline phase.[7]

Understand shareholder base. What do the ultimate owners of the stock want management to do with the excess FCF and payout ratios? In many sectors, such as utilities, telecom, REITs, and integrated oil companies, the investor base is a dividend-focused shareholder group. Having a materially lower payout ratio relative to peer firms could result in a lower valuation and more volatile stock.

Every management team and board should periodically ask its shareholders, especially its long-term shareholders, for input on capital allocation and capital returns. The input should not necessarily be the driving force in how a firm allocates capital, but it should be a consideration.

Cash flow volatility. Firms with volatile cash flows or firms that generate the majority of their cash flows late in the business cycle should pay a smaller regular dividend but should also consider paying out a regular-special dividend, which we will address in Chapter 7.

What are the alternatives? A management team and board should carefully examine both past and future uses of excess FCF to objectively measure the returns from acquisitions, share repurchase, and growth-orientated capital spending.

A firm that has significant opportunities to deploy capital at returns well in excess of the returns from dividends (see next section) should have a lower payout ratio than a firm that has fewer opportunities. However, management teams and boards must jointly monitor past and future return expectations given the strong academic evidence suggesting that firms that fail to return excess cash to shareholders underperform because they typically invest in low- or negative-return projects.

WHAT IS THE RETURN ON CAPITAL ASSOCIATED WITH DIVIDENDS?

The return on a dividend payment is a very difficult concept to grasp. When a firm builds a new plant, it is fairly simple to calculate the return on capital from the investment. If a firm invested $10 million in capital and the plant is producing $700,000 in FCF, the plant's initial ROIC is 7%. The same holds true for an acquisition. If a firm spends $2 billion on an acquisition that generates $160 million in FCF, the acquisition's initial ROIC is 8%. Even the return on a stock repurchase is easy to do. If a firm's shares are trading for $20 and the firm is producing $1.50 per share of FCF, the initial ROIC from share repurchase is 7.5%.

But what is the return on a dividend or special dividend? If a firm pays a $1 dividend to shareholders, what return are its owners likely to achieve on that $1 dividend?

In reality, a shareholder receiving a dividend has multiple options. She could acquire additional shares in the firm that declared the dividend, buy groceries, help pay junior's tuition bill at college, purchase a bond, put the cash in the bank, purchase this book, or consider a million other alternatives.

However, from a modeling perspective, the best way to conceptualize the return on a dividend should be based on the FCF yield of the S&P 500 or some other broad market index. In other words, if the firm's shareholders reinvest the dividends in the S&P 500, what is the cash-on-cash return they should expect to generate?

If the S&P 500 were trading at 20x forward operating earnings, it would have an earnings yield of 5% (inverse of P/E ratio). Nevertheless, it is important to consider the FCF yield of the S&P

500 (not the earnings yield) in order to compare cash-on-cash returns of all the various capital allocation options. The question is how to go from earnings yield to FCF yield for the S&P 500.

Over the 10 years from 2008 to 2018, the median FCF conversion for the S&P 500 ratio (FCF/adjusted, non-GAAP net income) has been about 85%.[†] In other words, for every dollar of "adjusted" net income (non-GAAP EPS), the median firm in the S&P 500 generates about $.85 of FCF.

The calculation for estimating the return on dividends/special dividends is shown in Tables 6.2 and 6.3.

TABLE 6.2

How to Calculate Return on Dividends/Special Dividends

Inverse of S&P 500 Forward Earnings Multiple
Multiple by 85% (LT S&P 500 FCF Conversion Rate)
Grow Organic S&P 500 FCF by Nominal GDP or 4%

Note: Used organic growth of S&P 500, not total return, to create more accurate apples-to-apples comparison to the cash-on-cash returns associated with other capital allocation alternatives.

TABLE 6.3

Calculating Returns on Dividends/Special Dividends

Market Multiple on Forward EPS	Year 1	Year 2	Year 3	Year 4	Year 5
16	5.3%	5.5%	5.7%	6.0%	6.2%
20	4.3%	4.4%	4.6%	4.8%	5.0%
10	8.5%	8.8%	9.2%	9.6%	9.9%

Assumptions: S&P 500 forward operating earnings valuation multiple; organic FCF growth of S&P 500 of 4% (consistent with nominal GDP growth); nominal GDP growth of 4%; FCF conversion rate of 85% consistent with 2008–2018 average.

---

† GAAP refers to generally accepted accounting principles. Every publicly traded company has to report its financials (earnings, statement of cash flows, balance sheet) in accordance with GAAP accounting. However, the vast majority of companies also report non-GAAP earnings and sometimes non-GAAP FCF. The difference between GAAP and non-GAAP earnings is usually driven by companies' desire to exclude amortization, restructuring charges, or one-time costs from their "adjusted" EPS.

While this calculation is complex, it is by far the best way I have come up with to conceptualize the expected return on dividends relative to the cash-on-cash returns from all the other capital alternatives available to the firm. **However, it is also by far the least relevant calculation.**

The appeal of dividends for shareholders is their consistency and long-term growth. Shareholders don't want companies to eliminate dividends when the stock becomes temporarily attractive or a large capital spending program is approved. As I discussed earlier in the chapter, the dividend and dividend payout ratio level should be set at a level that is sustainable through a downturn, consistent with industry-specific shareholder requirements, and reflects the ability (or inability) of the firm to generate strong returns on other capital allocation alternatives.

Boards and management teams should vary the level of growth capital spending, share repurchase, and acquisitions over time based on their cash-on-cash returns. There should be no preset rule for how much is deployed into these three areas. However, with dividends, the payout ratio should be set at a through-the-cycle, sustainable level and should never be cut except under extraordinary circumstances.

WHEN SHOULD A FIRM CUT THE DIVIDEND?

Consider the following factors when deciding whether to reduce the dividend.

- When dividend payments are greater than the current level of FCF the firm is producing and it is unlikely this will reverse in the very near term.
- When leverage is too high. A firm should cut the dividend to lower its bankruptcy risk, reduce the need to dilute existing equity holders through new share issuances, and to avoid a material increase in its interest expense from a potential downgrade to non–investment grade. Of the three reasons

mentioned, reducing bankruptcy risk and reducing equity dilution are no-brainer rationales to cut the dividend. A downgrade to non–investment grade is less clear-cut. If a firm will need to issue additional debt or refinance a considerable amount of debt in the short term, cutting the dividend to avoid being downgraded to non–investment grade might make sense. However, if the firm does not have significant near-term debt maturities to refinance or needs to issue new debt, a move to the non–investment grade market may not require a dividend cut.

- When the payout ratio is too high and this is limiting the firm's ability to invest in either maintenance capital programs or high-return growth projects.
- When the firm cannot maintain the current dividend through a cycle.

In addition, if you are going to cut the dividend, do it once. The stock is going to decline anyway. It is better to cut the dividend to a conservative, sustainable level that will allow the firm to reduce debt quickly and potentially limit the amount of dilutive equity raises. Dividend cuts tend to occur more frequently during economic downturns, when stocks come under considerable pressure. Having to issue a large amount of stock at the bottom of an economic downturn at a temporarily depressed level can be very negative for long-term shareholders.

CHAPTER 7

The "Regular-Special" Dividend: A New Way to Allocate Excess Capital

The Chicago Mercantile Exchange (CME) has a long history of innovation in the derivatives market. It can trace its origins to the founding of the Chicago Butter and Egg Board in 1898. In 1919, the Chicago Butter and Egg Board became the Chicago Mercantile Exchange, which was founded as a nonprofit owned by its members. One of its acquisitions, the Chicago Board of Trade (CBOT), created the first forward contract in 1851. In 1865, the CBOT began trading futures contracts, which were more standardized and easier to exchange than forwards, and thus provided traders with increased liquidity and strategic flexibility.

Over the next 100 years, CME and CBOT would launch a series of new futures contracts in pork bellies, live cattle, silver, foreign currencies, interest rates, and stock index futures. In 1992, CME would enable the first electronic trading platform for futures on its Globex system. This last innovation would facilitate explosive growth for

CME through much of the period from its IPO in 2002 right up until the Great Financial Crisis (GFC).

Before delving too deeply into the CME story, let's do some level setting to familiarize everyone with CME's essential business. At its core, CME facilitates the buying and selling of futures contracts.

WHAT IS A FUTURES CONTRACT?

A futures contract is a derivative that allows market participants to buy or sell a certain commodity, foreign currency, or financial instrument at a predetermined price in the future.

In deference to the classic Eddie Murphy and Dan Aykroyd film *Trading Places*, let's use orange juice futures in our example.

If I am an executive at a consumer staples firm that sells orange juice and I have just negotiated a price with Walmart to sell it for $3 a bottle, locking in the price for orange juice concentrate would make a lot of sense. If I can lock in a cost of $2 a bottle for the next 12 months through the purchase of orange juice concentrate futures, I reap multiple benefits. First, since orange juice concentrate is my largest component of cost of goods sold, I now have a fair degree of visibility on my profit margins on orange juice sales to Walmart and other customers. Second, if orange juice concentrate prices were to spike up (as Mortimer and Randolph Duke thought they would), I would not need to ask my key customers for an immediate price increase.

Since I had already locked in my orange juice concentrate costs through a series of futures contracts, I would be able to give Walmart and other customers an extended period of time to adjust to a pending price increase. Allowing key customers time to react to a commodity-induced price increase improves the odds that the price increase will be accepted, and also reduces the risk that the consumer staples firm's profit margin will compress. If the firm chose not to hedge its future cost of orange juice concentrate, a spike in its commodity costs would pressure near-term profit margins until it could renegotiate a price increase with its customers.

Futures Contracts Offer Multiple Benefits

By furnishing an infrastructure for trading, a legal structure of rules, contract specifications, and a clearinghouse to guarantee trades, futures exchanges provide a safe and efficient marketplace for traders. Benefits of futures trading include:

- Ensures near-term revenue or cost of goods certainty for producers
- Allows for the hedging of risk
- Provides valuable price signals for market participants (producers, buyers) that should reduce supply and demand imbalances in the market
- Offers a lower-cost way for investors to gain exposure to equity market returns

Who Might Buy or Sell a Futures Contract?

While futures markets were originally developed to help farmers and grain processors to hedge price risk, they have evolved to cover virtually every major commodity and financial market. Future contracts users include:

- Farmers: to lock in the price they will receive from crops or livestock
- Airline: to lock in the price of oil to minimize the impact of a spike in oil prices on profits
- Consumer staples firms: to lock in prices of key commodities that are used in their products (like orange juice)
- Fixed income portfolio managers: a low-cost way to alter a portfolio's duration (interest rate sensitivity)
- Equity portfolio managers: a low-cost way to gain exposure to the equity market
- Oil producers: to lock in the price of oil to make sure there is enough cash flow to support the drilling program

- Manufacturers: to lock in a set foreign currency exchange rate for a large overseas order to minimize the risk to profit margins if the currency depreciates

After a long history as a not-for-profit entity owned by its members, the CME Group transitioned to a publicly owned company in December of 2002. It went public with a market capitalization of $1.1 billion.

The CME Group stock performed impressively over its first four-plus years as a public company. A dollar invested in CME at the IPO was worth around $16 by the end of 2007. From 2003 to 2007, revenues more than tripled, operating margins expanded from 38% to 60%, net income increased almost fivefold, and earnings per share (EPS) increased from $3.60 to $14.93. For much of 2006–2007, the market awarded CME an earnings multiple on forward earnings between 32 and 37x. This was a significant premium—2.5x the S&P 500—reflecting CME's stellar revenue and earnings growth rate.

CME BENEFITED DURING THIS TIME FROM MULTIPLE POSITIVE TRENDS

After going public, CME trading volumes grew impressively as a result of better trading technologies and improved pricing.

Electronification

While futures exchanges had been around since before the Civil War, the use of futures for hedging or speculating was somewhat limited by the prevalence of open outcry markets that made trading difficult and expensive. The electronification of these markets was a significant positive trend for CME. It allowed investors as well as producers and firms that used or consumed these goods to enter orders electronically as opposed to having to send an order through a broker to buy on an open outcry market.

This greatly expanded the ease of buying futures, lowered bid-ask spreads, and increased liquidity in these markets, which drove a strong secular increase in demand for futures contracts. In 2000, only 10% of the contracts traded on CME's exchanges were done so electronically. By 2005, this would reach 70%.

Transition to For-Profit Business

When CME was a not-for-profit firm, it set the pricing for trading in its contracts at a low level to benefit its members. As a publicly traded company, CME set pricing on a commercial basis, reflecting the value of its exchange-trading platform. In addition, as volumes grew in what is primarily a high fixed-cost business, margins expanded dramatically.

The Great Financial Crisis (GFC) caused CME's business to slow, but CME was still able to grow revenues and operating profits in 2009.

Nevertheless, by 2010–2011, it had become clear that CME's growth rate was decelerating and the business was transitioning from an uber-growth stage to a more mature stage in its evolution. The strong secular growth in futures' demand was moderating. Quantitative easing by the Federal Reserve drove interest rates lower and reduced the need to hedge them, as the Federal Reserve was committed to keeping rates lower for longer.

THE CME'S ISSUANCE OF A SPECIAL DIVIDEND

Entering 2012, it was expected that CME's revenue growth would flatten out or potentially go negative. The stock, which, five years earlier had traded in the mid-30s on forward earnings, was now trading at 12–13x. In addition, there was speculation that CME might use its strong balance sheet to make potentially dilutive acquisitions to expand its business.

This weighed on investor confidence. The transition from a super-charged growth stock trading at a high valuation multiple to a more mature business facing near-term cyclical headwinds had been a painful experience for CME's investors. A $100 investment in CME in late 2007 was worth $38 at the end of 2011; the same $100 invested in the S&P 500 was worth $94.

In early February of 2012, CME reported disappointing fourth quarter earnings that missed consensus expectations. Nevertheless, CME's stock rose 8.4% when results were released as the company increased its regular dividend and announced a special dividend. CME now had a dividend yield of around 4.5% inclusive of the special dividend.

CME indicated that going forward it would return all excess cash on its balance sheet above $700 million in the form of an annual special dividend. In an environment of low interest rates, the ability to invest in a high-quality business with an attractive dividend yield was very compelling for investors. This capital return commitment also alleviated investor concerns about too much cash building up on the company's balance sheet (earning low returns) and the possibility that management would make dilutive acquisitions.

During CME's Fourth Quarter 2011 Earnings Conference Call, CME's CFO James Parisi said the following with regard to the announcement of the variable dividend and the increase in the regular dividend:

> We also want to, as I mentioned, invigorate our existing shareholders and attract new ones who are focused on yield. . . . Some shareholders will like the predictability of returns rather than the more sporadic buybacks. . . . The amount of the annual variable dividend will be determined after the end of each year and the level will increase or decrease from year to year based on excess cash on hand and will be impacted by operating results, potential M&A activity and other forms of capital return including regular dividends and share buybacks during the prior year. . . .

We want to continue to show that we are true to our word. We've said all along that we are going to return cash flow to our shareholders, and I believe the combination of the regular dividend and the variable dividend puts in place a mechanism that ensures we will continue to return excess capital in the future and keep our balance sheet strong and efficient. That, to me, is the most important takeaway that you have today, that we are committed to returning capital to our shareholders.[1]

This decision was a clear success. Between February of 2012 and the end of 2018, CME's forward earnings multiple doubled from 12–13x to 25x, even though the company's revenue growth rate decelerated over the next six years, as shown in Figure 7.1. CME's stock price rose 150% during this period relative to a 100% rise in the S&P 500 and a 125% rise in its exchange peers. The combination of increased capital return, reduced capital allocation uncertainty, and a structurally higher combined dividend (see Table 7.1) that could potentially support the stock during periods of weak exchange volumes created a compelling value proposition for investors.

TABLE 7.1

CME Dividend History (adjusted for stock splits)[2]

	Regular	Special	Total	Special as % of Total Dividends
2010	$0.92	$0.00	$0.92	0%
2011	$1.12	$0.00	$1.12	0%
2012	$1.79	$1.90	$3.69	51%
2013	$1.80	$2.60	$4.40	59%
2014	$1.88	$2.00	$3.88	52%
2015	$2.00	$2.90	$4.90	59%
2016	$2.40	$3.25	$5.65	58%
2017	$2.64	$3.50	$6.14	57%
2018	$2.80	$1.75	$4.55	38%

FIGURE 7.1

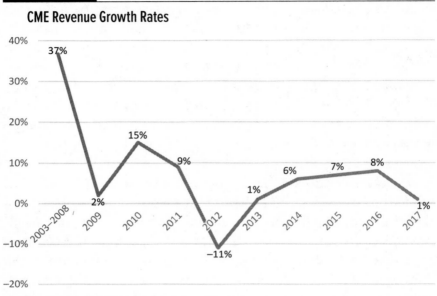

CME Revenue Growth Rates

Note: 2003-2008 CME growth rates are CAGR.

While this was a great outcome, was it the right decision from a process standpoint? It is fair to argue that when CME was trading at a depressed 12–13x earnings multiple that buying back stock might have generated more long-term shareholder wealth, given that returns on buying back stock would have been in the high-single digits immediately and increased into the double digits within a couple of years.

However, as exchange volumes started to grow again in 2013, it is likely CME's valuation multiple would have expanded, and the returns from buying back stock would have diminished. Moreover, a large stock repurchase program would not have attracted the yield-oriented investor or provided the downside support for the equity during a period of decreased exchange volumes. Buying back stock more aggressively or growing the dividend and instituting a regular-special dividend both had their advantages. However, CME's willingness to return more capital to shareholders, signaling a reduced risk of dilutive acquisitions and a lower likelihood of excess capital sitting on the balance sheet earning subpar returns was an important contributor to the excellent share price performance over this time period.

BRIEF HISTORY OF SPECIAL DIVIDENDS

For most of the period from 1930 to 1959, special dividends were neither rare nor special; they were often paid frequently, or in some cases, every year, as highlighted by an excellent research paper written by Harry DeAngelo, Linda DeAngelo, and Douglas J. Skinner in the *Journal of Financial Economics* in 2000.[3] Their paper highlights the following:

- Eastman Kodak paid out special dividends every year from 1954 to 1986.
- Around 28% of firms paying special dividends from 1926–1995 paid them almost every year.[†]
- More than half of firms paid special dividends more frequently than every other year.
- From mid-1926 through year-end 1995, special dividends represented 24% of all dividend distributions on average.

Their paper also highlights that special dividends reached their zenith in the 1950s when almost 3,000 special dividends were declared. However, by the 1980s, the number of special dividends fell by more than 90%. The low level of special dividends has continued for most of the last three decades as well, with the exception of periods when dividend tax changes occurred (driving companies to pay special dividends before the higher taxes went into effect) or periods when short-term tax changes allowed firms to repatriate overseas cash (i.e., trapped cash) at reduced rates.

---

† During the period in which they were paying special dividends. Not for the entire period 1926–1995.

Why Did Special Dividends Die Out?

Some people believe that special dividends died out as rule changes allowed firms to repurchase stock more easily, and repurchase activity took the place of special dividends. While this may have played a small role, special dividends were already declining before share repurchase activity started growing in the 1980s. Others believe that as institutional investors (mutual funds, hedge funds, pensions, etc.) came to own more shares than individual investors, institutional investors favored more regular, consistent dividends over less predictable special dividends.[4] While there is limited evidence to suggest a definitive conclusion as to why special dividends died out, I can appreciate the logic behind this latter view.

If you were to ask a CFO about capital allocation priorities and the benefits of various capital allocation alternatives, you might hear something close to the following:

- **Capital expenditures:** help me grow my business organically
- **Regular dividends:** increase attractiveness of my stock to yield-oriented investors
- **Share repurchase:** helps me grow EPS and increase returns on capital
- **Special dividends:** don't grow my business, don't increase EPS, and don't increase my ongoing dividend yield

While I don't necessarily agree with this logic, it does go a long way in explaining why special dividends have gone away.

Who Pays Special Dividends Today?

Generally, firms that pay special dividends today are those with:

- High insider ownership
- High cash levels

- Strong recent performance
- High returns[5]

These characteristics suggest that firms paying special dividends are often making the right decision. A company that has experienced strong recent earnings growth might have an expensive stock and/or its business is close to a cyclical peak, and thus overvalued on normalized, mid-cycle earnings. In that case, the decision to pay a special dividend is superior to buying back overvalued stock or increasing the regular dividend to a level that might not be sustainable during an economic or industry-specific downturn.

In addition, a company with high returns might be reluctant to spend additional capital on acquisitions or capital spending projects as these might dilute its already high returns. Finally, a company with high insider ownership is probably more aligned with shareholder interests and thus highly incentivized to deploy capital to generate the highest risk-adjusted returns.

Do Special Dividends Create Value?

In a 2009 article published in the *Quarterly Review of Economics and Finance*, researchers De-Wai Chou, Yi Liu, and Zaher Zantout assert, "Using essentially all declared extraordinary and special dividends between 1926 and 2001 which are not preceded or followed by the same for a period of three years, we find no robust post-declaration long-term abnormal stock returns."[6]

While this suggests that firms that issue infrequent special dividends do not outperform, many of the special dividends issued from 1926–1995 were recurring in nature and thus excluded from this study. A more limited study of special dividends from 2004–2012 found that firms declaring a special dividend outperformed by 2.61% over the three-day period following the announcement of the special dividend.[7]

As with all forms of capital allocation, the declaration of special dividends can be either value enhancing or value destroying depending on the characteristics of the firms declaring those dividends and the other options those firms have to deploy capital.

THE "REGULAR-SPECIAL DIVIDEND" OPTION

CME chose to provide forward commentary in connection with the special dividend announcement in February of 2012. This commentary suggested that CME would continue to pay the special dividend in most years and that investors could expect that at the end of the year, any excess cash on the balance sheet would be paid out in the form of a special dividend. This forward commentary essentially created a new class of capital allocation: the regular-special dividend.

For purposes of this book, I define the regular-special dividend as an informal commitment by a management team to return excess capital generated by the business in a given year to shareholders early in the following year via a special dividend payment.

That special dividend level can be set by:

- A certain cash level (as with CME)
- Excess capital beyond a certain leverage target (e.g., the firm will return excess capital to restore leverage to 1.5x net debt to EBITDA)
- A portion of the past year's FCF (e.g., return 50% of FCF to shareholders in the form of a special dividend)

The regular-special dividend is no longer one-off but instead something that investors can count on in most years and something that they can estimate. A yield-oriented investor, as in the case of CME, will value the special dividend and incorporate his assumption of the level of the special dividend into a total dividend yield calculation. As a result, the CFO's argument against issuing special dividends is no longer valid.

Given the success CME has had with its special dividend, it is somewhat surprising that more companies have not followed its example.

The regular-special dividend offers important advantages for firms:

Flexibility. A regular-special dividend provides a management team with tremendous flexibility. If the stock price falls and the returns from buying back stock increase, the firm has the ability to repurchase stock with excess capital and pay a smaller special dividend. If a very attractive acquisition opportunity comes along (e.g., CME made a large acquisition in 2018), the company can pay a smaller special dividend as well. The regular-special dividend gives investors increased certainty that excess capital will either be deployed each year or returned to shareholders the following year.

Attracts a more yield-oriented shareholder base. The ability of a more consistent regular-special dividend to attract a different and potentially more stable yield-oriented shareholder base could reduce the beta of the stock as well as increase a firm's valuation multiple.

WHAT TYPE OF FIRMS SHOULD CONSIDER PAYING A REGULAR-SPECIAL DIVIDEND?

Firms with volatile cash flows will benefit the most from issuing special dividends during period of excess cash accumulation.

Heavily Cyclical Businesses

There are numerous industries such as oil and gas exploration and production, chemical, agricultural, and banking that tend to generate significant earnings and FCFs late in the business cycle, and/or when the stock market/economy is strong or the underlying commodity price is above a mid-cycle, normalized level. These firms typically have significant excess capital to deploy at the wrong time in the cycle when their earnings, cash flows, and stock prices are elevated. Buying back stock during this period will likely mean overpaying for it at a disadvantageous time in the cycle. Putting in place a large regular dividend that is unsustainable in a downturn is not optimal either, as the dividend may later be cut. Increasing capital spending to take advantage of high commodity prices could backfire, given the lag time between the announcement and completion of the capital program if the commodity price returns to a more normalized, mid-cycle level or below.

Could a firm hold excess cash in the upturn and then use it in the downturn to buy back stock? While that is possible, in practice it is very challenging to execute. Sitting on cash earning very low, single-digit, after-tax returns while waiting for a downturn is not optimal and could attract activists. In addition, trying to predict when a downturn will occur is quite difficult. If a downturn does not occur for four to five years, the firm's return on capital will likely decline and its balance sheet will be highly inefficient.

A far better strategy would be for these firms to pay regular-special dividends with excess cash flow.

For example, an exploration and production company might commit to paying a regular-special dividend based on all excess cash on the balance sheet above $300 million at the end of the year. This informal commitment would allow an investment analyst to determine an approximate regular-special dividend the firm would pay based on different oil price averages over the course of the year, as shown in Table 7.2.

TABLE 7.2

Illustrative Example of Energy Company's Special Dividend

Oil Price	Potential Special Dividend	Incremental Yield
$40 and below	$0	0%
$50	$1	2.0%
$60	$1.75	3.5%
$70	$2.50	5.0%
$80	$3.25	6.5%

To recap, this strategy would do the following:

- Provide the Exploration and Production management team with some flexibility to make a high-return, value-creating acquisition during the course of the year.
- Provide improved clarity to its investor base around capital allocation, including the level of capital distribution at different oil price averages.
- Minimize risk of having cash pile up on the balance sheet earning subpar returns.
- Attract a more yield-oriented shareholder base to a volatile sector.
- Reduce the risk of buying back stock at high prices when oil prices are also high.
- Minimize the risk of a cut in the regular dividend by keeping it low.

Banks

Since the GFC, all of the largest US banks are required to go through extensive annual stress test of their capital adequacy in a theoretical future economic downturn. Firms that pass these tests are allowed to pay regular dividends and buy back stock.

Bank earnings are typically greatest near the end of an economic cycle when interest rates are high (thus net interest margins are high) and credit losses are low. As a result of this policy, banks are systematically forced to buy back stock at inopportune times or build up excess capital on their balance sheets. In a downturn, when credit losses are high and net interest margins are contracting, earnings often decline and potentially go negative, and stock prices are apt to experience considerable pressure. Unfortunately, the Federal Reserve would be unlikely to approve a significant capital return in the middle of a downturn for most banks as we saw in 2020 after the pandemic-induced economic downturn.

A far better strategy would be for the Federal Reserve to allow banks to pay regular-special dividends, or at a minimum, give them the option to do so, as opposed to buying back stock with their excess capital. Banks are typically bought by more value-oriented investors who are less focused on earnings growth and might be more attracted to a higher combined dividend (regular and regular-special).

Secularly Challenged Firms

The optimal capital allocation strategy for firms undergoing secular challenges to their business models will be thoroughly explored in Chapter 25; however, the regular-special dividend makes a tremendous amount of sense for these firms. For a firm with a business model facing secular challenges and limited options to address them, the management and board should do everything possible to bring forward capital returns to shareholders.

Finance theory teaches us that the value of any company is the present value of its future cash flows. If a firm never pays out dividends (regular or special) and then goes bankrupt 20 years in the future, from a financial theory standpoint the company is worthless today. However, if that same company paid out the vast majority of its cash flows to shareholders annually before going bankrupt, the firm would have considerable value to an investor today. The more risk and uncertainty about the sustainability of long-term cash flows, the greater the importance of returning excess capital to shareholders in the present.

A mall-based retailer with a strong management team that invests aggressively to sell its products online might still find itself with declining cash flows as mall traffic declines. A legacy-branded technology hardware manufacturer (PCs, servers, mainframes) might find its business under pressure as more and more of its customers' IT budgets shift to large cloud infrastructure providers who use predominantly white-label, commoditized hardware. While buying back stock at 8x FCF might produce strong cash-on-cash returns in year one, if cash flows are declining, cash-on-cash returns will diminish in future years. If the firm eventually goes bankrupt, the returns from buying back stock will be negative in the long term.

A far better strategy for these firms would be to pay out all excess capital to shareholders through an annual regular-special dividend, as opposed to buying back stock or making a Hail Mary acquisition in a different business where the management team has limited expertise. A company trading at 8x FCF with limited opportunities could enhance its shareholders' returns by issuing a 12.5% regular-special dividend. This would likely entice a new, yield-oriented shareholder base and could result in a higher valuation multiple as well.

Who Should Not Pay Special Dividends?

Paying special dividends is not advisable for many firms, including:

- Businesses with less volatile cash flows that can generate strong risk-adjusted returns buying back stock, increasing capital spending, making acquisitions, or paying a reasonable regular dividend that is not at risk of being cut.
- Businesses that are unlikely to pay the regular-special dividend in most years. A firm that creates an informal commitment to pay the regular-special dividend and pays it infrequently will disappoint its shareholder base.

CONCLUSION

CME's decision to pay a regular-special dividend beginning in 2012 has created a successful template for other firms to follow. Admittedly, the long-term academic evidence does not suggest significant outperformance for firms that pay special dividends. However, for a select group of firms that tend to generate material cash flows at the wrong point in the cycle, or for firms undergoing secular/structural challenges to their business models, the regular-special dividend is a logical option to consider as part of a sound capital allocation policy.

CHAPTER 8

The (Alleged) Seven Deadly Sins of Share Repurchase

S tock repurchases generate a great deal of heated commentary, as the following quotes attest:

> *Repurchases done on the open market, which constitute the vast majority of all buybacks, are nothing but manipulation of a company's stock price. That should be illegal, but it is obviously not.*
>
> **—William Lazonick,** "The Curse of Stock Buybacks"[1]

> *Stock buybacks are eating the world. The once illegal practice of companies purchasing their own shares is pulling money away from employee compensation, research and development, and other corporate priorities—with potentially sweeping effects on business dynamism, income, and wealth inequality, working-class economic stagnation, and the country's growth rate.*
>
> **—Annie Lowrey,** "Are Stock Buybacks Starving the Economy?"[2]

The surge in corporate buybacks is driving wealth inequality and wage stagnation in our country by hurting long-term economic growth and shared prosperity for workers.

—Senator Tammy Baldwin (D-WI)[3]

Unlike other ways of returning excess cash to investors, such as dividends, buybacks can distort financial measures, such as earnings per share. Fewer shares? Voila, higher earnings per share.

—Rita McGrath, "The Case for Banning Stock Buybacks"[4]

Stock buybacks create a sugar high for the corporations.

—Senator Elizabeth Warren (D-MA)[5]

The experts agree. Just a small sampling of my vast research on the subject confirms that share repurchase has become the most controversial and vilified form of capital allocation. It has been blamed for slower economic growth, increased wealth inequality, weak business investment, decreased R&D spending, lower employee compensation, earnings manipulation, and killing kittens. (OK, share repurchase has *yet* to be blamed for the untimely death of kittens.) If these critics were to prevail, in the near future, share repurchase could be banned. In fact, by the time you are reading this book, share repurchase may already have become a relic of the past. In many ways, share repurchase has become the Rodney Dangerfield of capital allocation in the last decade. It does not get any respect.

Most of the discussion around dividends, capital spending, and special dividends is quantitative in nature, with a plethora of academic analyses forming the foundation upon which to engage in a debate on the relative merits of each. These analyses are principally focused on returns, risk-adjusted returns, and the management incentives behind the capital allocation decision-making process.

The debate around share repurchase is altogether different. It has become political, emotional, and qualitative. Facts are less important.

Share repurchase suffers because it is less understood than the other forms of capital allocation. Dividends, special dividends, and capital spending have all been around for centuries. As a meaningful capital allocation alternative, share repurchase has been around since the early 1980s. The theory behind why a company might repurchase its own shares is less intuitive, and it suffers from the misguided belief that it does not create any economic value.

It is critically important to address the very serious charges leveled against share repurchase activity, and also to explain **why share repurchase makes sense in a limited number of circumstances.**

LEGITIMATE CONCERNS

There are some very legitimate concerns with regard to share repurchase.

Concern 1: Share Repurchase at the Aggregate Level Can Be Poorly Timed

Share repurchase activity among S&P 1500 companies grew dramatically from 1994 ($56 billion) to the peak of the dot-com bubble in 1999 ($215 billion). However, when stocks were on sale in 2001–2003, share repurchases averaged only $172 billion per year. Following that, share repurchase activity rose dramatically over the next four years reaching a peak of $673 billion in 2007 right as the stock market peaked and ultimately declined around 60%. In 2009, when stocks were at their lowest valuations on normalized earnings in at least two decades, share repurchase activity fell by more than 50% from its 2007 peak. The aggregate level of share repurchase activity among the S&P 1500 constituents did not pierce its 2007 peak until 2018. Buying back stock above fair value or when valuations are high is a recipe for value destruction and can result in suboptimal returns on capital.[6]

It should be pointed out that poor capital allocation timing is not unique to share repurchase. Spending on acquisitions often peaks near the top of the stock market and economic cycle. The level of capital spending, especially in heavily cyclical industries, tends to accelerate late in an economic cycle and decline during an economic correction.

Concern 2: Demand for Dividends Is Increasing at the Same Time That Dividend Payout Ratios Are Declining Due to Increased Share Repurchase

As interest rates on government bonds across most of the developed world have declined, the attractiveness of dividends as a source of income has risen. As Figure 8.1 demonstrates, the yield differential between US government bonds and S&P 500 has declined materially in the last decade. In countries such as Germany and Japan, where government bond yields are negative, this differential is even wider. Retirees across the globe who would have previously invested heavily in government bonds to provide safe, predictable retirement income are being forced to buy dividend stocks and/or invest in riskier bonds to achieve their income needs. The aging demographics of most of the Western world, with more and more people leaving the workforce, is only adding to the soaring demand for dividends.

In addition, over the long term, dividend payments should grow, whereas a bond is locked into a fixed level of interest. Currently, dividends are taxed at a lower rate than interest income in the United States, which only further enhances their after-tax attractiveness.

As demand for income from a secular demographic perspective is rising, dividend income is increasingly attractive relative to fixed income alternatives. Yet, management teams and boards of public companies are paying out a smaller percentage of earnings to shareholders in the form of dividends despite this insatiable investor demand. At the aggregate level, this does not make a lot of sense.

FIGURE 8.1

US 10-Year Bond Yields Have Fallen Dramatically in the Last Decade, S&P 500 Dividend Yields Have Declined Only Modestly

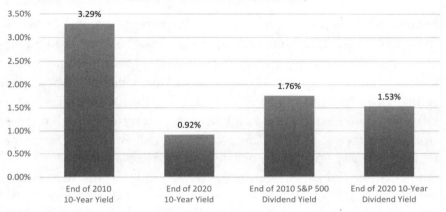

Source: FactSet financial data and analytics, accessed February 13, 2021

Concern 3: Certain Types of Firms Should De-emphasize Share Repurchase

There are two broad groupings of firms that should de-emphasize share repurchase relative to dividends and special dividends.

"Peakers." Firms that generate the vast majority of their FCF at the top of the economic, stock market, or commodity cycle are typically buying back stock when fundamentals and stock prices are trading above fair value. This helps explain why share repurchase activity was so strong in 2006–2007 and so weak in 2008–2010. These firms had a lot of FCF in 2006–2007 and spent it. Those same firms had less FCF in 2008–2010 and spent less on share repurchase.

Firms that produce FCF predominantly during these latter stages of an economic cycle are often structurally overpaying for their stock and thus generating poor returns on this investment. These firms should only buy back stock with FCF when the returns from buying back are justified, not on peak fundamentals but on mid-cycle fundamentals as well. A far better alternative to buying back shares at these firms is the regular-special dividend (see Chapter 7).

Secularly challenged. Firms that are undergoing secular pressure from new market entrants, changing consumer tastes, regulation, or technological change that is impeding their ability to grow and maintain profitability should not be aggressively buying back stock. A firm with $10 million of FCF and a $100 million market capitalization could easily look at the near-term returns of buying back stock as attractive (10% cash-on-cash returns). But if in five years FCF is down to $5 million (the 5% cash-on-cash return five years out), returns could look very poor. If the value of any firm is the net present value of its future cash flows paid to shareholders, then repurchase extends the duration of these cash flows further into the future for shareholders who choose not to sell. In contrast, dividends or special dividends bring forward cash flows to existing shareholders. For a company undergoing secular pressure, the future is more uncertain relative to the present, so bringing forward the duration of cash flows is optimal.

Concern 4: Recent Academic Evidence on Share Repurchase Is Mixed

The vast majority of academic research done on share repurchase pre-2000 demonstrated not only positive short-term outperformance, but more important intermediate-term outperformance as well. Essentially, following a share repurchase announcement, stocks reacted positively, but the stocks typically continued to outperform for multiple years into the future as investors systematically underreacted to these announcements. Many academics believed these announcements were a signal to the market that a firm's stock valuation was too low and that buybacks created value by acquiring shares for less than its intrinsic value. As discussed in Chapter 6, stock buyback programs were also a signal to the market of reduced risk of overinvestment consistent with Jensen's FCF theory (1986).[7]

However, Fangjian Fu and Sheng Huang, in a 2016 paper entitled "The Persistence of Long-Run Abnormal Returns Following Stock Repurchases and Offerings," reported no excess stock market returns for firms buying back stock during 2003–2012. Their research hypothesized that as buybacks grew in popularity, they became less about signaling undervaluation of their shares and more about returning excess capital to shareholders.[8]

Nevertheless, other, more recent studies have continued to see long-term excess returns from share repurchase activity. These include work by Peyer and Vermaelen (2009), Dittmar and Field (2015), and Manconi, Peyer, and Vermaelen (2019).[9] The last study is particularly interesting in that it found long-term excess returns among firms that bought back stock not only in the United States, but in the vast majority of 31 non-US markets as well.

One other factor to consider here is that growth companies, which typically buy back less stock, have dramatically outperformed value stocks, which typically buy back more stock since the Great Financial Crisis (GFC). It is quite possible that some of the underperformance of firms buying back stock is a function of growth stocks outperforming value stocks as opposed to share repurchase simply failing to create value. Moreover, from an anecdotal perspective, I have found in recent years an increasing amount of share repurchase activity among firms that are facing secular challenges to their business models. I believe that share repurchase in such cases is often misguided and in most cases generates a suboptimal long-term return on capital. This may also explain some of the mixed results of share repurchase in recent years.

ARE THE CRITICS RIGHT?

If I were a capital allocation deity, there would be less share repurchase and more dividends and special dividends. However, almost all of the decline in share repurchase would come from secularly challenged businesses and from companies with volatile earnings and cash flows and significant economic or industry-specific downside risk. Like all forms of capital allocation, share repurchase can be a very intelligent use of excess capital for certain companies and a suboptimal use of excess capital for other companies.

Despite the aforementioned concerns with regard to share repurchase at the aggregate level, I do find most of the criticisms of share repurchase to be misguided and/or unsupported by the vast preponderance of evidence.

THE (ALLEGED) SEVEN DEADLY SINS OF SHARE REPURCHASE

1. Dividends holy, share repurchase unholy.
2. Share repurchase is wasted cash.
3. Share repurchase negatively impacts R&D spending and capital spending.
4. Share repurchase drives EPS growth and can "distort" EPS.
5. Alternatives to share repurchase are far better.
6. Share repurchase hurts employee compensation.
7. Management teams use aggressive share repurchases to drive EPS growth to maximize their own compensation.

Let's address these sins one by one:

Sin 1: Dividends Holy, Share Repurchase Unholy

Share repurchase should hire whoever does public relations for dividends. I find it odd that share repurchase receives so much condemnation for allegedly impeding investment and R&D and slowing economic growth while dividends receive very little criticism. Both share repurchase and dividends are ways to return capital to shareholders, capital that could, theoretically, be retained for capital expenditures, employee compensation, or increased research and development.

Whether a firm pays a dividend to an investor or buys back stock from the same investor, the investor still receives cash from the company.

The investor then has a choice as to what he wants to do with that cash:

a. Redeploy (reinvest in another stock or bond)
b. Consume (spend)

Whether the dollar comes from a dividend or from selling share(s) back to the company does not matter to the investor. The only difference is that the investor receiving the dividend does not have to sell stock to receive cash to redeploy or consume.

Sin 2: Share Repurchase Is Wasted Cash

The cash that an investor receives from selling a share back to the firm is not lost to some parallel dimension or alternative universe. It does not disappear. It is often redeployed into one or more of the following options:

- Buying shares in another firm
- Participating in a capital raise for a firm looking to go public
- Participating in a secondary equity offering for a public company seeking additional capital
- Buying newly issued shares in a firm when an employee sells vested stock grants
- Participating in a convertible debt offering
- Buying shares in private companies prior to going public (more recently)
- Buying fixed-income securities (for investors that are not purely equity investors)

The key point is that the vast majority of capital returned to shareholders through a share repurchase program is recycled back into the capital markets. This recycling process is a very efficient way for capital that is not needed for reinvestment at mature companies to be funneled to firms that need additional funds for reinvestment.

Distinguished NYU finance professor Aswath Damadaran highlighted this point in a 2019 interview:

> *And so the question is not whether you want companies to invest or to buy back shares, but rather which companies you want investing: the aging companies of the last century, or the newer companies that have better investment opportunity today? Choosing the latter should redirect cash from bad businesses to good businesses, boosting the economy in the long run.*[10]

Share repurchase helps direct capital to firms that need it and away from firms that don't. Firms that deploy share repurchase are typically more mature, less capital-intensive businesses and in most cases, not "bad" businesses. Firms that need this capital are typically emerging growth companies and more capital-intensive businesses.

In addition, some of the cash investors receive by selling their shares back to the company will be consumed to pay for housing, groceries, medical care, college education for their children, and discretionary purposes. There is nothing wrong with this. Investors own stocks not merely for long-term capital appreciation purposes, but as a means to accomplish a multitude of financial objectives. This spending also helps support the economy and once again, highlights the point that excess capital returned by mature companies is not wasted or lost. This capital is either recycled into the capital markets for companies that need it or recycled into the real economy.

Sin 3: Share Repurchase Negatively Impacts R&D Spending and Capital Spending

In 1982, share repurchase limitations were relaxed in the United States. Since then, the level of R&D spending, especially business-funded R&D, has been steadily rising as a percentage of GDP. In fact, business-funded R&D spending as a percentage of GDP doubled from 1977 to 2017. In addition, while share repurchase is much more widespread in the United States than in Western Europe or China, US spending on R&D is 35% higher than Wester Europe and 30% higher than China as a percentage of GDP. Moreover, business-funded R&D represents almost three-quarters of all R&D spending in the United States. Business-funded R&D was only half of R&D spending at the time when share repurchase limitations were relaxed in the early 1980s.[11]

Recent evidence also suggests that firms buying back stock actually spend more on R&D and capital expenditures than firms that choose not to repurchase stock.[12]

In addition, in April 2017, the Federal Reserve released a paper by Joseph Gruber and Steven Kamin, in which the authors looked at the level of payouts (dividends + buybacks) and the level of capital investment in 26 OECD countries before and after the GFC. They sought to determine whether any relationship existed between the change in the level of shareholder payouts pre- and post-crisis and the change in the level of capital investment. In other words, did countries that saw the biggest increase in capital returns to shareholders (dividends + buybacks) see a decline in investment?

They did not. Gruber and Kamin found "little evidence that economies that have experienced larger shortfalls in corporate investment spending have experienced larger increases in share buybacks and/or dividend payments."[13] While the paper looked at total capital return, not just stock repurchase activity, it still supports the claim that returning excess capital to shareholders does not negatively impact capital spending.

There is simply no evidence that share repurchase activity is responsible for lower R&D or reduced capital spending in the developed world.

Sin 4: Share Repurchase Drives EPS Growth and Can "Distort" EPS

There is a view that buying back stock distorts earnings or is in some way a "free lunch" and an easy way for CEOs to drive EPS growth. Moreover, because CEOs are increasingly compensated on EPS growth, some argue that these executives use stock repurchase programs to artificially boost both EPS growth and their own compensation.

Can share repurchase support EPS growth? The answer is clearly yes, but *most* forms of intelligent capital allocation can drive EPS growth. While dividends and special dividends don't support EPS growth, they do drive total shareholder returns as I will show in the upcoming pages. The key is selecting the form of capital deployment that offers the greatest returns.

Regarding the claim that share repurchase distorts EPS, critics miss two important points:

First, share repurchase is not free. There is both an actual negative hit to the income statement as well as an opportunity cost related to share repurchase. A company that wants to increase its EPS by 5% cannot simply accomplish this by buying back 5% of its share on the open market. To fund a share repurchase program, the company will forgo interest income (if using cash on balance sheet to pay for it) or incur higher interest expense (if using debt to finance the program).

These incremental income statement costs will partially offset the benefits from the share repurchase program and result in a smaller benefit to EPS. In addition, there is an opportunity cost associated with share repurchase. Capital that is deployed on a share repurchase program could have been used for internal investments. If the return on these internal investments is higher than the return on share repurchase, a company would actually be slowing EPS growth by buying back stock.

Second, all forms of capital deployment can alter or distort EPS. A company that pays a special dividend or a regular dividend could see its EPS decline as it loses the interest income from the cash that was previously on its balance sheet. If the returns from a capital investment program and share repurchase program are the same, the impact on EPS would also be the same. A firm that makes an accretive acquisition will see its EPS "distorted" higher.

Let's provide an example here:

Company A
$100 million in earnings and FCF
100 million shares
$1 per share of EPS and FCF/share
$1.5 billion market capitalization
15x multiple on EPS and FCF/share
3% after-tax cost of debt

TABLE 8.1

Company A Decides to Repurchase 5% of Its Outstanding Shares for $75 Million

	Current State	Future State
Net Income	100	100
Incremental After-Tax Debt Costs		−2.25
Net Income After New Debt Costs	100	97.75
Existing Share Count	100	100
Change in Share Count		−5
New Share Count	100	95
EPS	$1.00	$1.03

The decision to repurchase stock has boosted EPS growth by 3% (see Table 8.1) but not the intended 5% level due to the higher interest costs associated with the program.

However, if the management team at Company A is really focused on growing EPS, there might be an internal investment the firm could make over the next year at a higher return than buying back stock. What if the firm spent that $75 million on renovating and expanding capacity at an older plant and was able to generate a 10% return on that investment?

TABLE 8.2

Company A Spends $75 Million Renovating and Expanding Capacity at a Plant

	Current State	Future State
Net Income	100	100
Incremental After-Tax Debt Costs		−2.25
Returns from Investment		7.5
Net Income After New Debt Costs	100	105.25
Existing Share Count	100	100
EPS	$1.00	$1.05

Given the high returns associated with this investment, Company A has boosted its EPS growth by more than it would have if it had bought back stock, as seen in Table 8.2.

Company A is also looking at making an acquisition of a complementary business in a new geography. Company A could spend $75 million on an acquisition that will generate $5 million in earnings and FCF (Table 8.3).

TABLE 8.3

Company A Spends $75 Million for an Acquisition

	Current State	Future State
Net Income	100	100
Incremental After-Tax Debt Costs		−2.25
Acquisition Earnings		5
Net Income After New Debt Costs	100	102.75
Existing Share Count	100	100
EPS	$1.00	$1.03

In this case, the EPS boost is similar to the benefit from the share repurchase program, but inferior to the EPS benefit from executing the renovation investment.

The last option Company A has under consideration is a special dividend payment to shareholders (Table 8.4).

TABLE 8.4

Company A Pays Out $75 Million in Cash to Shareholders Financed Through Adding Debt to Their Balance Sheet

	Current State	Future State
Net Income	100	100
Incremental After-Tax Debt Costs		−2.25
Net Income After New Debt Costs	100	97.75
Existing Share Count	100	100
EPS	$1.00	$0.98

In this case, EPS falls below the level of EPS in all of the other alternatives. However, investors care about total shareholder return, not just EPS growth. Total shareholder return is the combination of dividends + capital appreciation from the underlying stock.

In this last case, assuming a similar 15x valuation multiple, the underlying stock will decline in value from $15 (15x $1 in EPS) to $14.70 (15x $0.98 in EPS).

However, from a total return perspective, the investor received a 5% return from the special dividend that should more than compensate for an expected 2% decline in the underlying stock price, as shown in Table 8.5.

TABLE 8.5

Total Shareholder Return of Various Capital Alternatives Assuming Constant Valuation Multiples

	EPS	Stock Price	Capital Appreciation	Special Dividend	Total Shareholder Return
Current State	$1.00	$15.00			
Share Repurchase	$1.03	$15.45	3.0%	0%	3.0%
Acquisition	$1.03	$15.75	3.0%	0%	3.0%
Renovation Investment	$1.05	$15.75	5.0%	0%	5.0%
Special Dividend	$0.98	$14.70	–2.0%	5%	3.0%

The best way to drive EPS growth is to invest excess capital with the highest cash-on-cash returns whether that is internal investments, acquisitions, or share repurchase. While paying out dividends can reduce EPS growth, it does bolster total shareholder returns. **Share repurchase has no monopoly on driving higher EPS growth once the total cost of buying back stock (interest expense or lost interest income) and the opportunity cost of other alternatives is fully accounted for.**

Sin 5: Alternatives to Share Repurchase Are Far Better

If firms were no longer allowed to buy back stock, I do not believe that you would see any discernable difference in R&D or capital spending. The reason is simple: firms almost always prioritize high-return internal investments. Internal investments that generate higher returns than other capital allocation alternatives are frequently highlighted and prioritized in management presentations. In my 23-year investment career, I have yet to see a management team prioritize share repurchase, dividends, or acquisitions above high-return organic projects.

In a 2016 *ViewPoints* conversation on "Returning Capital to Shareholders" by members of the Audit Committee Leadership Network in North America, which represents some of the largest publicly traded companies in the United States, ACLN members stated "that in nearly every case, their companies try to exhaust their options for growth before returning capital to shareholders. . . . One member said, 'It is only after we consider all options for investing in the business and funding out liabilities that we might talk about a buyback.' "[14]

In his 2016 letter to Berkshire Hathaway shareholders, Warren Buffet wrote:

> As the subject of repurchases has come to a boil, some people have come close to calling them un-American—characterizing them as corporate misdeeds that divert funds needed for productive endeavors. That simply isn't the case. Both American corporations and private investors are today awash in funds looking to be sensibly deployed. I'm not aware of any enticing project that has died for lack of capital. (Call us if you have a candidate.)[15]

Returning capital return to shareholders (dividends, share repurchase, special dividends), and spending capital on acquisitions are almost always considered after firms have already exhausted all high-return internal investments. Eliminating the option for share repurchase might result in more acquisitions, higher dividends, and more special dividends, but is unlikely to result in additional low-return or negative-return projects.

While I might argue that having firms pay more dividends could be a good thing at the aggregate level, I do not believe that a surge in acquisitions would be a positive for shareholders or for society as a whole. Acquisitions typically generate subpar returns for shareholders relative to share repurchases and dividends.

Moreover, in order to justify paying sizable premiums to current stock price for an acquisition, most acquirers will announce a cost-cutting program in concert with the acquisition announcement. The cost-cutting program will often include plant closures, headcount reductions, and purchasing synergies.

I can still remember as a young child how scared my mother was when a large oil company attempted a hostile takeover of the firm that employed my father. My father worked at the corporate head-quarters of a midsized oil company in information technology and would most likely have lost his job if the hostile takeover had been successful. Of the prospective hostile acquirer, my dear mother half-joked with my sister and me that we should "pee on their floors when using their restrooms." While we did not follow through on that suggestion—or at least I don't remember doing that—it does highlight the consequences of a policy that reduces share repurchase activity and is likely to drive more M&A activity. I am not sure that is necessarily a good thing from a societal perspective, and it would clearly not be a positive for long-term equity investors.

In addition, one of the reasons why acquisitions may prove to be a less successful form of capital allocation is that employees of both firms may be distracted and distressed about losing their jobs. In many cases, the real winners from these acquisitions are the firm's competitors who see an opportunity to hire away talent from the firms that are combining. Just think how you would react tomorrow if your firm announced a large acquisition that involved significant cost synergies. Would you update your résumé, talk to your family about the potential need to leave your community, and pull back on spending? You might do all three of those things, especially if you work in an area that is likely to be synergized. But if your company announced a large share repurchase program, would you do anything different? I doubt it, because there would be no reason to fear for your job.

Acquisitions also create less competition and more oligopolistic industry pricing structures that may result in higher prices and fewer choices for consumers and businesses.

Sin 6: Share Repurchase Hurts Employee Compensation

One of the arguments against share repurchase is that if there is cash left that is not needed for reinvestment, it should be returned to employees rather than investors.

Few management teams and boards consider share repurchase, or for that matter dividends, special dividends, or M&A in this manner. For most management teams and boards, employee compensation and return of excess capital are in two completely separate buckets.

A firm must pay its employees a reasonable compensation level consistent with what its competitors pay and what its employees could earn in other industries. A firm that pays below the average rate for talent will systematically lose its best employees, experience high turnover, and struggle to fill vacancies. Any firm that engages in such a strategy will atrophy over the long run.

Management teams and boards think about how to deploy excess capital after all normal business expenses have been paid (utilities, maintenance capital spending, rent, taxes, and yes, employee compensation). What remains is a separate bucket of funds for the management team and board to allocate toward growth capital spending, dividends, special dividends, share repurchase, and M&A.

The larger issue is how do we as a society increase market-based wages? What happens when an employee in a high-labor cost country faces wage pressure or the loss of their job when an alternative is found in a low-cost emerging market country? Is the solution legislation aimed at a higher minimum wage? Is it tariffs that disrupt both the positives and negatives from free trade and globalization? Is it encouraging more unionization? Is it corporate tax policy? Is it employees serving on boards of directors?

This is not a policy-focused book, and there are no easy answers to these questions. These issues go far beyond the realm of capital allocation. However, I do feel very confident saying that banning share repurchase is unlikely to have any discernable impact on market-based wages. It will simply redirect excess capital toward larger dividends, more special dividends, and increased M&A.

Sin 7: Management Teams Use Aggressive Share Repurchases to Drive EPS Growth to Maximize Their Compensation

Once again, the evidence fails to support the accusation.

A majority of S&P 500 companies in 2018 did not tie executive compensation to EPS growth, and those that did actually spent less of their cash on share repurchase than those firms that did not have it is an incentive.[16]

A Stanford Business School Corporate Governance Research Institute study of S&P 500 long-term incentive programs found that only 28% of companies used EPS growth as a performance metric in determining long-term incentive compensation.[17]

While not directly tied to the seven deadly sins, critics of share repurchase tend to overstate the magnitude of corporate spending on share repurchase by not considering the role of stock-based compensation for employees.

When critics lament the hundreds of billions of dollars firms spend on share repurchase, they often fail to take into consideration that approximately a quarter to a third of all stock repurchase is undertaken to offset employee dilution in the United States.

In my experience, most companies have anywhere between 50 to 150 basis points of annual dilution from stock-based awards.

That means that if firms failed to buy back any stock, their outstanding diluted shares would increase 0.5% to 1.5% per year. As a general rule, the larger the firm, the less dilution. Many established firms that generate FCF will often use some of it to offset dilution.

Stock awards usually vest over a multiyear period and serve two purposes. First, they are a retention tool. If you leave the firm, you walk away from the value of unvested stock awards. Second, and maybe more important, stock awards incentivize all employees to drive long-term value creation for the firm, since employees will benefit from a rising stock price. With options and stock grants vesting over a multiyear period (3–10 years usually), employees are heavily incentivized to create long-term shareholder value as opposed to trying to maximize performance in one year or one quarter.

Now let's look at a simple example to illustrate this point (Table 8.6). There are two firms with the exact same income statement. In addition, both stocks are trading for $50 per share. The only difference is that Firm A employee compensation cost is 90% cash and 10% stock grants, and Firm B is 100% cash (no stock grants).

TABLE 8.6

Two Firms with the Exact Same Income Statement

Revenues	$1,000
Employee Compensation	−$400
Other Expenses	−$400
Pretax Income	$200
Taxes	−$50
Net Income	$150
Shares Outstanding	50
EPS	$3.00

Since stock awards are non-cash expenses, Firm A will report $40 million more FCF than Firm B, as shown in Table 8.7. However, if Firm A takes no action, its share count will increase from 50 million to 50.8 million ($40 million stock awards divided by $50 stock price).

TABLE 8.7

Firm A Employee Compensation Cost Is 90% Cash and 10% Stock Grants; Firm B's Is 100% Cash.

	Firm A	Firm B
Net Income	150	150
Non-cash Stock Compensation	40	0
Depreciation	100	100
W/C investments	−20	−20
Operating Cash Flow	270	230
Capital Spending	−120	−120
FCF	150	110

Firm A decides it wants to keep share count flat (like Firm B) and spends the $40 million to offset the dilution, shown in Table 8.8.

TABLE 8.8

Firm A Spends 40 Million to Offset Dilution

	Firm A	Firm B
Net Income	150	150
Non-cash Stock Compensation	40	0
Depreciation	100	100
W/C investments	−20	−20
Operating Cash Flow	270	230
Capital Spending	−120	−120
FCF	150	110
Buy Back Stock to Offset Dilution	−40	0
FCF After Offsetting Dilution	110	110

From an economic perspective, these two firms are exactly the same, excluding the potential benefits of higher retention and more motivated employees at Firm A. The FCF available to be deployed for the benefit of shareholders after offsetting dilution is exactly the same. Essentially, Firm A is giving employees stock in place of cash, then turning around and spending that cash to offset employee stock awards.

When one examines the level of share repurchase, especially relative to other countries that conduct less share repurchase and issue far fewer stock grants to employees, critics should take this dynamic into account. Net share repurchase—share repurchase net of stock awards—is a far more accurate way to think about the true amount of excess capital that is being deployed toward buying back stock.

SUMMARY OF SHARE REPURCHASE FINDINGS

Management teams, boards, investors, and critics of share repurchase should be aware of the following:

1. The timing of share repurchase activity by management teams at the aggregate level, similar to other forms of capital allocation, has not been stellar.
2. At the aggregate level, firms should spend less on share repurchase and more on dividends and special dividends.
3. Share repurchase is not responsible for lower R&D, capital spending, or employee wage growth.
4. Share repurchase has no monopoly on driving higher EPS growth for firms relative to other capital allocation alternatives.
5. Management compensation metrics are not driving increased share repurchase relative to other forms of capital allocation.
6. Banning share repurchase activity is likely to result in more M&A and lower returns on excess capital deployment for shareholders.

7. Share repurchase creates shareholder value only when the returns are greater than other forms of capital allocation over the intermediate term and when the shares are undervalued.

8. In the United States, given the extensive use of stock grants for employees, the level of share repurchase activity should be viewed on a net basis (net of employee stock issuance) as opposed to a gross basis.

CHAPTER 9

How Should Management Teams and Boards Think About Share Repurchase?

A number of factors should be considered:

- **Share repurchase versus alternatives**—Compare the cash-on-cash returns from share repurchase over the intermediate term (next five to six years) to other capital allocation options.
- **Secularly-challenged firms and heavy cyclical firms should avoid share repurchase**—Firms with secular challenges and volatile FCF are not great candidates for share repurchase. Companies facing secular challenges with long-term concerns about the sustainability, viability, and/or growth of the underlying business should favor special dividends over buybacks in order to bring forward cash distributions to shareholders. Firms with FCF that materializes only at the top of an economic cycle, commodity cycle, or stock market cycle should

favor special dividends over share repurchase unless the stock price is cheap on mid-cycle fundamentals/cash flows.

- **Share repurchase versus dividends**—Dividends should be set at a level that will not need to be cut in the future. The level of the dividend relative to the amount of share repurchase activity should be driven by the spread between the return on dividends (see Chapter 6) and the return on buying back stock. The greater the return spread on buying back stock vs. dividends, the more capital should be deployed toward share repurchase and vice versa.
- **The needs of your shareholders.** Do they want more dividend income or more capital appreciation?
- **The industry your firm operates in.** Is it a high-dividend sector or a low-dividend payout industry?
- **A mix that maximizes your risk-adjusted returns for shareholders.** Firms that pay limited dividends will have more of the present value of their future cash flows 20–30 years into the future, so small changes in fundamentals can have a greater impact on future cash flows resulting in a higher volatile stock. A firm that pays out a reasonable amount of dividends will have a greater proportion of their future cash flows paid out to its shareholders over the near-to-intermediate-term and thus its stock should be less volatile and less risky.

The best candidates to systematically buy back a significant amount of stock over the long run are firms that have the following characteristics:

- **Underlying business and cash flows are not overly cyclical.** This reduces the risk of poor timing of share repurchases, as the firm's cash flows are more sustainable throughout a cycle. In the event of a downturn, the firm will have the ability to buy back its shares at attractive prices. Unlike a more cyclical firm, the cash-on-cash returns from buying back stock are also more predictable as the underlying cash flows are more sustainable.

- **Firms in which acquisitions are not a viable alternative.** There are multiple reasons why this might be the case. It could be that the industry is already consolidated, and anti-trust concerns would hamper acquisitions. It could be that there is a supply/demand imbalance for acquisitions in the space, and the returns from acquisitions are poor. Or the firm might lack the management depth and expertise to successfully integrate acquisitions.

- **Firm operates in a mature market with moderate underlying growth without secular challenges.** As long as the business is generating consistent underlying growth over time, the cash-on-cash returns from buying back stock will compound and increase. A business that can improve underlying profits by 4–5% per year through a combination of organic growth and modest margin expansion that generates a year one mid-single-digit cash-on-cash returns by buying back stock with strong FCF conversion should be able to deliver high-single-digit to low-double-digit EPS growth annually. This rate can be higher or lower depending on the dividend payout ratio and the amount of debt in the capital structure.

- **Companies in which the stock price is fundamentally undervalued relative to the market.** One of the best ways to look at this is the year five cash-on-cash return from buying back stock versus the return from dividends (which are a proxy for market/index level cash-on-cash returns). The greater the spread between buying back stock and paying out dividends over the intermediate term, the more capital allocation should be spent on share repurchase versus dividends. In Chapter 10, I will explore the story of AutoZone that systematically bought back its undervalued stock and created significant shareholder value in the process while continuing to aggressively invest to grow its business.

- **Companies in which there is limited pressure to pay out a large dividend.** In certain sectors, there is significant interest in dividends (utilities, REITs, telecom) and in others there is less (growth and growth-at-a-reasonable price stocks). If the shareholder base is not interested in dividends and the returns from buying back stock are far superior to paying out dividends, firms should choose to buy back more stock.

Hypothetical Example of the Role of Share Repurchase

In 2009, the Greene family and a select group of friends decided to open a series of Italian restaurants in their hometown of Toledo, Ohio. Unlike most other towns at the time, Toledo had a dearth of Italian restaurants.

Their first eight restaurants were a financial success generating attractive returns on their investment. However, when they opened their ninth restaurant in 2018, they found it generated a subpar return. Sales at one of their existing restaurants were negatively impacted as the ninth location cannibalized a portion of its sales. In fact, once the adverse impact on the existing restaurant's profits was taken into account, the new restaurant generated only 7% returns.

While the family had planned on opening a tenth restaurant, the disappointing returns for the ninth suggested that they were getting close to saturating the greater Toledo market. Every additional restaurant they would open in the region would generate lower returns, as it would cannibalize sales and profits at the existing venues. Based on the results from the ninth restaurant opening, they calculated that if they opened another it would generate only a 5% return on capital.

Could they open Italian restaurants in Columbus, Findlay, Cleveland, Cincinnati, or Detroit? They could, but based on their research, all of those markets already had a sufficient number of Italian restaurants.

Could they diversify into Chinese or Thai restaurants? While that was a possibility, they had no special skill in running a Chinese or Thai restaurant, and there was a plethora of those restaurants in Toledo already. They correctly surmised that their odds of generating an attractive return on capital with a new concept in which they lacked expertise were quite low.

In 2018, the business generated $1 million in FCF after reinvestment in the nine existing restaurants. The family had originally planned to use this FCF to open a tenth restaurant, but now was less sure.

Of the 10 partners in the business, one partner indicated that he would like to leave the partnership and was willing to cash out his share in the business for $1 million. He wanted to move to Florida, open a Mexican restaurant with a friend from college, and run it independent of the Greene family. The partners were split on what to do. Many wanted to open the tenth restaurant. Others wanted to buy out the partner as opposed to opening a new restaurant with subpar economics.

What should they do with the $1 million in FCF? (See Table 9.1 and Figure 9.1.)

TABLE 9.1

Restaurant Options: Buy Out Partner or Open New Venue

	Open New Store	Buy out Partner
Existing FCF	$1,000,000	$1,000,000
New Store FCF	$50,000	0
FCF	$1,050,000	$1,000,000
Number of Partners	10	9
FCF/Partner	$105,000	$111,111

While opening up the additional store would increase the absolute level of FCF, it would result in less FCF per partner than if they were to buy out the partner.

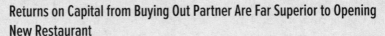

FIGURE 9.1

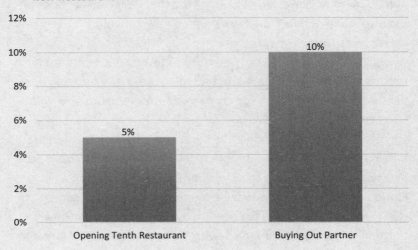

Returns on Capital from Buying Out Partner Are Far Superior to Opening New Restaurant

While opening up the new store would generate a 5% return on capital, buying out the partner would produce a 10% return on capital ($100,000 FCF/per partner divided by $1,000,000 purchase price).

In the end, the partners chose to buy out the partner. This partner took his $1,000,000 and opened his own, unique restaurant in Florida with his college buddy.

A majority of mature companies today find themselves in a similar situation. In most of the developed world, real GDP growth is 1–2% at best. This is not a function of underinvestment, but more a result of slowing population growth and an aging population. Most companies can serve their customers and continue to grow modestly without aggressive capital spending. Even after reinvesting in their businesses, they still have a significant amount of FCF left over. The expected returns from diversification into other areas that are already well supplied by existing participants, and where the management team has no unique skill set, differentiated product, or specialized service to offer prospective customers is poor at best.

As with the Greene family's partner, the return of excess cash in the form of a buyback of shares (or a partnership interest) was redeployed back into the economy with the opening of another restaurant in a different location. The partners generated a superior return on capital and higher FCF per partner going forward by reducing the number of partners, as opposed to taking on a subpar capital investment program.

Firms should not feel guilty about returning excess capital to shareholders after all high-return internal investments have been made. Squandering shareholder capital on low or negative capital return projects not only reduces return on capital and EPS and FCF/share growth rates, but reduces the amount of capital that can be recycled to other companies and industries where it is truly needed.

Very few shareholders and owners of businesses would argue that maximizing the size of the firm should be the primary objective of the management team and board. Growing bigger is actually rather easy. A company can issue debt or stock to make acquisitions, build additional plants, diversify into new businesses, or enter new geographies. The challenge is making sure these corporate actions truly generate satisfactory returns, and that is the hard part of capital allocation. Talented management teams balance growth and returns exceptionally well.

CHAPTER 10

AutoZone: The Power of Intelligent Share Repurchase

AutoZone serves as a prime example of how a sound strategy and an intelligent stock repurchase plan created enormous value for long-term shareholders.

If one examines AutoZone's sales from 1999–2018 (Figure 10.1), it would be fair to say that they looked fine but not spectacular at a 5.4% compound annual growth rate (CAGR). Similarly, the company grew its store base by a modest 4.3% CAGR over this time period.

FIGURE 10.1

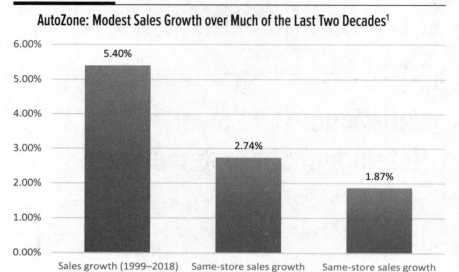

AutoZone: Modest Sales Growth over Much of the Last Two Decades[1]

Note: Refers to domestic comps only.

Then how in the world did AutoZone (AZO) produce a 2,445% return relative to 198% for the S&P 500 over this time period? How did AZO earnings per share (EPS) increase from $1.63 in 1999 to $50.34 in 2018?

The AutoZone plan was essentially to grow revenues, open new stores, improve margins, optimize the balance sheet, buy back stock with all available cash, and improve ROIC. The management team and board never wavered from that plan, and as a result they created significant long-term shareholder value for their investors.

WALKING THROUGH THE AZO VALUE-CREATION MATH

AZO grew sales at a 5.4% CAGR from 1999 to 2018 (sales grew from $4 billion to $11 billion). Management improved margins from 10.5% in 1999 to 19% in 2018 (ex-charges), or about 45 bps per year.

Net income and operating cash flow grew at 10.4% and 10.5% respectively. AZO maintained an optimal balance sheet leverage in the low-to-mid-2s (debt to EBITDAR—"r" indicates rent) for most of this period. As EBITDAR grew, AZO was able to carry more debt. Debt increased from $888 million to slightly more than $5 billion in 2018. While debt increased, debt to EBITDAR did not change much over this period, and AutoZone remained an investment-grade company throughout this time.

In addition, AZO leveraged its buying power to achieve improved working capital terms. For most companies, net working capital (inventory + receivables − payables) is a positive number. For a company with positive net working capital, the more the company grows sales, the more net working capital the firm needs to support the growth. For a company with $100 million in sales and 20% net working capital/sales, for every $5 million in sales growth, the firm will need to invest $1 million in working capital. This investment drag negatively impacts ROIC and results in less excess capital to be deployed to create shareholder value.

In 1998, AutoZone's net working capital was a positive $224.5 million. By the end of 2018, it was a negative $393 million. Over 20 years (see Table 10.2), AZO had grown sales by $7 billion and generated over $600 million in positive FCF from net working capital reductions.

This positive contribution from net working capital is one of the reasons AutoZone was able to generate an attractive 95% FCF conversion rate (FCF/net income) over this stretch, despite heavy capital spending to grow its store base.

Over this period of time, AZO spent $19.4 billion buying back its own shares, as shown in Table 10.1.

TABLE 10.1

AutoZone Buyback Machine[2]

Cash Spent Buying Back Stock (1999–2018) in billions	$19.4
Beginning Share Count (1999) in millions	150
Ending Share Count (2018) in millions	27
Decline in Shares Outstanding	82%
CAGR Reduction in Shares Outstanding (1999–2018)	8.60%

TABLE 10.2

AutoZone 1999–2018 Capital Deployment[3]

Operating Cash Flow in billions	$20.90
Capital Expenditures	($6.50)
FCF	$14.30
New Debt	$4.10
Asset Disposals	$0.20
Acquisitions	($0.20)
Other	$0.80
Share Repurchase	$19.40

The magic of the AZO model was modest growth, steadily improving margins, optimization of the balance sheet from a leverage and net working capital investment perspective, and aggressive share repurchase to create significant value for shareholders over the long term.

Now let's look at AZO through our share repurchase lens:

1. Is the Business Cyclical?

AZO is not cyclical; in fact, it is potentially modestly countercyclical. Sales grew every year, and same-store sales were positive every year with the exception of only two years.

2. Acquisitions Are Not a Viable Alternative

By 1999, AZO was already the largest US retail auto parts company and operated in 39 states. While it is possible AZO could have made small acquisitions that would not have invoked antitrust concerns, it is highly unlikely that the returns from those deals would have been nearly as strong as the returns from buying back stock and opening new stores. AZO's ROIC expanded dramatically from 12% in 1999 to 32% in 2018. Most acquisitions fail to generate double-digit returns, let alone 30%-plus returns.

3. Mature Business Without Secular Challenges

The auto parts business is a very mature business. While AutoZone and some of its competitors grew faster than the market through share gains, the underlying market was very mature. Until very recently, the business was not viewed as having secular challenges. However, the growth of Amazon and advent of electric cars could put pressure on the business over the long term. While AutoZone's capital allocation strategy has worked out very well for its long-term shareholders, it might make sense for the company to consider a dividend and/or special dividend going forward.

4. Company in Which the Underlying Stock Price Is Undervalued

The power of the AZO algorithm was aided by the rather consistent low valuation the market awarded AZO over this time period. AutoZone's average forward multiple during this period was only 13.5x. Despite growing EPS materially faster than the market with earnings and sales that were materially less volatile than the market (and less volatile than most highly valued consumer staples firms), AZO traded at a 10% discount to the S&P 500 average multiple over this time. This oversight by the market allowed AutoZone to buy back more stock at lower prices and generate a higher return on its share repurchases. First year cash-on-cash returns from buying back stock were over 7% on average (13.5x P/E times 95% FCF), and with cash flows growing by double digits annually, AZO's cash-on-cash returns were in the double digits by year four.

5. Limited Pressure to Pay Out a Dividend

In the late 1990s and the early part of the 2000s, much of retail was still viewed as a growth business. Few, if any retailers issued large dividend payouts. In addition, the return spread from buying back stock and the return its shareholders could receive reinvesting dividends in the market was so wide that it made a tremendous amount of sense for AutoZone management and board to buy back stock, as opposed to paying a dividend.

SHOULD AUTOZONE HAVE INVESTED MORE IN THE BUSINESS?

One question a skeptic of share repurchases might ask is: did AutoZone milk the business?

It is very hard to argue that AutoZone milked the business. Capital expenditures were 1.74x deprecation over this period. This is a very healthy reinvestment rate. The company increased the store base from 2,763 to over 6,000. It expanded in Mexico from 6 stores to over 600 and entered the Brazilian market as well. While AZO was mostly retail-focused, it aggressively expanded into the commercial sector.

In 2008, AZO had 2,200 stores with a commercial program (in which salespeople pursued commercial customers as opposed to purely retail customers), and by 2018, it had 4,700 stores operating a commercial program. The company even made an internet acquisition (Auto Anything) to try to learn more about this distribution channel.

AutoZone is certainly not alone in creating value through share repurchase, but probably no one has done it better over an extended period of time. In addition, there are few companies that more perfectly match the optimal criteria for aggressively buying back stock. Other companies such as Texas Instruments and Fiserv (see Table 10.3) have utilized share repurchase to create significant value for shareholders, despite being more cyclical (in the case of Texas Instruments) or trading for a higher valuation and having more acquisition opportunities (in the case of Fiserv).

TABLE 10.3

Texas Instruments and Fiserv Have Created Substantial Value for Their Shareholders Through Share Repurchase

	TXN	FISV
Period	2004–2018	2005–2018
Beginning FCF (millions)	$1,848	$432
Ending FCF (millions)	$6,058	$1,185
Beginning Diluted Shares	1,768	789
Ending Diluted Shares	990	414
Beginning FCF/Share	$1.05	$0.55
Ending FCF/Share	$6.12	$2.86
CAGR in FCF/Share	13.5%	13.6%
Total Shareholder Return	325%	631%
S&P 500 Return	207%	177%
Outperformance	118%	454%

Source: FactSet financial data and analytics

To embark on a successful share repurchase program, a company does not need to meet all of the aforementioned criteria. In the end, what really matters is that the share repurchase program generates the best risk-adjusted returns relative to other capital allocation alternatives.

CHAPTER 11

Acquisitions

Nearly all experts agree that the majority of acquisitions do not create value for the acquiring firm's shareholders. Here are some representative quotes.

> *The mass of research suggests that target shareholders earn sizable positive market returns, that bidders (with interesting exceptions) earn zero adjusted returns, and that bidders and targets combined earn positive returns. On balance, one should conclude that M&A does pay. But the broad dispersion of finding around a zero return to buyers suggests that executives should approach this activity with caution.*
>
> **—Robert F. Bruner[1]**

It's known as the winner's curse. When companies merge, most of the shareholder value created is likely to go not to the buyer but to the seller. Indeed, on average, the buyer pays the seller all of the value generated by a merger. . . . The main source of the winner's curse: the fact that the average acquirer materially overestimates the synergies a merger will yield.

—Scott A. Christofferson, Robert McNish, and Diane Sias[2]

Companies spend more than $2 trillion on acquisitions every year. Yet study after study puts the failure rate of mergers and acquisitions somewhere between 70% and 90%.

—Clayton M. Christensen, Richard Alton, Curtis Rising, and Andrew Waldeck[3]

Managers depend heavily on "promoters" to initiate structure and carry out the M&A transaction. Promoters for M&As are investment banks and top management consultancies. They have a vested interest in M&As and push companies into M&A deals in order to offer their services. Promoters convince managers that they can succeed, which may not be true in the end.

—Godfred Yaw Koi-Akrofi[4]

This small sampling of academic research and consultant articles on M&A is typical. Based on my review of multiple academic papers and consultant articles on this topic, the evidence suggests that more than half of all M&A transactions fail to generate a return equal to or greater than the acquirer's cost of capital. In addition, acquisitions that involved large transactions, or in which the acquirer used stock toward the purchase, performed the worst.

Of course, just achieving a return equal to the firm's cost of capital is a rather low standard by which to define the success of a transaction. Management teams and boards are tasked with making investments that generate returns *above* the firm's cost of capital.

Much of this academic evidence also ignores the alternatives to M&A and the expected relative returns on share repurchase, dividends, special dividends, and capital spending compared to M&A.

THE CHALLENGES WITH M&A

Why do the majority of acquisitions fail to generate returns above an acquirer's cost of capital? There are multiple challenges associated with M&A, which will be discussed in the following section.

Timing of M&A

Poor timing is one common challenge that almost all forms of capital allocation face.

- Companies buy back stock late in a cycle when their stocks are overvalued on normalized earnings or FCF.
- Firms increase capital spending late in a cycle to support future demand that often fails to materialize.
- Companies engage in more M&A later in a cycle when valuations tend to be extended.

M&A activity peaked around the top of the stock market during the dot-com bubble of the late 1990s and early 2000s and fell sharply during the market correction. This was again repeated in the lead-up to the Great Financial Crisis (GFC) in 2006–2007. In both cycles, M&A activity declined materially during the subsequent market correction when valuation multiples compressed to very attractive levels.[5]

Sellers Have Multiple Advantages over Buyers

With the exception of rare hostile transactions, selling firms have significant discretion as to when (or if) they choose to sell, and private companies in particular have complete discretion.

A firm can, and often will wait to sell until one or more of the following situations arise:

- Valuations are elevated.
- Industry cash flows are high and potential acquirers have more excess capital to deploy into M&A.
- Multiple potential bidders' balance sheets are in a good position to create a possible bidding war for the firm.
- Fundamentals (revenues, margins, backlog) are at their zenith. In a given industry sector, acquisitions tend to be completed within a fairly tight range of multiples. Later in an economic cycle, when acquirers are flush with cash, the valuation multiple a seller will receive often gravitates to the higher end of that range. A selling firm will often wait until it believes EBITDA levels are at or near the peak before it chooses to sell, especially in cyclical industries. A smart seller can thus achieve the high end of the valuation range on EBITDA that is at least elevated, if not peakish, to maximize the ultimate takeover price.

One common refrain I hear from management teams is that they plan to use their balance sheet aggressively the next time there is a downturn to buy assets on the cheap. In theory, that makes a lot of sense, and countercyclical capital deployment has the potential to create significant shareholder value (see Chapter 17). The only two problems are:

1. Few management teams and boards will choose to sell their company at the bottom of the cycle unless it is a distressed asset.

2. During a period of economic uncertainty and/or stock market downturn, boards and management teams often want to wait for more economic visibility or certainty before they deploy excess capital. This is frequently a mistake. The problem is that when economic uncertainty has been lifted, valuations tend to go much higher. Management teams and boards that engage in M&A should ignore near-term uncertainty when looking to acquire businesses that the firm will most likely own forever. This is especially relevant and advantageous when that near-term uncertainty allows the acquiring firm to buy a business for an attractive valuation and generate an above-average intermediate-term return.

Sellers Have More Information Than Buyers When It Comes to M&A

Sellers are almost always more knowledgeable about the strengths, weaknesses, and potential of their organization than prospective buyers.

- Is the management team really likely to stay and run the business?
- How strong is the next wave of new products, and will they result in accelerating, flat, or declining revenue and market share trends?
- Are profits artificially high? Has the company been making the right level of investments the last couple of years? Has the company pulled back on internal investments to boost profits in the short term to achieve a higher price upon takeout?
- Has the company stuffed the channel in an effort to artificially boost profits?
- What is the culture at the firm? Is it great? It is toxic?

An acquiring firm will almost certainly go through a due diligence process to learn more about the fundamentals of the firm prior to completing the acquisition. However, there is simply no way that the acquirer can know the business nearly as well as the seller after only a few weeks of due diligence.

Acquiring Public Firms Necessitates Paying a Premium over Market Prices

As an investor, I can buy just about any stock for a price very close to the currently quoted price. However, an acquiring firm almost always has to pay a significant premium to the currently quoted stock price in order to induce the board, management team, and shareholders to sell.

While the stock market is not perfectly efficient, the current stock price is, on average, a reasonable measure of the fair value of the firm. However, since more M&A tends to happen in the mid-to-late part of a stock market and economic cycle at higher valuations, I would argue that pre-takeout publicly traded market valuations tend to overstate the underlying value of acquired firms. Thus, a company might need to pay a sizable premium not only to the currently quoted market price, but also a potentially greater-than-appreciated premium to normalized fair value.

How can a firm justify paying more than the currently quoted market price for an acquisition? In many cases it comes down to synergies. Synergies are the scale benefits and efficiencies that accrue to the newly combined firm in the form of lower costs, higher profits, and potentially (but rarely) revenue gains. Let's look at an example (see Table 11.1)

Two very similar firms are combining, with Firm A buying Firm B for a 30% premium.

TABLE 11.1

Example: Acquisition Without Synergies

	Firm A	Firm B
Revenues	100	100
EBITDA	15	15
Current Valuation Multiple on EBITDA	10	10
Market Valuation	150	150
Shares	10	10
Price per Share	$15.00	$15.00
Firm A Pays 30% Premium for Firm B		195
Issues Shares @15 to Pay for Acquisition		15
New Shares Issued		13

	NewCo
Revenues	200
EBITDA	30
Apply 10x EBITDA Multiple	300
New Shares Outstanding	23
Price per Share	$13.04
Firm A Shareholders Value Destruction	−13.0%

Firm A shareholders' shares will likely decline by at least 13% in the absence of any synergies to justify the 30% premium paid for Firm B.

Now, how would the economics of the deal change if Firm A were able to take out 6% of the combined cost structure of the two businesses, as shown in Table 11.2?

TABLE 11.2

Example: Acquisition with Synergies

	Firm A	Firm B
Revenues	100	100
EBITDA	15	15
Current Valuation Multiple on EBITDA	10	10
Market Valuation	150	150
Shares	10	10
Price per Share	$15.00	$15.00
Firm A Pays 30% Premium for Firm B		195
Issues Shares @15 to Pay for Acquisition		15
New Shares Issued		13

	NewCo	Synergies @6% combined sales
Revenues	200	
EBITDA	42	12
Apply 10x EBITDA Multiple	420	
New Shares Outstanding	23	
Price per Share	$18.26	
Firm A Shareholders Value Creation	21.7%	

In this case, Firm A shareholders find that the deal has created value with their stock price likely to rise by almost 22%.

This very simple example demonstrates the power of synergies to overcome the premium an acquirer has to pay for a publicly traded company.

The greater the synergies, the more likely that an acquiring firm can justify paying a given premium for an acquisition and the higher the likelihood it will generate an attractive return on capital. Nevertheless, this is not lost on the board, management team, and investors of the firm being acquired. These parties are likely to push the acquirer (or multiple potential acquirers) to pay a larger premium so that their shareholders can receive a substantial share of the net present value of the synergies.

The preceding example is somewhat of an outlier in that the two businesses were exactly the same size, operated in the same industry, and had combined synergies that were very large. In most acquisitions, the acquiring firm is much larger than the firm being acquired, and the cost synergies would be considered in terms of the costs that would come out of the acquired business, not on combined revenues.

TABLE 11.3

Example: Acquisition with Larger Firm Buying a Smaller Firm

	Firm A	Firm B
Revenues	100	20
EBITDA	15	3
Current Valuation Multiple on EBITDA	10	10
Market Valuation	150	30
Shares	10	10
Price per Share	$15.00	$3.00
Firm A Pays 30% Premium for Firm B		39
Issues Shares @15 to Pay for Acquisition		15
New Shares Issued		2.6

	NewCo	Synergies @6% Acquired Firm's Sales
Revenues	120	
EBITDA	19.2	1.2
Apply 10x EBITDA Multiple	192	
New Shares Outstanding	12.6	
Price per Share	$15.24	
Firm A Shareholders Value Creation	1.6%	

In this example displayed in Table 11.3, Firm A's shareholders' stock should rise by 1.6%, as the synergy capture is able to overcome the 30% premium the firm needed to pay for the acquisition.

Regardless whether the forecast is for a large stock price decline (no synergy scenario), large stock price increase (large synergy scenario), or a modest increase (large buys small scenario), the level of accretion and dilution and subsequent stock price change should not be the most important consideration for the management team and board. The most important consideration should be the risk-adjusted returns that the transaction is expected to produce over the intermediate term and how attractive these are relative to other capital allocation options available to the firm.

Revenue Synergies Rarely Materialize

As Christensen et al. note in their 2011 article in the *Harvard Business Review*, "Acquisitions made for the purpose of cross-selling products succeed only occasionally."[6]

Measuring revenue synergies is often very difficult, especially from an external perspective. Most of the analyses on revenue synergies come from studies by management consultants and are based on survey work. There is a natural bias here, as companies are self-reporting the magnitude of revenue synergies they were able to achieve. This is analogous to asking my children how many sweets they ate at school in the last month. There is no way to verify the data and no one wants to admit how poorly their transaction panned out (or how many times they had sweets).

Nevertheless, despite this natural bias, most of the work from these surveys suggests that firms repeatedly fail to achieve their revenue synergy targets. As a survey conducted by Deloitte in 2017 reported: "Only 24% of firms achieve >80 percent of their goals."[7][†]

Why Do Revenue Synergies Fail to Materialize?

Acquisitions and the resultant integration and synergy capture can cause disruption inside an organization for the following reasons:

---

† Of the 528 firms surveyed, zero companies reported negative net revenue synergies (or revenue dis-synergies). It is unclear whether this was even an option for the survey.

- Consolidating firms can lose employees to competitors.
- Employees are more worried about losing their jobs than generating higher sales.
- Cultural challenges can arise during and after the integration.
- Sales force compensation schemes of the acquired firm are often altered to be more similar to those of the acquiring firm. This has the potential to trigger sales force disruption and increased turnover if a by-product of this is lower compensation for high-performing sales professionals from the acquired firm.
- The point of contact with the customer can be altered.

All of these things are more likely to result in revenue dissynergies than revenue synergies, at least initially. In addition, while revenue synergies might look good in a spreadsheet or on a PowerPoint slide, they may not materialize in a real-world setting. When thinking about revenue synergies, it is essential to ask the following questions:

- Does the end customer truly want to buy more from the combined enterprise? If so, why?
- Is there value for the end customer in buying more from the combined enterprise?
- Do the products interact together or integrate from a systems standpoint?
- Is there a common software overlay or interface that controls both products?
- Is the point of contact with a customer the same person? If not, revenue synergies are much less likely to materialize.
- Are the products bought at the same time?
- Are both products differentiated or is one more commoditized than the other?
- Does the end customer choose products on a best-of-breed approach? If the answer is yes, revenue synergies are far less likely to materialize.

- Do competitors already sell a bundled set of products to the customer? If yes, revenue synergies are more likely to materialize.
- Is the size and strength of the firm's balance sheet an important consideration for the customer? If yes, it is possible that an inadequately capitalized firm could benefit from being part of a larger firm with a stronger balance sheet.

Approach to Revenue Synergies

It's critical to examine potential revenue synergies realistically.

- If you need revenue synergies to justify the economics of a transaction, you probably should not be making the transaction.
- The best acquirers have zero or minimal revenue synergies in their financial projections. Revenue synergies are a potential source of upside, but never in the base case projections.
- Achieving revenue synergies often involves costs or a level of investment to achieve those synergies. A management team and board should consider those costs as part of the ultimate purchase price of an acquisition. Alternatively, they should reduce the gross cost savings from the acquisition to account for these additional investments.

THE BASICS OF ACQUISITIONS FOR BOARDS AND MANAGEMENT TEAMS

When evaluating potential acquisitions, leadership should concentrate on several key factors.

Focus on Cash-on-Cash Returns over the Intermediate Term

The most accurate and intellectually honest way to look at M&A is to assess how attractive the cash-on-cash returns from the transaction are over the intermediate term. This is not to say that boards should ignore the long-term returns on acquisitions, but the quality and accuracy of the inputs are likely to diminish over time. Trying to measure growth rates accurately 10 or 20 years into the future is unlikely to yield truly actionable insights, given how the business, economy, customers, technology, and competitors are likely to change over an extended period of time.

Cash-on-cash returns make the most sense because a board should be highly focused on them, and it is easy to compare returns against other alternatives. Many firms use different metrics such as discounted cash flow (DCF) or internal rate of return (IRR) metrics that may apply a terminal value calculation.

The terminal value calculation is a rather arbitrary valuation on what the business will be worth at some point in the future. In many cases, these analyses place a value on near-term cash flows and then put a terminal value multiple on year 6 or year 10 cash flows to generate an IRR or DCF valuation. The problem is that you can justify just about any M&A transaction valuation by using a very high terminal value. If you buy something for 12x EBITDA and use a year six terminal value multiple of 14x, *voilà* your DCF or IRR looks great.

Garbage in and garbage out calculations relying on terminal value assumptions should not be used to justify an acquisition. Moreover, an IRR or DCF analysis that uses a terminal value assumption makes it very difficult to compare the attractiveness of an acquisition to alternative deployments of excess capital.

TABLE 11.4

What Is in the Numerator and Denominator for Return Calculations?

Numerator

Acquired FCF (including capital spending, but excluding interest expense)

Add after-tax net synergies

Reduce by lost FCF from divested assets

Exclude any short-term, unsustainable tax savings

Denominator

Purchase price + assumed debt

Reduce by cash/marketable securities

Add after-tax cash cost of achieving synergies

Add investment banking/advisory fees

Add costs associated with equity + fixed income issuance

Reduce by after-tax proceeds of divested assets

Reduce by net present value of short-term, unsustainable tax synergies from deal

Add in risk-weighted breakup fee

The last part of the denominator in Table 11.4, the risk-weighted breakup fee, might be a little bit of a surprise. It should be included in the denominator if the acquiring firm has to pay a breakup fee in the event that the transaction is unable to be consummated due to regulatory and/or anti-trust issues. This is only material if there is a risk that the transaction might be rejected by the regulatory authorities.

A firm attempting to make an acquisition of a rival for $10 billion might have to pay a $400 million breakup fee ($300 million after tax) to the acquiring firm if it fails to gain regulatory approval—shown in Table 11.5. If the acquiring firm and its advisors believe the deal faces 25% odds of failing to gain regulatory approval, they should increase the denominator by $75 million (25% × $300 million), regardless of whether the deal receives antitrust approval. Ignoring this embedded option liability in the transaction is not intellectually honest or financially accurate.

TABLE 11.5

Risk-Weighted Breakup Fee Example

$10 billion deal
4% breakup fee
$400 million breakup fee if deal blocked
25% tax rate
$300 million after-tax breakup fee
25% odds of deal rejected
$75 million (25% × $300 million)

Every once in a while, I encounter firms using very dubious ways to account for their acquisition returns. Sometimes I find firms that ignore taxes or capital spending. That is great if the acquired asset no longer has to pay taxes or has any capital spending needs, but that is not consistent with economic reality. EBITDA is not the same as after-tax FCF. Earning a double-digit return on investment using EBITDA in the numerator is a rather meaningless number.

Focus on Returns More than Accretion/Dilution

To say that investors can often be short-term-oriented is an understatement. Routinely, when an acquisition is announced, investors capitalize the accretion/dilution at the valuation multiple of the acquiring firm and the acquiring firm's stock price appreciates or declines in line with the level of accretion or dilution associated with the deal. In fact, when a firm announces a dilutive acquisition, the stock price often goes down by more than the level of dilution would warrant because investors absolutely despise dilutive acquisitions and the management teams that enter into them.

With a mildly accretive acquisition, if Firm A was expected to earn $1 per share next year, is trading at 15x earnings ($15 per share), and announces an acquisition that is 5% accretive to earnings, it is more than likely that the stock price will appreciate by some amount up to the level of accretion (in this case to $15.75 as a reasonable upper bound). This short-term focus ignores both the returns from the acquisition and the potential returns from various other capital deployment alternatives. It has been my experience that the first-day stock price change following a deal announcement is often not a great harbinger for the ultimate value creation of an acquisition, or even how the acquiring firm's stock is likely to perform over the intermediate term.

In the developed world, the after-tax cost of debt is very low, especially relative to the after-tax cost of equity. Investment grade firms with operations in Europe can often raise debt globally with total after-tax costs of debt around 2.5% or less. When the after-tax cost of debt is that low, it is hard not to make a deal accretive to earnings. I am convinced that the acquisition of a ham sandwich could somehow be made accretive to earnings these days.

In a world where just about every deal is accretive to earnings, the threshold for deal success should be transactions that generate attractive returns relative to alternatives, not simply earnings accretion.

Think Externally About Assumptions

If there were one book I would recommend that every investor, management team, and board member read it would be Daniel Kahneman's *Thinking, Fast and Slow*.[8] Although he is a psychologist, Kahneman won the 2002 Nobel Prize in economic science. His book does a fabulous job of illustrating how the human mind makes decisions quickly based on emotions, underlying biases, over-confidence, and a lack of good external data. The resulting decisions are often quite poor. This book is extremely relevant for management teams and boards as they analyze potential acquisitions, and for investors as they analyze publicly announced acquisitions.

Kahneman speaks of an inside view and an outside view of potential outcomes. The inside view is the expected outcome based on the observations and experiences of a select few people involved in making a projection. It looks at "specific circumstances" in trying to determine a baseline projection.[9] The outside view uses external data and outcomes of similar events in the past to make a baseline projection.

Not surprisingly, a baseline projection based on the outside view is much more likely to be accurate than a baseline projection based on the inside view.

Let's use the example of a consumer staples firm that is looking to purchase a faster-growing, privately owned consumer business with $200 million in sales. The acquiring firm expects to achieve $400 million in sales by year five in the deal model. The business has been growing 14–15% and the management team believes that is a reasonable level of growth to extrapolate into the future. This assumption is based on the inside view.

But how good is that underlying assumption? Is it too aggressive due to the law of large numbers? Is it too conservative because the larger parent will be able to expand distribution and potentially take the newly acquired business global? This is where the outside view becomes critically important to help gauge how reasonable the underlying forecast is.

A board that is willing to take an outside view should ask the following questions:

- In looking at the last 10 years of data, how many private consumer staples firms that were growing in the mid-teens with $150–$250 million in revenues were able to double their revenues in the next five years? How many actually declined? What was the average/median change in revenues from year zero to year five?
- What has been the success rate of larger consumer staples firms buying faster-growing private companies over the last 10 years?
- Do acquired private consumer staples companies' growth rates accelerate, decelerate, or decline relative to private companies that stay private?
- How many of these transactions resulted in a write-down within five years due to underperformance, or an outright sale of the business?

Wouldn't it be extremely valuable to know that the odds of a $150–$250 million consumer staples company doubling its revenues over the next five years are only 15%, and the median growth rate is 5%? Wouldn't it be helpful to know that after being bought, private consumer staples companies' growth rates decelerated more than private companies that were not acquired? In other words, the acquisition of a fast-growing consumer staples firm by a large global consumer staples firm actually impaired its natural growth rate.[†]

This information can help provide valuable insights into how conservative or aggressive the underlying assumptions in the deal model are. Better insights into the underlying assumptions will generate a more informed and reasonable expected return on the investment.

I would recommend that on just about every potential acquisition a firm looks at, the underlying assumptions should be informed by both the inside view and the outside view. It is crucial to look at the success rate of similar acquisitions in the industry and sector.

Focus on Process More Than Outcomes and Be Willing to Invest Countercyclically

I have always been surprised by the high correlation between CEO confidence levels and M&A activity. There are a number of factors that contribute to this correlation, but a fear of having an acquisition underperform in the short term has to be one of the most important. Hence, if you announce an acquisition during a period when fundamentals and the economy are doing well, there is a perception that the risk of near-term disappointment is lower. No one wants to announce a deal, then two quarters after it has been completed, see it underperform. This leaves the CEO with egg on his face.

I understand that fear, but extrapolating near-term fundamentals for the foreseeable future in the economy or in the business you are acquiring is not sensible either. Fundamentals felt great in 1999 and 2006 and early 2020, and within a couple of years or months the

---

† Note: these are hypothetical numbers used to illustrate the concept, not facts on the expected revenue growth rates of private consumer staples firms.

economy was in recession. In 2018, the European economy appeared strong, and a year later, growth disappointed. In 2008 and 2009, it felt like the world was ending, and yet a decade later, the United States enjoyed 10 years of continuous, recession-free growth.

Near-term certainty is a false god, and all that pray at its altar are likely to be disappointed. The future is far more uncertain than economists, stock market strategists, or executives fully appreciate. Often the stronger the near-term outlook, the worse the intermediate outlook, and vice versa.

The impact of CEO confidence is particularly troubling as acquisition multiples/valuations are typically expanding when confidence is high. Hence, you are paying a higher price and ultimately getting a lower long-term return for near-term visibility with limited-to-no ultimate value. Near-term visibility is a structurally overvalued asset that should be heavily discounted when considering long-term decisions, such as making an acquisition.

Boards must empower management teams to undertake investments with attractive long-term returns even if that means short-term uncertainty with regard to the fundamentals. I would much rather have a firm buy a company for 10–12x EBITDA during a period of economic uncertainty when EBITDA could potentially fall another 10–20% than pay 14–15x EBITDA late in a cycle when things feel good.

Boards need to focus on process. If the underlying process behind an investment is sound, CEOs should not fear for their jobs in the event that external forces (currency, economy) cause the acquisition to underperform in the short term.

Hostile Versus Friendly Deals

Friendly deals are always preferred for several reasons:

- Hostile deals limit the amount of due diligence the acquiring firm can undertake prior to the announcement.
- A hostile deal can make integrations more challenging because animosity often develops during the takeover process.

- Hostile deals typically result in higher takeover premiums.[10]
- A hostile deal can bring out additional buyers for the target company. This can result in a rising price tag for the acquisition, and consequently, lower returns.

A hostile deal can require a significant time commitment from management, and there is an opportunity cost associated with management's time. A management team that initiates a hostile takeover bid will often need to spend considerable time "selling" its bid not only to its shareholders, but to the target firms' shareholders as well. In addition, this considerable investment of time can make it harder to walk away at the end if the price tag becomes too rich or the due diligence picks up some negative data points. While a good management team and board will correctly view the investment of time as a sunk cost and irrelevant to the future returns of the acquisition, not every management and board will prove to be as rational amid a heated battle for control. **Some of the best decisions a management team and board will make over their careers is the decision to walk away from a deal regardless of whether it was hostile or friendly. In many cases, the best "deals" are the ones they have the discipline to walk away from when valuation, cultural fit, or business risk reduce the attractiveness of the deal.**

As previously mentioned, sellers typically have considerable control over when they choose to sell their firm. A hostile acquisition proposal does negate this natural seller advantage.

Hence, if a company is ever planning to go hostile, it makes the most sense to do so under the following conditions:

- Early in a cycle when earnings or EBITDA might still be depressed or below normalized mid-cycle levels
- During a downturn in the economy or sector
- When sector valuations are depressed
- When the acquisition target's stock price or fundamentals are under pressure

- At a time when other potential acquirers are unlikely to be able to bid for the asset because of other factors, for example, they are already integrating an acquisition and/or their balance sheet capacity for another deal is limited

However, it is important to remember that the acquiring firm's stock price might also be depressed and the expected returns on the acquisition should be compared to the returns from buying back shares. Also, regarding the outside view, it is essential to consider how often hostile transactions are successful in general and how successful hostile transactions have been in the particular industry and/or sector.

A hostile bid may also make sense following a friendly takeover bid if the management team is unwilling to engage with the acquirer in a constructive manner due to management entrenchment. A newly minted CEO who is in his early fifties making $10 million a year is likely to be disinclined to sell the company and forgo 10 to 15 years of attractive compensation. Conversely, a 65-year-old CEO might be too open to being acquired as she nears retirement and could receive 3x or more her annual compensation due to change of control provisions.

In fact, a 2015 article in the *Journal of Finance* highlighted a 32% increase in the odds of a takeover when the CEO is between the ages of 64 and 66. Authors Dirk Jenter and Katharina Lewellen note that "results show that bidders are more likely to target firms with retirement-age CEOs, possibly due to these CEOs' greater willingness to accept takeover bids."[11]

While CEO age should be irrelevant for a strong board focusing on creating shareholder value, the reality is that the CEO's view of the potential takeover is likely to have a bearing on how the board views the attractiveness of the offer. A hostile offer at a material premium to the current stock price that creates value for the existing shareholders of the target firm and generates an attractive return for the shareholders of the acquiring firm may be the only way to overcome this.

Minimize Disruptive Impact on Organizations

While synergies are often one of the most important contributors to generating attractive returns for the acquiring firm, they are also often the biggest contributors to near-term disruption and sales dis-synergies.

A good acquirer will look to minimize the disruptive impact on both organizations involved in an acquisition. This can be accomplished in the following ways:

First, limit head-count reductions in parts of the business that directly touch the end customer and are most critical to long-term revenue growth. This means that material head-count reductions should be avoided in the sales force, new product development, customer support, and R&D. Sales force commissions and incentives should be altered over time, as opposed to day one, to minimize disruption.

This does not mean that the acquiring firm should forgo changes in areas like R&D, but a change in R&D strategy and priorities and increased R&D accountability is far less disruptive than significant layoffs. In many cases, a good acquirer will actually reinvest some of the synergies back into the business in these critical areas to accelerate long-term revenue growth.

Second, a strong management team can often generate significant cost savings in the short term by combining purchasing to negotiate better prices, and by reducing corporate costs (in a public acquisition), finance, and other G&A expenses. In the intermediate term, consolidation of manufacturing, distribution, and office space can be another source of synergies to help drive higher returns on investment. These synergies can also give the acquired business additional resources to invest in R&D, sales force, and geographic expansion to fuel the top line over the long term.

Measure Returns from Deals

For a number of reasons, it is imperative that firms actively monitor how their acquisitions' returns are trending in both absolute terms and relative to the deal plan:

- Boards should hold management teams accountable for delivering on the deal plan over the intermediate term.
- If a deal fails to perform up to expectations or outperforms expectations, the board and management team should undertake a root cause analysis. This should seek to determine why the outcome was different from what was expected, and what insight can be gleaned that the firm can apply toward future transactions. If a company is routinely making acquisitions, these insights can make the company a better acquirer. What are the common characteristics of deals that outperformed the deal model versus deals that underperformed the deal model?
- This monitoring allows the firm to see whether the returns from a given transaction or a series of transactions were superior to the alternatives at the time. If the vast majority of acquisitions are generating higher returns than buying back stock, the firm should pursue more acquisitions and engage in less share repurchase. If deals are routinely generating returns below the returns from returning cash to shareholders, the firm should de-emphasize acquisitions, pay higher dividends, and conduct more share repurchase.

A management team and board should be committed to continuously improving and becoming smarter about how they deploy capital every year. Measuring returns and learning from the successes and failures with capital allocation will drive a dynamic, engaged board to make better decisions for its shareholders and avoid repeating the same mistake again and again. A mistake is only a mistake if you fail to learn from it.

Equity Versus Debt Financing Acquisitions

In a returns-focused boardroom, the question of how the deal is financed is theoretically irrelevant as the choice of debt or equity financing does not ultimately impact the expected return on the investment. However, from a practical standpoint, while prospective deal returns are the most important consideration, the choice of debt versus equity is important for a number of reasons.

In most cases, the cost of debt capital (after tax) is much lower than the cost of equity (inverse of P/E ratio or inverse of price to free cash flow). Thus, a debt-financed transaction is likely to result in higher earnings and higher FCF than an equity-financed transaction.

Academic research finds that firms that undertake equity-financed transactions experience weaker stock price performance than firms with debt-financed transactions.[12] However, since most stock-financed transactions involve large deals (relative to the size of the acquirer) and are more to be likely public companies rather than private company acquisitions, it is quite possible that this under-performance is not due purely to the method of financing. It may partially be explained by the fact that large acquisitions and public company acquisitions tend to underperform compared to small and private acquisitions. It would also be very logical to assume that firms with overvalued stock prices are more willing to enter into acquisitions using their inflated currency to finance deals. This initial overvaluation could help explain subsequent stock underperformance as well.

When a firm uses equity to finance a transaction, existing shareholders are surrendering a portion of their claims on the future cash flows of the existing company in return for a claim on the future cash flows of the acquired company. If a management team overpays for an acquired company's cash flows relative to the value of the existing firm's cash flow, it will be value destructive.

Rules for Determining Whether to Use Equity or Debt Financing for M&A

When considering how to finance an acquisition, the management team should follow a few basic rules:

- When there is balance sheet capacity to use low-cost debt to make an acquisition, given the higher earnings and FCF per share accretion, a debt-financed transaction is generally preferred.

- A board and management team should not add excessive leverage just to maximize near-term accretion. The post-acquisition balance sheet should be strong enough to support the dividend and minimize the need for issuing new shares at discounted prices if the economy and/or underlying business enter a downturn following the acquisition.
- The intermediate-term returns from the equity-financed acquisition must be superior to buying back stock, increasing dividends, or paying special dividends.

CONCLUSIONS

The academic evidence suggests that most acquisitions fail to achieve returns greater than the firm's cost of capital—this is an important "outside view" for boards and management teams to recognize. However, this does not mean that companies should avoid M&A altogether. While there are numerous examples of companies that have destroyed massive amounts of shareholder value through M&A (such as GE, see Chapter 18), there are also numerous companies that have used M&A to build large businesses and create significant long-term value for their shareholders. In the coming chapters, I discuss the strategies that many successful acquirers have used to beat the odds and create significant shareholder value through M&A.

In the end, an engaged board that looks at deals with a returns-focused lens, compares deals with other capital return alternatives, creates baseline forecasts consistent with the outside view, monitors deal success, and learns from success and failure is far more likely to create long-term shareholder value.

Over the next series of chapters on M&A, the focus will be on the types of acquisitions most likely to create significant shareholder value and those least likely to do so. Each chapter will highlight acquisitions that produced either attractive or poor results.

However, I will not focus purely on the outcomes, but rather on the decision-making processes and characteristics of those deals that led management teams and boards to make these capital allocation decisions. A board or management team that employs a good process for selecting acquisitions will still make mistakes, but is far more likely to create shareholder value over time.

CHAPTER 12

Complex Transactions

What we have achieved is an asset swap which allows both companies to build on their existing strengths while at the same time creating significant value for GSK assets which we have built up over time. Transactions like this are incredibly complicated to execute, but when you do, it can have tremendous benefits for the businesses and for patients and consumers.

—David Redfern, Chief Strategy Officer, GlaxoSmithKline[1]

On April 22, 2014, Novartis and GlaxoSmithKline announced a series of asset swaps.

- Novartis agreed to sell its $900 million vaccine business to GSK for $5.25 billion with the potential to increase the total purchase price up to $7.05 billion based on the achievement of various future milestones.

- GSK agreed to sell its $1.6 billion oncology business to Novartis for $14.5 billion with the potential to increase the total purchase price to $16 billion depending on the clinical outcome of a specific ongoing trial.
- GSK and Novartis agreed to combine their consumer over-the-counter pharmaceutical businesses into a joint venture with GSK owning 63.5% and Novartis owning 36.5%.

In addition, Novartis agreed to sell its animal health business to Eli Lilly for $5.4 billion in a separate, unrelated transaction.

For GSK, the transactions accomplished the following:

- Accretive to EPS.
- Allowed GSK to double down in two scale businesses—consumer over-the-counter (OTC) medicines and vaccines—in which they were now number one globally.
- Created a more stable business portfolio with "more durable revenues, greater annuity businesses."[2]
- Allowed them to exit a business (oncology) in which they were the fourteenth largest player at an attractive valuation of 50x earnings.[3]
- Generated $1.7 billion of gross synergies ($1.35 billion net of reinvestment), some of which would accrete to Novartis through the consumer JV.
- Allowed the firm to return £4 billion ($6.72 billion) in excess capital to shareholders.

For Novartis, the transactions accomplished the following:

- Accretive to EPS.
- Allowed them to exit or joint venture three smaller businesses (including animal health) with below average operating margins that lacked scale in their respective markets.
- Increased operating margins on a pro forma basis by 250 basis points.

- Added to its oncology business where it had scale as the second largest oncology pharmaceutical company in the world.
- Offered an opportunity to "significantly" improve operating margins of the acquired oncology assets.
- While the deal created a consumer JV structure that would enable Novartis to exit the business in the future, Novartis was well positioned to benefit over the intermediate term from synergy capture that was expected to increase the consumer joint venture's operating margins from 15% to 20% over the next five years. Novartis would likely to able to divest the business at a much higher price in the future.
- Tax benefits of $2 billion.

What I find fascinating about these transactions is that both companies clearly emerged from them competitively and financially stronger, and they accomplished multiple strategic objectives while creating substantial value for long-term shareholders. This is very unusual with M&A, and highlights the powerful "win-win" potential of an asset swap.

Vaccine business. GSK was able to buy a business that, while currently losing money, was expected to grow significantly between 2013 and 2020 based on sell-side estimates. With substantial synergies, GSK was expected to generate a double-digit cash-on-cash ROIC in an attractive business within the healthcare space.[4]

Oncology. Novartis's oncology franchise was already at scale in this very attractive market segment. As a result, it was highly likely that much of the cost structure associated with the legacy GSK assets could be eliminated, which would allow the acquired revenues to drop to the bottom line at a very high incremental margin. Using consensus estimates for these acquired drugs at the time of acquisition, I estimated cash-on-cash returns in the high-single digits to low teens within five years.[5]

Consumer JV. Novartis received a disproportionate share of the consumer JV in return for giving up control and becoming a minority investor in the business. The Novartis assets represented 25% of the $10 billion pro-forma JV sales. Its businesses had operating margins of around 10% versus the GSK assets in the high teens. Novartis was able to secure a much higher share ownership (36.5%) relative to its sales contribution (25%) or operating profits contribution (15%).

While it is debatable which firm achieved a better deal on the individual transactions, it is clear that the collective asset swap was value accretive to both parties:

- Both firms doubled down in scale businesses in which they were market leaders.
- The transactions generated significant cost synergies for both firms and tax synergies for Novartis.
- Both companies achieved strategic goals (GSK: more stable revenue mix; Novartis: refocused portfolio on core business).
- Both firms were able to generate earnings accretion from the deals.

The GSK/Novartis deal is a great example of a complex transaction that can create significant value for boards and management teams that are willing to explore such opportunities.

While all transactions involve risks, complex transactions tend to have some of the best risk-adjusted returns.

The following sections present three examples of complex transactions.

ASSET SWAPS (GSK/NOVARTIS)

Two or more firms swap assets to generate scale and synergies. Most M&A transactions involve a winner and a loser (usually the seller and buyer, respectively). When a firm has to outbid multiple parties for a business, it is unlikely that it will be able to generate an attractive return on that transaction, and thus it encounters the winners' curse challenge with M&A. What makes an asset swap so compelling is that you are not competing with four other motivated bidders for a business. It is most likely a one-on-one negotiation. Both firms can generate synergies and emerge financially and strategically stronger from the transaction.

Boards and management teams should proactively seek out these opportunities by asking the following questions:

- What assets are owned by other conglomerates or companies with multiple subsidiaries that would fit well in our portfolio?
- How many of these assets are small relative to the size of the conglomerates' other assets?
- How many of these assets are subscale with below-average margins?
- Have any of these assets struggled recently from a performance perspective? Often, management teams, boards, and shareholders tire of an underperforming, smaller asset. They ask why they are spending 30% of their time and 40% of the quarterly conference call focused on a business that accounts for only 10% of revenues. As long as the issues are fixable, and not structural or secular, this is a great time to approach the firm with an asset swap or an outright purchase.
- Do we have subscale or smaller businesses that would fit well with these same conglomerates to facilitate a value accretive swap opportunity?

DEALS THAT COME WITH NON-CORE ASSETS (HON/NOVAR)

When an asset or firm is put up for sale, it may come with multiple subsidiaries or different businesses. An acquirer may have an interest in one or more of the businesses, but not all. In 2005, Honeywell bought Novar PLC, a British conglomerate with three businesses. Honeywell only wanted the $1.2 billion Intelligent Building Systems (IBS) and planned to divest the other two businesses with $1.5 billion in revenues. While that might sound risky, it only paid $2.4 billion for the entire acquisition. Even if the other businesses were worthless, HON would still have generated a year five cash-on-cash return of between 5–6%. While this level of return would have been disappointing, it would not have been a disaster.

In the end, HON sold the two non-core businesses for $1.25 billion. Thus, the net investment including the present value of the costs to achieve the synergies was around $1.2 billion. Assuming management delivered on their synergies and grew the business by 3% per year, they should have achieved an attractive 11%-plus cash-on-cash return by year five (see Table 12.1) for a highly complementary business that strategically increased their market presence in Europe.

TABLE 12.1

Financial Projections of Honeywell Acquisition of Novar PLC[6]

Honeywell Acquisition of Novar PLC	Year 1	Year 2	Year 3	Year 4	Year 5
IBS Division	1,273	1,311	1,351	1,391	1,433
Operating Profits Before Synergies	76	79	81	83	86
Operating Margin Before Synergies	6%	6%	6%	6%	6%
Synergies	20	40	60	80	100
Operating Profits After Synergies	96	119	141	163	186
Operating Margin After Synergies	7.6%	9.1%	10.4%	11.8%	13.0%
Honeywell Tax Rate	26%	26%	26%	26%	26%
Taxes	25	31	37	43	48

(continued)

Financial Projections of Honeywell Acquisition of Novar PLC (*continued*)

Honeywell Acquisition of Novar PLC	Year 1	Year 2	Year 3	Year 4	Year 5
Net Income	71	88	104	121	138
FCF Conversion Rate	100%	100%	100%	100%	100%
FCF	71	88	104	121	138
Cash-on-Cash Return Assuming Midpoint of Divested Proceeds	**5.9%**	**7.2%**	**8.6%**	**10.0%**	**11.3%**
Cash-on-Cash Return Assuming High-End of Divested Proceeds	7.4%	9.1%	10.8%	12.5%	14.3%
Cash-on-Cash Return Assuming Low-End of Divested Proceeds	4.9%	6.0%	7.1%	8.3%	9.4%
Cash-on-Cash Return Assuming Divested Assets Are Worthless	2.9%	3.6%	4.2%	4.9%	5.6%
Purchase Price + Assumed Debt	2,400				
After-Tax Cost of Achieving Synergies	66				
Total Investment Without Proceeds	2,466				
Total Investment with Midpoint of Divested Proceeds	1,216				
Total Investment with High End of Divested Proceeds	966				
Total Investment with Low End of Divested Proceeds	1,466				

Assumptions:

$100 million in synergies

3% revenue growth off 2003 base

26% tax rate, consistent with HON 2004 tax rate

100% FCF conversion, HON had FCF above 100% for four straight years ending in 2004

Management guided to $1 to $1.5 billion in proceeds, ultimately received $1.25 billion

No guidance on timing of synergies or cost of achieving, assumed five years

Many firms don't want to go through the headache of owning a non-core asset and trying to find a seller. This irrational bias creates a sustainable inefficiency for boards and management teams willing to exploit this. As long as the underlying assumptions for the sale of the non-core business are conservative and the returns from acquiring the core business are attractive, boards and management teams should be very open to these types of transactions. It may be possible to do a joint bid for a company with multiple businesses using private equity or another strategic buyer to further reduce the non-core asset sale risk.

CARVE-OUTS (DUPONT/AXALTA)

Many larger conglomerates provide corporate services such as human resources, finance, legal, and information technology for their various subsidiaries. These costs also include headquarters expenses (CEO, CFO, their staff, M&A), finance, IT, human resources, and sometimes corporate R&D as well. When they choose to sell a subsidiary, they will often continue to provide many of these services to the subsidiary for a specified amount of time (12 to 24 months) for a fee. The new owner of the divested business will need to re-create these corporate services once these transition services go away. While this involves time and complexity, it is also an opportunity.

The costs allocated to a subsidiary for HR, finance, information technology, and legal should, in theory, be very low relative to the cost of the subsidiary providing these services on its own, given the scale benefits of spreading these corporate services costs across multiple subsidiaries. However, in many cases, this simply is not the case. The most famous example of this is probably DuPont's sale of its automotive aftermarket coatings business to private equity in 2012. An activist investor, Trian Partners, published a white paper that showed that the coating business (with only $339 million of reported EBITDA in 2011) was being charged with $229 million in excess corporate costs/services as part of DuPont. By 2014, the coating business, now called Axalta, was earning $852 million in EBITDA.[7]

What I see time and time again with these carve-out transactions is that in most cases, the removal of these corporate services and corporate costs is a source of margin expansion. However, it is even better than that. For most M&A transactions, there is a cost to achieving the synergies that should be added to the cost of the transaction, severance being the largest expense.

A good rule of thumb for a firm is that it will spend a dollar for every dollar of cost savings it hopes to achieve as part of a transaction. The costs to achieve synergies in Europe will tend to be higher than in the United States. With a carve-out transaction, the costs of achieving the synergies are much lower as you are not technically laying off employees, but instead replacing high-cost corporate services from the previous owner with lower-cost corporate services for the subsidiary. There might still be costs associated with plant closures, but much of the traditional G&A savings will be achieved at limited cost. This lowers the all-in cost of the transaction and all else being equal, generates a higher ROIC on the transaction.

Hence, carve-outs are very attractive opportunities in most cases. The number of potential bidders is limited by the complexity of replacing the corporate services that were delivered by the parent, and the costs to achieve the synergies are materially lower as well. The odds of generating attractive returns rise materially with fewer bidders and lower integration cash costs. As a result, boards and management teams should not be deterred by the complexity of these transactions, but instead should embrace these opportunities.

Throughout these chapters on acquisitions, a common theme should emerge: a key to generating attractive returns in M&A is to find situations in which supply and demand favor the acquirer or are at least balanced.

Whether it is an asset swap, acquiring a business with one or more non-core businesses, or a corporate carve-out transaction, all of these involve a limited set of competitors for the asset. Balancing supply and demand and entering into negotiations with a firm as the only potential buyer, or one of a few, materially increases the odds of success in M&A.

CHAPTER 13

Superior Businesses with Lower Valuations

Industrial conglomerates are often misunderstood and underappreciated. While they frequently report their financial results within four or five different segments, they may operate multiple independent businesses within a given segment. Although industrial conglomerates will occasionally spin off one or more segments into its own separately traded company, many of the underlying businesses within an industrial conglomerate would be too small to exist as public companies on their own.

Industrial conglomerates effectively serve as holding companies that allow people to invest in a variety of industrial assets that would not otherwise be available to public investors. These collections of businesses also provide some degree of diversification by geography and end market, and between short and long industrial cycle end markets. Common operating and managerial disciplines and the training of future business leaders, who may move from one business to another, can result in the value of an industrial conglomerate being worth more than the sum of its parts.

These firms also tend to be much less capital intensive than other cyclical industries such as autos, energy, chemicals, and materials. Combined with a relatively modest level of underlying organic growth, they produce significant FCF. Furthermore, the volatility of their cash flow tends to be less pronounced due to their lower capital intensity. Even in an economic downturn when profits decline, their cash flows frequently fall at a more modest rate as capital spending drops and working capital becomes a source of cash. This lower level of cash flow volatility allows most industrial conglomerates to support a reasonable amount of debt throughout an economic cycle.

With strong FCF, modest organic growth, and balance sheets that can support a reasonable level of debt, capital allocation can become a source of massive alpha generation for shareholders if executed well. However, it can also be a driver of significant underperformance if executed poorly, as in the case of General Electric (see Chapter 18). With strong FCF generation that is often deployed toward acquisitions, industrial conglomerates in many ways resemble living, breathing creatures that are constantly evolving. Roper Technologies (ROP) is one such industrial conglomerate, and its differentiated approach to capital allocation created significant long-term shareholder value under the leadership of CEO Brian Jellison.

ROPER'S TRANSFORMATION

Roper Technologies CEO Brian Jellison did an unparalleled job of deploying capital to transform his company. No book on capital allocation would be complete without a thorough examination of the transformation of Roper under Brian Jellison's leadership and vision.

Jellison joined Roper as CEO in November of 2001 after a 26-year career at Ingersoll-Rand. During this period, enticing an executive to leave General Electric to become CEO at a smaller firm was viewed as a coup; Home Depot, Stanley Works, SPX, and 3M all experienced stock spikes when GE executives joined their firms.

No one viewed bringing in a CEO from Ingersoll-Rand as a coup. Ingersoll-Rand was seen as, at best, an average industrial conglomerate known for making two large acquisitions over the prior five years at each business's fundamental peak, only to see results falter shortly after both acquisitions were completed. Ingersoll-Rand would repeat this mistake once again with its acquisition of Trane in 2008. The increased debt associated with this large acquisition caused significant financial distress for Ingersoll-Rand during the Great Financial Crisis (GFC). If a board were looking for a leader from a firm with capital allocation prowess, Ingersoll-Rand would have been the last place to look at the time.

When Jellison joined Roper in 2001, the company had $587 million in sales, $130 million in EBITDA, $95 million in FCF, and a 52.7% gross margin (see Table 13.1). Roper reported its results in three segments: analytical instruments, industrial controls, and fluid handling. Its largest end market was the oil and gas sector with 31% of its sales, including 8% from Russian gas giant Gazprom (which would soon go away). Lower volatility sectors, including medical and research, comprised only 21% of Roper's sales.

In 2018, Roper would report $5.2 billion in sales, $1.8 billion in EBITDA, $1.37 billion in FCF, and a 63.2% gross margin (see Table 13.1). Its two largest business segments would be application software and network software and systems, representing 59% of its EBITDA. Its measurement and analytical solutions businesses that included Roper's medical products, water meter, material analysis, and research businesses represented another 28% of its EBITDA. Roper's more volatile legacy fluid handling and industrial controls divisions represented only about 12% of EBITDA.

TABLE 13.1

Portfolio Transformation at Roper[1]

	2001	2018	CAGR
Sales	587	5199	14%
Gross Margin	52.7%	63.2%	
Cap Ex	7.5	58.6	
FCF	95	1371	17%
Current Assets Minus Current Liabilities	110	−200	
Cap Ex/Sales	1.3%	1.1%	
FCF/Share	$1.51	$13.13	14%
Current Assets Minus Current Liabilities % of Sales	19%	−3.9%	

Notes: Current assets minus current liabilities is the difference between (current assets minus cash) − (current liabilities minus short-term debt). It is a broader definition of net working capital. Sales, cap ex, FCF, and current assets minus current liabilities in millions.

Between 2001 and 2018, Roper used acquisitions to fundamentally alter its business composition and financial metrics, and to drive substantial growth in revenues and cash flows. Not surprisingly, Roper's stock price significantly outperformed the market and its peers during this period. If an investor put $100 into Roper when Brian Jellison joined the firm in 2001, and left it there until September of 2018 when Jellison left, he or she would have seen it grow to a value of $1,932, including reinvested dividends.

So how did Brian Jellison create so much value at Roper, and what can we learn from what he accomplished?

Brian Jellison was a proponent of the importance of cash return on investment and brought this mindset to Roper; it was this mindset that heavily influenced his acquisition strategy.

Cash Return on Investment Definition

A company with a high cash return on investment (see Table 13.2) is unique in that it derives value not from its metal-bending prowess, manufacturing plants, or balance sheet, but from its brand, its intellectual property, unique customer value proposition, and strong market share of a relatively small, niche business. Brian Jellison wanted companies with exceptionally high cash return on investment. He strongly believed that the stock market and his industrial peers structurally undervalued these high-quality companies and wanted to take advantage of this inefficiency.

TABLE 13.2

Cash Return on Investment[2]

Numerator	Net Income + Depreciation + Amortization − Maintenance Capital Spending
Denominator	Gross PP&E + Net Working Capital

Many of his industrial conglomerate peers looked at businesses through an EBITDA lens, and valued firms on an EBITDA multiple. However, EBITDA does not equal after-tax cash flow as it ignores the capital intensity of the business as well as the cost to grow the business from a working capital perspective.

Table 13.3 illustrates this point. It looks at three different firms with 3% organic growth, 20% EBITDA margins, and different levels of capital intensity and working capital/sales ratios.

TABLE 13.3

Three Different Firms with 3% Organic Growth and 20% EBITDA Margins

Firm A, $100 million in revenues, 20% EBITDA, 4% cap ex/sales, 20% W/C to sales, 25% tax rate, 1.2x cap ex/D&A

Year	0	1	2	3	4	5
Revenues	100	103.0	106.1	109.3	112.6	115.9
EBITDA	20.0	20.6	21.2	21.9	22.5	23.2
EBIT	16.7	17.2	17.7	18.2	18.8	19.3
Taxes	−4.2	−4.3	−4.4	−4.6	−4.7	−4.8
Net Income	12.5	12.9	13.3	13.7	14.1	14.5
D&A	3.3	3.4	3.5	3.6	3.8	3.9
Cap Ex	−4.0	−4.1	−4.2	−4.4	−4.5	−4.6
W/C		−0.6	−0.6	−0.6	−0.7	−0.7
FCF		11.6	11.9	12.3	12.7	13.0
Cumulative FCF	**61.5**					

Firm B, $100 million in revenues, 20% EBITDA, 2% cap ex/sales, 10% W/C to sales, 25% tax rate, 1.2x cap ex/D&A

Year	0	1	2	3	4	5
Revenues	100.0	103.0	106.1	109.3	112.6	115.9
EBITDA	20.0	20.6	21.2	21.9	22.5	23.2
EBIT	18.3	18.9	19.5	20.0	20.6	21.3
Taxes	−4.6	−4.7	−4.9	−5.0	−5.2	−5.3
Net Income	13.8	14.2	14.6	15.0	15.5	15.9
D&A	1.7	1.7	1.8	1.8	1.9	1.9
Cap Ex	−2.0	−2.1	−2.1	−2.2	−2.3	−2.3
W/C		−0.3	−0.3	−0.3	−0.3	−0.3
FCF		13.5	13.9	14.3	14.8	15.2
Cumulative FCF	**71.8**					

Firm C, $100 million in revenues, 20% EBITDA, 1% cap ex/sales, 0% W/C to sales, 25% tax rate, 1.2x cap ex/D&A

Year	0	1	2	3	4	5
Revenues	100.0	103.0	106.1	109.3	112.6	115.9
EBITDA	20.0	20.6	21.2	21.9	22.5	23.2
EBIT	19.2	19.7	20.3	20.9	21.6	22.2
Taxes	−4.8	−4.9	−5.1	−5.2	−5.4	−5.6
Net Income	14.4	14.8	15.3	15.7	16.2	16.7
D&A	0.8	0.9	0.9	0.9	0.9	1.0
Cap Ex	−1.0	−1.0	−1.1	−1.1	−1.1	−1.2
W/C		0.0	0.0	0.0	0.0	0.0
FCF		14.6	15.1	15.5	16.0	16.5
Cumulative FCF	**77.7**					

Even with the same level of organic growth, EBITDA margins, and tax rate, Firm C generated 26% more FCF than Firm A and 8% more FCF than Firm B over a five-year period.

FIGURE 13.1

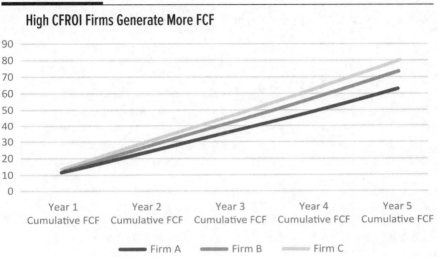

High CFROI Firms Generate More FCF

Over the next 17 years, Roper's cash return on investment would increase from 30% in 2001 to 521% in 2018 as Roper used its free cash flow, debt capacity, and working capital to fundamentally reshape its portfolio.†‡

---

† I highlight Roper's high cash return on investment to demonstrate the quality of businesses they were acquiring. These were businesses with low capital intensity, high margins, and in some cases negative working capital. However, it is important to highlight that the right way to look at the returns from acquisitions is by calculating cash-on-cash returns as I have stressed before. The CROI return ignores the full purchase price of the acquisition and uses only the net tangible assets and net working capital associated with the acquisition in the denominator of the calculation. Roper's returns on its acquisitions were good, but not 521% good.

‡ Roper does not disclose maintenance capital expenditures, so I used total capital spending. Given how low capital spending is, the impact would be very minor on the calculation.

As one can see in Table 13.4, Roper was consistently able to buy better businesses in attractive, low-cyclical end markets for a lower valuation than the company was trading for at the time.

TABLE 13.4

Roper Buying Better Businesses at 15% Discount to Roper's Valuation[3]

Acquisition	Announce Date	Price	EV/ EBITDA Price	ROP EV/ EBITDA	Business
Neptune	Oct 03	$475	8.0	12.7	Water meters
TransCore	Oct 04	$600	8.2	12.2	Tolling systems
CIVCO	Jun 05	$120	8.5	11.3	Medical products
MEDTEC	Dec 05	$150	8.8	11.4	Cancer care products
CBORD	Feb 08	$344	11	10.3	Smart card systems for food transactions in universities
Verathon/ UTS	Nov 09	$356	9.4	10.7	Medical products + tolling systems
iTRADE	Jul 10	$525	9.5	10.4	Software for food industry
Northern Digital	May 11	$204	10	11.8	3-D measurement tech for medical applications
Sunquest	Jul 12	$1,415	10.1	11.1	Diagnostic and laboratory software
MHA	Apr 13	$1,000	10.5	12.6	Services, software for acute care healthcare providers
Aderant	Oct 15	$675	12	14	Software for legal industry
Construct Connect	Oct 16	$632	12	13.9	Software for commercial construction industry
Deltek	Dec 16	$2,800	14	14.5	Software for government contractors
PowerPlan	May 18	$1,100	16	18.6	Software for asset-centric companies
		Average	10.6	12.5	

Note: Verathon and UTS were two separate transactions, but Roper announced both acquisitions at the same time and only disclosed the combined financials.

INGREDIENTS OF ROPER'S ACQUISITION SUCCESS

Buying better businesses for a lower valuation than where your firm is trading is a very difficult proposition. It requires taking advantage of multiple market arbitrages and inefficiencies.

Private/Public Arbitrage (See Chapter 14)

All of Roper's large acquisitions were of private companies. This is the one area of M&A that most academic evidence suggests is ripe for value creation. Private company cash flows are valued lower than public company cash flows due to an illiquidity discount. A smart acquirer can take advantage of this arbitrage opportunity by acquiring private company cash flows. This instantly creates value by converting those cash flows into higher valued, more liquid public company cash flows. Roper took advantage of this.

Supply/Demand

As an analyst covering Roper from 2000–2007, I was always surprised at the quality of businesses that Roper was able to acquire at very reasonable valuations. At the time, I did not fully appreciate the supply/demand dynamics that allowed them to achieve this. In the vast majority of cases, these businesses had no logical strategic owner and were too small to go public. Most of Roper's acquisitions did not fit nicely into the existing segments of their industrial conglomerate peers. Moreover, while they might have fit into technology, healthcare, or software companies, these niche businesses typically produced "only" mid-single-digit organic growth. While this is an attractive organic growth rate relative to the growth rate of most industrial assets, many of the firms within the technology, healthcare, or software industries sought acquisitions that would grow materially faster.

As a result, in many cases, ROP was the only logical buyer outside of private equity whose high return threshold limited the valuation multiple they could pay for these businesses. Hence, ROP was able to acquire these businesses for reasonable prices due to a lack of sufficient and strategic competition.

Few Failures

Roper does not report on the organic growth of all of its various operating businesses. However, from 2005–2018, it reported an impressive 4.45% organic revenue growth CAGR. This growth rate is very consistent with the GDP+ growth rate in most of its acquisitions' end-markets. While difficult to prove, it is logical and highly likely that Roper's legacy assets grew slower than the businesses the company acquired during the Jellison era. Out of all of the acquisitions completed during the Jellison era, only Sunquest (due to competition) stands out as a failed acquisition. Nevertheless, given the aforementioned 4.45% organic growth rate, other acquisitions likely outperformed expectations and more than offset Sunquest's challenges.

One of the challenges for companies that spend the vast majority of their cash flows on acquisitions is that management can become too focused on the next deal and neglect the health of the existing businesses. Over time, the organic growth rate and competitiveness of the underlying business decays. Roper did not experience this common challenge for acquisition-driven firms due to management's relentless focus on organic growth as well as the quality of the assets that the company acquired. It is much harder to damage a really sound business than an average or below-average business. A strong business will often require less time and attention from senior management than its weaker counterparts.

Optimized Balance Sheet

At the end of 2001, Roper had a debt/EBITDA ratio of 2.5x and at the end of 2018, it had debt/EBITDA ratio of 2.7x. Roper was able to deploy $4.6 billion extra debt capital between 2001 and 2018 as it maintained an optimized balance sheet. While leverage increased slightly on a debt/EBITDA basis, the Roper of 2018, with significant exposure to high-recurring software business and less volatile medical and municipal end markets, was much better positioned to handle an economic downturn than the Roper of 2001.

Limited Divestitures

Jellison, with minor exceptions like Petrotech, chose not to sell Roper's legacy industrial, scientific research, and energy-related businesses. He believed that these businesses' cash flows allowed Roper to spend more on acquisitions, support a larger balance sheet with more debt capacity, and were valued by the market more highly as part of Roper than if they were spun off or sold. It is a testament to Jellison's leadership as well as the leadership of those legacy businesses that they did not atrophy inside of Roper, where their FCF was consistently siphoned off for corporate M&A.

ADVANTAGES TO BUYING BETTER BUSINESSES AT A LOWER VALUATION THAN THEIR TRADING LEVEL

If a firm can buy a higher growth, less capital-intensive, and less cyclical company than the firm's existing business for a lower valuation, share repurchase makes no sense. As a result, capital deployment decisions become relatively easy. While the firm should still make sure that acquisitions generate higher returns than dividends or incremental capital expenditures, in most cases, the firm should be deploying the bulk of their excess capital toward acquisitions.

There are two mathematical ways to create shareholder value: EPS/FCF growth and P/E or P/FCF multiple expansion. This M&A strategy accentuates both.

A stock price is a function of a firm's EPS or FCF per share and the valuation multiple the market awards the company. A company with $1 of EPS trading at 12x earnings will produce a $12 stock. A company that is buying better businesses with higher organic growth rates, better FCF characteristics, and less volatile cash flows is likely, over time, to be awarded with a higher valuation multiple. This reflects the improvement in the underlying company's financial characteristics, and is exactly what happened to Roper.

In 2003, ROP was trading at 13x NTM EBITDA (more industrial controls and fluid handling). In 2018, it was trading at 18x NTM EBITDA (more software). In addition, by paying reasonable prices for great businesses and continuing to grow organically in the mid-single digits, Roper was able to increase FCF per share at a 14% CAGR for 17 years.

However, Roper was able to compound shareholder wealth at an 18.4% CAGR during Brian Jellison's reign through the following combination of factors:

- A 14% CAGR in FCF per share
- A higher valuation placed on the company reflecting its improved portfolio and Jellison's M&A acumen

Firms that can acquire better businesses at valuations lower than their own trading levels can create a powerful flywheel of shareholder value with a combination of strong earnings and cash flow growth accompanied by an expanding valuation multiple (see Table 13.5).

Roper is not the only industrial conglomerate that has transformed its portfolio over time. At one time, Danaher was essentially a tools and industrial controls company. Today, it is predominantly a healthcare company with leading businesses serving the life science, diagnostics, water, and product identification end markets. Teleflex shed its auto and industrial assets to focus on growing its healthcare business both organically and inorganically. Both firms saw their stock prices outperform significantly over time.

The principle of trying to acquire superior businesses for a lower valuation than a firm's current trading level is not unique to Roper or even to industrial conglomerates. It can be applied in every sector and industry to create shareholder value. Nor does it have to be as extreme as in the case of Roper, which transformed from an energy and industrial controls firm to a software-focused firm in less than two decades.

Buying businesses with a little faster growth, a little less cyclicality, and better FCF characteristics, can, over time, drive portfolio enhancement or transformation. Moreover, it can also serve as an important guardrail to prevent management teams and boards from overpaying for growth assets that result in poor returns on capital, slower EPS/FCF growth, and heightened risk of write-offs in the future.

TABLE 13.5

M&A Focused Firms Value Creation Flywheel

Action	Impact
Buy firms growing faster than existing business	Higher multiple, faster EPS/FCF
Buy firms with less cyclicality than existing business	Higher multiple, more debt capacity
Buy firms with lower capital and W/C intensity	Stronger FCF, higher multiple, faster EPS/FCF
Generate high-single-digit to low-double-digit returns by Year 5–6	Supports strong EPS/FCF growth
Don't buy a firm for a materially higher valuation than where your company is trading on a post-synergy basis	Supports strong EPS/FCF Growth

As a young industrial analyst covering Roper, then as portfolio manager and owner of Roper shares in the T. Rowe Price Capital Appreciation Fund, I had the pleasure of interacting with Brian Jellison from the day he started at Roper until 2018. While Brian created significant shareholder value for T. Rowe Price mutual fund shareholders, I will always remember him as an executive with a passion for capital allocation. When I would fly down to visit him in Georgia, I would often miss my returning flight, as Brian would become so enthusiastic about Roper's acquisition strategy and value creation formula that a one-hour meeting would extend to two hours or more. Brian passed away in November of 2018 at the age of 73. He will be missed as a great leader, an excellent capital allocator, and a good man.

CHAPTER 14

Private Deals

Despite all the compelling academic evidence suggesting that most acquisitions fail to achieve a return above the acquiring firm's cost of capital, there is an entire category of acquisitions for which this is not true. Academic studies consistently demonstrate that firms acquiring non-public traded firms can generate attractive returns for their shareholders. In their paper in the *Journal of Finance*, Kathleen Fuller, Jeffrey Netter, and Mike Stegemoller address this distinction:

> *Using a sample of 3,135 takeovers, we find that bidders have significantly negative returns when buying public targets and significantly positive returns when buying private or subsidiary targets. . . . One explanation for the differing market reactions to the acquisitions of private and subsidiary targets versus public acquisitions is that bidders receive a better price when they buy nonpublic firms.*[1]

The authors correctly hypothesized that this was due to a liquidity discount that is routinely applied to private businesses but not to larger, more liquid public companies. In other words, the future stream of cash flows of a private company can be acquired for a lower valuation than the future stream of cash flows of a public company.

By paying a lower valuation for a private company, the acquiring firm generates a higher return on capital, all else being equal, and is more likely to generate a return greater than its cost of capital. Consequently, an intelligent management team and board can create value for its shareholders by exploiting this liquidity discount. Once a private company is acquired by a public company, the liquidity discount that was previously applied to the private firm's cash flow goes away.

A McKinsey study of the 1,000 largest nonbanking companies' acquisitions from 1999–2010 (over 15,000 deals) found that firms using a programmatic approach to M&A that involved a large number of small acquisitions accrued the greatest excess total shareholder returns. Companies that had completed at least one large deal greater than 30% of their market capitalization underperformed by 1.7% per year and underperformed the programmatic acquirers by 4.5% per year.[2]

WHY PRIVATE DEALS GENERATE BETTER RETURNS

So why are small, private acquisitions far more likely to generate attractive returns than larger, public acquisitions?

Public-Private Arbitrage

As Fuller, Netter, and Stegemoller correctly hypothesized in their paper, the cash flows from a public company are more highly valued than the cash flows from a private company due to the liquidity discount that is applied to the latter. In every Finance 101 class at university, students are taught that the value of a business is the present value of its future cash flows. However, not all cash flows are created equal. Liquidity matters. Less liquid bonds trade at wider spreads relative to their more liquid counterparts, even with the same underlying credit risk.

If I own a 5% stake in a local grocery store that is generating $500,000 in profits (my share is $25,000) and I want to sell my interest in the store, finding a buyer would likely be time consuming and expensive, and the bid-ask spread would probably be wide. If after selling my interest, I changed my mind the next day and wanted to buy my 5% interest back, it would be very costly for me, confusing to the buyer, and virtually impossible.

However, if I owned $250,000 of stock in Kroger, I could liquidate the position or initial a new position in seconds with a bid-ask spread likely less than $0.01 per share without needing to pay a commission to an online broker. By the same token, if my partners and I chose to sell our local grocery store to Kroger, those cash flows would magically lose their liquidity discount and likely be valued at the same valuation multiple as the rest of Kroger's cash flows.

Supply/Demand

In many industries, there are numerous small, private businesses and few buyers. While some private companies may choose to hire a small, regional investment bank to auction themselves off to the highest bidder, many will engage in one-on-one discussions with a single bidder they know and respect or have been courted by in the past. Often, there is a fairly tight range of EBITDA multiples for small, private companies that public companies are willing to pay in certain industries; this negates the need for auctions. In addition, there might be a natural buyer due to geographic, product, customer, or synergy-extraction potential that is recognized by all of the potential bidders.

Less Likely to Be Optimized

A small, private company is far less likely than a large, publicly traded company to have taken advantage of global sourcing to lower its cost of goods. It is also far less likely to be selling its products or services globally. It may also have less professional management. Small, private firms are apt to have low-hanging cost synergies that enable operating margin improvement for the acquirer.

In some cases, family-run private firms are being run as cash cows. These firms are systematically underinvesting in high-return capital and expansion opportunities in order to maximize short-term cash distributions to the family. It is typically much easier to improve the top- and bottom-line trajectory of a private company post-acquisition than it is a public company for all of the aforementioned reasons.

Ametek, an industrial conglomerate under the leadership of Frank Hermance from 1999 to 2016, had a simple but effective model of using the bulk of the company's FCF to buy private companies and, in many cases, double their operating margins over a couple of years. The strategy drove significant excess returns for Ametek's shareholders. During Hermance's tenure as CEO, the S&P 500 had a total return of 112% or 4.6% annualized. Over the same period, Ametek's total return was 1,604% or 18.5% annualized.

Not Always About Price

When asked why Republic Services' acquisition activity had increased, President Jon Vander Ark replied:

> We treat employees that we acquire with dignity and respect and they understand that this is a great place to work. And listen, owners care about money, but they don't just care about money. They care about legacy and how people are going to take care of the businesses they built and we've proven ourselves to be very good stewards of the business they're selling to us.[3]

When a public company is sold, it is almost always sold to the highest bidder. It would be very hard for a public company board to agree to sell their company to an acquirer offering $45 per share and spurn the advances of a prospective acquirer offering $50 per share. Shareholders, whose approval is needed for the sale of the company, would almost never agree to take a lower price. However, that is not always true for a private company. While price is still important, it may not be paramount.

If a founder or family is selling a company, trying to find an acquisition partner that will maintain the brand, treat employees fairly, and give the business the capital and attention to expand and thrive over the long term can, in many cases, be just as important as price. This can result in the business being sold for a lower valuation than if it went to auction and is more likely to result in a one-on-one negotiation. In the end, this can enable a higher return for the buyer with the right qualitative attributes for the seller.

I will discuss two companies, PerkinElmer and Marsh & McLennan, both of which have created significant long-term shareholder value by buying private companies.

CREATION OF MARSH & MCLENNAN AGENCY (MMA)[†]

In 2009, MMC's biggest subsidiary, Marsh Brokerage, the world's largest insurance broker, already had a strong market share of Fortune 1000 customers. This was a good business with low-to-mid single digit growth, low cyclicality, high customer retention, and good margins. However, it operated in a concentrated space with a handful of insurance brokerage firms that controlled the vast majority of the market and, given high retention rates, it was hard to grow much faster than the market. The customers tended to be very price aware and sophisticated with regard to the costs of the services that Marsh Brokerage provided.

---

† Note: In this example, there are multiple subsidiaries discussed and one holding company mentioned, and I acknowledge that this might be confusing. Marsh & McLennan (MMC) is the publicly traded holding company that owns Marsh Brokerage, an insurance brokerage company. Marsh Brokerage embarked on an acquisition strategy to build a separate subsidiary called Marsh & McLennan Agency (MMA) to develop a presence in US middle market insurance brokerage.

However, Marsh Brokerage was missing out on an even more attractive and ultimately larger part of the insurance brokerage industry: the middle market. This is a much more fragmented area with greater potential to grow faster than the underlying market. Customers are smaller, slightly less sophisticated, and price is often less important than long-term relationships and the power of the local brand. Operating margins also tend to be higher in the middle market. This segment of the market also offers the opportunity for a good insurance brokerage firm to provide both insurance broker services and employee benefits for the client.

It would have been very easy for Marsh to scratch this strategic itch by making a large acquisition to expand into the more attractive middle market insurance arena. Its competitor, Willis Group, had done just that by agreeing to purchase Hilb Rogal & Hobbs Company (HRH) for $1.7 billion in 2008 for what was promised to be 10x EBITDA. However, reality delivered closer to 13–14x EBITDA due to poor acquisition timing, the loss of contingent commission profits, poor revenue trends, and employee departures.[4]

Marsh could have bid for the largest publicly traded middle market brokerage firm, Brown & Brown. However, Marsh would have had to pay at least $6–$7 billion for a company whose organic revenues had declined for three straight years. Marsh also could have attempted to buy private-equity-backed roll-ups. But it didn't.

In many respects, even if one ignores elevated valuations for large middle market brokerage properties, the largest acquisition opportunities were structurally less attractive than the market they served. Most of these larger firms were built up through an aggressive acquisition roll-up strategy that focused on quantity over quality and getting the next deal done over driving sustainable organic growth. So, while many of these acquisitions would have given MMC an instant presence in a more attractive part of the insurance brokerage market, the underlying assets were typically below-average.

The head of the insurance brokerage division and future CEO of Marsh & McLennan, Dan Glaser, decided to take a different approach to building the business over the long term through a "string of pearls" strategy:

This is a five year and longer view of how we're going to be building our performance and our capabilities within the small commercial and middle market. So, it's not an extraction exercise for Marsh. It's actually building a separate business. . . .

[David Eslick, Chairman & CEO of MMA] is under no obligation to close deals at any sort of pace. This is a strategy based upon finding quality organizations that will join Marsh & McLennan Agency.[5]

Glaser's patience would be well rewarded. Over the next decade, Marsh McLennan Agency (MMA) would be transformed into a $1.5 billion business built through 72 small, private acquisitions.[6†]

While Marsh does not break out MMA's organic growth rate, over the last decade the management team at MMC has made multiple public comments suggesting that the business is growing in the mid-single digits organically.[7‡] This is more than twice the organic revenue growth rate of Brown & Brown over this period.[8]

At Marsh's 2014 investor day, CEO Dan Glaser explained the firm's overall acquisition strategy:

The philosophy that we have been following is really a string of pearls, 57 pearls since 2009. You can see we've been a good steward of your capital. Aggregate purchase price of $2.5 billion, giving us revenue of $1.2 billion, an average price of 2.1 times revenue and an average deal size of $43 million.

---

† 72 through first quarter of 2019.

‡ In the presentation, MMC showed a pie chart showing that 25% of their revenues came from growth business, and MMA was included within this 25% sleeve, which included other fast-growing businesses and regions such as Cyber, Data & Analytics, Latin America, and Africa.

So, you can see from that we are not trying to hit a home run. We want to hit many singles with the occasional double and the occasional triple. And why is that? Well, one, it's got less risk.[9]

On the first quarter of 2018 conference call, Glaser, outlined his acquisition priorities:

*[O]ur philosophy is that we have no budget or timetable. Quality is the number one thing that we focus on. **We prefer companies growing faster and that are trading below our multiple** and where we have really good chemistry [emphasis added].*[10]

What Marsh Brokerage was able to create through a string of pearls, disciplined M&A strategy is remarkable. Glaser identified a strategic hole in the portfolio and then had the patience to address it over the long term, which created a strong collection of assets with an attractive organic growth rate at very reasonable multiples. No one felt pressure to close a deal, and notably, in 2013, Marsh Brokerage completed only two middle market deals. The focus on small deals allowed shareholders to benefit from the private-public arbitrage. In addition, the focus on acquiring faster growth assets for a lower multiple than MMC's is a recipe for value creation (see Chapter 13).

PERKINELMER'S ACQUISITION OF EUROIMMUN

In June 2017, PerkinElmer (PKI) announced the acquisition of EUROIMMUN, a German manufacturer of autoimmune and allergy diagnostics, for $1.3 billion in cash.

EUROIMMUN had all the characteristics of a great business:

- 19% organic growth over the last five years with no year less than 15%
- 90%+ recurring re-agent/consumable mix

- EBITDA margins higher than PKI's
- Unique relationship with over 100 research partners
- Culture that resulted in exceptionally quick new assay development (essentially new tests).
- Significant exposure to emerging markets where penetration of diagnostics is still low[11]

The addition of EUROIMMUN to Perkin would materially improve PKI's fundamentals:

- Add 100+ basis points to PKI's organic growth rate
- Increase PKI's profit mix from diagnostics to more than 45% from 30%
- Increase PKI's mix of recurring revenue and lower its cyclicality
- Potentially lower PKI's tax rate

PKI management also indicated that it expected EUROIMMUN's operating margin (then 19%) to move up over the long term to a level more consistent with PKI's diagnostics margins (around 30%).

Last, while most diagnostics companies generate around half of their revenue from the United States, EUROIMMUN generated only 5% of its revenues from the United States. This was not due to competitive forces or a failure of its products to gain acceptance, but rather a conscious decision by EUROIMMUN's management to focus on Europe and China first. With PKI's established US presence and strong regulatory expertise, the acquisition could accelerate EUROIMMUN's expansion in the United States and give it another growth lever to support its strong organic growth rate.

PKI, which was trading at around 15x 2018 EV/EBITDA at the time, paid about 16x 2018 EV/EBITDA for EUROIMMUN. In many respects, this can best be described as a coup for PKI. Perkin bought a business with a growth rate more than twice its own, with significant margin expansion potential, and with 90%+ recurring revenue for only a fraction higher valuation than where PKI was trading, even if one ignores the potential tax benefits. In addition, given EUROIMMUN's strong organic growth and high incremental margins, operating margin expansion would play out naturally over time without the need for large restructuring cash outflows.

The life science and diagnostics spaces are generally viewed as attractive due to their low cyclicality, high recurring revenue, and mid-single-digit organic growth. As a result, acquisition multiples are generally in the mid-to-high teens on EBITDA, and good acquirers strive to generate high-single-digit returns on investment by year five. In contrast, PKI announced that it expected to generate a double-digit return on investment by year five.

So how was PerkinElmer able to acquire EUROIMMUN for such an attractive price?

First, there was no auction. This was a one-on-one negotiation between Perkin's CEO Robert Friel and EUROIMMUN's CEO and founder Winfried Stöcker.

Second, before you think PKI CEO Rob Friel must be an excellent negotiator (which he may be), Dr. Stöcker's comments demonstrate very clearly that price was not his top priority during the sale process.

On June 21, 2017, Dr. Stöcker explained this position on his blog:

I need not fear about the distant future—provided that EUROIMMUN does not fall into the wrong hands after my retirement. . . .

I would therefore prefer to entrust the company to proven experts, who, according to my assessment, are capable of ensuring the continued existence of what we have successfully built up over the past 30 years. We have found these experts in PerkinElmer, a renowned company of global significance, which is headquartered in Boston, USA, but has also some prosperous divisions located in Germany.[12]

Dr Stöcker went on to explain that the decision to sell to PerkinElmer was based on the fact that there would be no job losses, no subsidiary closures, and no overlap in businesses between the two companies. He never once mentioned price. Instead, it was about finding the right company with the right attributes to ensure the continued success of the firm he built and its employees across the globe.

It is clear that EUROIMMUN, which Dr. Stöcker founded in 1987, was his baby. In only 30 years, Dr. Stöcker built a business with over $300 million in revenues that created significant value for patients, customers, and employees. Once he was no longer running the company, he wanted to make sure that the business would continue to prosper, that its culture would persist, and that its employees would be protected. He trusted that Rob Friel from PerkinElmer would do just that, and that was more important than money.

In the end, Perkin bought a great business for a very attractive price because it offered Dr. Stöcker the right combination of cultural alignment, minimal business overlap, and employee security. As a result, the acquisition proved a true win-win for Perkin-Elmer shareholders, EURIOMMUN employees, and Dr. Stöcker.

CHAPTER 15

Distressed Sellers

The General Electric Co. Ltd (GEC) had a long, proud history as a British conglomerate. In many ways, the triumph and tragedy of the British General Electric Company is not unlike the story of the American General Electric Company (see Chapter 18).

GEC's origins stretch back to the early 1880s, when German immigrants Gustav Binswanger and Hugo Hirst opened a wholesale business called the Electric Appliance Company. In 1884, they brought in another partner and started a separate electric wholesale distribution business called the Electric Apparatus Company Limited. Within a few years, the Electric Apparatus Company bought a factory to manufacture telephones, bells, and switchboards as it expanded into the manufacturing of electrical equipment. In 1889, it was incorporated as the General Electric Company Limited, and in 1900, it went public.

GEC soon became a leading electrical equipment manufacturer, and within a couple of decades, it had become a global company generating revenues on multiple continents. GEC was a major supplier of electrical equipment to the British government during the First World War. During the Second World War, it manufactured sophisticated electrical and communications equipment, radar, and other defense products to help England defeat the Nazis.

In the years following the Second World War, the company struggled, and by the early 1960s, it was operating at a rather low 3% operating margin. However, the future of General Electric was about to change. In the early 1960s, the GEC board directors sought new leadership to turn the company around.[1] In 1961, they settled on Arnold Weinstock, a promising young executive who had been running Radio and Allied Industries since the mid-1950s.

Weinstock was the son of Polish immigrants to the United Kingdom. His father died when he was five, and his mother died from breast cancer five years later. He was initially sent to live with his older brother and his wife, Annie. This arrangement lasted a couple of years, after which he resided with Annie's relatives until the outbreak of the Second World War.

Despite these hardships, Weinstock excelled in school, particularly in mathematics. He was accepted to the London School of Economics, graduated in 1944, and immediately went to work for the Navy. In 1954, after a brief career in real estate, Weinstock joined Radio and Allied Industries. Despite his lack of experience, he found himself running the company's day-to-day operations almost from day one.

Under Weinstock's leadership, Radio and Allied Industries achieved rapid, highly profitable growth at a time when many large electrical equipment companies struggled with low growth and low profit margins. Radio and Allied Industries went public in 1958, and in 1961 it merged with GEC in a stock-for-stock transaction that offered an attractive premium for Radio and Allied Industries shareholders. Radio and Allied was just one-twentieth the size of GEC at the time of the merger.

Less than two years after the merger, Weinstock was running GEC. In 1962, the year before he became managing director, GEC generated £135 million in revenue with around £4 million in pretax profits. In the late 1960s, with the blessing of a Labour government looking to assert British dominance in specific strategic industries,

Weinstock led GEC through a series of acquisitions, and operational consolidations of many of the largest British electrical equipment companies.

Following these consolidations, Weinstock would further reshape GEC's portfolio through a series of acquisitions that increased the company's presence in the defense, communications, and general industrial sectors. During Weinstock's tenure, a relentless focus on controlling costs, M&A acumen, and disciplined business planning and oversight drove significant shareholder value. When Weinstock retired in 1996, he left a business with revenues of £11 billion ($17.1 billion USD),[†] just under £1 billion of profits, and a very strong balance sheet with more than £1.4 billion in cash. He increased GEC's profits by almost 250x, tripled operating margins, and increased revenues by 81x.

A pound invested in General Electric in 1963 was worth 50 in 1996. From a purely outcomes perspective, GEC's acquisition of Radio and Allied Industries may have been one of the best deals in history. Former Deputy Prime Minister Michael Heseltine called Lord Weinstock "one of the greatest industrialists of the second half of the 20th century."[2]

In 1996, Lord Weinstock was succeeded by Lord George Simpson, a former executive at Rover and Lucas, who also reshaped the GEC portfolio through a series of divestitures and acquisitions. From 1996 to 1999, Lord Simpson sold off a variety of general industrial, defense, rail, and power businesses. In 1999, he chose to double down on the firm's telecommunications equipment business by making two large US acquisitions, Reltec and FORE Systems, for $6.6 billion.

At the end of 1999, Lord Simpson changed the name of the firm to Marconi PLC to reflect this transition from a traditional industrial conglomerate to a more focused telecommunications company.[‡] By 2001, 89% of Marconi's revenues came from its communications

---

[†] Based on 1.5597 pound to dollar ratio on September 2, 1996, accessed via the web resource poundsterlinglive.com.

[‡] Weinstock had acquired English Electric in 1968, which in turn had purchased Marconi in 1946.

network, communications services, mobile communications, and data systems segments. Interestingly, Marconi's non-data and telecommunications businesses, which represented 11% of revenues, were lumped together in a segment called "other," reflecting their lack of strategic importance within the new Marconi PLC. In 1999, Michael Harrison, writing for the *Independent*, said, "Once the Fore Systems and Marconi defence deals are complete, GEC will be virtually unrecognizable from the company Lord Simpson inherited in September 1996."[3]

Unfortunately, Lord Simpson's timing could not have been worse. The dot-com bubble burst, and demand for telecommunication and datacom equipment plummeted. In September of 2000, Marconi's stock price was £12.50, and it sported a £35 billion ($50 billion USD)[†] market capitalization. By August of 2001, the company's stock price hit a low of 53 pence, its market capitalization had collapsed by a staggering 96%, and its debt was downgraded to junk.

In March of 2001, the end of Marconi's fiscal year, the company had over $5 billion in long-term debt and short-term borrowings, and only $530 million in cash. During fiscal year 2001, Marconi produced an astonishing $1.6 billion in negative FCF. Lord Simpson, along with Marconi's chairman Sir Roger Hurn, resigned in September of 2001. By the middle of 2002, Marconi had laid off more than half of its workforce.[4]

In an article in the *Telegraph*, Dan Sabbagh and Sean O'Neill described "[t]he fall of Marconi, formerly GEC," as "perhaps the most dramatic industrial collapse seen in Britain since the Rolls-Royce crisis 30 years ago."[5] The company was now losing money and had $5 billion in debt. It needed to sell assets, and quickly.

Luckily for Marconi, Lord Simpson had not sold off all of the firm's non-telecom/datacom businesses. On December 20, 2001, Marconi announced that it would sell its Gilbarco fuel dispenser business to Danaher for $325 million. On February 5, 2002, Marconi

---

† Based on 1.43 pound to dollar ratio on September 7, 2000, accessed via the web resource poundsterlinglive.com.

announced the sale of its Videojet product identification business to Danaher for $500 million.

Table 15.1 is a very conservative return analysis based on publicly available information at the time of the acquisitions.

TABLE 15.1

Danaher's Acquisitions of Videojet and Gilbarco from Marconi PLC[6]

Annualized Revenues at Acquisition	$800
Assume Organic Growth Rate	4%
Normalized Operating Margins	15%
Purchase Price for Acquisitions	$825
DHR 2001 Cash Tax Rate	10.9%
Estimate of NPV of After Cost Costs to Improve Margins	$40
Year 5 Projected Financials	
Revenues	$973
Operating Profits	$146
After-Tax Profits	$130
Total Investment	$865
ROIC	**15%**

Note: Danaher's cash tax rate was low in 2001, and it is unclear what the right cash tax rate for these acquisitions would be over the following five years. However, even if I use a 15% cash tax rate, the return would still be 14.3%. If I use a 20% cash tax rate, the return would still be 13.5%. This analysis also excludes the working capital improvements Danaher typically achieves with its acquisitions, which would lower the total investment and increase the return as well. No matter what assumptions one uses, these were very attractive transactions for Danaher and its shareholders.

Videojet was a well-above-average business with high gross margins, low cyclicality, and a large consumables aftermarket stream. At its 2017 investor day, Danaher highlighted that it had generated greater than a 20% return on capital in its product identification business, which included not only Videojet but also all of the additional accretive bolt-on acquisitions that the transaction had enabled. In 2017, the product identification platform, of which Videojet was the largest business, generated 25%+ operating margins versus the low-teens level prior to being acquired.

While Gilbarco was a slightly below average business with low-single digit growth and some cyclicality, Danaher bought it for a bargain price of 0.65x revenues. Gilbarco is one of the businesses that Danaher spun off in 2016 to create Fortive. It was the largest business within Fortive's industrial technology segment, which generated around a 20% operating margin in 2018.

Danaher and its CEO Larry Culp acquired these assets for an exceptional price from a distressed seller. One of the many challenges with M&A is timing (see Chapter 11). Sellers almost always have the advantage over buyers. They can choose to sell when valuations are high, when multiple bidders are well positioned to bid, or when the economy or business feels peakish. With a distressed seller, none of those advantages apply. Here the buyer has the advantage and an enhanced opportunity to generate attractive returns.

HOW CAN MANAGEMENT TEAMS AND BOARDS TAKE ADVANTAGE OF DISTRESSED ASSETS?

Leadership should always be identifying assets that would be logical acquisition candidates whether private, public, or part of a conglomerate. This list should be compiled and discussed as part of a board's annual capital allocation review process.

If one of these assets is held by a financially distressed firm, proactively reach out to the firm about acquiring it. Be willing to pay for the asset in cash, and promise to move quickly to complete the acquisition. In distress situations, the ability to close the transaction quickly can be as important as the price tag.

Even in non-distress situations, conditions exist in which a firm has made a large acquisition in a different business and potentially leveraged up the balance sheet to do it. The acquisition may also indicate a change in the strategic direction of the acquiring firm, and signal that a portion of its portfolio may be less strategic than it used to be. If there is a business inside the conglomerate that your firm would like to acquire, consider approaching the company with an offer.

Boards, management teams, and investors prefer to avoid elevated leverage, even if there is a plan to reduce it to a more normalized level within a couple of years. A management team and board are likely to be far more receptive to a reasonable offer for a business if it accelerates debt reduction and improves financial flexibility, especially if the business is less strategic going forward.

Hostile Bid for Distressed Asset

There are many risks associated with a hostile acquisition. These include a lack of sufficient due diligence, relatively low odds of actually completing the transaction, and integration/cultural challenges even if the hostile bid is successful.

The main advantage of a hostile transaction is that it can be launched at an opportune time for the prospective buyer. One such opportune time might be when a target is in financial distress. Financially distressed firms are likely trading at attractive valuations. Even if the potential acquirer must pay a material premium to the target's current stock price, the investment still has the potential to generate attractive returns. Few boards and management teams would ever choose to sell from a position of weakness; however, in the case of financial distress, they may not have a choice.

CHAPTER 16

Non-Core Divestitures

O n March 9, 2017, Canadian Natural Resources (CNQ) announced the acquisition of a majority stake in the Athabasca Oil Sands project (AOSP) and a hodgepodge of additional oil sands and heavy oil assets from Royal Dutch Shell and Marathon Oil.[†] The total cost of this acquisition was $C12.74 billion with $C4 billion of the purchase price in CNQ stock.

The Athabasca Oil Sands project is an integrated oil sands mining operation that involves the following production steps:

- Excavate energy-rich earth
- Place that energy-rich earth onto large trucks
- Detach energy-rich bitumen from the earth using a separation process
- Put the bitumen through an upgrader to create commercially salable oil

---

† Note: Following the transaction, CNQ would own 70% of AOSP, Chevron 20%, and Royal Dutch Shell 10%.

While clearly not the most environmentally friendly way to produce oil, this mining process does have some favorable business attributes relative to other forms of oil production, which will be addressed in subsequent pages.

As the owner of Horizon, an existing mining project located near the Athabasca site, CNQ was the natural buyer of these assets. Its close proximity created the opportunity for significant operational synergies, since AOSP had 2,800 employees on location and Horizon had 2,400. Even more important, CNQ was simply a better operator when it came to the oil sands. CNQ's Horizon project was able to produce oil at a cash cost of \$C22.50 a barrel relative to \$C30–32 for AOSP. A lower operating cost allowed CNQ's Horizon project to generate more FCF per barrel of oil than AOSP. CNQ should have been able to reduce operating costs at AOSP and boost FCF even before factoring in the potential operational synergies between the two facilities.

The economics of the deal were very attractive for CNQ, as shown in Figure 16.1.

FIGURE 16.1

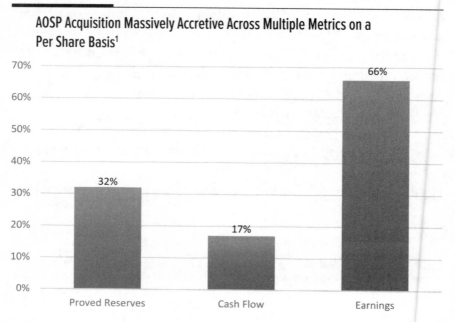

AOSP Acquisition Massively Accretive Across Multiple Metrics on a Per Share Basis[1]

While this deal did increase debt to EBITDA from 1.8x to 2.2x pro forma, the significant increase in the FCF of the business following this acquisition would allow CNQ to de-lever to pre-deal levels within a year.[2]

CNQ paid 5.9x EBITDA (pre-synergies) when it was trading closer to 7x EBITDA prior to the announcement, as shown in Figure 16.2. If CNQ could lower the operating costs at AOSP by $5 per barrel, this would lower the multiple to around 5.1x EBITDA. If AOSP's operating costs could be lowered to the same level as Horizon's, the acquisition multiple would decline to 4.65x EBITDA.

Another way to look at the price paid is to examine CNQ's cost to build its Horizon mining project. CNQ spent $102,000 of up-front capital per barrel of daily oil production at Horizon. It bought AOSP for $61,000 per barrel of daily oil production. In other words, it bought AOSP for a 40% discount to the cost of building its own mining project.

FIGURE 16.2

CNQ Paid Significantly Lower Multiple of EBITDA for AOSP Relative to Where CNQ Was Trading

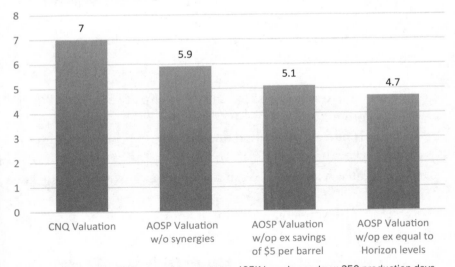

Note: Doing the math: CNQ ownership generates 195K barrels per day × 350 production days per year, resulting in a total of 68.25 million barrels of oil per year. Each $1 reduction in cash costs creates an additional $68.25 million in EBITDA.

But did it buy a lower quality business relative to the rest of the portfolio?† No, in fact, it bought a better business for a lower multiple.

To understand this dynamic, you must understand that there are multiple challenges with traditional oil drilling:

- It is very possible to drill a dry hole. The returns on drilling a dry hole are about as bad as they come.
- Production from traditional oil wells tends to peak very early after the well is brought online and then declines very sharply over time. A well that produces 1,000 barrels a day in the first year might produce only 50–100 barrels a day 5–6 years down the road. Hence, most energy firms are on a treadmill that requires the continual drilling of new wells just to maintain production levels. This is very capital intensive.
- Traditional oil drilling requires a firm to constantly find new, drillable energy resources. Many of these resources are either already held by state-owned enterprises like Saudi Aramco, are in less stable and more dangerous parts of the world, and/or require the energy company to share a disproportionate amount of the economics of the drilling with the host government.

A mining project like Horizon or AOSP has multiple advantages relative to traditional drilling:

- There is no dry hole risk, as the oil is already confirmed to be in the ground.
- There is no natural decline rate as with traditional drilling.
- The project has a long reserve life.
- It operates in a stable Western democracy where rule of law exists.
- There is low ongoing capital intensity (once the project is completed).

---

† I am not trying to argue here that oil sands mining is a great business. This is not Nike or Microsoft or Apple from a quality of business perspective. However, relative to the rest of CNQ's portfolio, this was clearly a better business. CNQ is a world-class operator when it comes to the oil sands and it bought this asset for a very attractive valuation.

The advent of shale oil in the United States has lowered the marginal cost of oil to the point that it no longer makes sense to build a new oil sands mining facility with an upgrader. However, once all the capital has been deployed, maintenance capital spending and operating costs are the only ongoing cash expenditures. On that basis, CNQ could still generate very attractive cash returns on this acquisition.

Thus, from a portfolio perspective, this acquisition increased the quality of CNQ's holdings as:

- CNQ's decline rate fell from 11.7% to 9%.[†]
- Its mix of long life, low-decline crude production increased from 60% to 70%.
- Cash flow increased by $1.9 billion while maintenance capital spending rose only $400 million. FCF increased by $1.5 billion.

Hence, CNQ was able to do the impossible with this acquisition:

- Increase portfolio quality
- Achieve a material increase in EPS, cash flow per share, and reserves per share
- Pay a lower valuation for AOSP than where CNQ was trading pre-synergies
- Experience no material change in leverage or risk profile
- Buy a mining project at a 40% discount to the cost of building one

Not surprisingly, CNQ shares rallied 10% on the day of this announcement. How did CNQ pull this off?

In many ways, this transaction became a necessity because of a strategic decision Royal Dutch Shell made two years earlier. In April

---

† Decline rate refers to how much lower production would be in one year if the company chose not to drill additional wells across its entire portfolio. A mining operation does not require the drilling of additional wells.

of 2015, Royal Dutch Shell announced the acquisition of BG Group for $70 billion. BG was a leader in LNG (liquefied natural gas), and with this acquisition, Royal Dutch Shell would become the largest global producer of LNG.

Natural gas, used primarily for power generation, burns more cleanly than other fuels. It was viewed at the time to have a stronger long-term growth profile as it was increasingly displacing coal and oil for power generation. Like oil sands mining, LNG tends to exhibit a low decline rate, and once the initial capital has been deployed, it generates strong, consistent cash flows.

While this deal made sense strategically at the time, Royal Dutch Shell paid a hefty 52% premium (to 90-day average stock price) that equated to tens of billions more than the market had valued BG prior to the deal. The transaction also left Royal Dutch Shell with over $80 billion in net debt on a pro forma basis right before oil prices, which are linked with LNG prices, fell sharply to near decade-low levels (see Figure 16.3).

Royal Dutch Shell's adjusted earnings fell from $23.1 billion in 2014 to $7.2 billion in 2016. In 2015 and 2016, Shell's earnings failed to cover its dividend payments and there was risk of a dividend cut if oil prices did not recover.

At the time of the acquisition announcement, Royal Dutch Shell said that it had planned to sell $30 billion of assets to pay down debt. The decline in oil prices following the acquisition announcement resulted in deteriorating cash flow (see Figure 16.4) and higher than expected debt levels. This backdrop clearly increased the urgency for these asset sales. Royal Dutch Shell's divestiture of its majority interest in AOSP was triggered by this need to pay down debt.

Shell was by no means a distressed seller in the way that Marconi PLC was in 2002 (see Chapter 15), and still sported an investment-grade balance sheet and a pro forma market capitalization of around $190 billion. Nevertheless, the company still had too much debt. If the global economy entered a recession or oil prices remained in the thirties, Shell's cash flows would have declined further, and its

FIGURE 16.3

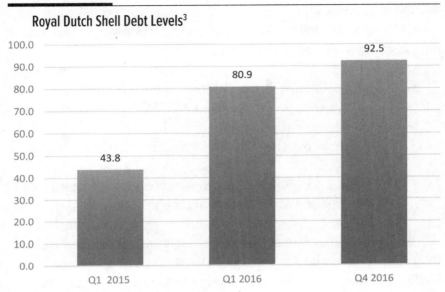

Royal Dutch Shell Debt Levels[3]

Note: Numbers in billions.

FIGURE 16.4

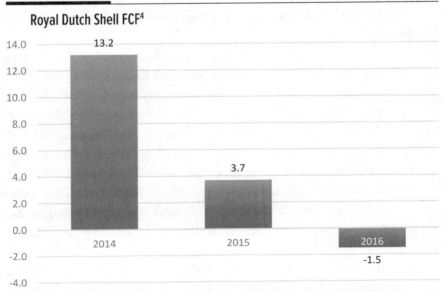

Royal Dutch Shell FCF[4]

Notes: Definition of FCF is operating cash flow minus capital expenditures. This is before dividends payments as well. Numbers in billions.

ability to sell assets would have become very challenging. Shell still needed to move quickly.

CNQ was the logical buyer for the AOSP project as it had a unique combination of the following:

- A strategic interest in the oil sands at a time when other large oil companies were focused on LNG, US shale oil, and deep-water development projects
- The ability to pay the $C12.7 billion price tag ($C8.7 billion in cash)
- The ability to generate the most synergies given the geographic proximity to its Horizon project

While we do not have behind-the-scenes information on how many other potential buyers looked at this asset, given the fit for CNQ, it is likely that this was a one-on-one negotiation. The lack of a serious second or third bidder is likely part of the reason that CNQ was able to secure such an attractive price. What are the lessons from this transaction?

Non-core divestitures are a potential source of value creation for buyers. Why?

- **Not selling business/asset at optimal time.** One of the challenges with M&A is that, in most cases, the seller can choose to auction off the business or asset when valuations are high, when there are multiple bidders who can pay a high price, or when fundamentals feel peakish. In the case of a non-core divestiture, that is rarely the case. The decision to divest the business is much more likely to be driven by strategic considerations such as wanting to refocus the portfolio, reinvest the proceeds in another area, or as in this case, pay down debt.
- **Non-core divestitures usually don't occur in a "hot" space.** When firms decide to divest a non-core business, in most cases, the business they are divesting is not hitting on all cylinders,

is out of favor cyclically or secularly, or is viewed as a lower-quality asset by its shareholders. The result is fewer bidders and a more favorable valuation for the buyer. One company's trash is another company's treasure, as was the case with AOSP.

- **Shares many characteristics with spin-offs of less strategic or cash cow businesses.** The non-core business may have not received sufficient resources (investment, talent, attention) under its previous corporate owner. As a result, the business likely was not optimized from an efficiency or margin perspective. Case in point with AOSP, where the cash operating cost per barrel was 40–50% higher than that of the Horizon project. Once a non-core businesses is acquired, a management team with the time, resources, and attention should find significant low-hanging fruit.

How should a management team or board approach the acquisition and potential sale of non-core businesses?

On the buy side:

- Be open to these types of transactions.
- Proactively approach companies about the availability of non-core assets if the company has excess debt (as was the case with Royal Dutch Shell) or is strategically moving in a different direction.

On the sell side:

- If there are a limited number of buyers for the asset and the ultimate sale price is too low, consider spinning off the asset to shareholders. Allow existing shareholders to participate in the potential value creation. This is particularly attractive if a sale would trigger a large tax bill. However, if the rationale for an asset sale is debt reduction, as in the case of AOSP, a spin-off is not advised (see Chapter 23).

- If a sale will create significant synergies between the buyer and the seller, consider taking stock as opposed to cash to allow your firm to participate in the upside. Shell took $C4.0 billion in CNQ shares as part of the transaction and benefitted from the upward move in CNQ's stock price following the transaction announcement.
- Try to improve the margins and revenue trajectory of the business prior to selling, even if this requires restructuring dollars or modest investments. A higher-margin business with improving near-term trends is more likely to command a higher valuation and purchase price.
- Try to sell the non-core business in an environment where industry fundamentals are not depressed and when there are multiple potential bidders with healthy balance sheets.
- Try to avoid selling from a position of weakness when the buyer(s) know you have to unload the asset. A distressed seller is likely to receive a lower price than a seller who has the ability to walk away if the offer is not sufficient. While I understand why Royal Dutch Shell management felt that they needed to announce the $30 billion divestiture target after the BG acquisition announcement, this large financial target did not put them in a position to optimize the valuation multiples they received on their asset sales.

CHAPTER 17

Short-Term Challenges, Long-Term Benefits

Marc Casper may not be a household name, but when it comes to deploying capital wisely, he probably should be. He became the CEO of Thermo Fisher Scientific (TMO) in October 2009. From the time he became CEO through the end of 2020, Thermo generated an impressive total shareholder return of 932%, compared with the S&P 500's total return, which was 333%.

Many of the principles that I have discussed throughout this book show up regularly in a careful examination of Thermo's capital allocation during Casper's tenure as CEO:

Public/private arbitrage. TMO bought One Lambda in 2012 for an attractive multiple of 8.7x 2011 EBITDA including tax benefits but excluding synergies. Most acquisitions within the life sciences industry are completed for a mid-to-high teens multiple of EBITDA.[1] One Lambda was a leader in transport diagnostics, a market with high-single-digit growth.[2]

Optimal capital structure. TMO averaged 3x debt/EBITDA during Casper's tenure. This level of debt is optimal for a company with around three-quarters of its revenue coming from highly predictable consumable and service revenue. In 2009, in the midst of the Great Financial Crisis (GFC), TMO's sales and EBITDA only declined by 4% and 7% respectively.

Opportunistic stock repurchases. TMO repurchased $3.4 billion of its shares between 2009–2012 when the share price was depressed, trading between 10 and 14x forward earnings. Between 1998 and 2018, TMO traded for an average of 17.6x forward earnings. Most of the repurchases completed in 2009–2012 occurred while TMO's valuation multiple was one standard deviation or more away from its long-term average.

Willingness to walk away from strategic deals when valuations became elevated. TMO was rumored to have bid for both Millipore (2010) and Pall (2015) but had the discipline to walk away when valuations became too elevated. In the case of Qiagen, it was reported that Thermo Fisher Scientific made a bid for the company in November 2019, but in December walked away when the price tag became too high. However, when the stock market and economy came under pressure from the COVID-19 pandemic, Thermo Fisher Scientific pounced on Qiagen and was able to reach an agreement to acquire it at a much more reasonable valuation. Even though Qiagen's shareholders eventually voted against a modestly higher revised offer from Thermo Fisher Scientific, the decision to pursue Qiagen during the pandemic as well as its decision to increase its bid only modesty demonstrated sound capital allocation process and discipline.

Token dividend. TMO initiated a small dividend in 2012. Given the strong returns that TMO had been able to achieve on its acquisitions and share repurchase program, a small dividend was logical. The return the company could generate through acquisitions and share repurchase was far greater than the return investors could achieve by redeploying dividends.

Revenue synergies. Based on more than 20 years of investment experience, I am generally very skeptical of the ability of firms to achieve revenue synergies. It is rare for an acquired business to become more valuable to its customers and to generate a stronger organic growth rate after being acquired. However, that is exactly what Thermo Fisher Scientific did with its acquisition of Life Technologies in 2014 and Patheon in 2017. Patheon is a contract manufacturer of pharmaceuticals for predominantly small to midsized pharmaceutical companies. It became more valuable inside of Thermo Fisher Scientific due to Thermo's strong balance sheet, its manufacturing expertise, and its close relationships with C-suite pharmaceutical executives. As a result, Patheon's organic growth has steadily improved from the mid-single digits before the acquisition to the high-single digits a couple of years post acquisition. In addition, Thermo's unique position as a manufacturer and distributor of life science tools and supplies has often enabled it to generate revenue synergies by adding acquired firms' products to its Fisher Scientific catalogs.

Countercyclical capital deployment. Thermo Fisher Scientific's acquisition of FEI Company (FEIC) in 2016 and Life Technologies are great examples of buying good businesses with attractive long-term fundamentals at a time when near-term fundamentals are challenged. Thermo Fisher Scientific was able to buy both of these businesses right before growth was poised to reaccelerate.

THE STORY OF LIFE (TECHNOLOGIES)

Life Technologies, a leading provider of research consumables, next-generation sequencing equipment, and bioproduction consumables that enable the manufacture of biologic pharmaceuticals, was created in 2008 when Invitrogen acquired Applied Biosystems.

At the time, the future looked bright for Life Technologies. The legacy Invitrogen business had grown an impressive 8% organically in 2008. The combined Life Technologies company did not miss a beat in 2009, growing an equally impressive 3% organically during a horrific global recession. This growth was aided by its 85% consumable revenue mix and pricing power. As the economy recovered in 2010, the business grew organically by 7%. But in 2011 and 2012 the business hit a wall with organic growth slowing to 2%. The outlook for 2013 was not much better.

While there were multiple minor short-term and nonrecurring headwinds that chipped away at Life Technologies' revenue growth during this period, the most important factor was the weakness in the company's academic and government business. This was Life Technologies' largest end market, representing slightly less than half of its revenues. This end market is driven mainly by government, academic, and foundation spending on scientific research.

In the United States, the largest provider of funding for scientific research is the National Institutes of Health (NIH). NIH funding declined in 2011 and 2012, and would fall another 5% in 2013. The 2013 decline was a result of the failure of Democrats and Republicans to come to an agreement to cut $1.2 trillion in spending as required under the Budget Control Act of 2011. This triggered automatic cuts in defense and discretionary spending, which included NIH. With another year of lower NIH funding, Life Technologies looked poised to generate another year of subpar low-single-digit revenue growth in 2013.

Life's stock price had been relatively flat for five years by the end of 2012. By mid-January of 2013 (before rumors emerged in the press that Life was considering selling itself), the company was trading at a large discount to its peers, as shown in Figure 17.1.

However, this combination of a low valuation and a relatively weak stock price caught the attention of multiple interested parties. In fact, during the summer of 2011, the first party to reach out to Life was not a strategic buyer, but a private equity buyer.

FIGURE 17.1

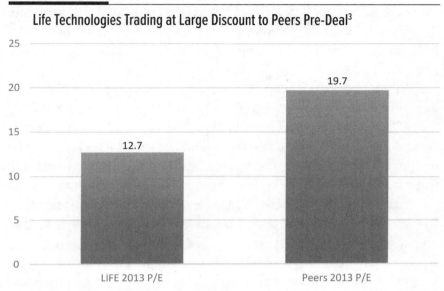

Life Technologies Trading at Large Discount to Peers Pre-Deal[3]

Note: Peers include Agilent Technologies, Bio-Rad Laboratories, Bruker, Illumina, Perkin-Elmer, Qiagen, Sigma-Aldrich, Thermo-Fisher, and Waters.

In most cases, a private equity (PE) buyer would struggle to acquire a large life science tools company given PE's 15–20%+ required return threshold, as well as a lower level of synergy capture relative to a strategic buyer already operating in the sector. This demonstrates just how cheap and out of favor Life Technologies was at the time. Over the next 20 months, multiple private equity firms and strategic buyers would express some level of interest in acquiring either Life Technologies or its next-generation sequencing business.

However, only three parties (Thermo Fisher Scientific, Strategic Party A, and Sponsor A) would submit binding bids for the firm. Not surprisingly, Sponsor A (private equity firm) was only able to bid $65, but in the end said it was willing to very modestly increase its bid. The two strategic bidders offered $75 and $76. Thermo Fisher Scientific bid $76 in cash and Strategic Party A bid $75, with 86% in cash and 14% in stock. On April 14, 2013, Life Technologies' board agreed to sell the company to Thermo Fisher Scientific.

Thermo Fisher Scientific's $76 bid represented a 38% premium to where Life's stock price was in mid-January and it valued Life Technologies at 3.9x revenues, 12.3x EBITDA, and 17.2x P/E on estimated 2013 results. Looking at trailing 12-month results, it represented 4.1x sales and 13.7x EBITDA.

While Thermo Fisher Scientific's stock reacted positively to the deal rumors and continued to perform well after the deal announcement, there was one big concern. Had Thermo Fisher Scientific just diluted its organic growth rate by purchasing Life Technologies? The deal was very accretive to earnings (initially projected to be $0.90 to $1.00 on a $6+ base in 2014), but it increased Thermo's exposure to an academic and government end market that was struggling. Maybe Thermo had paid a low valuation, but bought a lower quality business?

On the conference call announcing the acquisition, there were multiple questions around this topic. Thermo Fisher Scientific CEO Marc Casper said at the time that TMO was using a 3% organic growth assumption for the Life business but hoped to do better.[4] In the proxy, Life Technologies' internal projections called for mid-single-digit growth through 2016, but proxy projections are often too high.

Life Technologies grew 2% organically once again in 2013, despite an accelerated decline in NIH spending. However, in 2014–2016, Thermo Fisher Scientific's Life Sciences Solution Segment, comprised primarily of Life Technologies, grew 5%. In 2017–2018, this segment grew 7% organically.

What happened here? Why did growth accelerate meaningfully after Thermo Fisher Scientific acquired the business in 2014? There are four main reasons:

1. The Acquisition by Thermo Allowed LIFE to Make Investments to Grow the Business

At the Thermo Fisher Scientific 2019 analyst day, Mark Stevenson, the chief operating officer at Thermo (who had worked at Life

Technologies prior to the acquisition), highlighted one of the drivers of this accelerated revenue growth. He emphasized the company's ability to make strategic investments internally in bioscience, bioproduction, and genetics, and to expand operations in key emerging markets.[5] While this is more qualitative than quantitative, the old Life Technologies management team was overly focused on trying to win big in next-generation sequencing. But Illumina had already won the next-generation sequencing market. Instead of accepting that their business would serve more niche applications, Life Technologies management held out too much hope that they could challenge Illumina in this market. As a result, Life management may have taken its eye off the ball of the core business, and growth suffered as a result. It is eye-opening just how quickly growth accelerated once the core business was given the resources it needed to compete more effectively.

2. NIH Academic and Government Funding Improved

NIH spending rebounded after 2013 and grew from $29 billion in fiscal year 2013 to $39 billion in fiscal year 2019, as displayed in Figure 17.2. This was not a surprise or a lucky break for TMO, but a very logical outcome. NIH spending is one of the few government expenditures that both Democrats and Republicans support.

3. Minor Headwinds

In 2011–2013, Life Technologies was facing a series of minor headwinds from lower royalty income and loss of patent protection in parts of the PCR business.[†] Many of these headwinds dissipated or disappeared completely after Thermo Fisher acquired the business.

---

† PCR stands for polymerase chain reaction and is a scientific technique used to amplify small segments of DNA for various laboratory tests and procedures.

FIGURE 17.2

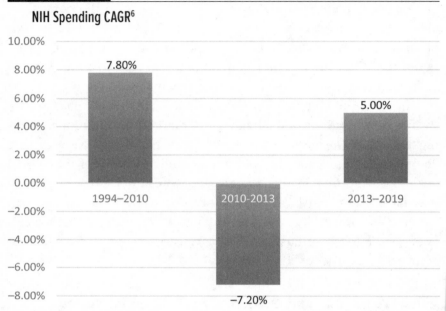

NIH Spending CAGR[6]

Note: NIH spending in 2009–2010 includes the supplementary spending from the American Recovery and Reinvestment Act.

4. Revenue Synergies

While I am very skeptical of revenue synergies, in this case it is probable that TMO was able to generate them. Thermo Fisher Scientific is somewhat unique in that it manufactures life science tools and consumables as well as distributing them through its Fisher Scientific catalogs and websites. Even before Life Technologies was acquired, about 1% of its sales came through the Fisher Scientific catalogs. It is quite possible that Thermo was able to place more legacy Life products in its catalogs and use the Fisher Scientific sales force to push those products more aggressively.

A HOME RUN OF A DEAL

What TMO CEO Marc Casper pulled off was an acquisition of a business with short-term challenges, but long-term attractive fundamentals at a very advantageous valuation. If the academic and government business had been growing more in line with its long-term growth rates, Life Technologies would not have been trading at such an attractive valuation (see Figure 17.3). If its organic growth rate had been stronger, there might have been more strategic bidders for the asset.

FIGURE 17.3

Strategic Buyers of Life Science Tool Businesses (Trailing EBITDA Multiple)[7]

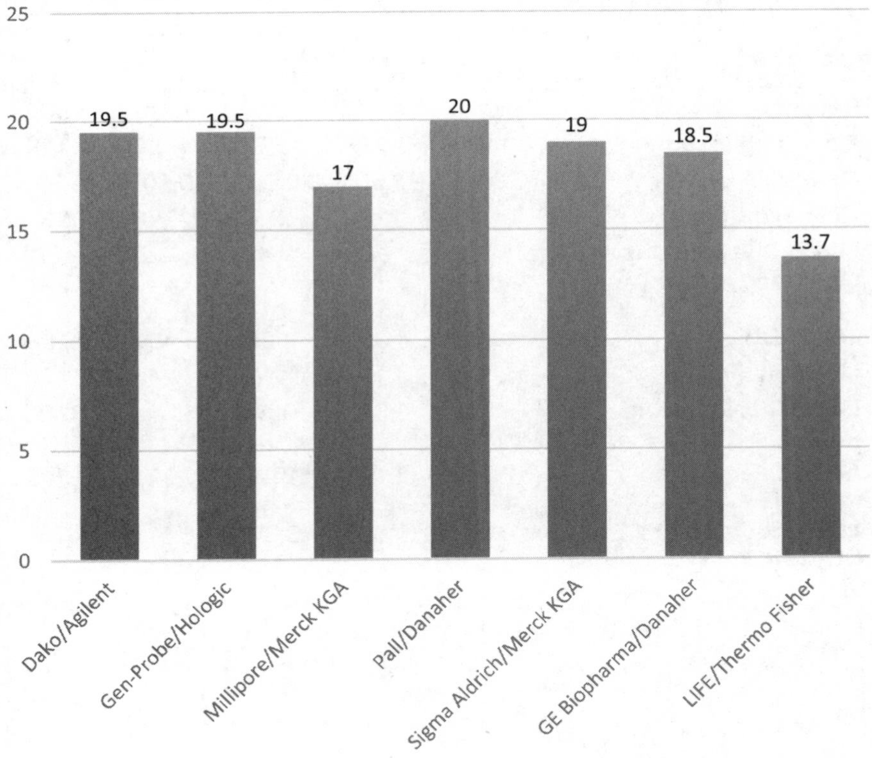

In the end, Casper created a very positively skewed scenario for his investors. If the business continued to grow at 2–3%, as shown in Table 17.1, it would:

- Still generate an attractive return on his investment (year five return of 8.7%)
- Significantly increase TMO EPS
- Reduce cyclicality (61% vs. 55% consumables/service post deal)
- Only modestly lower organic growth rate (4.4% vs. 5%)

TABLE 17.1

TMO Acquisition of Life Technologies Initial Financial Projections Assuming Growth Did Not Accelerate

	Year 1	Year 2	Year 3	Year 4	Year 5
Revenues	4,000	4,120	4,244	4,371	4,502
Operating Income	1,180	1,215	1,252	1,289	1,328
OI Margin	29.5%	29.50%	29.50%	29.50%	29.50%
Cost Synergies	85	165	250	250	250
Minus Divested Business Operating Income	−62	−68	−75	−82	−91
Total EBIT	1,203	1,312	1,427	1,457	1,488
LIFE Net Income	1,029	1,122	1,220	1,246	1,272
LIFE FCF/Net Income Ratio	98%	98%	98%	98%	98%
LIFE FCF	1,008	1,100	1,196	1,221	1,246
LIFE Acquisition FCF ROIC By Year	7.0%	7.6%	8.3%	8.5%	8.7%

(continued)

TMO Acquisition of Life Technologies Initial Financial Projections Assuming Growth Did Not Accelerate (*continued*)					
	Year 1	Year 2	Year 3	Year 4	Year 5
Thermo Net Investment					
Purchase Price	$13,600				
Net Debt Assumed	$1,500				
After-Tax Proceeds from Divested Asset	–$906				
After-Tax Cost to Achieve Synergies, NPV	$200				
Net Investment	$14,394				

Notes: Life FCF conversion rate is average of 2011 and 2012 FCF/adjusted net income. TMO was required to divest a business it already owned to complete the transaction. I did not have details on investment banking/advisory/securities fees associated with transaction. Does not include revenue synergies.

However, if Marc Casper could accelerate organic growth at Life through a combination of internal initiatives and reversion to a more normal growth rate in its largest end market (see Table 17.2), he could:

- Achieve even higher returns on investment (9.8% cash-on-cash returns by year five)
- Increase earnings accretion
- Reduce cyclicality
- Experience no degradation in organic growth rate

TABLE 17.2

TMO Acquisition of Life Technologies Assuming Acceleration in Organic Growth to 5%

	Year 1	Year 2	Year 3	Year 4	Year 5
Revenues	4,000	4,200	4,410	4,631	4,862
Operating Income	1,180	1,260	1,345	1,435	1,532
OI Margin	29.5%	30.00%	30.50%	31.00%	31.50%
Cost Synergies	85	165	250	250	250
Minus Divested Business Operating Income	−62	−68	−75	−82	−91
Total EBIT	1,203	1,357	1,520	1,603	1,691
LIFE Net Income	1,029	1,160	1,300	1,371	1,446
LIFE FCF/Net Income Ratio	98%	98%	98%	98%	98%
LIFE FCF	1,008	1,137	1,274	1,343	1,417
LIFE Acquisition FCF ROIC By Year	7.0%	7.9%	8.8%	9.3%	9.8%

Thermo Net Investment	
Purchase Price	$13,600
Net Debt Assumed	$1,500
After-Tax Proceeds from Divested Asset	−$906
After-Tax Cost to Achieve Synergies, NPV	$200
Net Investment	$14,394

Note: Assumes mid-single-digit organic revenue growth and 50 bps of core operating margin expansion per year in addition to synergy capture. Does not include the investment banking, legal, and securities issuance costs associated with the transaction.

From an outcomes perspective, this deal was a home run given Life's previously highlighted acceleration in growth in 2015–2018, higher than initially anticipated cost synergies, and the benefits from tax reform that lowered TMO's (and thus Life's) tax rate. As a result, the acquisition of Life Technologies almost certainty outperformed the more optimistic deal model (5%+ growth model). That was a great outcome for TMO's shareholders.

However, from a process standpoint, it was an even better transaction and something all management teams and boards should look to emulate. Buying an undermanaged business when a large part of that business is struggling due strictly to short-term challenges is about as surefire a way as there is to create long-term value in M&A.

FISERV BUYS FIRST DATA

In April 2007, private equity firm KKR announced it would acquire First Data for $34 per share. This represented 27x projected forward earnings and 14x EBITDA. KKR loaded up First Data's balance sheet with $24 billion in debt to fund the transaction and to maximize returns on its equity investment. This equated to more than 10x First Data's EBITDA. This was an excessive amount of leverage even for a private equity-backed company. In order to make the math work, First Data would need to cut costs aggressively and continue to grow revenues at a healthy rate. This would lower its leverage by growing EBITDA and eventually put First Data in a position to generate FCF to pay down debt.

Unfortunately, within nine months of announcing the transaction, the US economy entered a deep recession that would last for a year and a half. While First Data's business was more resilient than most, the company struggled to grow, deleverage, and produce meaningful FCF during and immediately after the GFC.

In 2013, the company still had $22.6 billion in long-term debt. In addition, the company had gone through a series of CEOs before recruiting Frank Bisignano, the highly respected former J.P. Morgan executive, to lead the firm in 2013. In March of 2014, KKR disclosed that it was valuing its equity investment in First Data business at 80 cents on the dollar almost seven years after making its initial investment.

However, underneath the surface, there were glimmers of hope. In December 2012, First Data acquired Clover, a startup manufacturer of next-generation point-of-sale systems for small merchants. The 2013 arrival of CEO Frank Bisignano was a positive development. In 2014, KKR doubled down and injected another $3.5 billion of equity that enabled First Data to pay down a portion of its high-coupon debt. This equity injection put First Data in a position to go public again with a still elevated, but manageable level of debt. In October 2015, First Data went public by selling 160 million shares at $16 per share.

But First Data's rebirth as a public company did not go well. The stock fell below its IPO price almost immediately and was below $10 per share in early 2016. The stock spent most of 2017–2018 in a range of $14–$20 with the exception of a brief spike mid-2018. On Christmas Eve of 2018, the stock closed at $15.52, slightly below its IPO price.

Why Did First Data Shares Struggle?

A number of factors contributed to First Data's valuation struggles.

Too much debt. While First Data's debt load was no longer a risk to the solvency of the business, it was still excessive relative to its peers at 6.8x debt to EBITDA at the time of the IPO. As a high-yield issuer, First Data made large interest payments that limited the amount of FCF it had left over to make acquisitions, buy back stock, or pay dividends.

Losing market share. First Data's largest division was its merchant acquiring business. Merchant acquirers are an important cog in the payments ecosystem that enable businesses to accept electronic payments for goods and services. This is an end market with strong secular growth as debit cards and credit cards continue to take market share from cash and check payments.

Unfortunately, First Data's North American merchant acquiring business was losing share. It was overexposed to a distribution channel that was losing share (the bank channel), was underexposed in e-commerce and integrated payments that were outpacing the growth rate of in-person or onsite retail commerce, and was struggling to retain its highly profitable small business book of business. First Data's North American merchant acquiring business experienced minimal growth from 2012 to 2015 and actually declined in 2016.

KKR overhang. Following the IPO, KKR still owned 61% of the shares in First Data. Investors feared that any time the stock bounced, KKR would pounce on the opportunity and hit the market with a large slug of stock.

In 2018, fundamentals began to improve.

- **Organic growth accelerated.** First Data's organic growth accelerated to 6% in 2018 from 4% in 2017. The global merchant acquiring business accelerated to 7% organic growth in 2018 from 4% in 2017. Even the North America merchant acquiring business accelerated to mid-single-digit growth as it had much better success in retaining and winning small business customers thanks to its Clover point of sale platform.
- **Balance sheet improved.** By the end of 2018, net debt to EBITDA had declined from 6.8x at the time of the IPO to 5.2x.
- **Increased FCF.** First Data's FCF rose from $1.1 billion in 2016 to $1.5 billion in 2018.

Despite First Data's improved growth, lower leverage, and increased cash flow, the stock was going nowhere. But even before this inflection in fundamentals, First Data management and KKR were exploring strategic alternatives. In December 2017, First Data's CEO and KKR's Co-President Scott Nuttall began having discussions to sell First Data to a company operating within the financial services ecosystem. Those discussions lasted until April 2018, but ultimately failed to lead to a deal. The deal fell apart due to cultural differences, the price this strategic buyer was willing to pay, concerns about integration execution, and the acquirer's insistence that its management team run the combined entity.

In September of 2018, Nuttall reached out to Fiserv CEO Jeff Yabuki about the potential of merging First Data and Fiserv. Over the next three and a half months, the management teams of Fiserv, First Data, and KKR negotiated a transaction that would ultimately value First Data shares at $26 per share. However, since it was a stock-for-stock transaction, First Data shareholders would be able to benefit from the potential value creation this deal could unlock.

From a process standpoint, this is one of the best large transactions I have come across in my career. This is the case for a number of reasons:

The business was getting better. The underlying health of First Data business was clearly getting stronger in 2018, and the market had failed to recognize this. Fiserv was able to take advantage of a situation in which the market's perception of First Data was rooted in the past as opposed to the present or the future.

It allowed for reinvestment at First Data. The best acquirers almost always take a portion of the synergies from an acquisition and reinvest back into the acquired business to drive improved long-term growth. Fiserv management initially promised that the transaction would generate $900 million in annual cost synergies and they soon raised that to $1.2 billion. However, Fiserv management also committed to reinvest a total of $500 million back into the business to accelerate growth ($100 million per year). First Data's business had turned the corner in 2018, due in part to internal investments around its Clover platform that were clearly paying off.

However, it would be very logical to assume that because of First Data's significant debt load and high interest expense burden that the company was limited in the amount of internal investments it could it make. Inside of Fiserv, however, that would change. The $1.2 billion in cost savings would allow First Data to make internal investments that it could not have dreamed of inside a highly leveraged firm. These investments, if executed well, would strengthen the long-term health and competitiveness of the First Data business. First Data could become a stronger business inside of Fiserv as a result.

KKR overhang diminished. Post the closure of the acquisition, KKR owned only 16% of the combined company.

It became investment grade. Following the transaction, the new Fiserv/First Data business had an investment grade balance sheet. This allowed Fiserv to refinance First Data's $17 billion in non–investment grade debt and reduce annual interest expense by hundreds of millions of dollars.

First Data's organic growth rate became similar to Fiserv's. While the market fixated on First Data's North America merchant acquiring business, even as that business struggled, First Data generated a similar, if not slightly better organic growth rate than Fiserv (see Table 17.3).

TABLE 17. 3

Fiserv and First Data Organic Growth[8]

	2014	2015	2016	2017	2018
Fiserv	4%	4%	4%	4%	5%
First Data	4%	5%	4%	4%	6%

And even with the North American businesses' challenges pre-2018, First Data's global merchant acquiring business was still producing reasonable organic growth in aggregate, as shown in Table 17.4.

TABLE 17.4

Organic Growth Rate of First Data Global Merchant Acquiring Business[9]

2014	2015	2016	2017	2018
4%	4%	1%	4%	7%

Note: Assumes constant currency organic revenue growth.

Fiserv essentially bought a business with a similar, if not faster organic growth rate for a much lower valuation than where Fiserv was trading. A few other important points:

There was more to First Data than the North American merchant business. While North American merchant acquiring received all the focus from investors, there was more to First Data than just this business. First Data had two other, higher-margin segments that collectively generated 42% of its EBITDA. These businesses were very similar to the core Fiserv business of providing outsourced, scaled services to bank and nonbank customers for fraud protection, card services, and loan and debit processing. Fiserv and First Data each owned their own debit networks as well.

Similar to Fiserv, these businesses tend to have a slightly slower organic growth rate than the merchant acquiring business, but with more recurring business. In addition, about a quarter of the First Data merchant acquiring business's revenues came from outside of North America (see Figure 17.4), where the growth rate was substantially faster due to lower penetration of merchant acquiring and electronic payments in general. In 2017–2018, these businesses continued to produce solid results.

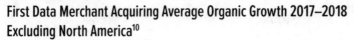

FIGURE 17.4

First Data Merchant Acquiring Average Organic Growth 2017–2018
Excluding North America[10]

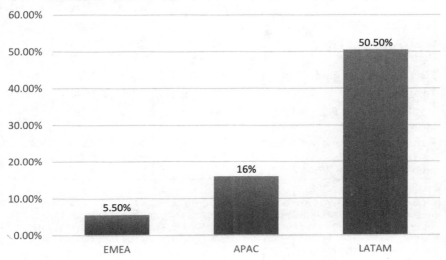

The deal was very accretive to earnings. FISV provided guidance that the deal would be more than 20% accretive to EPS in its first full year and 40% accretive to EPS once all the synergies were taken into account.

Strong returns on capital were expected. Fiserv should be able to generate high-single-digit to low teens returns on invested capital by year five (see Table 17.5).

TABLE 17.5

Fiserv's Anticipated Returns on Capital on First Data Deal[11]

	2020	2021	2022	2023	2024
First Data EBIT	2,750	2,904	3,069	3,241	3,423
Cost Synergies Net of Reinvestment	300	500	750	1,000	1,100
EBIT Post-Synergies	3,050	3,404	3819	4,241	4,523
Taxes @20%	−610	−681	−764	−848	−905
Net Income and FCF (100% conversion)	2,440	2,723	3,055	3,393	3,618
Return on Investment Capital	6.4%	7.1%	8.0%	8.8%	9.4%

Invested Capital: 38,417

Notes: Numbers in millions. Returns are likely to be higher than presented as I did not include revenue synergies and used a conservative 100% FCF to net income conversion ratio. Adding revenue synergies would add 50 bps to year five returns and using Fiserv's historic 108% target of free cash to net income would returns by another 100 bps. I also did not include the cost of achieving the synergies or the benefit from the First Data net operating carry-forward (NOLs) which should roughly offset each other.

CONCLUSION

One could argue that Fiserv CEO Jeff Yabuki bought a business with similar or slightly better organic growth rate relative to his own company for about half of the multiple FISV was trading for at the time. Using contemporaneous consensus expectations, Fiserv was trading in early 2019 for 19–20x 2020 FCF. Fiserv bought First Data for 12–13x 2020 FCF inclusive of first year synergies and 9x 2020 FCF on a fully synergized basis.

In addition, one could argue that the 50%+ of First Data's revenues and profits that came from its international merchant processing, global financial solutions, and network and security solutions businesses were worth a similar multiple of FCF to FISV (19–20x). If you agree with this, you could argue that Fiserv purchased the North American merchant acquiring business for free or less on a sum-of-the-parts, fully synergized basis. Even adjusting out the value of the

First Data's NOLs, which were expected to temporarily boost First Data's FCF in 2020, Fiserv paid a negligible price for an improving business with expected revenues of $5 billion and EBITDA margins in the 30%+.[†]

Time will tell if Fiserv's acquisition of First Data turns out as well as Thermo Fisher Scientific's acquisition of Life Technologies. However, from a process standpoint, they were very similar and provide a blueprint for other companies to follow.

Both firms bought companies whose stocks had flatlined for multiple years. Both firms bought companies in which the market's perception of the long-term attractiveness of the assets was heavily skewed by challenges in each firm's largest business (Life's academic and government end market, First Data's North America merchant acquiring). Both firms were in a position to generate reasonable returns on capital, even if fundamentals failed to improve. And they both had the potential to generate even stronger returns if growth accelerated, as in case of Life, or remained at the 2018–2019 run-rate, as in the case of First Data.

Both Fiserv CEO Jeff Yabuki and Thermo Fisher Scientific CEO Marc Casper created significant value for their shareholders by deploying capital where returns were highest. Fiserv does not pay a dividend, and Thermo Fisher only recently started to pay a very small dividend. Thermo Fisher Scientific bought back a significant amount of stock when its valuation was extremely cheap relative to history. But when Life Technologies became available, Marc Casper was able to pounce on that opportunity and generate very attractive returns for his shareholders. Fiserv, as discussed in Chapter 10, was a prolific acquirer of its own shares during Jeff Yabuki's tenure and this helped to drive material outperformance versus the market. But when the opportunity to purchase First Data arose, Yabuki was willing to issue shares to pay for it, as the returns from buying First Data far surpassed the returns from continuing to buy back stock.

---

† First Data did not break out EBITDA margins by region, but total GBS EBITDA margins were in the 30s and North America is the largest component of GBS.

Great capital allocators are not locked into one capital strategy or capital allocation preference. Great capital allocators such as Jeff Yabuki and Marc Casper deploy capital where the risk-adjusted returns are the best.

The "short-term challenge but long-term benefits acquisition scenario" can deliver value-creating M&A transactions for boards and management teams willing to embrace it. Short-term weak fundamentals create a lower valuation over which sellers need to offer a premium. In addition, short-term weak fundamentals result in fewer bidders for the business, which means that the company can be acquired for a more reasonable price. In the case of First Data, fundamentals had already inflected positively, but the market either did not believe in the sustainability of this growth or simply did not care.

The biggest challenge consummating these transactions is that few management teams and boards will choose to sell when fundamentals are temporarily depressed. It is hard to know why the Life management and board chose to sell the company in 2013. They were likely influenced by multiple parties expressing interest in the company, the fact that the stock was flat for a long time, and the fact that the fundamental outlook was going to be weak for the third straight year. In the case of First Data, KKR had owned it for over 11 years when the deal with Fiserv was announced. In addition, with the stock-for-stock transaction, KKR and First Data shareholders were positioned to benefit not only from the initial takeout premium, but also from the long-term value creation potential of the deal as well.

Important considerations before pursuing a company with weak short-term fundamentals include:

- **Can you ensure that the issue is short term, not long term or secular?** What are the detailed reasons for the short-term deceleration in growth? What do you expect to improve? How confident are you that growth will accelerate and why? Are you sure the issue is not secular or structural? Has the company grown faster in the last five years than it is growing now?

- **If growth does not accelerate, can I still generate an attractive return?** Or do I need growth to accelerate in order to generate an attractive return? Look for a situation that can:

  1. Generate an adequate-to-good return on investment if growth does not accelerate
  2. Generate a great return on investment from accelerating growth

  This is exactly what Thermo saw in Life Technologies and Fiserv saw in First Data.

- **Is this better than buying back stock, paying a special dividend, or making capital investments from a ROIC perspective?** Before making an acquisition, the board and management team must be convinced that the risk-adjusted returns from the acquisition are greater than those for all of the other capital allocation alternatives available to the company.

CHAPTER 18

The Rise and Fall of the General Electric Empire

In April of 1981, Jack Welch became the eighth CEO in the history of the General Electric Company. In 1980, the year before Welch took the reins at GE, the company generated $25 billion in sales, $1.5 billion in profits, and paid out $670 million in dividends to its investors.

The largest profit center for the company that year was the consumer products and service division, which manufactured appliances, air-conditioning equipment, lighting, and housewares. This segment also included the General Electric Credit Corporation. This nonconsolidated business, which was the forerunner to GE Capital, produced $115 million in profits and had $9 billion in assets. General Electric's operating margin was a rather uninspiring 9%, down from 10% in 1978.

However, the most surprising financial metric to emerge from a review of GE's 1980 annual report was that GE's industrial businesses generated only $65 million in FCF on $1.4 billion in industrial profits, or a 5% FCF to net income ratio. GE's FCF in 1980 did not even cover its dividend payments.

Over the next two decades, Welch would transform General Electric into an industrial and financial giant with a reputation for managerial excellence that delivered consistent, strong returns for shareholders.

In 2000, Welch's last full year with GE, the company generated $130 billion in revenues and $12.7 billion in profits and paid out $5.4 billion in dividends. Most important, in 2000, GE's industrial businesses generated $11 billion in FCF, or 170x the level of FCF produced in the year before Welch became CEO. The market capitalization of GE rose from $14 billion to $410 billion during his tenure. GE's stock price generated a 5,000% total return during the Welch era and outperformed the S&P by almost 10x. In 2000, General Electric was the largest company in the United States by market capitalization, and *Fortune* magazine named GE the world's most admired company for the fourth time in a row.[1] That same year, the *Financial Times* named GE as the world's most respected company for the third time.[2]

SIX ELEMENTS DEFINE THE WELCH ERA AT GE

There are six notable elements that define the Welch era at General Electric; most observers fail to appreciate the first five:

1. Consistency of earnings outperformance
2. Conservatism of the GE Industrial balance sheet
3. Quality of GE Industrial's FCF
4. Improvement in returns on equity at GE Industrial
5. Transformation of GE Industrial portfolio
6. Managerial excellence and talent cultivation

Consistency of Earnings Outperformance

GE consistently delivered double-digit growth over multiple rolling four- to six-year periods through a variety of different macro environments that included three recessions, as shown in Table 18.1 While the growth of GE Capital may have played a role in these consistent results, particularly in the 1990s, it was still a relatively small part of the company's earnings throughout most of the 1980s.

TABLE 18.1

GE: Consistent Earnings Growth Outperformance[3]

	GE EPS Growth	S&P 500 EPS Growth Rate	GE Outperformance
1979–1984	10%	5%	5%
1985–1988	10%	7%	3%
1989–1993	11%	–2%	13%
1994–1998	15%	12%	3%
1999–2000	17%	15%	2%
2001	11%	–20%	31%

Conservatism of the GE Industrial Balance Sheet

The company that Jack Welch inherited had a very strong balance sheet with $2.2 billion in cash and marketable securities and only $2.1 billion in debt. Despite being an active acquirer of businesses and transforming the portfolio during his tenure, Welch actually left the GE Industrial balance sheet stronger in 2000 than it was when he became CEO 20 years earlier.

In 2000, GE's industrial balance sheet held $8.2 billion in cash and $1.8 billion in debt. Gross debt levels declined over Welch's tenure, and cash and marketable securities more than tripled. In addition, GE's pension plan was well funded, with $50 billion in assets relative to a $28 billion projected benefit obligation in 2000. When Welch became CEO in 1981, there were approximately 60 non-financial companies with a AAA rating. When he departed, that number was down to six, and GE was one of them.

Quality of GE Industrial FCF

I have already discussed the 170x increase in GE Industrial's FCF from 1980 to 2000. However, the impressive FCF generation in 2000 (shown in Figure 18.1), while elevated, was not a fluke.

FIGURE 18.1

GE Industrial: Impressive FCF to Net Income Conversion Ratio[4]

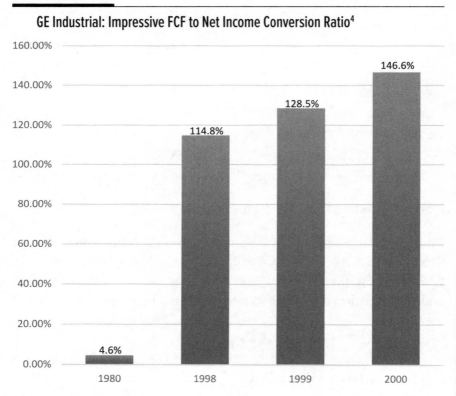

Most industrial companies generate less than 100% FCF conversion. In the late 1990s, GE's industrial FCF generation was substantially greater than its reported net income. This speaks to the high-quality nature of its earnings.

Improvement in Returns on Equity at GE Industrial

In 1980, GE's industrial businesses produced an impressive 20% return on average shareholder equity. In 2000, GE's industrial businesses produced $7.5 billion of profits on just under $25 billion in average shareholder equity, which equated to a 30% return on average shareholder equity.

If you were to define return on average shareholder equity using FCF instead of net income (FCF divided by average shareholder equity), returns would have been a remarkable 44%. Moreover, the returns were actually weighed down by the $8 billion in cash and marketable securities on GE's industrial balance sheet at the time.

5. Transformation of GE Industrial Portfolio

By 2000, the coal mining and natural gas production businesses were gone, and the combined profit mix of appliances and industrial products had dropped by half, as shown in Tables 18.2 and 18.3.

The mix of good businesses (Aircraft Engines, NBC, Technical Products, Power Systems) with either strong secular growth, large aftermarket streams, and/or pricing power, increased to around two-thirds of the industrial profit mix by 2000. In 1980, this was somewhere between a quarter and a third of the total.

Profit Mix of GE Businesses in 1980[5]

	1980 Profit Mix	Businesses
Consumer Products	20.7%	Appliances, lighting, air conditioning
Industrial Products	22.3%	Motors, electrical equipment
Power Systems	10.0%	Steam, gas, and nuclear turbines and reactors
Technical Systems	26.4%	Aerospace, plastics, healthcare
Natural Resources	15.9%	Coal mining, uranium, and natural gas production
Foreign	4.8%	

Note: Excluded GE Credit Corporation profits that were reported within the consumer products segment.

Profit Mix of GE Businesses in 2000[6]

	2000 Profit Mix	Businesses
Aircraft Engines	18.0%	Aircraft engines for commercial aerospace and defense
Appliances	5.0%	Appliances, air-conditioning
Power Systems	20.7%	Gas and steam turbines
Technical Products	12.7%	Mostly healthcare
Industrial Products	16.1%	Lighting, locomotives, motors
NBC	13.2%	NBC network and cable channels
Plastics	14.2%	Plastics for multiple industries

Managerial Excellence and Talent Cultivation

In addition to the five aforementioned and often overlooked elements that define his tenure, Welch's ability to identify, train, develop, nurture, and promote excellent managerial talent really set GE apart.

Authors Derek Lehmberg, W. Glenn Rowe, Roderick E. White, and John R. Philips assert this position in an article entitled "The GE

Paradox: Competitive Advantage Through Non-Fungible Non-Firm-Specific Investment" published in the October 2009 edition of the *Journal of Management*:

> *The results of our stock price study support the proposition that GE has a leadership development capability superior to other firms. . . . Our results imply that GE has a pool of general management talent that is superior, on average, to that available in the general labor market.*[7]

Similarly, in April 2005, E.F. Kratz wrote in *Fortune* magazine, "When a company needs a loan, it goes to a bank. When a company needs a CEO, it goes to GE."[8]

GE CAPITAL INSURANCE

While the Welch era at GE was a success, the one major blemish on Welch's record relates to GE Capital's insurance business. In the mid-to-late 1990s, GE and many other insurance and reinsurance companies wrote policies that would lead to large losses in future years as the premiums received were insufficient to cover future losses. Many of GE's reinsurance contracts had a long tail with profits accrued up front based on estimates for insurance claims far in the future. When future losses ended up being far greater than expected, GE was forced to recognize more than $10 billion in insurance losses between 2001 and 2005. In 2017, GE was forced to record another $15 billion in losses on its legacy insurance business from policies written for long-term-care insurance. Many of these policies were reinsured during the Welch era.

Despite these large insurance reserve additions, GE Capital would still report $42 billion in cumulative profits and pay out more than $26 billion in dividends to GE to help fund the GE dividend between 2001 and 2006.

THE FUTURE LOOKED BRIGHT

At the end of 2000, despite the announcement that Jack Welch would retire in September of 2001 and be replaced by Jeff Immelt, the future looked bright for GE. GE's industrial businesses were generating $11 billion in FCF. GE Capital was generating $5 billion in profits and paying a dividend of a little less than $2 billion to GE to help fund the GE dividend.

In short, after Jack Welch retired, GE's largest businesses seemed well positioned to continue to grow.

The crown jewel of the industrial portfolio was the aircraft engines business. This was a classic razor and razor blade business with high margins and pricing power. GE was the exclusive engine provider on the Boeing 737, virtually guaranteeing market share gains for the foreseeable future in GE's high margin aftermarket business. Interestingly, despite the sizable decline in commercial air travel post-9/11, this business was still able to maintain relatively stable profits from 2001 to 2003.

Strong demographic forces propelled GE's healthcare business. In addition, GE Healthcare was well positioned in emerging markets where the utilization of advanced medical imaging equipment was still low but growing.

GE's power systems business manufactured industrial gas turbines. This business was in the midst of a robust up cycle that would last for multiple years. Even when the cycle ended, it appeared poised to generate a steady stream of aftermarket profits for the next decade and beyond.

NBC, GE's communications holding, was the number one network in the United States in 2000, and CNBC, its business cable channel, was a major success as the dominant cable channel for financial news.

In addition, in 2000, GE announced it would acquire Honeywell in an all-stock transaction. This acquisition was expected to strengthen GE's aerospace business as well as adding attractive automation and specialty chemical franchises to the GE portfolio. The

Honeywell deal was expected to be double-digit accretive to GE's EPS, lower the percentage of earnings that came from GE Capital, and accelerate GE's growth rate.

Investors were confident in GE's future and awarded the company with a very healthy 25x multiple on forward earnings on the day that Jack Welch retired. This was well ahead of the mid-teens multiple that GE traded for in the early to mid-1990s.

YET 18 YEARS LATER, GE WAS IN DISARRAY

GE's AAA-rating was gone. Portions of its industrial debt were trading at spreads consistent with junk-bond levels. GE's industrial gross debt and after-tax pension deficit had swelled to $68 billion. In 2018, GE was expelled from the Dow Jones Industrial Average after being a part of the index for 111 years. Industrial FCF had deteriorated from $11 billion in 2000 to a negative $1.4 billion in 2018 ($4.5 billion in adjusted FCF, see the following box). The dividend was cut to a penny per quarter to conserve cash. GE would pay out fewer dividend dollars in 2019 than it did in 1980. Management was forced to sell $40 billion in industrial and healthcare businesses to strengthen the balance sheet in order to maintain its investment grade credit rating.

What Is the Right Way to Define GE's FCF?

Unlike net income or EPS, which are reported using generally accepted accounting principles (GAAP), there is no standard definition for FCF or FCF per share. As a result, how one investor or management team defines FCF could be very different from how another investor or management team defines it. However, in my experience, the most common definition of FCF is operating cash minus capital expenditures. Throughout this book I have used this relatively common definition.

However, GE adjusts its FCF figure to include asset sales, exclude most pension contributions, and exclude the taxes it pays on businesses that it sells. This latter issue is very defensible. It does not make sense to deduct taxes paid on a divested business from ongoing operating cash flows while the proceeds from the divested business are counted in cash flow from investing. However, asset sales are very discretionary and should not be included in free cash flow.

In 2018, GE reported $4.5 billion in adjusted FCF but using a more standard definition, its FCF was actually negative $1.4 billion. The biggest difference between GE's adjusted FCF and its actual FCF was due to $6 billion in pension contributions.

Should pension contributions be excluded from FCF calculations?

From an economic perspective, the after-tax pension deficit of a firm is in many ways equivalent to the firm's debt and both should be included in a firm's enterprise value calculation. When a firm uses its FCF to retire debt, few, if any, financial analysts would exclude this payment from the firm's FCF. However, if a firm makes a large contribution to its pension plan and reduces its after-tax deficit, under the traditional FCF definition, this will reduce a firm's FCF in the year of the payment. The correct way for firms to account for pension contributions in their adjusted FCF definition should be to include pension contributions that are needed to maintain the after-tax pension deficit at its current level and exclude any pension contributions that actually reduce the after-tax pension deficit.

In this chapter, we will show both GE Industrial's FCF using the standard definition and GE's adjusted FCF in 2018.

GE's board of directors, which now included an activist investor, brought in an outside CEO to turn the company around. GE was no longer the largest market capitalization company in the United

States. It was not even in the top 50. In 2000, when GE announced the acquisition of Honeywell (which was subsequently rejected by European antitrust authorities), its market capitalization was more than 10x that of Honeywell. At the end of 2018, Honeywell was larger than GE.

From the end of the Welch era through the end of 2018, GE's stock price declined 81%. At the same time, the S&P 500 increased by 131%. GE's total return trailed the S&P 500's total return by an astonishing compounded annual rate of 13.2% per year.

WHAT HAPPENED TO GE?

Most observers would point to three contributing factors that brought GE to its knees:

Valuation Too High

GE's valuation rose steadily in the final years of the Welch era. At the end of 1994, GE was trading at 13x earnings, and at its height in 2000 it was awarded an eye-catching multiple of 43x earnings. At the end of 2000, GE was still trading over 30x, or more than twice the multiple it had traded for only six years earlier. GE was trading at a large premium in relation to the sum of its parts, and this was not sustainable. Balance sheet intensive financial businesses typically trade between 8 and 12x earnings, and GE Capital represented 41% of GE earnings. Even within GE's industrial earnings, more commoditized businesses such as plastics and appliances still made up 19% of earnings, and these businesses were not worth 30x earnings. While GE likely deserved to trade at a premium to the sum of its parts due to superior management talent, strong industrial FCF, and a history of consistent earnings growth, in the late 1990s and 2000, that premium became too high and was destined to collapse over time.

GE Capital

GE Capital went from earning over $5 billion in 2000 to losing money in 2016–2018. GE Capital's reinsurance business had under-reserved for policies underwritten in the mid-to-late 1990s, resulting in more than $10 billion in write-offs from 2001–2005. During the Great Financial Crisis (GFC), GE was forced to inject $15 billion into GE Capital. In 2009, this led to the loss of the GE AAA rating and a painful dividend cut. In 2017, GE was forced to significantly increase reserves on its legacy long-term-care insurance book of business. This would require a cash injection of $15 billion over 2018–2024 to bring reserves to a level consistent with expected future claims. In 2019, GE injected $4 billion of cash into GE Capital to help fund these reserve additions and other GE Capital liabilities.

There is no question that in 2000, GE Capital's embedded valuation within GE was too high, given where other balance sheet intensive financial companies traded at the time. In addition, GE Capital's insurance operations were significantly under-reserved.

It is very difficult to estimate the embedded earnings multiple the market placed on GE Capital at the end of 2000, but it was likely in the 15–20x range. This implied that GE Capital was being valued between $80 to $110 billion. At the end of 2018, two sell-side analysts' sum of parts analyses valued GE Capital at a negative.[9]

Power Systems Collapse

The power systems business was a strong contributor to earnings for most of the period between 2000 and 2016 with segment profits rising from $2.8 billion to $5.0 billion (3.6% CAGR). However, this business was on the wrong side of secular change. While GE had a renewables business, it was small relative to the legacy power business. GE only compounded this challenge by doubling down on this business through the acquisition of Alstom's power assets in November of 2015. Alstom's power business was even more secularly challenged than that of GE's industrial gas turbine division. By the end of 2017, the global demand for industrial gas turbines would fall sharply as renewable sources of power generation soaked up the vast majority of new energy needs, particularly in the United States and Western Europe.

The power business struggled for two additional reasons. First, GE power started recognizing large up-front gains on long-term service agreements that resulted in stronger reported earnings, but weaker cash flow. In the first three quarters of 2017, these non-cash gains represented almost half of the profits from the power segment. The power business also artificially boosted near-term cash flow by pulling forward future customer cash flows on these long-term service agreements through intracompany receivable transactions with GE Capital. Second, the business faltered operationally with frequent warranty issues, poor productivity, project execution challenges, and failing blades on some of its newer turbines.

Coming into 2017, GE management had initially issued guidance that this business would earn $5.5–$6 billion in segment profits. Less than two years later in 2018, the power system business posted $808 million in losses and lost $2.7 billion in FCF.

ROLE OF CAPITAL ALLOCATION

Most observers have stopped there in examining the fall of GE. GE Capital and Power Systems were disasters from a financial perspective over this period, and GE was trading for an unsustainably high valuation level in 2000. GE Capital was under-reserved in its insurance business by tens of billions of dollars. All of that is 100% accurate.

However, the oft-missed explanation for GE's fall from grace, and maybe the company's most powerful shortcoming, comes down to capital allocation.

What is fascinating about GE's acquisitions over the course of 2001–2018 is that the majority of the acquisitions completed over this period were also divested over this same time period. In the vast majority of cases, these divestitures were completed at prices well below what GE original paid or, in the case of Alstom, had more than 100% of the purchase price completely written off. This cycle of paying up for deals and then divesting the businesses at lower prices years later also had a cascading negative impact on the returns associated with GE's $105 billion in share repurchase as industrial FCF declined precipitously in the decade of the 2010s. The result was an extremely low return on the bulk of the share repurchase completed over this period. The compounding impact of this poor capital allocation will become apparent over the remainder of the chapter.

Throughout the following analysis, I attempt to isolate GE's industrial business from GE Capital.

What Should GE Industrial's FCF Have Been in 2018?

There are a few important variables:

1. In 2000, industrial FCF was $11 billion.
2. In 2018, industrial FCF was –$1.4 billion.
3. In 2018, "adjusted" industrial FCF was $4.5 billion.
4. US nominal GDP CAGR was 4% during this period.

Let's make the following assumptions:

1. GE Industrial was able to grow its FCF organically over this period at the rate of nominal GDP growth. This assumes no underlying margin expansion.
2. GE Industrial invests all available FCF after paying its share of the GE dividend and buying back enough stock to offset the dilutive impact of employee stock and option grants.
3. With all the FCF left over, GE makes investments (acquisitions, repurchase of stock, etc.) that generate cash-on-cash returns of 5%, 10%, and 20% in year five as shown in Table 18.4.

TABLE 18.4

Returns on Excess Capital

Returns on Excess Capital	Year 1	Year 5
Poor	3%	5%
Attractive	5%	10%
Best in class	10%	20%

Note: Assumes after year five, growth in line with GDP.

Based on my readings of all the annual reports from 2000–2018, many of these assumptions seem very conservative. CEO Jeff Immelt said that GE had historically grown revenues organically at 5% and that he aimed to take this to 8% over time. In the 2004 annual report, he highlighted a goal of generating 20% returns on investments. The range of these returns on excess capital are displayed in Table 18.4.

Now, before running the numbers here, to be fair, it's important to make a couple of adjustments to GE Industrial's baseline FCF level. I've already highlighted that GE Industrial's FCF conversion was an exceptionally high 147% rate in 2000. This is not a sustainable level of FCF conversion rate for any industrial firm over the long run. Moreover, demand for GE's industrial gas turbines was running well above mid-cycle, normalized levels, and this was not sustainable either. If you reduce GE Industrial's FCF conversion rate to 110% and further reduce power systems profits by $500 million, you arrive at a more reasonable mid-cycle baseline for GE Industrial's FCF of around $7 billion as a starting point in 2000.

Using this more conservative starting point for GE Industrial's FCF generation, how much FCF per share should GE Industrial have generated in 2018, assuming different returns on excess capital deployment?

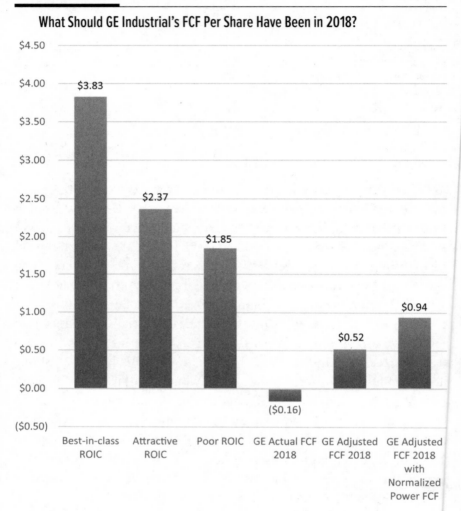

FIGURE 18.2

What Should GE Industrial's FCF Per Share Have Been in 2018?

As discussed previously, GE Industrial's FCF was a negative $1.4 billion in 2018 and, even using GE's adjusted industrial FCF definition, was only $4.5 billion. As Figure 18.2 demonstrates, GE's FCF generation was abysmal.

Assuming GE had deployed capital at poor rates of return over this period, its FCF should still have been around $16 billion in 2018![†]

Moreover, this miss cannot be attributed to the weakness of the power business alone, which had $2.7 billion in negative FCF in 2018[‡]. Even if I were to very generously assume that the power business was able to deliver on its 2017 operating profit target of $5.5 to $6 billion and hold that flat in 2018, this would only make up a small part of the shortfall. In the first three quarters of 2017, a significant portion of the profits of the power division were coming from non-cash accounting profits on adjustments to long-term service agreements, and Alstom's cash flow was materially worse than its income statement results. After adjusting for these factors, the power division's normalized FCF would have been closer to $1 billion. This would increase GE Industrial's adjusted FCF in 2018 to $8.2 billion (still well less than $1 per share) and actual FCF to $2.3 billion.

Now let's try to put this massive FCF shortfall into a shareholder value destruction context.

At the end of 2018, GE had a market capitalization of a mere $66 billion. In the fourth quarter of 2018, there were only two published sell-side analyst sum-of-the-parts analyses that included an estimate for GE Capital.[10] The average of the two analyses valued GE Capital at a negative $5.3 billion. This implies that GE Industrial was valued at around $71 billion at the end of 2018.

If you take what GE Industrial's FCF generation should have been in 2018 and apply a conservative 20x multiple on trailing FCF, you can arrive at what GE Industrial should have been worth at the end of 2018 (see Figure 18.3).

---

† I arrived at this by multiplying the poor ROIC FCF per share of $1.85 per share by 8.7 billion diluted shares outstanding for 2018.

‡ This massive miss cannot be blamed on weakness in GE's organic growth rate either. GE disclosed its industrial growth rate (not organic) in 2001–2002, disclosed total organic growth rate (inclusive of GE Capital) in 2003–2007, disclosed industrial organic growth rate in 2008 for the first time, stopped disclosing industrial organic growth in 2009–2010 when it was most likely negative, and then reported industrial organic growth from 2011 onwards. My best estimate is that GE Industrial's organic growth from 2001 to 2018 was a little more than 3%. However, unlike every other number in this book, this should be viewed as an intelligent guestimate.

FIGURE 18.3

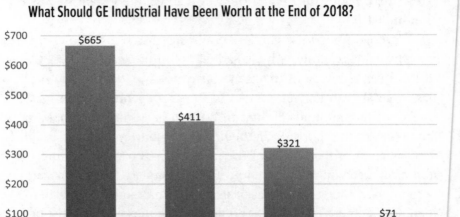

What Should GE Industrial Have Been Worth at the End of 2018?

Notes: Assumes 20x multiple on FCF/per share and 8.7 billion diluted shares outstanding.
Numbers in billions.

Even assuming GE had deployed capital poorly from 2001–2018 with initial returns on capital of 3% and 5% returns by year five, its market value should still have been worth $250 billion more than it was at the end of 2018. If GE had been able to deploy capital and generate double-digit returns by year five, its market capitalization should have been $340 billion more than it was at the end of 2018.

Moreover, this massive market cap and FCF shortfall cannot be blamed on GE Capital. While GE Industrial did have to inject cash into GE Capital in the Great Financial Crisis (GFC) and again in 2019, GE Capital, even excluding the normal GE Capital dividend, was a net capital contributor to GE Industrial over this period, as shown in Figure 18.4.

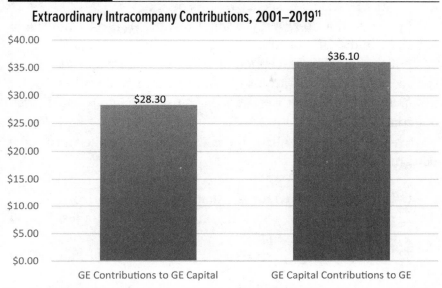

FIGURE 18.4

Extraordinary Intracompany Contributions, 2001–2019[11]

Notes: Includes $20.4 billion Synchrony exchange offer that retired 671 million shares. Excludes regular GE Capital dividend to support GE dividend. Numbers in billions.

One last comment, as you might suspect, the best-in-class ROIC on excess capital scenario was not realistic. There are very few companies that can invest large amounts of capital that generate 20% cash-on-cash returns. I only included this because CEO Jeff Immelt had highlighted his focus on generating 20% returns on investments in the 2004 GE Annual Report. If he had been able to pull off this stretch goal, GE Industrial would likely have had a market capitalization of $665 billion at the end of 2018.

How did this happen?

EXTREMELY POOR CAPITAL ALLOCATION

In reviewing GE filings, sell-side analyst reports, investor presentations, and press releases, I was able to identify 59 businesses that GE acquired between the years 2001 and 2018 (shown in Table 18.5) that collectively added up to $95.4 billion of capital deployment or about 87% of its M&A dollars spent over this period.

By the end of 2020, only a small number of these acquisitions remained in the GE portfolio.

With the possible exception of seven of those acquisitions (life sciences and aerospace acquisitions), I feel confident stating that the vast majority of the rest were failed acquisitions and, in most cases, materially value destructive.

Eventually, almost all of these acquisitions resulted in a poor outcome:

1. They were divested for less than the purchase price.
2. They were part of a business unit that was sold for less than its collective purchase price.
3. They had a large portion of the purchase price written off.

Moreover, the level of value destruction is even more pronounced when one considers the time value of money and the fact that these businesses should have been accreting value over time.

In a world where more than 50% of deals struggle to generate attractive returns for shareholders, General Electric's success rate on M&A was significantly worse than average.

But why was this?

From a process standpoint, GE made three mistakes in M&A that resulted in consistently poor or negative returns.

TABLE 18.5

GE Acquisitions, 2001–2018[12]

	Number of Deals	Outcome	Comments
Water	4	Negative Returns	Sold more than a decade later for less than original purchase price
NBC	7	Negative Returns	Announced divesture to Comcast right after recession
Oil & Gas	12	Horrible Returns	Worth a fraction of the capital deployed to build business
Security	3	Negative Returns	Divested for less than original purchase price
Healthcare	5	Negative Returns	Three businesses sold for less than original purchase price, paid high valuations for all deals
Renewables	3	Negative Returns	Renewables business had $1 billion of negative FCF in 2019, partially due to Alstom joint ventures
Power	4	Horrible Returns	Alstom purchase price completely written off
Aviation	3	OK to Good Returns	Limited visibility, but end-market has been healthy and initial prices paid were reasonable
Life Sciences	4	OK to Good Returns	Sold majority of business to Danaher in 2020 for $21.4 billion
GE Digital	2	Likely Negative Returns	Bought ServiceMax for high valuation in 2016 and sold to Silver Lake a few years later
Other	12	Negative Returns	Series of bad deals, many sold near or below original purchase price years later

Note: Returns are defined here as initial purchase price relative to eventual sale price or cash-on-cash returns for assets still owned by GE.

1. Acquiring Poor Businesses

GE Oil and Gas. GE acquired an oil and gas business in 1995 but started to invest aggressively in this space in 2007, beginning with the acquisition of Vetco and concluding with the combination of its oil and gas businesses with Baker Hughes in 2017. The problem with the oil and gas service business is that it is highly cyclical, is very capital intensive, and generates consistently less FCF than earnings. While GE did not disclose its oil and gas businesses' FCF to net income conversion rate, Baker Hughes, GE Oil and Gas's eventual merger partner, can serve as a proxy to demonstrate just how poor FCF is within the oil and gas services sector. Between 2008 and 2015, Baker Hughes produced $8.9 billion in adjusted earnings, but only generated $3.5 billion in FCF, even using a very expansive definition of FCF that includes asset sales. This equates to an abysmal 39% net income to FCF conversion rate.

From a quality standpoint, GE's aggressive expansion into the oil and gas business was dilutive to the quality of its industrial assets. In addition, as Figure 18.5 demonstrates, these acquisitions generated a negative return for GE shareholders.

Alstom Power. In 2014, GE announced it would acquire Alstom's power assets for a price of around $13.7 billion. GE announced that the asset was expected to generate high-teens returns on the capital employed. The problem was that the business had experienced only one year of positive organic growth in the previous four. It was overexposed in thermal/coal plants at a time when coal was in clear secular decline, and GE was forced to take a reserve for contracts in Alstom's backlog that were expected to lose more than $1.1 billion over the next couple of years.

FIGURE 18.5

More Than $13 Billion of Value Destruction at GE Oil and Gas

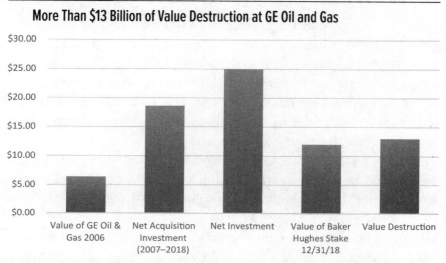

Notes: Used 8.2x multiple of EBITDA for GE Oil & Gas value in 2006 as this is consistent with where Haliburton was trading at the time. Net investment equates to existing value of GE Oil & Gas 2006 and acquisition dollars spent on oil and gas businesses minus first sale of Baker Hughes shares in 2018. Numbers in billions.

Essentially, Alstom had already entered into multiple utility construction contracts that were expected to cost more to build than the company would be paid for building them. GE was now on the hook for these money-losing contracts. In addition, after closing, GE would need to materially increase its reserves beyond its initial estimates for these contracts and other legacy liability costs associated with the Alstom acquisition. The business generated negative operating cash flow in 2016, and GE ended up writing down more than 100% of the purchase price of Alstom in 2017–2018.[14] While GE does not break out Alstom Power specifically, the acquisition of Alstom likely produced significant negative FCF in 2017 and 2018.

2. Paying High Valuations for Growth Assets

There is nothing inherently wrong with paying higher valuations for growth assets. While the returns in the early years may be somewhat lower, the growth rate in the outer years combined with good synergy capture can generate attractive returns by year five or six. However, paying high multiples for growth assets can produce poor returns if growth fails to materialize and/or synergy capture falls short of expectations.

Unfortunately, some of GE's forays into new, higher-growth businesses such as water, security, healthcare, IT, Spanish broadcasting, and industrial internet/digital fell into the latter bucket.

GE Water. GE started acquiring water assets in 2002–2003 through the purchase of Betz Dearborn and Osmonics for a little more than $2 billion. In the 2002 GE annual report, CEO Jeff Immelt said these two businesses should grow organically at 15% per year and that he aimed to have the water business generate $4 billion in revenues by 2005. GE would make two additional large acquisitions in the water space in 2004 (Ionics) and 2006 (Zenon Membrane Systems) for another $1.9 billion. In 2017, GE disclosed that its water business had $2 billion in revenues and was sold that same year for $3.1 billion to Suez Environmental. GE had spent more than $3.9 billion for water assets in the early-to-mid-2000s and sold them for 20% less than the original investment in 2018. Figure 18.6 shows the extent of the value destruction attributable to its water acquisitions.

GE Security and Healthcare Acquisitions. The acquisitions of Interlogix and Edwards gave GE a foothold in the attractive and fast-growing security business. Clarient gave GE a presence in molecular diagnostics with a promising breast cancer test. In addition, GE paid a hefty 45x earnings for Vital Signs, a manufacturer of anesthesia equipment and single-use consumables. According to Omar Ishrak, president and CEO of GE Healthcare's clinical systems unit, the Vital Signs acquisition was expected to generate double-digit

FIGURE 18.6

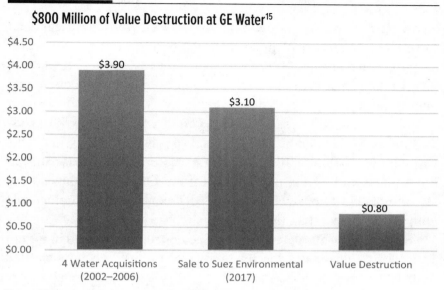

$800 Million of Value Destruction at GE Water[15]

Notes: GE received after-tax proceeds of $3.1 billion. Numbers in billions.

organic growth.[16] Five years later, it had grown at less than half the anticipated rate, and GE divested the business to Carefusion for $358 million less than it had paid for it.

All four of these were attractive businesses with robust underlying market growth rates, low cyclicality, recurring revenue, and strong brands. However, due to a combination of paying high valuations up front (which led to low initial returns on capital), overly aggressive sales growth assumptions, and poor operational execution, GE ended up selling all of these businesses for far less than what it paid. If you are going to pay high valuations for acquisitions, growth and margin expansion are essential in order to generate acceptable returns.

3. Buying High, Selling Low

NBC. NBC provided a growth platform for GE for many years and served as a consumer of more than $12 billion in acquisition capital in the early-to-mid 2000s. GE spent aggressively to expand into Spanish-language television, cable channels, movie production, and internet sites.

GE announced the sale of NBC Universal business to Comcast in 2009 only six months after the end of a horrific recession. This was not the ideal time to sell NBC if garnering a good price was an important priority. Just one month earlier, GE had announced the sale of its security businesses to United Technologies in another sale with proceeds less than the original purchase price.

However, the absolute level of value destruction, shown in Figure 18.7, vastly understates the magnitude of the true economic value destruction for long-term shareholders.

FIGURE 18.7

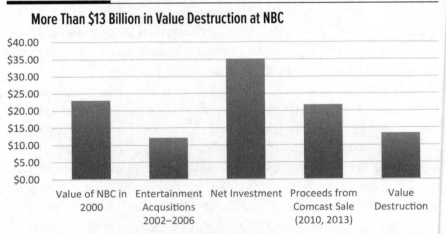

More Than $13 Billion in Value Destruction at NBC

Notes: Valued NBC at 12x EBITDA in 2000 consistent with where the business was valued in the formation of the joint venture with Vivendi. Entertainment acquisitions are net of $300 million GE received from selling its interest in Sundance channel. Proceeds from Comcast are after-tax. Numbers in billions.

Remember, from 2001 to 2018, US nominal GDP growth averaged around 4% and many emerging market economies grew significantly faster. In a growing global economy, GE's industrial assets and acquisitions should have been accreting value at a rate at least equal to US GDP growth. The static absolute value destruction numbers above fail to capture what these businesses should have been worth when GE sold them.

GE spent a total of $110 billion on acquisitions during this period. It is clear that the vast majority of these acquisitions were worth considerably less than the price GE paid. By the time GE sold many of these assets, the decline in investment value was massive both versus the prices originally paid and relative to what they should have been worth, as displayed in Figures 18.8 and 18.9.

FIGURE 18.8

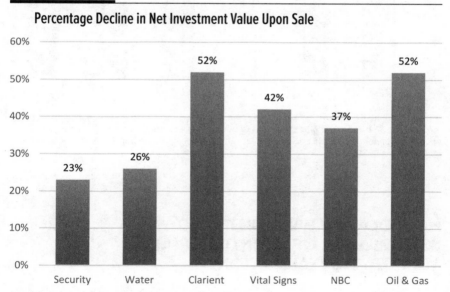

Percentage Decline in Net Investment Value Upon Sale

Notes: The math behind this analysis is the value of the existing assets + net acquisition investment relative to GE's eventual divestiture proceeds. Oil & Gas reflects GE's remaining interest in Baker Hughes as of December 31, 2018.

FIGURE 18.9

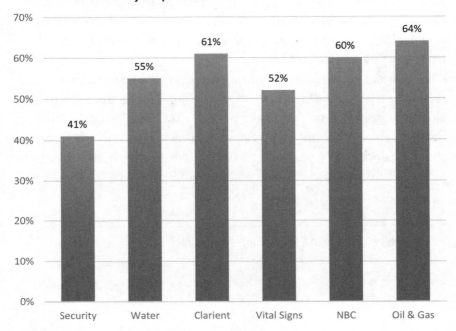

Percentage Decline in Net Investment Value upon Sale Assuming Assets Accreted in Value by 4% per Year

Notes: The math behind this is exactly the same as last example except that it assumes that the existing GE businesses plus the acquired businesses accreted in value by 4% per year prior to being sold by GE. Oil and Gas reflects GE's remaining interest in Baker Hughes as of December 31, 2018.

HOW DO YOU WIPE OUT $250–$340 BILLION OF GE INDUSTRIAL'S MARKET CAPITALIZATION?

It is impossible to parse exactly how much of this shortfall is due to poor capital allocation versus poor operational execution. In many ways, they are linked. Over this period, GE spent $110 billion on acquisitions. If GE had been able to improve margins and grow these businesses organically, the returns would have been better—not good, but better. The $105 billion GE spent buying its shares during this time (shown in Figure 18.10) would have generated reasonable returns on capital if FCF had continued to grow, as opposed to declining and ultimately going negative. If the power business had been more focused on cash generation, not acquired Alstom, and produced a reasonable amount of FCF in 2018–2019, GE might not have needed to divest as many industrial and healthcare assets from a position of weakness. Interestingly, the best-run business and best operating segment in the GE portfolio, GE Aviation, received a limited amount of acquisition capital over this time period.

FIGURE 18.10

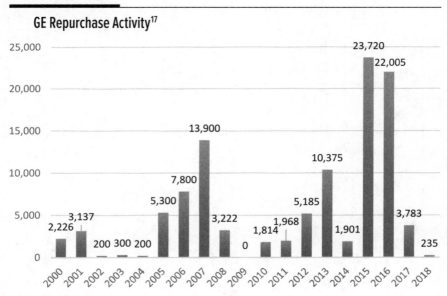

GE Repurchase Activity[17]

Note: Numbers in millions.

What is crystal clear is that if you systematically acquire bad businesses, pay high multiples for growth assets that you don't have the ability to integrate and grow, and are constantly buying high and selling low, you have a recipe for value destruction.

TABLE 18.6

Four Phases of GE Capital Deployment[18]

Description	Objective	Period	Acquisition Examples	Divestitures	Share Repurchase	Acquisitions
Growth at Any Price	Accelerate Growth	2001–2007	Telemundo Amersham Vivendi Ionics EST	Plastics Advanced Materials GE Supply	$30.8	$56.7
Oil & Gas	Grow Oil & Gas	2008–2014	Hydril Dresser John Wood Lufkin Wellstream	NBC Security	$24.5	$27.0
The Pivot	Get to $2 of EPS Grow Industrial Shrink Capital	2015–2018	Alstom Service Max Baker Hughes Meridium	Water Appliances	$49.7	$26.5
Oh Crap	Save Company Pay Down Debt Avoid Junk Credit Rating	2019–2021		Biopharma Rail	TBD	TBD

Notes: Numbers in billions.

THE LESSONS FROM GE'S FALL

There are two more important lessons to be gleaned from the decisions that contributed to the fall of the General Electric Corporation. First, acquisitions, or any form of capital allocation, should be justified on the merits of the transaction alone. When transactions become a necessity to enable some broader strategic objective, all too often the deal fails not only to achieve an attractive financial return for long-term shareholders, but frequently fails to achieve its stated strategic objective(s) as well. This will be a common refrain throughout this book.

Second, firms, especially cyclical firms, should be reticent to provide long-term financial targets such as EPS or revenue targets for some distant future year. A singular focus on a financial objective can lead to multiple, poor short-term decisions. These can compromise the financial health of the business, result in poor cash-on-cash returns on capital deployment, and ultimately harm long-term shareholders.

The GE management team wished to reduce the size and scope of GE Capital prior to the announced acquisition of Alstom's power assets in 2014.[19] However, GE Capital was an important contributor to GE's earnings, and the GE Capital dividend payment to GE helped fund the overall GE dividend. A material reduction in the size of GE Capital would have been massively dilutive to earnings and potentially risked the sustainability of the GE dividend in the future. These challenges drove the GE management team to make a series of poor decisions.

The acquisition of Alstom's power assets can be referred to as an "enabling transaction." It was a large industrial business that was expected to generate significant industrial earnings and cash flows that would partially offset the dilution caused by the reduction in the size of GE Capital. Enabling transactions such as this can allow a firm to accomplish one or more strategic objectives. But all too often, these strategic objectives become the overriding force for entering into such a transaction, and they supersede the financial returns or industrial logic of the acquisition. That is exactly what happened with GE's acquisition of Alstom: strategic imperatives overwhelmed financial and business quality considerations.

While the Alstom transaction was expected to partially off-set the dilution from the reduction in the size of GE Capital, it was not going to be enough. GE had provided long-term earnings guidance of $2 per share in 2015 following the completion of the Alstom transaction. To achieve this financial objective, GE needed to use the proceeds from GE Capital asset sales to buy back stock, increase debt at GE Industrial to make accretive industrial acquisitions and buy back even more stock, and grow the core industrial business at a healthy rate. The $2 per share objective became GE's true north star.

The problem was that the core business was in trouble. The oil and gas and transportation businesses were struggling to grow earnings as both end markets were pressured by weak oil and commodity prices. Simultaneously, GE started to recognize an increasing amount of non-cash, cumulative adjustments on its long-term service contracts. These low-quality one-time gains boosted reported earnings but had no impact on cash flows.

In 2015 and 2016, GE spent $46 billion on stock (shown in Table 18.7) and continued buying back stock aggressively into 2017 to increase EPS, even though the cash-on-cash returns were deteriorating. The returns on this large share repurchase program would decline to the low-single digits in the upcoming years as FCF deteriorated.

In mid-2017, CEO Jeff Immelt stepped down and his CFO stepped down six months later. GE recorded a large write-off on its acquisition of Alstom in 2018. The company turned from acquisition and share repurchase mode to an asset sale focus to pay down debt. The large non-cash cumulative gains that had been used to bolster earnings returned to more normal pre-2014 levels. The power, energy, and transportation businesses continued to weaken, with power's reported operating profits falling off a cliff. In 2018, GE reported a GAAP operating loss of $2.43 per share and even on an adjusted basis earned only $.65 per share. In addition, the Securities and Exchange Commission announced an investigation into GE's accounting practices.[†]

TABLE 18.7

GE Spent $46 Billion Buying Back Stock in 2015–2016 at Low Single-Digit Returns on Capital[20]

2015–2016 Share Repurchase (in millions)	$45,725
Number of Shares Repurchased	1507
Average Price of Shares Bought Back	$30.34
Average Value of GE Capital at 1x Book Value	$3.74
Value of GE Industrial	$26.60
Average Industrial FCF/Share 2015–2016	$0.81
Initial Cash-on-Cash Returns from Share Repurchase	**3.0%**

When GE's singular focus became the achievement of $2 per share in 2018, earnings quality suffered, a focus on cash-on-cash returns on acquisitions and share repurchase suffered, and a focus on balance sheet management suffered.

A company's true north star should be deploying capital at the highest possible risk-adjusted returns, while maintaining an optimized balance sheet. Any financial objective that eclipses this objective, whether it is some arbitrary EPS or revenue objective, is a mistake.

No one set out to destroy shareholder value at GE. Blaming GE's entire downfall on capital allocation would be a mistake. New management had to deal with billions of inherited losses at GE Capital Insurance between 2001 and 2005, and they had no responsibility for those underwriting decisions. While GE had to inject $15 billion

---

[†] In December 2020, the SEC would find that "GE violated the antifraud, reporting, disclosure controls, and accounting controls provision of the securities laws." (Source: General Electric Agrees to Pay $200 Million Penalty for Disclosure Violations, Dec 9, 2020, Washington, DC, US Securities and Exchange Commission.)

into GE Capital during the Great Financial Crisis (GFC), this was far less than what many other banks and investment banks had to raise. Moreover, GE Capital lived to fight another day, whereas many large banks and investment banks such as Bear Stearns, Lehman Brothers, Wachovia, National City, and Washington Mutual went under or were sold to other firms for a fraction of their 2006–2007 values.

Moreover, not every acquisition was a failure. General Electric's purchase of Amersham in 2004 for $10.7 billion formed the foundation of GE's high-growth, highly profitable Biopharma business. The largest component of this business was sold to Danaher for over $20 billion in 2020 to help pay down debt.†

CONCLUSION

It is important to point out that no matter how well Mr. Immelt deployed capital, he was still destined to underperform his peers. The combination of an unsustainable level of FCF to net income, becoming CEO in the middle of a very robust power cycle, the fact that GE was trading at a massive premium to its sum of parts, and the aforementioned GE Capital insurance reserve shortfalls all doomed any possibility of GE outperformance during his tenure as CEO.[21] In many ways, Mr. Immelt was dealt a very difficult hand upon becoming CEO, but he, his management team, and the GE board of directors made the situation so much worse through extremely poor capital allocation.

In the end, GE failed because of a variety of external and internal factors as well as a deeply flawed capital allocation process.

Before moving on from GE, it is important to point out that not all is lost. GE is not bankrupt. GE has not defaulted on its debt or pension commitments. As of the publication of this book, GE has retained an investment grade credit rating. GE still possesses two strong businesses in its aviation and healthcare divisions. In late

---

† GE acquired Amersham with GE stock. At time of the announcement, the stock was worth $9.5 billion, but at deal closing it was worth $10.7 billion.

2018, GE announced the hiring of former Danaher CEO Larry Culp as its chairman and CEO. Culp has a well-earned reputation for operational excellence, turning around businesses, and understanding the power of capital allocation to create long-term shareholder value.

GE lost its way, and I am sure that its customers, investors, employees, retirees, and all stakeholders are hoping that the new leadership can restore the company's former glory. I count myself among those rooting for better days ahead.

Inferior Businesses with Higher Valuations

We see lots of opportunity in our data connectivity businesses. Residential broadband and business services, which combined generate over $20 billion in revenue per year growing right at around 10% and are accretive to our margins. . . . In broadband we expect a strong end of the year and are on track to add over 1 million net new customers for the 12th year in a row.

—Brian L. Roberts, Chairman and CEO, Comcast Corporation[1]

Broadband is a fantastic business for Comcast and many other cable companies. It has become a virtual necessity for most households to enable high-speed internet surfing, video games, virtual assistants like Alexa, and media consumption on an ever-increasing number of devices.

In the majority of its footprint, Comcast's broadband offering has a significant speed advantage over legacy telecom operators and satellite providers. In many of its markets, Comcast has a virtual monopoly on true high-speed broadband.

In addition, as Roberts made clear during the October 2017 earnings conference call quoted above, this business is not fully penetrated within Comcast's commercial and consumer customer footprints. Comcast continues to add new high-speed residential and business customers at an impressive clip. The combination of a growing subscriber base, customers mixing up to higher-speed packages, and annual price increases drove double-digit growth in this business.

This business is also higher-margin and less capital-intensive than the rest of the cable business. There is no set-top box or remote control involved as with a video subscription, and there is very limited variable cost. While the management of Comcast does not break out the profitability or FCF characteristics of this business, it would be logical to assume that high-speed broadband generates a disproportionate share of Comcast's EBITDA and FCF.

In contrast, Comcast's traditional video subscription business is the polar opposite of a quality business. It is capital-intensive, with high variable costs in the form of programming fees it pays to Disney, Discovery, Fox, Viacom, and other cable networks. Cable networks have raised prices well above inflation and well above what cable systems like Comcast can pass onto their subscribers, which has pressured video margins. These price increases have occurred despite the fact that the amount of time the average American spends watching linear[†] television declined every year between 2014 and 2017.[2]

And it gets worse. The growth of high-speed broadband has reduced the barriers for new market participants to enter the video business and decreased the need for cable video subscriptions. As cable networks have raised programming fees over time, the cost of a cable television subscription has increased. Additionally, the value proposition has diminished as Americans watch less and less linear television.

---

† Linear television includes traditional cable channels and the large broadcast networks. Streaming services like Netflix, Amazon Prime, Disney Plus, and YouTube have been and will likely continue to take share from traditional linear television.

In many markets, customers who don't care about sports pay bills that embed high prices for ESPN and their regional sports channels. This has spurred new market entrants that offer a lower-cost alternative or a "skinny bundle" with fewer channels through an over-the-top (OTT) solution that uses a customer's broadband to deliver channels virtually.

However, the bigger long-term threat is that the customer will no longer need a video subscription due to the plethora of diverse, high-quality content provided by low-cost services such as Netflix and quasi-free services such as Amazon Prime and YouTube. In addition, many of these services are commercial-free. This threat became even more pronounced in 2019–2020 when many of the strongest entertainment firms such as Disney (Disney+) and AT&T/Warner (HBO Max) launched their own premium streaming services centered around their extensive libraries of accumulated content and their unique ability to create new content from existing franchises.

A family could subscribe to Netflix, Disney+, and HBO Max for a fraction of what they paid for cable television, and have access to YouTube and Amazon Prime as well. The combination of declining viewership, increased pricing, and a more viable, lower-cost alternative appears to be creating a tipping point for traditional cable video subscriptions.

Cable video subscriptions had been declining at an accelerating rate even before the launch of Disney+ and HBO Max. The percentage of US households with a cable or satellite video subscription dropped from 87% in 2009 to 75% in 2017.[3]

The fundamentals and outlook for the broadband business and the video subscription business could not be more divergent.

If one were going to do a sum-of-parts analysis on a cable company trading at 8x EBITDA, it would be quite reasonable to put a materially higher valuation on the broadband business and a much lower valuation on the video subscription business.

As a result, no returns-focused management team or board would ever choose to double down on a video subscription business. Furthermore, no company with a majority of its cash flows coming from a high-multiple broadband business would pay a higher valuation multiple than where it is trading for a video subscription business. But that is exactly what Comcast did.

ENTER RUPERT MURDOCH

In 2017, media mogul Rupert Murdoch did something most media moguls would never do: he downsized. He decided to sell Fox's movie studio, regional sports networks, entertainment-focused cable networks, as well as its 39% interest in Sky Broadcasting (a UK, German, and Italian pay-TV satellite operator), and additional international assets. The new, much smaller Fox would be left with the Fox network, Fox News, and Fox Sports. This raises the question: when someone as smart as Rupert Murdoch is selling, do you really want to be buying?

Murdoch negotiated with both Comcast and Disney before coming to an agreement with Disney in December 2017 for a price of $52.4 billion. Comcast announced a competing bid of $65 billion, but in the end all it did was push up the price Disney paid to $71.3 billion. Comcast would drop its bid for Fox's assets in July of 2018 when it became clear that its chances of prevailing were extremely low.

In the middle of this bidding war for Fox, Comcast decided to make a bid for Sky Broadcasting. While Murdoch owned a majority stake in the voting shares of Fox and would have the final say on whom he would sell to, this was not true with Sky Broadcasting. Moreover, while there were potential antitrust concerns with Comcast buying Fox's cable channels, there was no overlap or antitrust risk associated with Comcast buying Sky Broadcasting.

Fox already owned 39% of Sky Broadcasting and had made multiple attempts to acquire the remaining 61% interest in the past. In fact, at the time Murdoch was negotiating with Disney and Comcast to sell a large portion of the Fox entertainment empire, Murdoch and Fox had an outstanding bid of £10.75 per share for the 61% of Sky Broadcasting that Fox did not own. Since Disney would now be acquiring Fox's 39% interest in Sky Broadcasting, Disney announced that it would honor Fox's existing bid for the remaining 61% of Sky Broadcasting. However, Comcast was eager to gain control of Sky Broadcasting and engaged in a bidding war with Fox/Disney.

As seen below, Comcast would repeatedly increase its bid and by September it would emerge victorious (see Figure 19.1).

FIGURE 19.1

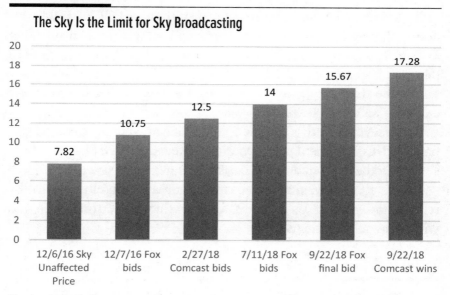

The Sky Is the Limit for Sky Broadcasting

Sky share price in £.

Note: While Fox was technically the bidder for Sky Broadcasting, it was bidding on behalf of Disney after Fox and Disney had come to an agreement on the sale of the majority of Fox's entertainment assets to Disney.

Source: Douglas Mitchelson, Brian Russo, Meghan Durkin, and Grant Joslin, *Comcast "Wins" Sky*, Credit Suisse, September 24, 2018, 5, accessed via FactSet.

THE COST OF VICTORY

However, victory here is in the eye of the beholder.

This price represented a 125% premium to Sky Broadcasting's unaffected stock price from two years earlier. On a USD basis, Comcast paid about $48.5 billion for Sky, including the assumption of debt.

At first glance, this appeared to be approximately 15x calendar year 2018 EBITDA of around $3.2 billion. However, due to accounting differences between IFRS and GAAP and other factors, Sky's pro forma EBITDA was only $2.9 billion. Moreover, this was a decline of 5.3% year-over-year on a constant currency basis.

In reality, Comcast had paid closer to 17x calendar year 2018 EBITDA for Sky.

While Sky never reported calendar year 2018 FCF, we know that in fiscal year 2018 Sky reported £456 million in FCF or £704 million excluding interest expense. This implies that Comcast paid 54x FCF to enterprise value and 69x on price to FCF basis (including interest expense).

At the time, Comcast was trading for 7.5x EBITDA and at 14x calendar year 2018 FCF.

Even if you were to add in the $500 million in synergies that Comcast promised, Comcast still paid 14x calendar year 2018 EBITDA on a fully synergized basis, excluding the costs to achieve those synergies.

Table 19.1 shows that Comcast paid a massive premium for Sky relative to where its own shares were trading at the time, with and without synergies included.

TABLE 19.1

Comcast Pays Huge Premium for Sky Relative to Its Own Valuation

	2018 EV/EBITDA	2018 Price to FCF
Comcast	7.5	14
Sky	17	69
Sky Premium	**127%**	**393%**
Sky (with synergies)	14	41
Sky Premium	**87%**	**193%**

Note: Using Sky's fiscal year 2018 for price to FCF versus Comcast calendar year. Used Sky calendar year EBITDA for 2018 (which Comcast disclosed) for the EV/EBITDA comparison. On a FCF basis this equates to a $40 billion purchase price divided by $581 USD FCF. In fiscal year 2018, Sky Broadcasting reported net cash from operating cash flows of £1.766 billion, capital expenditures and purchase of intangible assets of £1.185, dividends from joint ventures of £131 million, funding to joint ventures of £8, and interest paid of £248 million. Used conversion rate of 1.2746 Pounds to USD.

In addition to this premium, there other issues that made this a problematic acquisition, at best.

Slow growth in UK and Ireland market. In fiscal year 2018, the UK and Ireland represented 88% of Sky's operating profits. Sky's operating profits in this more mature market had grown over the last three years at less than 1% per year.

No competitive advantage in broadband assets. Unlike Comcast in the United States, Sky does not own its broadband assets and instead leases them from British Telecommunications. This reduces the profitability of the business and its competitive moat, in contrast to Comcast's near monopoly on true broadband in the United States within the majority of its footprint. In addition, although Sky was leader in broadband in the United Kingdom in 2018, there were multiple industry participants that were building or expanding their own broadband fiber footprints in the United Kingdom, including Liberty Global. This may erode Sky's market share over time.

All in all, Comcast paid a significant premium to the level at which its own shares were trading for an inferior business (see Table 19.2).

TABLE 19.2

Comcast Is Superior Business to Sky

	Comcast	Sky
2013–2018 Adjusted EPS Growth	15.5%	2.4%
2013–2018 FCF per Share Growth	10.5%	−16.7%
2018 EBITDA Margins	31.9%	17.3%

Notes: Sky reported £1.063 billion in FCF in 2013 and £456 million in FCF in 2018. Sky results represent fiscal years 2013–2018; Comcast results represent calendar years 2013–2018. Sky's growth rates were impacted by what appears to have been a dilutive transaction to buy out the public shareholders of Sky Italia and Sky Deutschland in November of 2014. The consolidation of these businesses appears to have been very negative on a FCF per share metric.

While Sky Broadcasting shareholders received a 125% premium,[†] Comcast shareholders suffered. Comcast shares underperformed the market by 15% between the initial bid for Sky in February and the "winning" of Sky in September. This cost equates to a roughly $26 billion relative loss for Comcast shareholders.

Yet, there must be something missing here. This just does not make sense.

When Comcast first announced that it was bidding for Sky Broadcasting, Comcast CEO Brian Roberts gave the following reasons:

1. Sky is an "outstanding" business
2. Gives Comcast scale
3. Likes Sky's content business
4. International diversification[4]

However, upon closer examination, these four claims were not entirely sound.

- **Sky is an "outstanding" business.** While there are undoubtedly worse businesses out there, Sky is not a great business. Great businesses grow revenues, earnings, and FCF at a faster pace than Sky has, and they don't face secular challenges.
- **Comcast needed scale.** In 2018, Comcast generated $30 billion in EBITDA and $12.6 billion in FCF. Acquiring Sky added $2.9 billion in EBITDA and far less than $1 billion in FCF. Even if scale were a strategic objective (which it probably should not be), Sky would not really move the needle.
- **Sky content.** Paying $48.5 billion for Sky's content is like buying a Ferrari because you need a cup holder for your coffee or going on vacation to get free shampoo. Sky's content generated only 6% of its revenues.

---

† Refers to where Sky's shares were trading before the Fox 2016 offer was made.

- **International diversification.** Investors own Comcast because it is a domestic, low-beta, low cyclical, steady-growth business. Investors who want more international exposure can diversify independently. International diversification also adds foreign exchange volatility to the financial results. This may make sense if the international business is growing faster—faster growth with added volatility may be a reasonable trade-off—but not when the business is a drag on overall growth.

  In addition, an international acquisition would make sense if it generated an attractive return on capital that more than compensated for higher foreign exchange volatility. In this case, the initial cash return on investment was less than 2%.

  Moreover, Comcast added a predominantly UK-based business during a period of heightened uncertainty surrounding Brexit. At the time, Comcast was taking on additional risk that a disorderly Brexit could pressure the UK economy, as well as reduce the value of the British pound. Both could put pressure on Sky's USD EBITDA and FCF.

  While I generally support firms deploying capital during a period of uncertainty, it makes sense only if the uncertainty creates the potential for an elevated return on capital. This is clearly not the case with Comcast's acquisition of Sky Broadcasting.

Now, to be fair to Mr. Roberts and Comcast, Sky Broadcasting is not as poorly positioned as a US satellite operator or even a US cable television subscription business. Sky Broadcasting has non-pay-TV businesses like high-speed internet, as well as an entertainment and news content business. Cable and satellite penetration in markets such as Germany, where Sky operates, is still much lower than in the United States.

In addition, Comcast management has created significant value for its shareholders over the last decade, despite the 2018 Sky-induced drawdown. Over the 10-year period ending in December of 2018, Comcast delivered a total return of 387% relative to a 243%

total return for the S&P 500. During that time, Comcast returned over $55 billion to shareholders in dividends and share repurchases.

Furthermore, there is a reasonable possibility that Comcast will improve Sky Broadcasting beyond what it has publicly articulated, if history is any guide. The management of Comcast has a well-earned reputation for being good operators. They turned around NBC Universal after buying it from GE in 2011 (announced in December 2009). NBCU's EBITDA increased from $3.1 billion in 2009 to $8.6 billion in 2018. NBCU almost certainly generated more FCF than all of GE Industrial in 2018.

The problem is, no matter how well Comcast runs Sky, the returns from buying it will be inferior to buying back stock under almost every conceivable scenario. In addition, Comcast diluted the quality of its portfolio by increasing exposure to the secularly challenged pay-TV business and, in doing so, diluted the portion of cash flows coming from the monopoly broadband business. In the end, this was empire building by a company and its controlling shareholder that destroyed shareholder value.

In Chapter 13, I talked about the powerful M&A flywheel of value creation when a firm can buy better businesses for lower multiples than its own trading level. However, a negative flywheel of value destruction can also be created when a firm consistently buys lower quality businesses for higher valuations. The addition of lower quality businesses will result in slower revenue and cash flow growth and/or higher cyclicality/volatility. In addition, investors will put a discounted valuation on the firm relative to its peers in an attempt to compensate for the risk of value-destructive M&A in the future.

CHAPTER 20

Low-Return, Strategic Acquisitions: A Cautionary Tale

While competitors poured flames on our market share, what happened at Nokia? We fell behind, we missed big trends, and we lost time. At that time, we thought we were making the right decisions; but with the benefit of hindsight, we now find ourselves years behind.

The first iPhone shipped in 2007, and we don't have a product that is close to their experience. Android came on the scene just over two years ago, and this week they took over our leadership position in smartphone volumes. Unbelievable. . . .

Our competitors aren't taking our market share with devices; they are taking our market share with an entire ecosystem. This means we're going to have to decide how we either build, catalyze or join an ecosystem."

—**Stephen Elop,** CEO of Nokia, "Burning Platform" Memo[1]

Fifteen years prior to Elop's (infamous) memo, Nokia had become the global market leader in mobile phones. It experienced explosive growth between 1996 and 2001 with sales increasing almost fivefold. At its zenith, Nokia had a market capitalization of greater than $250 billion.

However, by the summer of 2013 Nokia was struggling and was in a far worse position financially and competitively than when CEO Stephen Elop had written his "Burning Platform" memo in 2011. This proud Finnish company that had started as a paper mill almost 150 years earlier was bleeding hundreds of millions of cash in its core mobile phone business per quarter with no end in sight.

The mobile phone business had begun to evolve in the mid-2000s with the emergence of smartphones that could do more than simply make phone calls, email, and text. Today, we tend to think of the launch of the Apple iPhone in 2007 as the start of the smartphone era. However, less feature-rich smartphones had been around for years, and in fact, in 2007, Nokia had around a 50% market share of the global smartphone market.

However, by the summer of 2013 Nokia's market capitalization had declined by more than 90% from its highs, its stock price was languishing in the low-single digits, and it was bleeding market share. Nokia's share of the global smartphone market had collapsed to 3%. The launch of the iPhone from Apple in 2007 and Google's commercial launch of the Android operating system in 2008 had squeezed Nokia at both the high and low ends of the smartphone market.

THE NOKIA MICROSOFT BET

Two years earlier, Nokia had made a big bet to turn around its mobile phone business by partnering with Microsoft (MSFT). Microsoft, which owned the dominant operating system for personal computers used by consumers and businesses for decades, was very worried about its almost nonexistent market share of mobile phone operating systems. Microsoft had entered this market very late. In fact, Microsoft CEO Steve Ballmer had famously laughed at the iPhone upon its introduction in 2007 and said it had "no chance" of gaining significant market share. However, by 2011, Ballmer was keenly focused on improving Microsoft's market share in mobile phone operating systems. Meanwhile, Nokia was debating whether to standardize around Android, continue with its own Symbian operating system, or partner with Microsoft.

In 2011, Nokia bet the company on Microsoft. Nokia agreed to transition all of its smartphones to the Microsoft operating system over a two-year period and discontinue its own Symbian operating system. Microsoft would, in turn, pay Nokia "billions" to help facilitate this transition as well as prevent Nokia from adopting Android. Nokia would also agree to make Microsoft Bing the default search engine on all Nokia phones. Additionally, Nokia would contribute its mapping business to the Microsoft mobile operating system to strengthen it.

From the Microsoft perspective, this deal would be compelling if Nokia could stabilize its smartphone share. Nokia still had a high-twenties share of global smartphone units in the fourth quarter of 2010, and Microsoft needed scale in its operating system to be a viable long-term player.

Why was share so important? Operating systems are essentially the brains of a smartphone. When an app like Uber, Weather Channel, or MarketWatch is developed for a smartphone, every operating system requires a specific version to be written for it. If there were 10 operating systems and a developer wanted to be on all mobile phones, it would need to re-create the app 10 times. This could be cost prohibitive. However, if it could write the app for two or three operating systems that represented 95% of all mobile devices, it could simply ignore the last 5% of the market. This is especially relevant for smaller developers and lower-volume apps.

While the quality of the hardware still mattered, for consumers, having a robust app store with a competitive number of apps was quickly becoming table stakes. Why would consumers choose to buy a phone if only 30 of the 50 apps they used were available on it? The answer is, in most cases, they wouldn't. Microsoft needed scale in mobile phone operating systems or it was dead. If it did not capture scale, Microsoft would never have a competitive app store. Nokia was its last hope.

Not only would this partnership provide Microsoft with much-needed scale, but it would be able to earn a "competitive" license fee of around $10 per phone for its operating system software. If Nokia had been able to maintain its high-twenties market share and convert all of its smartphones to the Microsoft operating system, this could have generated hundreds of millions in high-margin software revenue for Microsoft in a rapidly growing market as consumers moved from traditional mobile phones to smartphones. Making Bing the default option on Nokia phones might have helped on the margin, but consumers could just use the Google app instead of the default search option.

While we don't know how much Microsoft was paying Nokia, except that it was in the billions, it is fairly likely that this was a strategically and financially reasonable deal for Microsoft at the time. If Nokia had chosen to go with Android, Microsoft's chances of ever achieving a sufficient share of mobile phone operating systems to have a viable long-term business would have been close to zero.

WHY THE DEAL FAILED

Unfortunately for Microsoft and Nokia, this agreement did not work out. In retrospect, it was consummated too late. Nokia's smartphone market share fell dramatically between the fourth quarter of 2010 (high-twenties share) and the second quarter of 2013 (3% share). While Nokia still sold 54 million mobile phones in the second quarter of 2013, only 12 million were smartphones and only 7 million of those used the Microsoft operating system.

Consumers did not want a phone with the Microsoft operating system. And so, despite the billions in payments from Microsoft to Nokia, Nokia's core mobile phone business was still burning cash. Nokia needed a new strategy.

Nokia basically had three options:

1. Attempt to exit the agreement with Microsoft and adopt the Android operating system, which would allow its users to access a competitive number of apps.
2. Double down on the partnership with Microsoft in return for more cash and financial support.
3. Sell the money-losing business to Microsoft.

By far, the best-case scenario was to sell.

On September 3, 2013, Microsoft announced that it would acquire Nokia's mobile device business and license many of its patents for $7.2 billion and hire 32,000 Nokia employees. Not surprisingly, MSFT investors were disappointed about doubling down on a failed strategy. Microsoft's stock price fell by 6%, and it lost $13 billion in market capitalization (almost twice the cash it would pay to Nokia). Microsoft was adding a money-losing business with 23% gross margins, while at the time MSFT's core business was generating very attractive 74% gross margins. The acquisition would be dilutive to earnings, potentially reduce capital return to shareholders, lower margins, and lower returns on capital.

While MSFT promised the deal would be nicely accretive to EPS by 2016, the justification was based on some very aggressive assumptions. MSFT said it would need to sell 50 million smartphones with the MSFT operating system to reach breakeven levels, well up from the current 30 million annualized pace. Microsoft also estimated that it would be able to increase smartphone unit sales with its operating systems to 250 million by June 2018. That would represent an amazing 833% growth in five years. Whenever you need 833% growth to justify an acquisition, you probably shouldn't be making the acquisition.

Nokia shareholders reacted very positively to this news. Nokia's stock price rallied 34%, adding $5 billion to the company's market capitalization. Most of the sell-side analysts covering Nokia raised their sum-of-parts analyses and price targets. Overnight, Nokia was transformed from a negative cash flow business with a low 4% operating margin to a pure-play telecom equipment business with positive cash flow, a strong balance sheet, and double-digit operating margins. In addition, Nokia kept its $500 million annual royalty revenue from the licensing of its mobile phone patents.

If Microsoft had the better deal in the 2011 agreement, Nokia clearly had the advantage in 2013.

The problem for Microsoft was that the die was already cast. Consumers did not want phones with the Microsoft operating system. Apple and Google/Android had become the dominant smartphone operating systems, and app developers were designing for those two operating systems. Microsoft was never going to have a competitive app store offering, and without that the business just was not viable.

In addition, the smartphone business had become much more competitive, especially at the low end of the market. The launch of Google Android as a low-cost operating system had enabled more hardware-focused Chinese OEMs to enter the market. These new players were successfully manufacturing low-cost smartphones and leveraging the Android operating system to run their devices. Without Android, they would have faced the same challenges as Microsoft and Nokia: insufficient scale to entice developers to write apps for their phones and incremental costs associated with designing and maintaining their own operating systems.

This wave of Chinese OEMs flooding the market with low-cost smartphones led to commoditization at the low end of the market and drove significant downward price pressure. This was the business in which Microsoft had chosen to double down—a more commoditized hardware business with an operating system that lacked sufficient scale to be viable.

By 2015, Microsoft had new leadership, and it had written off almost the entire Nokia acquisition purchase price. Of the 32,000 Nokia employees that had joined Microsoft in the acquisition, more than 80% had been laid off. In 2016, Microsoft would sell its remaining mobile phone business for $350 million to HMD and Foxconn.

The Microsoft acquisition of Nokia's mobile phone business is an example of a low-return, strategic acquisition.

But what does *strategic* really mean? The Merriam-Webster online dictionary entry for *strategic* includes the following definitions: "necessary to or important in the initiation, conduct, or completion of a strategic plan" and "of great importance within an integrated whole or to a planned effect."[2] I would certainly hope that all the acquisitions a firm undertakes can be defined as strategic. Acquisitions should fit with a firm's long-term strategy as well as enable the business to grow, generate attractive returns, and enhance long-term shareholder wealth.

THE PROBLEM WITH STRATEGIC ACQUISITIONS

For whatever reason, however, the term *strategic acquisition* has come to represent something completely different over time. Today, when a firm characterizes an acquisition as "strategic" it is all too often a euphemism for low return.

I would also argue that larger companies such as Microsoft with Nokia are more willing to enter into strategic acquisitions, especially if the deal is small relative to the size of the existing business or the free cash flow the firm generates. Firms with significant excess cash flow or balance sheet flexibility are often more willing to lower their return thresholds to make a low-return, purely strategic acquisition. While Nokia was a large deal in absolute terms, it was small relative to Microsoft's cash on the balance sheet, its market capitalization, and its free cash flow.

The tragedy of these deals for companies is that the cumulation of a series of relatively small strategic deals can still torpedo returns on capital, operating margins, growth rates, and, in the case of General Electric, its balance sheet.

Purely strategic acquisitions tend to have one or more of the following four characteristics:

1. Undertaken for purposes other than generating an attractive ROIC on a deal.

2. Entry into a new business or market that is tangential to the firm's existing business.
3. Defense. If the firm does not make the acquisition, the long-term health and potentially the viability of the existing business could be negatively impacted.
4. Pursuit of limited opportunities. There are few potential acquisitions in an attractive, fast-growing market niche, and if the firm does not make the acquisition, it will struggle to gain significant share or participate in the growth of the attractive market niche.

The Microsoft acquisition of Nokia's mobile phone business had all four of these characteristics. The "strategic" rationale for the deal was the long-term risk that increasingly sophisticated phones and other form factors such as tablets could reduce consumer, and maybe even business, demand for personal computers. Microsoft dominated both the operating system software for PCs as well as the most-used PC application software such as Word, Excel, Exchange, and PowerPoint. Collectively, these software franchises generated a massive profit pool for the company. Microsoft had to win in mobile phone operating systems to protect this profit pool from this potential long-term risk. Or so it thought.

Even if one ignores the negative consequences of deploying shareholder capital with unattractive returns, there are four main reasons for boards and management teams to avoid the purely strategic acquisition.

The Tendency to Overestimate the Need for the Acquisition

Time and again, firms that enter into purely strategic acquisitions with low returns for defensive purposes structurally overestimate the importance of the acquisition. In most cases, the acquisition, even if executed perfectly, fails to achieve its strategic objective.

Microsoft is a perfect example. The failure of the Nokia acquisition and its inability to gain a foothold in smartphone operating systems did not doom the company. Within six years of the Nokia acquisition announcement, Microsoft's stock price had more than quadrupled and the company achieved a market capitalization of greater than $1 trillion. It turns out that being a viable player in mobile phone operating systems really did not matter. Microsoft's keys to success were:

- Making the right investments in the core business
- Building a world-class cloud platform with Azure
- Developing consumer productivity software that its customers could access on non-PC devices, competitors' devices, and in the cloud
- Returning excess capital to shareholders

In 2018, the year Microsoft was supposed to sell 250 million phones and instead sold none, Microsoft's revenues grew 14%, operating profits grew 20%, and EPS grew 18%. This is a truly amazing feat for a company the size of Microsoft with $110 billion in sales.

Acquisitions Rarely Help the Core Business

If there is one thing just about everyone agrees on with acquisitions, it is that revenue synergies rarely come to fruition. Buying an asset to jump-start growth in the core business or to strengthen the core business is a flawed strategy.

The Desire to Enter a More Attractive Niche Without a Return Threshold Does Not Make Sense

Every once in a while, a company will announce an expensive strategic acquisition using the justification that it is entering an attractive space with limited available acquisitions—essentially "it is now or never." I dispute the "now or never" argument for a couple of reasons.

First, an important part of value-accretive M&A is finding situations in which supply and demand are on your side. If there are only one or two companies in an attractive market niche, the chance of generating a good return for shareholders is very low, as multiple industry participants will likely bid for these attractive properties.

Second, if your firm operates in markets that are growing 3% and you are exploring the acquisition of a business operating in a market growing 6%, how many years do you have to extrapolate the growth of the new business to justify the acquisition?

Essentially, how far in the future do you need to forecast this strong growth rate to justify the acquisition as a better use of capital than other alternatives? If it is within 5 or 6 years, that makes a lot of sense. However, when you need 10 or 15 years of 6% growth to justify the acquisition, that seems like a stretch. The future is far more uncertain than what the acquisition spreadsheet might say. Businesses with abnormal growth rates attract new competitors and the law of large numbers sometimes catches up to these market niches.

The Curse of White Space

In June of 2016, it was reported that Mondelez made a $23 billion bid to acquire Hershey for $107 per share. At the time, Mondelez had a strong share in chocolate in Europe and many emerging markets but lacked a strong presence in the United States. Hershey had a strong presence in chocolate in the United States but had struggled to gain a presence internationally.

The acquisition of Hershey by Mondelez would have been strategic in that it would have allowed Mondelez to gain a stronger presence in the United States. However, is filling a geographic hole in the portfolio a reason to make an acquisition? I would argue that, in and of itself, it is not. In the case of Mondelez, being bigger in US chocolate would not have helped the European or emerging market chocolate business unless you believe in revenue synergies, and you should not. In fact, in this case, there would be sizable revenue dis-synergies because Hershey would most likely have lost its perpetual license for Kit Kat in the United States in a takeout.

The acquisition would also slow Mondelez's organic growth rate by diluting the percentage of its business coming from faster growth emerging markets by doubling down on a primarily domestic business. While we don't have all the details on the proposed transaction, we do know the deal would have involved Mondelez leveraging up its balance sheet to more than 4x debt to EBITDA. This would have limited financial flexibility for multiple years following the acquisition. It would most likely have been significantly dilutive to returns on capital as well.

Last, increasing Mondelez's presence in chocolate with an industry backdrop of accelerating online grocery delivery might result in lower future revenues as impulse sales, like candy and chocolate, could be negatively impacted long term. Children, and sometimes even adults, waiting in a long checkout line all too often succumb to the guilty pleasure of a chocolate bar. Unless your six-year-old handles your online grocery ordering, the chances of adding a chocolate bar to your purchases are much lower than when checking out in an actual grocery store.

If Mondelez had been successful in acquiring Hershey, it would have created a truly global chocolate business with leading market shares in Europe, the United States and many emerging markets. But filling this strategic white space would have come at a significant cost. It would have resulted in a lower return on capital, a slower growth rate, a much more leveraged balance sheet, diminished financial flexibility, and a more structurally challenged business in the long term.

There is absolutely nothing wrong with plugging a hole in a portfolio, whether it is a product, location, or service that the company is missing. However, filling a hole or white space should never be the sole or primary determinant of whether to make an acquisition.

WHEN IS IT ACCEPTABLE TO MAKE A LOW-RETURN STRATEGIC ACQUISITION?

Are there circumstances when it is acceptable to make a low-return, purely strategic acquisition? Yes, in the following two scenarios:

Compelling Evidence That Not Acquiring Would Negatively Impact the Core Business

There could be a situation in which customers' purchasing behaviors evolve to require a bundled set of solutions, products, or services. If the business lacks one or more of these products or services, it may be necessary to make a low-return, strategic acquisition. In this case, while the return on the acquisition might be low, the overall returns might suffer even more if the firm failed to consummate an acquisition that delivers the competitive solution, product, or service. This scenario is exceedingly rare, however, and companies often overplay the importance of a bundled solution when their customer base increasingly wants best of breed solutions.

Potential for New Industry Participant That Could Negatively Impact Industry Economics

It is possible a firm could find itself in a situation in which a firm known for aggressive pricing is bidding for a competitor. If that competitor were to fall into the hands of a firm with a reputation for aggressive pricing, a willingness to accept lower operating margins, or a plan to use the acquired goods or services as a loss leader to strengthen its core business, existing industry participants would suffer. For example, there could be an industry in which six to eight businesses control 80% of the market and all earn 15–20% operating margins with double-digit returns on capital. If one of those firms were sold to a firm willing to accept 5% operating margins and low-to-mid-single-digit returns on capital, there could be a real risk that industry cash flows would reset materially lower upon this transaction. In such a case, it might make sense for one industry participant to outbid a new price-aggressive entrant even if that meant generating a low return. Again, while the return might be subpar when viewed in isolation, the aggregate returns for the company (and the industry) would likely be higher in the long run. Still, I would characterize this as a very rare scenario.

CONCLUSION

In a perfect world, firms would not feel the need to make low-return, strategic acquisitions. If a firm feels compelled to make such an acquisition, it should be small relative to its market capitalization and enterprise value. Such situations should be exceedingly rare. Management and the board should also be highly confident, using both an inside and outside view, in achieving their ultimate strategic objective with the acquisition. Trying to solve a strategic challenge by throwing a Hail Mary pass, as Microsoft did with Nokia, is rarely a panacea for the company. It is far more likely to be a recipe for disaster and result in a firm's failure to achieve its financial and strategic objectives.

CHAPTER 21

Supply/Demand Imbalance

Prostate cancer is the most common form of cancer in men. With the exception of lung cancer, it kills more men than any other form of cancer. According to a paper published in the *World Journal of Oncology*, in 2018 alone, 1.3 million men were diagnosed with prostate cancer and 359,000 died.[1]

Metastatic prostate cancer is prostate cancer that has spread to other organs such as the lymph nodes, bones, lungs, or liver. While prostate cancer survival rates have improved dramatically over the last couple of decades, especially in developed countries, metastatic prostate cancer is more serious and has a lower survival rate.

Given the high incidence of prostate cancer, and in particular the dangers associated with metastatic prostate cancer, this area has been viewed as a large market opportunity for any pharmaceutical company that could develop a drug to treat patients burdened by this disease. Medivation had such a drug.

MEDIVATION'S STORY

In 2012, Medivation, a midsized pharmaceutical firm, received approval for Xtandi, a drug used to treat post-chemotherapy prostate cancer patients. Two years later, Medivation received a label expansion that allowed Xtandi to be used prior to chemotherapy.

In the pre-chemotherapy setting, a patient was likely to be on the drug longer than in the post-chemotherapy setting. The number of potential patients was also much larger.

In the six months following the label expansion, Medivation's stock rose from the mid-forties to the mid-sixties.

In addition to its indication for the treatment of metastatic prostate cancer, Medivation had multiple ongoing trials, including one that could extend Xtandi into non-metastatic and hormone-sensitive prostate cancers as well as advanced triple-negative breast cancer. If these trials were successful, they would expand the drug's addressable market and increase its peak sales potential.

Xtandi competed against Zytiga from Johnson & Johnson and a generic drug called Casodex. Medivation's patents on Xtandi were scheduled to last through 2026 in Europe and 2027 in the United States.

Medivation shared the economics of Xtandi with Astellas, a Japanese pharmaceutical company, as part of a 2009 agreement whereby Medivation would sell Xtandi in the United States and receive 50% of the revenues. Astellas was responsible for international sales and paid royalties on these ex-US sales to Medivation. Medivation had one drug in its pipeline: an earlier stage immuno-oncology agent called pidilizumab. It purchased another pipeline asset in 2015 from BioMarin called talazoparib that was in a phase 3 trial for BRCA-mutated breast cancer.

US Xtandi sales had risen rapidly from $57 million in the fourth quarter of 2012 to $144 million in the second quarter of 2014, before any benefit from the new label expansion. With the expanded label, sales rose to $230 million in the fourth quarter of 2014. As a result of this explosive growth, by mid-2015, the sell-side analyst consensus estimates for 2019 US Xtandi revenues had risen to more than $3 billion.

But beginning in the fall of 2015, something unexpected occurred. Prescription trends for Xtandi, which were anticipated to continue growing rapidly, didn't. Xtandi's US sales grew much more slowly than expected over the next three quarters, as shown in Figures 21.1 and 21.2. This slowdown would call into question the ultimate market opportunity for Xtandi. By February of 2016, Medivation shares had declined by 60% from their recent peak.

US Xtandi sales beat sell-side expectations almost every quarter between the first quarter of 2012 and the fourth quarter of 2014. However, US Xtandi sales would go on to miss sell-side consensus expectations four out of the next six quarters, between the first quarter of 2015 and second quarter of 2016.

Why were US Xtandi revenues stalling out?

- **Xtandi vs. Zytiga:** Xtandi was more expensive than Johnson & Johnson's Zytiga, which made it difficult to gain market share.
- **Urologists:** Medivation struggled to persuade enough urologists to prescribe Xtandi over other alternatives.

In addition, there were other concerns about Xtandi that weighed on Medivation's stock price:

- **Generic Zytiga:** There was some concern about the future competitive environment. Johnson & Johnson's patent protection on Zytiga was expected to expire in 2018 or 2019, which could facilitate the introduction of a low-cost generic version onto the market. A much lower-cost alternative to Xtandi could have a negative impact on Xtandi's market share. If Xtandi was already struggling to gain significant market share from Zytiga, what would happen in the future when a low-cost generic version of Zytiga was available?
- **New competition:** Both Johnson & Johnson and Bayer were running phase 3 trials for new drugs to treat prostate cancer. If either of these drugs were superior to Xtandi with respect to efficacy, side effects, or both, they could limit Xtandi's sales potential or cause revenues to decline.

FIGURE 21.1

US Xtandi Sales[2]

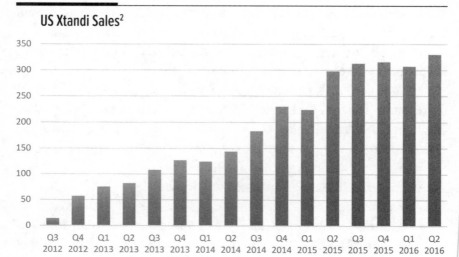

Note: In millions of dollars

FIGURE 21.2

US Xtandi Q/Q Sales Growth[3]

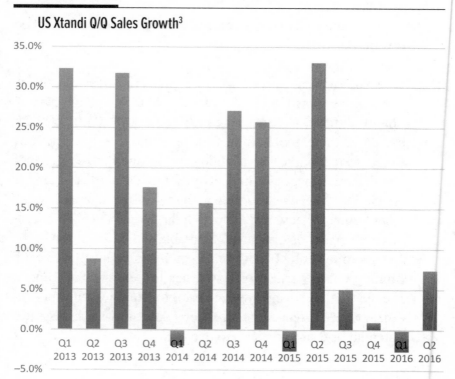

However, fundamentals would soon take a backseat to the prospect of Medivation being acquired.

MEDIVATION TAKEOVER BATTLE TIMELINE

Takeover battles often move quickly and dramatically. The Medivation takeover was no exception and involved multiple players and multiple bids.

- On March 22, 2016, Olivier Brandicourt, the CEO of Sanofi, a French pharmaceutical company that was struggling with declines in its diabetes franchise, contacted Medivation's CEO David Hung, MD. Sanofi was interested in buying Medivation, which set off a fierce takeover battle for control of Medivation and its cancer drug.
- On March 24, Medivation's board responded by hiring JP Morgan as an advisor.
- In late March, the press got wind of Sanofi's interest in Medivation and the fact that Medivation had hired bankers.
- On April 3, Dr. Hung informed Olivier Brandicourt that Medivation was not interested in discussing a potential sale of the company.
- On April 15, Sanofi offered to buy Medivation for $52.50, subject to future due diligence. This offer was not disclosed publicly at the time.
- On April 20, an executive from Pfizer reached out to Dr. Hung to say that Pfizer would like to be included in any strategic review process that Medivation would undertake. In other words, if Medivation chose to sell, Pfizer wanted a seat at the bidding table.
- On April 28, Sanofi publicly announced its $52.50 bid for Medivation.
- On April 29, Medivation announced that its board of directors had rejected Sanofi's bid.

- On May 5, Sanofi went hostile. Sanofi threatened to "remove and replace" the board of Medivation if it did not engage with Sanofi concerning its takeover bid. After the stock market close on May 5th, Medivation reported Xtandi's US sales were $308 million in the quarter. **This represented a quarter-over-quarter decline of 3%.** It was 7 points below consensus expectations and reflected the third consecutive quarter of lower than anticipated sales for Medivation's only approved drug. Xtandi had effectively stopped growing. In addition, Medivation missed consensus EPS expectations by 50%. But Sanofi kept coming.
- On May 25, Sanofi followed through with its threat to start a process that could lead to the removal of Medivation's eight board members and their replacement by directors selected by Sanofi.
- On June 21–22, the Medivation board reversed course and began a process that would eventually lead to the sale of the company. The board directed its bankers to determine who might have an interest in acquiring Medivation and what they would be willing to pay.
- In late June, Medivation and its bankers contacted 12 companies, including Pfizer and 4 others that had expressed interest after the press reported on Sanofi's interest.
- On June 27, Sanofi offered $58 per share along with a $3 contingent value right (CVR), dependent on the achievement of various future revenue targets. A CVR should be thought of as an option. If a company hits a revenue target or if a future clinical trial outcome is positive, the holder of the CVR can receive up to the face value of the CVR (in this case $3). Following an acquisition, a CVR will trade like a stock or an option in the open market until the revenue target is met or missed, or the clinical trial succeeds or fails.
- On June 30, Medivation once again rejected the Sanofi bid. However, the board also invited Sanofi to join in the strategic review process.

- Between July 7 and July 13, Medivation entered into confidential agreements with five potential acquirers, which provided them access to nonpublic information and allowed them to perform due diligence on Medivation.
- From July 15 to 21, the management team of Medivation gave a series of in-person presentations to each of the potential bidders.
- On July 19–20, Medivation's bankers asked for preliminary bids by August 8 from the five parties.
- On August 3, CVS Health announced that Xtandi would be one of 29 drugs that would be excluded from its 2017 formulary. This action would make it more difficult for CVS Health's tens of millions of pharmacy benefit members to receive Xtandi for the treatment of prostate cancer. Did this impact the bidding? Nope.
- On August 8, Pfizer bid $65 in cash for Medivation. Two other firms offered purely cash deals, one for $71 and another for $62–$64. Two other firms offered cash plus contingent value rights, one for $60 in cash and a $10 CVR and another for $63 and a $5 CVR.
- On August 9, Medivation reported that US Xtandi sales once again missed consensus estimates.
- On August 10, Medivation's board planned to reduce the bidders from five to three. However, the next day, the two firms that had been told their bids were not high enough revised them to $70 and $70.50 in cash.
- On August 14, Medivation bankers asked for definitive proposals from the five remaining bidders.
- On August 19, four of the five firms submitted bids with Pfizer at $77 and the other three at $72.50, $73, and $75.50. On that same day, the four bidders were told to send in their final and best offer. That night, one of the four remaining decided that it would not increase its bid.
- On August 20, Pfizer bid $81.50 and the two other companies offered $80.25 and $80. All the bids were in cash and there were no CVRs. On that same day Medivation's board accepted the Pfizer bid and publicly announced its decision.

In the end, Pfizer won the takeover battle with a bid of $81.50, which valued Medivation at $14 billion on an enterprise value basis.

FIGURE 21.3

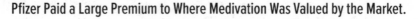

Pfizer Paid a Large Premium to Where Medivation Was Valued by the Market.

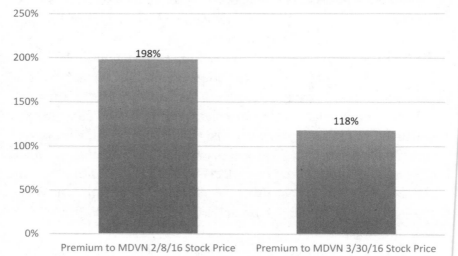

Note: The March 30, 2016, price was the "unaffected price" or the price where Medivation shares were trading prior to press reports that it had been approached to sell the company.

The Medivation management team provided its bankers with internal projections for sales, margins, and FCF through 2032. Medivation's bankers used these inputs to create a discounted cash flow (DCF) valuation for Medivation's shares under three scenarios, shown in Table 21.1.

Based on my reading of the proxy statement, all of these scenarios assumed different degrees of success for Xtandi in multiple new indications/therapies as well as the successful launch of its two pipeline products. It does not appear that Medivation's bankers used additional inputs beyond management's internal projections when creating these discounted cash flow (DCF) analyses.

TABLE 21.1

Scenarios for Medivation's Performance[4]

	2022 Sales	2027 Sales	Low-End DCF	High-End of DCF
Scenario 1	3,634	5,721	$62.70	$76.70
Scenario 2	3,699	7,347	$68.50	$84.40
Scenario 3	3,870	8,523	$74.10	$93.25

What I find fascinating about these management projections is that they are substantially higher than the consensus estimates from the sell-side analysts who covered Medivation. While most did not publish a 2027 estimate in 2016, their 2022 estimates indicate how aggressive these management assumptions appear. (See Figures 21.4, 21.5, and 21.6.)

FIGURE 21.4

Medivation's 2022 Consensus Revenue Expectations[5]

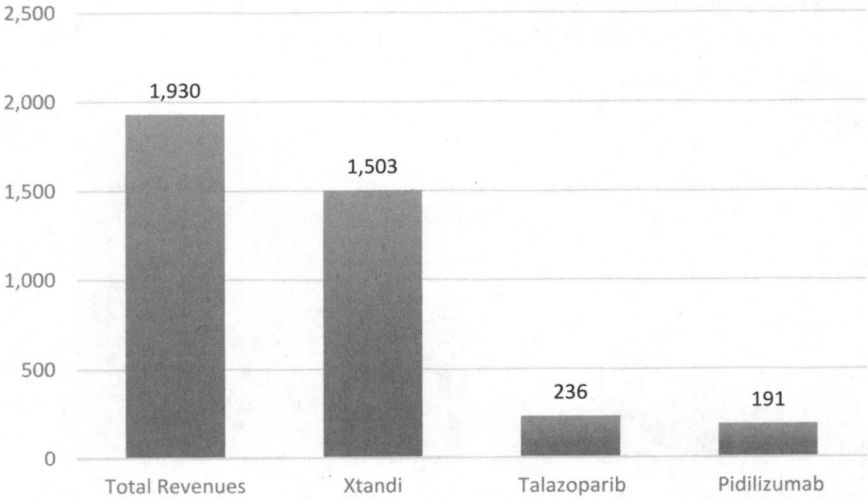

Notes: Bloomberg consensus expectations as of April 28, 2016, as cited in Eric Schmidt and Cristina Ghenoiu, *Medivation: Caution Ahead: All Signs Point to a Xtandi Slowdown*, Cowen and Company, July 29, 2015. Xtandi sales are 50% of total Xtandi US Sales + International Xtandi royalties.

FIGURE 21.5

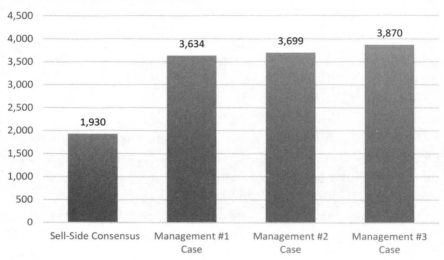

2022 Medivation Revenue Expectations[6]

FIGURE 21.6

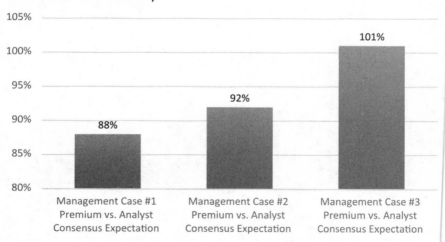

Management Revenue Projections Appear Aggressive (Percentage Premium Versus 2022 Consensus)[7]

Note: Comparing Medivation proxy projections in 2022 with sell-side consensus estimates as of April 28, 2016.

Management estimates were not just a little bit higher than consensus, they were 88–101% higher than the consensus estimates for 2022. Extrapolating these industry-expert estimates out to 2027, it would be very easy to argue that the proxy's DCF values were more than double what they would have been if the bankers had used sell-side industry analyst projections instead of management projections.

Another way to illustrate this point is to consider that Medivation's 2016 revenue projections were $922 million according to the proxy. Scenario 2 (see Table 21.1) predicted revenues ramping up to $7.3 billion by 2027. That is a 21% annual growth rate for the next 11 years!

To be fair, it would be logical to assume that Pfizer's cost of capital would be lower than Medivation's. Thus, the Medivation portfolio would be worth more inside of Pfizer than as a stand-alone entity. If Medivation management's far-above-consensus projections ended up being accurate, it is likely that the DCF value to Pfizer would be greater than the high end of the DCF value used in the three scenarios.

In addition, one might argue that I am ignoring the potential cost synergies that Pfizer might be able to wring out in this acquisition, which is a fair observation. However, the three scenarios already assumed extremely high operating margins in 2027 (79.5%, 79.7%, and 77.3% respectively). Pfizer's operating margins in 2015 were 36.3%. Best-in-class biotech firms can sometimes achieve mid-fifties operating margins.

Even assuming a lower cost of capital and cost synergies from the transaction, it still appears that Pfizer paid a hefty price for Medivation that would require extraordinary sales growth, sky-high margins, success with Xtandi indication expansion, and future pipeline success to generate reasonable cash-on-cash returns for Pfizer.

Why was Pfizer willing to pay a 118% premium (see Figure 21.3) to Medivation's unaffected stock price and, more important, why were two other companies willing to pay almost the same price? Remember, this is not a situation in which Pfizer paid a massive premium to the other bidders. Pfizer and two other companies were all willing to pay essentially the same price.

The answer comes down to these firms' desperation for a growing asset with intermediate-term patent protection in an attractive part of the pharmaceutical market. These types of assets can support a firm's revenue growth and help overcome the headwinds associated with patent protection expirations.

Pfizer's acquisition of Medivation highlights the challenge of engaging in M&A in a space where there is a supply/demand imbalance that heavily favors sellers. While this challenge is not limited to the pharmaceutical industry, it is most pronounced there, given past consolidation, structural industry changes, and the limited patent life of most pharmaceutical products.

BIG PHARMA'S QUEST FOR GROWTH

One of the challenges for big pharma and increasingly big biotech (Biogen, Abbvie, Amgen, Gilead) is the companies' massive size, with each having more than $10 billion in revenues. Many large pharmaceutical companies such as Pfizer, Bristol-Myers, GSK, and Astra-Zeneca are products of large, mostly cost-driven mergers and, in some cases, multiple, large mergers. In addition, many are victims of their own success. They develop a drug with good clinical outcomes, such as Lipitor or Crestor to lower cholesterol, but then struggle to develop a new drug that is materially better once their innovative drug goes generic and the price drops dramatically.

In 2005, about 60% of drugs dispensed in the United States were generics. By 2018, 90% were. From a purely dispensing perspective, branded pharmaceuticals have lost 75% of their market share to generics over the last 13 years![8]

As a result of mergers and past success in developing efficacious drugs, many of these companies have struggled to replace their massive revenue bases through organic, internal R&D. Pharma companies, unlike most other businesses, operate on a treadmill. If they fail to introduce new, innovative drugs that are safe and much more effective than low-cost generic alternatives, their business can literally vanish in a little more than a decade.

Today, the pharmaceutical industry faces two additional structural challenges.

The PBM Industry

The pharmacy benefit manager (PBM) industry has consolidated over the years, and its power and influence over drug pricing has become a thorn in the side of the pharmaceutical industry. Each of the large PBMs operates a formulary that functions like an "auction for volume" for a class of drugs that are not highly differentiated. In these cases, the PBM will provide a pharmaceutical company with increased market share in return for a big volume discount.

While the PBM's clients can still access drugs that are not on the formulary, the consumer may have to pay higher out-of-pocket costs and/or the prescribing doctor may have to jump through multiple hoops.

In addition, new drugs that are only modestly better than the generic alternative struggle to gain acceptance because cost-benefit analysis does not justify their use. This issue is most pronounced in areas such as cholesterol and respiratory, which once generated multiple billions in revenues annually but have since seen a rise in the availability of highly efficacious generics. This has greatly diminished the ability of pharmaceutical companies to re-create large revenue drug franchises.

Biosimilars

There are two main kinds of drugs: small-molecule and large-molecule/biotech drugs. Small-molecule drugs are relatively easy for a generic company to manufacture. Once patent protection expires, pricing typically drops dramatically and the innovative pharmaceutical company's revenues fall 90%+.

However, a large-molecule/biotech drug is much more difficult for a generic company to manufacture, and a branded biotech drug might be protected not only by patents on its chemical composition (like small-molecule drugs) but on its manufacturing process as well. The result is that many biotech drugs can continue to generate revenue well past the expiration of their original chemical composition patent.

Even when a generic company is able to manufacture a biotech drug, it often struggles to gain a regulatory pathway to market. To enter the market, they need to prove that it is producing exactly the same drug as the original. This often requires running multiple trials, which is costly and time-consuming. This ultimately results in less competition, and even when there are biosimilars available, the price of the drug tends to decline materially less than with a small-molecule generic.

However, this is changing. Europe has implemented an improved regulatory mechanism to enable lower-cost biosimilars to come to market, and a similar trend, although with a lag, is emerging in the United States. This only adds to the challenges for big pharma and big biotech as biosimilars put pressure on revenue streams previously thought to be protected from real competition.

THE CHALLENGES FACING BIG PHARMA AND BIG BIOTECH

Large pharmaceutical companies today find themselves with less pricing power than in the past, emerging competition for their biotech drugs, and limited opportunities to re-create large revenue streams in important therapeutic areas. As a result, they face the titanic challenge of trying to replace and grow their massive revenue base organically through internal R&D.

This has forced pharmaceutical firms to price innovative new drugs at higher price points to support their top line. Long term, this strategy could create a backlash from consumers and politicians that could curtail pharmaceutical firms' pricing power.

Faced with these multiple challenges, many large pharma and large biotech companies have chosen to invest aggressively in oncology (cancer) R&D and also to invest inorganically in oncology acquisitions.

Cancer/oncology is one of the few remaining frontiers for pharmaceutical companies to invest in for several reasons:

- Cancer involves life or death, so price is less important. Annual costs of these drugs can now run in the hundreds of thousands or even millions of dollars per patient for some of the newest, most innovative drugs.
- Within the oncology space, there have been recent advances in immuno-oncology that, from a very high level, involve supercharging the body's own immune system to fight cancer. This has opened up a whole new area for researchers to explore in the battle against cancer.
- Small innovations and mild improvements in expected survival periods can generate billions in incremental revenues for pharmaceutical companies. Modest improvements in other therapeutic areas struggle to gain widespread acceptance, given the aforementioned cost-benefit analysis and the power of PBMs.
- PBM power is more limited relative to other categories, although this did not stop CVS Health from excluding Xtandi from its formulary in 2017.

This has set off a mad dash for oncology assets with large pharma and large biotech paying increasingly high prices and valuation multiples. There is simply too much demand and too little supply. As a result, when a business like Medivation becomes available in the oncology space, just about everyone wants it and, in the end, the winning bidder is cursed with a poor return on capital.

But this is not limited to Pfizer/Medivation.

Celgene, facing its own portfolio cliff scenario in the mid-2020s, paid a 93% premium for Juno Therapeutics in 2018.

Even GSK, which exited its oncology business in a value-creating asset swap with Novartis (see Chapter 12), could not resist the temptation to reenter the oncology space. GSK bought Tesaro in 2019 for a 110% premium to its 30-day average stock price. Investors were so disappointed with this acquisition that they knocked $10 billion off GSK's market value, even though GSK paid only $5 billion for Tesaro.

Eli Lilly bought Loxo Oncology in 2019 for a 68% premium.

Even in non-oncology acquisitions, large pharma and large biotech tend to pay hefty multiples and extremely high premiums to their targets' trading levels.

In the Medivation proxy, there were 15 medium-size acquisitions listed from 2011–2016, the majority of which were non-oncology related. The average target company was taken out at a 62% premium to its unaffected stock price.

Generally, the market price for a company is a reasonably good proxy for its underlying value. When paying a premium, normally 25–30% in recent years, an acquirer will typically try to justify the deal premium based on deal synergies. But with premiums in the pharmaceutical space ranging from 60% to 120%, there is simply no way the synergies can justify the purchase price.

Moreover, this takeover supply/demand imbalance is not lost on investors. Given the number of acquisitions and the magnitude of the premiums paid, it would be logical to assume that investors price at least some embedded takeover option value in the shares of these companies. Hence, a buyer must not only pay a big premium to the discounted value of its future cash flows, but likely a premium above the already embedded takeover optionality as well (see Table 21.2).

TABLE 21.2

Acquirers of Pharmaceutical Assets Paying Massive Premiums

DCF value	$100
Investors embed 15% odds of takeover at $190 in stock	$13.50
Unaffected stock price	$113.50
Acquirer pays 90% premium to unaffected stock price	$215.65
Acquirer pays premium to DCF value	116%

To clarify, this is not an argument against pharmaceutical companies investing in oncology. In fact, given the fact that cancer is a leading cause of death globally, it makes sense that R&D resources are allocated there. From a financial perspective, the size of the revenue streams available to big pharma and big biotech for innovative oncology drugs justifies significant focus on cancer treatments. However, I am critical of the M&A decisions in this arena. Whether big pharma and big biotech companies buy smaller firms or allow them to remain independent, these innovative drugs will still come to market to benefit patients. The only thing that changes is the corporate ownership of these drugs.

Another reason to be somewhat critical of these oncology acquisitions is the massive cost of the treatments. How sustainable are $2 million annual price tags? While going from $922 million in revenues to $7.3 billion might look great in a spreadsheet, management teams and boards should at least be aware of the risk that extremely high price points for treatment could be curtailed in the future. That is where the returns on these acquisitions go from bad to downright ugly.

HOW SHOULD BIG PHARMA AND
BIG BIOTECH RESPOND?

So, there is an incredible M&A supply/demand imbalance for big pharma and big biotech. Revenue bases are too big to grow without M&A, and a limited number of M&A targets exist to drive growth.

Here are some suggestions on what Big Pharma and Big Biotech can do:

Be willing to be smaller. If a firm is too big to grow or even maintain its current revenue base without M&A, it is OK to shrink over time. Returning excess cash to shareholders in buybacks, dividends, or special dividends prior to or during this shrinkage process can deliver substantially higher returns than value-destructive M&A and is a far more viable path than most investors or pharmaceutical executives appreciate. Reduce the firm to a size that enables it to maintain its revenue trajectory over the long term and concentrate R&D in areas of strength and differentiation.

Create a growth company/cash cow structure. If the firm is unable to sustain its top line organically, it should consider splitting into two or more companies. The growth company can have the stronger pipeline and fewer patent cliffs, and focus its R&D resources where the firm is strongest and most differentiated versus peers.

The cash cow business may have limited revenue growth or even shrink, but can pay out large dividends and potentially special dividends to a more yield-focused investor base. In 2019, Pfizer did exactly this by combining its low-to-no-growth off-patent pharmaceutical portfolio with Mylan. In 2020, Merck announced a spin-off of its women's health, legacy brands, and biosimilars into a separate publicly traded company as well.

Asset swaps. Follow the value creation example of GSK/Novartis. Be willing to trade drugs and pipeline assets in areas where your firm is not a leader for drugs and pipeline assets where you are a recognized scientific leader and innovator. This makes a tremendous amount of sense in the pharmaceutical industry.

Take advantage of non-core divestitures. With oncology the most important focus of many large pharmaceutical companies, these firms may be willing to part with less strategic assets at reasonable prices to help fund organic and inorganic investments in oncology. Scooping up non-core divestitures is exactly what Biogen, a leader in neurology, has done in recent years:

- Paid $75 million up front and as much as $515 million in the future for a Pfizer schizophrenia drug in phase 2b clinical trials.
- Paid $300 million up front and as much as $410 million in the future for a Bristol-Myers anti-tau drug for the treatment of progressive supranuclear palsy (PSP).
- Paid $4 million up front with another $18 million option and as much as $335 million in the future to Japan-based TMS for a stroke drug.

While the ultimate fate of these drugs in the marketplace is important, my focus is on the soundness of the decisions that led Biogen to acquire them. From a purely process standpoint, these appear to be intelligent acquisitions given small up-front payments, non-core divestitures by sellers, and good fit with Biogen's differentiated capabilities and scientific expertise in neurology.

Split company into smaller entities focused on a specific therapeutic area. This approach offers multiple advantages:

- Brings more focus to the organization
- Lessens bureaucracy
- Reduces the need for large, expensive acquisitions, given the smaller size of the new business

- Allows for smaller acquisitions and partnerships that can move the top line and potentially generate higher returns on capital

Furthermore, some of these spin-offs might become takeover targets in the future and allow the shareholder base of the spin-off to benefit from the supply/demand imbalance.

Focus on parts of business that have more steady revenue streams. Many pharmaceutical companies own non-branded pharmaceutical businesses such as vaccines, over-the-counter medications, and animal health. These businesses tend to have more stable revenue streams and reasonable growth rates, and they face materially less long-term pricing risk.

When Democratic (and increasingly Republicans as well) politicians decry the high cost of prescription drugs, they typically are not targeting over-the-counter medicines such as Tylenol, vaccines, or medicines for cats, fish, and dogs. Big pharma has been selling or spinning off these assets in recent years to take advantage of the higher valuations they command.

For example, in 2013, Pfizer IPOed and then spun off its animal health business, Zoetis, to its shareholders. Over the next five years, Zoetis's share price almost tripled. While such spins-off make sense in the short term, the challenge is that the remaining business becomes more vulnerable to patent cliffs, and this can drive more value-destructive, high-priced M&A. From a portfolio perspective, pharmaceutical firms are divesting their "good" businesses for a premium to their own valuation multiple only to then pay exorbitant premiums for weaker pharmaceutical assets with finite life spans that generate low returns on capital.

WHAT ARE THE BROADER TAKEAWAYS FOR NON-PHARMACEUTICAL FIRMS?

Companies in other industries can learn from the challenges facing pharmaceutical firms.

- **It is difficult to create long-term shareholder value when the supply/demand imbalance favors the sellers.** This is where the winner's curse comes into play. Be open to other forms of capital deployment when the returns from M&A are poor, even if that means the revenue base of the company declines for a time.
- **M&A decisions should be completely independent of what is happening in the core business.** Whether the top line is growing at 5% or declining at 5% should have no bearing on the return threshold for M&A. M&A should not be utilized to fill a hole in the core business. Entering into M&A for the wrong reasons rarely produces long-term shareholder wealth.
- **Look at other options for value creation if you cannot maintain the current revenue base or if the business is struggling to grow as in the past.** Splitting the firm into a growth company and a value company with different growth rates, different capital allocation strategies, and different shareholder bases can be an intelligent alternative to low-return M&A.

CHAPTER 22

Short-Term Plug Deal

In some cases, it can be problematic to fully ascertain a management team's motivation for making an acquisition. Perrigo's acquisition of Entocort is one such case in point.

In April 2015, Perrigo, a manufacturer of generic drugs and over-the-counter private label medicines, was the subject of an aggressive hostile takeover attempt by Mylan. To understand the nature of the bid, one must first understand the environment in which the bid was made.

This was a period of rapid consolidation within the pharmaceutical industry. Valeant Pharmaceuticals had pioneered the strategy of acquiring drug companies; slashing costs, including R&D; raising prices; and operating as a non-US company to minimize taxes. This strategy produced massive short-term returns for its shareholders and helped set off a consolidation wave:

- In 2013, Perrigo purchased Elan Pharmaceuticals for $6.7 billion largely to facilitate Perrigo's redomicile in Ireland and slash its tax bill, even though its headquarters remained in Michigan.

- In 2015, Mylan bought a European-based subsidiary from Abbott Laboratories to lower its tax rate.
- In 2015, Teva Pharmaceuticals made a hostile bid for Mylan but eventually dropped the bid and instead acquired Allergan's generic business for $40.5 billion.
- In 2015, Mylan, in turn, made a hostile bid for Perrigo.
- In November 2015, Pfizer attempted to acquire Allergan in a $160 billion transaction to lower its tax rate and cut costs.

In short, an epidemic of "deal fever," fueled by a desire to lower tax rates, cut costs, and generate materially higher profits for shareholders spread through the whole pharmaceutical industry.

Perrigo's board unanimously rejected multiple offers from Mylan that valued Perrigo between $188 and $205. Prior to the first public offer of $205, Perrigo shares were trading at an unaffected stock price of $162 per share. Mylan launched a tender for Perrigo shares in September of 2015 and threatened to delist non-tendered shares from the exchange as an enticement—or more accurately, a threat—to force Perrigo shareholders to tender their shares to Mylan. In the end, the hostile takeover failed as Mylan's stock price experienced considerable pressure, which, in turn, reduced the value of the cash and stock offer made to Perrigo shareholders.

PERRIGO WINS THE BATTLE, BUT LAYS OUT AGGRESSIVE TARGETS

During this process, however, Perrigo felt the need to offer its shareholders a compelling "stay independent" alternative to the value creation Mylan was promising in a takeover. So in October 2015, Perrigo announced a $2 billion multiyear share repurchase program, a restructuring that would cut 800 jobs, and tax savings from a supply chain consolidation in Ireland. The company forecast this help would drive 20%+ growth in EPS to $9.45 in 2016.

Near the end of the Mylan tender process, Perrigo CEO Joseph Papa said the following during a Credit Suisse Health Care Conference on November 10, 2015:

> *And we came out most recently with our 2016 guidance. We revealed that on October 22, which I think for most people I've talked to was significantly above their guidance expectations. We came out with a 20% increase over the mid-point of our 2015 [guidance] of $7.75. That 20% translated into $9.30 by putting an additional share repurchase there, a $500 million share repurchase we would deal with this year between November and December 31 to get to you to about $9.45 of earnings per share.*
>
> *We think this is significantly preferable to the Mylan transaction both in the near term and midterm simply because as we get through this and we decouple ourselves from Mylan, we think our historical run rate for both growth, earnings per share, and importantly our P/E multiple revert back to what it's been before. We think that's an important distinction, so we transfer something back to let's call it a 19 or 20 times P/E multiple based on $9.45, and you're in the $180s–$190s, you trade right through this transaction. So, we think that's an important comment.[1]*

Perrigo's CEO was making a strong argument for why shareholders would be better off not tendering their shares. However, a critical part of the calculus for shareholders was the ability of Perrigo to deliver on its EPS commitments that were much higher than expected at the time Perrigo provided them.

On November 13, 2015, Mylan's seven-month bid to acquire Perrigo failed as it was unable to entice enough Perrigo shareholders to tender their shares.

On November 23, 2015, Perrigo announced it would acquire AstraZeneca's Entocort capsule business for $380 million in cash. The business sold Entocort branded and authorized generic drugs for Crohn's disease and generated approximately $90 million in sales. The deal was estimated to be $0.35 accretive to EPS at the time.

Perrigo was facing multiple challenges by the end of 2015. Its $4.4 billion acquisition of Omega, a European over-the-counter (OTC) medicine business, was underperforming expectations. Perrigo was forced to write off part of the acquisition price less than a year after the deal. In addition, Perrigo's core OTC medicine business faced pressures in its smoking cessation private-label product line as a branded competitor reentered the market. Perrigo also faced margin headwinds due to faster growth in of its some lower-margin products.

Management guidance for 2016 was very back-half weighted with less robust results expected in the first half of 2016, but significant earnings growth in the second half of the year. In the end, Perrigo would earn a very disappointing $7.10 per share in 2016 (see Figure 22.1). CEO Joseph Papa left Perrigo for the CEO job at Valeant, the CFO resigned, and the company had to delay the filing of its 10-K due to accounting issues. Perrigo's stock price declined by 42% in 2016.

However, what I find most intriguing about this series of events is the acquisition of Entocort. The risk of a hostile takeover by Mylan had passed, but management still had to deliver on its aggressive target for EPS growth made during the heat of battle for control of Perrigo. At the same time, the Omega acquisition was underperforming expectations and there were some competitive headwinds in Perrigo's core OTC business.

Did either of these challenges play a part in the Entocort acquisition? We cannot know precisely what Perrigo's leadership team was thinking at the time. However, it is quite logical to assume that the Perrigo management team did not want to miss its recently issued 2016 guidance, and that the highly accretive Entocort acquisition announced in November of 2015 would provide an added margin of safety for earnings in 2016.

FIGURE 22.1

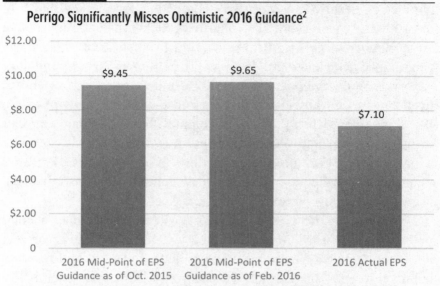

Perrigo Significantly Misses Optimistic 2016 Guidance[2]

Note: It does not appear that Perrigo actually disclosed an adjusted EPS result for fiscal year 2016. This was due to the accounting issues that delayed the publication of the 10-K, as well as the announced sale of the Tysabri royalty stream. This sale required Perrigo to restate prior years' earnings to reflect this cash flow stream as a discontinued business. Management had originally provided preliminary 2016 earnings of $7.10 to $7.25 per share (note: this is after FY 16 was already over inclusive of Tysabri) prior to filing its 10-K, but I was unable to find any information in press releases or filings to demonstrate what Perrigo actually earned in 2016 on an adjusted basis. The $7.10 adjusted EPS result in the table is the average of three sell-side analyst reports, whose authors all came up with different results ($7.18, $7.15, and $6.98).

In the generic pharmaceutical business, the price of a drug and the ultimate margin the manufacturer can earn is heavily influenced by how complex it is to manufacture. Perrigo's generics business earned an impressive 43.8% adjusted operating margin in 2016, in part because the company was a leader in hard-to-manufacture drugs with a particular focus on creams and gels. This resulted in less competition for its generics portfolio, better pricing power, and higher returns.

Perrigo's Entocort acquisition was expected to generate a double-digit return on capital in the first year and $0.35 of earnings accretion.

But was this sustainable?

The profitability of generic drugs is heavily influenced by the number of generic manufacturers competing for market share. In most cases, when a branded pharmaceutical's patent runs out, a large number of generic firms swoop in to manufacture the newly genericized drug and drive down its price dramatically. An influx of generic manufacturers competing for a finite market almost always results in a materially lower price for consumers. It usually plays out like this, except when the drug is complex, hard to manufacture, or difficult to prove equivalency to the existing drug, as in the case with a biologic drug. For Entocort's cash flows to be sustainable, Perrigo's management needed to believe that new entrants would be unable to bring competing generic drugs to the market.

However, in the case of Entocort, Mylan already had a competing generic in the market. In addition, Entocort was a capsule, not a cream or gel (where Perrigo excelled). Teva also had received approval to enter the market, but had yet to launch its generic. The inevitable entry of Teva into a two-player market would almost certainly have resulted in a loss of market share, a reduced price for Perrigo's Entocort generic, and a reduction in cash flows. As it happened, within two years, five new generic manufacturers would gain FDA approval to sell a generic version of Entocort.

As a result, within a year of being acquired, the Entocort business encountered significant pressure from new competition. Management wrote off $342 million of the $380 million purchase price, and projected an additional $72 million revenue decline in 2017, even after a sharp drop in the fourth quarter of 2016. For all practical purposes, the business was vanishing.

Had management made a low quality, highly accretive acquisition to support its aggressive guidance? In Perrigo's 2016 10-K, management indicated that the new competition was "significant and unexpected."[3] Maybe it was unexpected, or maybe it was unexpected so soon after the acquisition. But whether new competition arrived in the fourth quarter of 2016 or at some point in the near future, Perrigo had bought a lower-quality generic asset lacking the complexity that defined its core generics portfolio. All of the circumstantial evidence points to Perrigo's acquisition of Entocort as a short-term plug deal as opposed to a long-term, value-creating acquisition for shareholders.

WHAT ARE THE LESSONS FROM THE PERRIGO/ ENTOCORT STORY?

Don't make short-term plug deals. If earnings expectations are too high and the core business is underperforming, a company may be tempted to make an acquisition to fill a short-term earnings hole. In a world with low interest rates, generating earnings accretion in the short term is relatively easy. These earnings may help overcome near-term weak fundamentals in the core business. However, that is the wrong mindset with which to approach M&A.

A short-term plug deal might placate investors, support earnings and maintain the stock price in the short term, but real value creation comes from generating attractive returns on capital that benefit shareholders over the long term. This is not to say that a firm should avoid M&A when its core business is under pressure, but rather that a firm should not lower its return objectives during this period.

Moreover, it is critical that the board of directors reiterates a returns-focused mindset to management during this time. Management teams face considerable external pressure to reach their earnings guidance and continue to grow earnings.

A returns-focused board needs to make sure the management team is doing everything in its power to optimize the business in the short term without taking actions that could damage the business over the long term. Board members should make it clear to management that they would rather miss earnings in the short term and suffer the consequences than make an accretive, but low ROIC acquisition to support near-term earnings.

Making an acquisition for the wrong reasons is a surefire way to destroy long-term shareholder value, as Perrigo experienced with the Entocort acquisition.

Be intellectually honest in your targets when subject to a hostile takeover offer. Whether it is with Perrigo/Mylan, Astra-Zeneca/Pfizer, or Allergan/Valeant, I have seen management teams time and again provide aggressive long-term guidance to justify not being acquired. While that may seem like the right strategy if the sole objective is to avoid being acquired, it is not in the best interests of shareholders.

Management teams should provide a reasonable target, not the best-case outcome, for the coming years. They should have faith in the shareholders of their businesses to come to a sensible conclusion based on reasonable assumptions, as opposed to dangling a best-case outcome that is often rejected by sophisticated investors anyway.

The problem for a management team that defeats a hostile takeover is that they now have to deliver on a new, aggressive multiyear plan. Trying to achieve this ambitious plan can often result in excessive cost cutting, taking on too much debt, reducing strategic investments, and pushing the business to grow faster than it is capable of growing. These actions can actually damage the business, limit financial flexibility, and be counterproductive to long-term value creation.

CHAPTER 23

Spin-Offs

Yum! Brands, the parent company of Taco Bell, KFC, and Pizza Hut, delivered significant long-term shareholder value from the time it was spun off from PepsiCo in 1997 until the end of 2012.

Yum! Brands (YUM) delivered an impressive 954% cumulative total return to shareholders versus a 99% total return for the S&P 500. The firm's operations in China contributed significantly to this growth. YUM management made an early and aggressive bet on the Chinese market, and this investment drove spectacular growth in China and for all of Yum! Brands. In 1997, YUM's Chinese operations had fewer than 200 restaurants and less than $20 million in operating profit. By the end of 2012, Yum China had more than 5,700 restaurants and slightly more than $1 billion in operating profit; China represented 42% of YUM profits.

In 2012 alone, YUM added 889 new restaurants in China. The front cover of the Yum! Brands 2012 annual report featured four people on the Great Wall of China with the caption "Staying the Course: China and a Whole Lot More."[1]

However, YUM's Chinese subsidiary operated a very different business model than most of the non-Chinese businesses at YUM.

Within the restaurant business, there are two distinct operating models: company-owned and franchised, as shown in Table 23.1. A restaurant company can choose to build its own stores and operate them on a day-to-day basis. A well-run quick-service restaurant can typically generate a mid-teen operating margin. This was the predominant model that YUM had employed in China, with around 90% of restaurants owned and operated by YUM.[†] Yum China's owned-and-operated restaurants had an impressive high-teens operating margin in 2012.

TABLE 23.1

Economics of New Restaurant Opening to Brand Owner

	Company-Owned Store	Franchise
Revenues	100%	4–6%
Operating Margin	10–20%	70–80%
Cost to Build New Restaurant	100%	0%
ROIC	10–20%	Infinite

	Company-Owned Store	Franchisee Store
Revenues	$750,000	$37,500
Operating Profits	$112,500	$28,125
After-Tax Profits	$84,375	$21,094
Net Investment	$550,000	0
ROIC	15.3%	Infinite

Note: This is a generic comparison between a franchise model and a company-owned store model and not YUM-specific.

Alternatively, with a franchise model, a franchisee provides the capital, builds the store, operates it, and pays the brand owner (restaurant company) a royalty, usually around 5% of revenues. This

---

† This excludes unconsolidated affiliate restaurant stores in China (of which there were 660 at the end of 2012). Excluding these stores, YUM had a little more than 5,000 restaurants in China at the end of 2012.

was the predominant model for YUM restaurants outside of China, with roughly 90% of non-China stores franchised.

The company-owned model usually generates higher profits per store for the restaurant company. However, the restaurant company has to put up all the capital to build the stores and run them day to day. Additionally, the cash flows are much more volatile due to labor inflation, food input inflation and deflation, and changes in same-store sales trends. The company-owned model generates higher profits, but lower returns on capital and greater cash flow volatility.

The stock market tends to put a much higher valuation on royalty revenues and royalty profits due to their predictability and low capital intensity/high FCF.

YUM had moved forward with a company-owned model in China. At the time, China was very much a developing economy and lacked significant franchisee capital and expertise in running stores.

None of these differences really mattered until the end of 2012 as Yum China was opening new stores at a rapid pace and growing same-store sales at very healthy rates. In 2011, China's same-store sales growth was up an amazing 19% versus a 1% decline in the United States. The future looked bright, as penetration of YUM's stores in China was still a fraction of that (on a per capita basis) in the United States and Western Europe.

However, between the end of 2012 and 2015 the Chinese business hit a wall, or more accurately, a series of walls. The first blow to Yum China operations came in December 2012. Its KFC business was rocked by a report on Chinese television that a number of farmers were injecting poultry with excessive levels of antibiotics, and the poultry had been purchased by KFC suppliers. This news drove the Shanghai FDA to investigate and led to a series of recommendations for YUM to improve its supply chain safety. In January 2013, KFC's China same-store sales plummeted 41%.

Over the next three years, a combination of avian flu, supplier quality issues, negative press coverage, currency weakness, and, to a lesser extent, increased competition, drove same-store sales negative.

Yum China profits fell from over $1 billion in 2012 to $757 million in 2015, despite the opening of almost 1,500 new restaurants. Chinese comps nosedived 13% in 2013, fell another 5% in 2014, and 4% further in 2015. The most important growth driver of YUM had turned into a headwind. Whereas, in the past, YUM had consistently surpassed its long-term earnings guidance of 10% EPS growth, Chinese profit weakness caused the company to miss this target for three straight years. Indeed, adjusted EPS actually declined from $3.25 in 2012 to $3.18 in 2015.

The stock that had been a monster for a decade materially underperformed the market and its consumer discretionary peer group between 2013 and 2015. China was not prominently featured on the front cover of YUM's annual reports anymore.

YUM CHINA SPIN-OFF

The management team announced a strategic review of the China business in 2015, and in October 2015 announced it would spin off Yum China in 2016.

In the press release announcing the decision to separate, YUM CEO Greg Creed said:

> *Following the separation, each standalone company will be able to intensify focus on its distinct commercial priorities, allocate its own resources to meet the needs of its businesses, and pursue distinct capital structures and capital allocation strategies. This will provide a clear investment thesis and visibility to attract a long-term investor base suited to each business.*
>
> *Yum! Brands will have a more stable earnings stream typical of a franchise company powered by industry-leading brands, while also benefiting from the development of the China business as a unique growth engine. In turn, our China business is self-sufficient and scalable with strong*

leadership in place, and is well-positioned to realize its full potential as a standalone business to capture the compelling opportunities in China."[2]

The separation of YUM's China operations from the rest of Yum China enabled the following:

- Yum China was spun off with a strong investment-grade balance sheet and a net cash position that enabled it to continue to open new stores.
- Yum China was headquartered in China and added multiple Chinese nationals to its board. Importantly, Yum China went from being a subsidiary of an American company to a truly Chinese company.
- Stand-alone YUM was able to increase leverage to 5x debt/EBITDA given the stability of its earnings and FCF stream, and commit to returning $13.5–$14 billion of capital back to shareholders from 2016 to 2019. This represented more than 45% of its market capitalization the day before the spin-off announcement.
- Stand-alone YUM's FCF potential moved from 85% to 100% by 2019 as ongoing capital spending was expected to decline from $1 billion to $100 million. For the new Yum! Brands going forward, franchisees, as opposed to the company, would put up the vast majority of capital to open new restaurants.
- Stand-alone YUM's franchise mix moved from 77% to 93% after the China separation, with a planned increase to 98% by 2019.

In the first couple of years following the spin-off, the stand-alone YUM outperformed Yum China, but both Yum China (up 40%) and YUM (up 53%) significantly outperformed the total return of the S&P 500 through the end of 2018. Moreover, Yum China returned to prosperity with CAGR EPS growth of 11% from 2016 to 2019, despite challenges at Pizza Hut and increased competition. The supplier issues and negative press coverage that plagued Yum China when it was part of YUM went away when it became a Chinese company.

Yum! Brands has transitioned its business model to more of a pure franchise model, enabling the company to spend its time and resources on accelerating new store development. For a restaurant company, there are two ways to drive top-line sales growth: same-store sales growth and new store openings. With less focus on China and operating company-owned stores, management has been free to focus on growing stores and, in some cases, forming partnerships with master franchisees to penetrate key new markets. As a result, net new store growth accelerated from 2% to around 4% in 2018–2019. Returns on new store openings are extremely high, as YUM does not need to invest any shareholder capital in them.

The YUM split-up is a great example of the value creation opportunity that can exist in situations where two or more businesses have significant differences in cyclicality, capital intensity, capital allocation priorities, growth rates, optimal balance sheet leverage, and potential shareholder bases (see Table 23.2).

TABLE 23.2

New YUM and Yum China Businesses Differ Greatly

	New YUM	YUM China
Cyclicality	Low	Medium
Capital Intensity	Low	High
Capital Allocation	Buybacks, Dividends	Open New Stores
Balance Sheet Leverage	High-Yield, 5x Leverage	Investment-Grade, Low Debt
Top-Line Growth Goals	7%	Double-Digit
EPS Growth Goals	Low-Teens	15%
Shareholder Base	US, GARP/Growth	US/Chinese, Growth
Exposure to China Comps + Currency Volatility	Low	High

Note: GARP refers to growth at a reasonable price.

The long-term historical performance of spin-offs is rather compelling. What is particularly interesting is that not only does the spun-off asset (NewCo) outperform the market, but the parent company also tends to outperform as well.

A report from Credit Suisse in 2012, for example, looked at spin-off and parent performance between 1995 and 2012. It found that on average the spin-off and parent outperformed the market by 9.6% and 13.4%, respectively, in the year following the spin-off.[3]

WHAT TO CONSIDER WHEN THINKING ABOUT A SPLIT

There is usually a catalyst for the decision to split a company into two or more publicly traded companies. It is often a function of two forces: sum-of-parts discount and short-to-intermediate-term stock performance (see Table 23.3).

TABLE 23.3

Spin-Off Matrix: How Much Pressure to Spin?

	Small to No Sum-of-Parts Discount	Moderate to Large Sum-of-Parts Discount
Outperforming Stock	No Pressure	Modest Pressure
Underperforming Stock	Modest Pressure	**Significant Pressure**

While stock price performance and sum-of-parts discount are two of the most important catalysts to initiate a split-up, these should not be the most important considerations for a management team or board.

A management team or board should consider the following relevant questions:

- Are both businesses (or in some cases more than two businesses) being run optimally inside the parent company?

- Would the businesses be optimized inside or outside the parent company over the long term?

With many spin-off situations, there is a growth business and a no-growth/slower-growth business, or an attractive business model (stand-alone YUM) and a less attractive business model (Yum China). In many cases, one of the businesses is a cash cow that helps to fund capital expenditures or M&A of the faster-growing, more-dynamic business.

Being a cash cow or slower-growth asset in a corporation with a faster-growth business can be difficult. Often the cash cow will be both a source of financial capital for the growth asset and also a source of intellectual capital—because the best and brightest at the cash cow move to work at the growth asset. The potential for greater compensation and advancement can be drivers of this. If profits are not growing as rapidly at the cash cow as with the growth asset, it may be hard to grow the bonus pool as fast. There may be more opportunities for advancement in a growing organization than in a slow-growth organization, and it is more likely that the next CEO will come from the growth asset than the cash cow. In addition, will the cash cow really get the requisite time and attention of senior management? Will the cash cow receive its fair share of investments to grow market share, invest in R&D, participate in bolt-on acquisitions, and restructure to increase profitability?

All too often the answer to these questions is no. Frequently the cash cow business lacks management talent, senior management focus, and capital. As a result, it atrophies over time.

Much of the long-term success of spin-offs has less to do with sum-of-the-parts discounts and more to do with what happens when the cash cow or low-growth asset gets the talent, resources, capital, and focus it has been lacking. In Chapter 8 on share repurchase, I referenced a group of treasurers who said they always prioritized high-return internal projects over returning excess capital to shareholders. However, with a cash cow, that is often not the case.

When the cash cow is spun off it often finds a sizable backlog of very high-return projects that it should have been doing all along. Now, as a newly public company, it will frontload these initiatives over the next one to two years. Those high-return projects may involve introducing new products, consolidating manufacturing facilities, adding sales resources, and engaging in accretive bolt-on acquisitions. In addition, management talent is often injected into the cash cow prior to the spin-off as the attractiveness of working there increases. As a public company, the spin-off controls its own destiny as opposed to being a second-class citizen inside its former parent.

TO SPIN OR NOT TO SPIN—THESE ARE THE QUESTIONS

A number of factors should be considered when considering to spin off a business:

Is the asset of a sufficient size? Spinning off a $100 million business that might need to incur an additional $5–$10 million in public company costs should probably be sold as opposed to being spun off.

Does a sale create more value than a spin? In most cases the answer is no. A spin-off is usually structured as a tax-free transaction, whereas a sale may incur tax leakage. If a business has sufficient size to be an independent company, there are only two reasons to sell as opposed to spin. First, if a bidder is willing to pay a higher price on an after-tax basis than the value the spin will create for shareholders over the short to intermediate term, then a sale makes sense. However, that this is rare. Second, if the parent company has too much debt and needs to divest the business to pay down debt to improve its balance sheet, a sale also makes sense.

In all other scenarios, a spin-off allows existing shareholders to participate in the upside potential of the NewCo in a tax-efficient way. In addition, a reverse Morris transaction—in which one business is combined with another public company—is also a creative way to generate significant shareholder value because there are usually cost synergies generated in the transaction with no tax leakage. Finally, with an IPO it is also possible for a parent firm to sell up to 19.9% of its ownership in a NewCo before a full spin-off down the road. The proceeds from this transaction are tax-free as well.

Is the cash cow business being run as well inside the parent company as it would be outside? Does it have the management talent and capital to invest to outperform its peers and create shareholder value?

Does a spin-off hurt either business's customers? Are their goods and services bundled? Do competitors bundle so that a spin-off would impair the new businesses' ability to compete in the marketplace? Don't spin off a business if this would hurt customers and negatively impact either business's competitiveness in the market.

Are the products sold by a common sales force, and would the two entities need to double the sales force as two public companies? Spinning off a mustard business from a ketchup company does not make sense.

Is there a sum-of-parts discount? While this is unlikely, even if there is not, a board should be open to spinning off the cash cow or lower-growth asset if it is not being optimized inside the parent.

How different are the businesses? The greater the difference in cyclicality, capital intensity, growth rates, capital allocation priorities, and expected shareholder bases, the greater the urgency to separate the businesses.

The Stranded Corporate Costs Myth

You might be surprised that I did not mention the potential for stranded corporate costs as a reason to avoid spinning off an asset.

Many large firms have dedicated corporate departments for functions such as technology, human resources, R&D, and finance. In an effort to take advantage of scale, a conglomerate with multiple divisions will often centralize some of these operations and allocate a portion of the costs to each of its divisions. If a conglomerate were to spin off 20% of its sales, in theory, there should be some level of stranded costs, as these corporate costs are not 100% variable.

I have been surprised again and again that when a business is sold or spun off from a larger conglomerate, the corporate allocated costs become a source of margin upside for the divested business. The NewCo is able to replicate these corporate functions at a lower cost than what the corporate parent charged.

When DuPont sold its paint refinishing business to a private equity firm, there was massive margin upside from the reduction in corporate allocated expenses. When Fortive bought Johnson & Johnson's ASP subsidiary in 2019, a reduction in corporate allocated costs was a material driver of the expected operating margin expansion.

This tells me two things:

1. Stranded costs are a weak reason not to spin off a business.
2. Corporate costs at large conglomerates are not delivering the scale benefits that they should be. When company after company that is divested from its parent is able to replicate these functions at a lower cost with less scale, it suggests there is substantial savings potential in corporate costs at many conglomerates. In reality, allocated costs are not only critical functions, but the costs of a large corporate bureaucracy that has likely grown over decades. These large corporate allocations also limit the ability of business units to fully control their own P&L when a meaningful part of their expense is allocated costs over which they have no control. The best conglomerates have limited allocated costs to their businesses and minimize corporate overhead. The best corporate headquarters is a small corporate headquarters.

Spin-Off or Split-Off

The last item to consider here is whether to do a spin-off or a split-off. Both create a new publicly traded company, but they facilitate its separation from the parent company in a slightly different way.

A spin-off distributes shares in the newly public company to the existing shareholder base.

A split-off is a slightly more complex transaction in which shareholders are able to tender all or a portion of their shares in the parent company in exchange for shares in the spun-off business. A split-off occurs only when the parent company has already IPO'd the NewCo business and essentially swaps the remaining parent company ownership of NewCo (usually 80.1%) for shares in the parent. It acts like a quasi–stock buyback and can minimize earnings dilution from the spin.

The advantage of the split-off is that it gives the shareholder base of the parent some discretion as to whether they want to keep the parent shares, hold some of the parent and NewCo, or exit the parent and only own NewCo.

I do not have a strong preference for spin-offs versus split-offs. A split-off may make more sense if the shareholder base of the parent and NewCo are very different (e.g., one is growth and one is value, or one is large-cap and one is small- or mid-cap) and may make the NewCo shares trade better at the start. But over the long term, both companies will naturally find the right shareholder bases anyway.

Regardless of the method chosen, if a company meets the right criteria, a spin-off or a split-off is an excellent way to optimize shareholder value and improve the long-term health and competitiveness of both entities.

CHAPTER 24

Restructuring

I disapprove of companies that abuse the practice of excluding extraordinary, nonrecurring restructuring charges from their adjusted earnings. If a firm takes charges every year and in some cases, multiple times per year, are the charges truly extraordinary or nonrecurring? Unfortunately, there are no standards for such charges. As long as a firm can create a footnote in an earnings release that shows how the company got from GAAP to non-GAAP earnings, it can usually exclude whatever it wants.

Newell Brands (NWL) excluded nonrecurring restructuring costs from adjusted EPS every year from 2006–2018.[1] Non-GAAP cumulative EPS during this period were a healthy $25.37, but GAAP earnings were just $3.16, as shown in Figure 24.1.

FIGURE 24.1

Newell Rubbermaid 2006–2018 GAAP EPS, FCF Per Share, and Non-GAAP Adjusted EPS

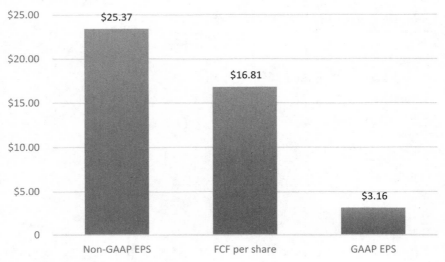

Source: FactSet financial data and analytics

FIGURE 24.2

Newell Rubbermaid 2006 Versus 2018 FCF Per Share

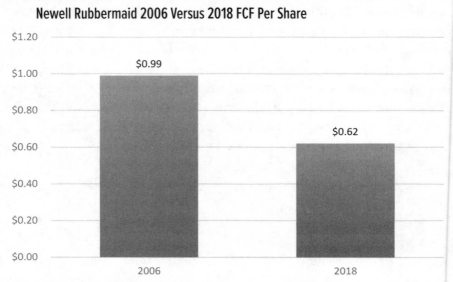

Source: FactSet financial data and analytics

Moreover, the quality of non-GAAP EPS was low; NWL converted only converted 64% of its non-GAAP EPS into FCF. Recurring "nonrecurring" restructuring charges and the disastrous large acquisition of Jarden were the principal reasons for these disappointing financial results.

In the end, what really matters for the vast majority of companies is not the level of GAAP or non-GAAP earnings, but the FCF behind those earnings. A company cannot pay dividends, make acquisitions, buy back shares, or invest in growth-oriented capital projects out of earnings. A firm needs real, tangible FCF to deploy capital and generate attractive returns.

Companies that are constantly in restructuring mode may appear earnings rich, but are often cash-flow poor. As discussed in the second chapter, the EPS and FCF growth rate of a company with a given level of organic profit growth is directly related to not only the returns it can generate on excess capital deployment but also to its FCF to net income ratio.

The Newell example highlights some of the challenges that arise when companies exclude recurring "nonrecurring" cash expenses from EPS.

First, EPS tends to be the most important metric investors use to compare valuation across companies. Frequent charges distort the quality of EPS and make the figure far less useful.

Second, frequent charges distort the calculation of return on invested capital. To improve ROIC, a company can simply write off the goodwill from the underperforming large acquisition. This lowers shareholder equity and *voilà,* ROIC is higher. That plant the firm built near the top of the last economic cycle that is not needed or well utilized? Write it off and returns go up.

Beyond the accounting distortions, there is a cost to the company and its culture. Any firm that continually announces layoffs and plant closures will find its culture challenged and its employees worried about their jobs. This distracts them from driving higher sales, developing new products, and collaborating across the organization. It also hampers the firm's ability to retain the best and brightest and attract outside talent. In general, as with Newell, it is hard to restructure your way to prosperity.

You might ask: "Why are we talking about restructuring and accounting in a book about capital allocation?" First, restructuring usually involves a cash outlay with an expected return similar to that from M&A, share repurchase, dividends, and special dividends. Second, restructuring reduces the cash available for other value accretive actions to create long-term shareholder value.

WHEN RESTRUCTURING PROGRAMS ARE WARRANTED

There are several circumstances when restructuring makes sense.

Right-Sizing a Business to a Level Consistent with Long-Term Demand

It is critically important to differentiate between a short-term, cyclical downturn and a long-term, structural decline in demand. If the downturn is temporary, as in a shallow recession, there should be no need for a large restructuring program to lower costs.

Firms can lower costs during a cyclical downturn by not replacing workers who retire or voluntarily leave, by limiting discretionary expenditures such as travel and entertainment, and by cutting back on bonuses and other forms of variable compensation. Taking more extreme steps such as closing multiple plants and laying off hundreds or thousands of workers is likely to be a mistake. Once demand returns to more normal levels, the firm will need the capacity at those plants. It will also need to hire and train new employees. Once you factor in the severance costs and the inefficiency associated with a less-seasoned workforce, the returns from mass layoffs and rehiring are likely to be quite poor. That said, a restructuring plan may be needed when longer-term demand has declined for structural reasons and is unlikely to recover.

GE's power business is a great example of this. GE Gas Power and Alstom, GE's acquired steam power business, face structurally lower demand for their products and services. This is especially true on the Alstom part of the business where coal is in steep secular decline. Renewables such as wind and solar power are capturing market share due to climate change concerns, lower wind and solar capital costs that make them far more price competitive, and to a lesser extent, government subsidies.

On its 2018 fourth quarter conference call, GE announced that its power business had negative FCF of $2.7 in 2018 and projected a similar outflow in 2019.[2] GE really had no choice but to consolidate facilities, right-size its workforce, and build a cost structure that would make this business sustainable in a new world of lower demand.

Optimizing Supply Chain

For most manufacturing firms, the decision on where to locate plants and distribution centers was made in the distant past. If a firm has made acquisitions, which come with their own plants and distribution centers, it is very common to find that the expanded firm has a disjointed supply chain.

In most cases, if the firm were starting from scratch, it would not build its current supply chain and manufacturing and distribution infrastructure as it exists today. But closing all of the plants and distribution centers to optimize their locations would disrupt its supply chain, operations, and customer service. Additionally, the cost would be prohibitive.

A far better solution is to identify low-hanging fruit and eliminate smaller, less efficient, and higher-cost plants and distribution centers that may be more geographically remote from customers. Opening a new state-of-the-art plant to absorb some of this less efficient capacity is also a potential solution. (See Chapter 5; this is essentially what Hershey did, and the returns from this program were very high.)

Improving Efficiency to the Level of Peers

Every board should go through a detailed annual benchmarking study that compares the firm to its industry and sector peers as well as to the market (as defined by the S&P 500, Russell 1000, or a broader index of companies). The benchmarking process should identify actions needed to close gaps with peers.

If a firm is growing slower than its peers, it may need to invest in R&D, develop new products, expand the sales force, or broaden geographic reach, all with an eye on the size of the investment and expected cash-on-cash returns over the intermediate term. If a firm's FCF conversion is lower than its peers, one or more of the following actions may be required: a greater focus on inventory turns, a push to extend payables, or a change in management compensation to drive accountability. But if margins are below peers', a restructuring action to lower the cost structure of the business to a level more consistent with the peer set may be required.

RESTRUCTURING CATALYSTS

Over the last two decades, I have observed that there is usually a catalyst for large restructuring programs that aim to close the performance gap between a firm and its peer group. This catalyst may take the form of:

- Significant underperformance of the stock versus its peers.
- Change at the management or board level with a mandate to improve the company.
- An activist in the stock who pushes the firm to address its cost structure.
- A looming hostile takeover. A firm may announce a large restructuring program to boost earnings power in an effort to thwart a hostile acquirer. This is designed to placate investors worried that the stock will retreat lower if the hostile

transaction fails to materialize. This was part of Allergan's strategy when Valeant attempted to acquire the firm in 2014.

The issue with most of these catalyzing events is that they could have been prevented. If the board and management team had been serious about benchmarking analysis, taken actions to close performance gaps, monitored progress, and held management accountable, in most cases, a large restructuring program would not have been necessary.

Pushing a firm to improve its performance usually does not require massive restructuring actions. Small changes in the supply chain, holding G&A dollars flat, and closing or consolidating a plant or distribution center can help margins and also free up resources for investment to drive the top line.

FUEL TO DRIVE IMPROVED TOP-LINE PERFORMANCE

For a returns-focused management team and board, the decision to make investments to drive the top line (R&D, sales force expansion, geographic expansion) and the decision to implement a restructuring action should be separate processes. Both decisions should be based on the expected intermediate-term returns from each action, viewed independently.

However, from a practical standpoint, the returns from investments to drive the top line are likely to take longer to materialize and may be lower than the returns from restructuring. Proactively reducing margins over the next three years with an expected payoff in years 5–6 is unlikely to be met with rousing applause by investors. This is especially true if the stock has underperformed in recent years and if the company's margins are already below its peers. That is why combining a restructuring program with a top-line accelerant plan often makes the most sense, as long as the returns from both programs independently generate attractive returns over the intermediate term.

The restructuring announcement allows the company to improve margins and bottom-line results, and at the same time provides fuel to enhance the organic growth rate of the firm for the intermediate term. This is essentially what Hershey did when prior management cut advertising and marketing dollars and the company found itself losing market share while its top line decelerated. Hershey was able to reinvest in the business to drive faster organic top-line results and improve margins at the same time, which led to strong earnings growth and a sizable upward movement in its stock price.

BEST PRACTICES FOR RESTRUCTURING

Boards and senior managers should adhere to the following practices when considering restructuring.

- Large, nonrecurring restructuring actions should be rare.
- A well-run company should take small, high-return restructuring actions when necessary to improve operational performance, but also to provide resources to fund accelerated top-line growth. Companies should not exclude these charges from their adjusted EPS.
- A hands-on board should have an intermediate and long-term strategy for improving the company and its various subsidiaries. The board should monitor the investments required and hold management accountable for improved results. Small restructuring actions may be part of this process.
- Management and the board should compare the returns on restructuring actions to the returns on alternative uses of capital (capital spending, share repurchase, dividends, special dividends). A restructuring action is likely to reduce the amount of capital available for other potentially value-creating alternatives.

- There are ways for a company to cut costs that do not require a restructuring program and can be less traumatic on an organization. Hiring freezes, not replacing employees who retire or leave voluntarily, consolidating suppliers to negotiate better terms, reducing travel and entertainment expenses, and using fewer outside consultants can generate significant cost savings without the trauma of firing workers or the cash costs associated with severance programs.
- Restructuring actions should minimize the impact on the parts of the organization that drive revenues and are customer-facing. R&D, new product development, marketing, and sales force should, in most cases, be excluded.

CHAPTER 25

Secular Challenges

I t is difficult to know exactly when the management team and board of Eastman Kodak came to the realization that their enterprise was in serious jeopardy. In 1999, revenues from Kodak's consumer imaging and professional segments were still growing. The company would buy back around $2 billion of its stock between 1999 and 2000. Kodak increased its dividend per share from $1.76 to $2.21 in 2001.

KODAK UNDER PRESSURE

However, soon after Kodak's business started experiencing significant pressure. Its core consumer film business began to be negatively impacted by digital photography, which allowed consumers to take digital photographs without the need to capture these images on high-margin Kodak film. Kodak's FCF would decline from $1.3 billion in 2001 to less than $700 million by 2004. The company would reduce its dividend annually for the next four years, ultimately cutting it by more than 75% to $0.50 per share. It was very clear by the early 2000s that Kodak's core business was under stress and the company needed to reposition itself.

With Kodak's core business under assault, the management team and board did what so many companies do when their core business suffers from secular pressures: they turned to acquisitions to reposition. Between 2001 and 2005 (see Table 25.1), Kodak spent $2.93 billion on acquisitions with the majority of this spent in 2005 on two large assets.

TABLE 25.1

Kodak 2001–2005 Cash Flows[1]

Kodak 2001–2005 Cash Flows	
Cash Flow from Operations	$8,290
Capital Expenditures	$2,758
FCF	$5,532
Uses of Cash	
Dividends	$1,785
Acquisitions	$2,928
Share Repurchase	$304

Note: Acquisitions include $500 million in future cash payments associated with Kodak's purchase of Sun Chemical's 50% stake in Kodak Polychrome Graphics. These payments were scheduled to be made between 2006 and 2013.

When strategic repositioning becomes the sole mission of a management team and board, acquisitions are regarded as a necessity to save the company. When acquisitions turn into necessities to save the company, return thresholds become less important than grander strategic objectives. These acquisitions repeatedly fail to achieve their broader strategic objectives and typically generate very disappointing returns, as they did with Kodak:

Lucky (2004). Kodak paid $167 million for a 20% stake in China's largest manufacturer of photographic film. The following year, Kodak would write off $44 million of the purchase price.

Practice Works (2003). Kodak paid $475 million for this dental practice software and digital dental equipment business. Based on the Kodak 2004 10-K, this business generated around $13–$14 million in net income, meaning that Kodak paid over 35x 2004 net income. Kodak's cash-on-cash return on this business one year after purchase was likely less than 3%. In 2007, this business would be included in the sale of Kodak's healthcare business to a private equity firm for a very low multiple of 4.3x EBITDA.

NextPress, Creo, Kodak Polychrome, Scitex Digital Printing (2004–2005). Kodak spent around $2.1 billion on these four acquisitions. NextPress and Kodak Polychrome were buyouts of existing Kodak joint ventures with other companies. Kodak paid 23x earnings for Kodak Polychrome and 35x earnings for Creo. The purchase price for Creo represented a 100% premium to where its stock was trading prior to the deal announcement.

These latter four acquisitions formed the base of a new graphic communications segment for Kodak that sold prepress equipment, software, and document scanning equipment to the commercial printing industry. While these businesses were viewed as more promising enterprises than Kodak's core business, they were still well-below-average businesses with high cyclicality, very low underlying growth, and limited recurring revenue.

Before the end of the decade, this business segment faced pricing pressure and declining sales of large presses, and would go on to report annual losses each year between 2009 and 2011. These acquisitions added debt to the balance sheet and contributed to four credit ratings downgrades between 2005 and early 2006, leaving Kodak's debt at the single B level, just one level above the lowest rating for a non–investment grade credit.

These acquisitions and the burden they placed on Kodak's already stretched balance sheet led Kodak to sell its healthcare business to a private equity firm in 2007 to pay down debt. By 2013, the buyer of Kodak's healthcare business would report that it had already generated a return of 2.6x its original investment simply through the dividends it had received over the past six years.[2]

Kodak Declares Bankruptcy

In 2007, Kodak reported negative FCF, and from 2008 to 2011 Kodak reported negative operating cash flow. This culminated in a massive $1 billion negative operating cash outflow in 2011. Back in 2007, Kodak, despite all its challenges, still had a pension plan that was overfunded by $1.5 billion. But the Great Financial Crisis (GFC) hit and decimated Kodak's pension plan. The plan's assets fell from $10.7 billion in 2007 to $7.5 billion in 2008 as global equity markets plummeted. The massive decline in interest rates in the years that followed put further upward pressure on Kodak's pension liabilities. Unfortunately, Kodak did not have any cash flow to inject into its pension plan, as it was not generating any at the time. By the end of 2011, Kodak's pension plan was underfunded by $1.7 billion.

On January 19, 2012, almost 128 years after George Eastman received his first patents for storing film on a roll and 124 years after he made his first camera to use this new technology, Kodak declared bankruptcy.

Nineteen months later, upon Kodak's emergence from bankruptcy with creditors receiving pennies on the dollars and pensioners receiving diminished retirement benefits, US Bankruptcy Court judge Allan Gropper would declare that "Kodak's decline and bankruptcy is a tragedy of American economic life."[3]

There is no question in my mind that Kodak's demise was inevitable and there was nothing the board or management team could have done to make it a viable long-term business. Kodak generated revenue and profits primarily from consumer and professional film and related photofinishing, healthcare film, and motion picture film. Digital cameras and ultimately smartphones would reduce the marginal cost of capturing an image to close to zero. Movie theaters would replace analog projectors with digital projectors, massively reducing demand for motion picture film. While Kodak would sell its health imaging business in 2007, this business also faced secular challenges as digital x-rays, software, and storage would dramatically reduce the need for analog healthcare film. Kodak's move into the tangential business of graphic communications was the action of a desperate management team and board trying to find growing cash flows to replace the declining cash flows of its core business. However, even if Kodak had not bought into this business, it would not have altered its inevitable demise.

WHAT CAN BE LEARNED FROM WHAT HAPPENED TO KODAK?

While Kodak's bankruptcy was inevitable, there are still lessons to be learned from its demise.

First, after 2001, Kodak's management correctly turned off share repurchase (with the exception of $301 million of ill-timed share repurchase in 2008) and did not buy back any stock between 2003 and 2007. Buying back stock of a declining business is frequently a capital allocation error. While the returns can look attractive in the early years, if cash flows are declining, the returns in the subsequent years will look progressively poorer. In the case of a company that goes bankrupt, the return on buybacks is negative.

Second, when acquisitions are made to reposition the company for strategic purposes, deal return thresholds are sacrificed to save the company. In the end, these acquisitions frequently generate poor returns and fail to achieve their Hail Mary strategic objective.

Third, Kodak's massive expansion into a tangential business (graphic communications) was a mistake. Management teams and boards focused on making acquisitions to fix a company are often rightly hesitant to enter into brand new businesses. As a result, they often limit acquisitions to markets where they already have a presence or that are tangential to their existing business. In the case of Kodak, while graphic communications was a better business than the company's core business, it was still a poor, capital-intensive business that generated low and eventually negative returns on capital.

It would have been much better if Kodak had simply returned this capital to shareholders. Overpaying for a "new business" does not create shareholder value. If investors previously owned a business with declining cash flows and now own a business with declining cash flows as well as a new business worth far less than what it was acquired for, they are not on a path to shareholder value creation.

Fourth, when a firm's cash flows are under pressure, an aggressive acquisition strategy can put the balance sheet at risk and cause financial instability. This is exactly what Kodak's $2.93 billion of acquisitions between 2001 and 2005 did. These acquisitions, which were done at high valuations, ended up pressuring Kodak to sell its healthcare business for a low multiple to repair the company's balance sheet. The loss of this healthcare EBITDA also negatively impacted Kodak cash flows. Kodak would mostly likely have survived longer if it had not gone on an acquisition spending binge and instead kept the healthcare business.

Fifth, Kodak's aggressive acquisition program forced it to cut back on dividends. This limited the amount of cash flows that could be returned to shareholders. A declining stream of cash flows still has value for shareholders, but only if that cash is returned to shareholders. If a company's value is the present value of its future cash flows, a company that does not return capital to shareholders for 10 years and subsequently declares bankruptcy is essentially worthless day one.

Firms facing declining cash flows should return excess capital to shareholders and bring forward cash flows to maximize the present value of the cash flow stream. Buying back stock or making strategic repositioning acquisitions with poor returns materially reduces the present value of future cash flows and ultimately destroys shareholder value.

KODAK AND THE ISSUE OF SECULAR RISK

While Kodak may be an extreme case, many companies these days face some degree of secular risk. Secular risk is the emergence of a new competitive force, technological advance, change in customer habit, or regulatory change that is structural and long term and that results in a slower top-line growth rate, margin compression, and/or valuation multiple contraction.

Importantly, this is not a situation in which a business's growth slows due to the law of large numbers or a temporary loss of market share to an established competitor. Secular risk represents something structural and long term in nature.

When I first joined T. Rowe Price as a young associate analyst in 1998, secular risk was a rather minor investment issue. Companies such as Polaroid and Sears were viewed as having various degrees of secular risk. However, this risk was not widespread. At the time, technology hardware companies and many retailers were still viewed as growth companies. At the height of the dot-com bubble in the late 1990s and early 2000s, many companies in distribution industries were temporarily believed to face secular risk from the rise of the internet. However, with the collapse of the internet and tech bubble, this concern largely disappeared.

When I became a portfolio manager in 2006, secular risk was still viewed as a relatively minor issue. Amazon was beginning to have an impact on select retailers, newspapers were under threat, and imaging companies such as Kodak, Polaroid, Pitney Bowes, and Xerox were struggling as demand for their goods and services declined. However, secular risk was still not widespread. In my first years as a portfolio manager, the topic of secular risk came up in less than 5% of the meetings I had with management teams.

But a decade later secular risk had exploded onto the scene. It was mentioned much more frequently in meetings. My team and I decided to apply the definition of secular risk explained previously to all of the companies in the S&P 500. In late 2016 and early 2017, we were surprised to find that around 20% of the market capitalization of the S&P 500 had some degree of secular risk. We updated this analysis every quarter and by early 2019 estimated that 31% of the S&P 500 faced secular risk. In the last two years, this percentage has actually declined, even as we have added additional companies to the secular risk list, as the secular risk group has systematically underperformed the market.

Why Secular Risk Has Expanded Enormously in the Past Decade

Major forces that have contributed to secular risk include:

Amazon. Amazon has disrupted multiple industries including retail, technology hardware, and on-premise software due to the growth of its Amazon shopping site and Amazon Web Services (AWS) business.

Netflix. Netflix offers a low-cost digital platform for commercial-free quality television that is far superior to traditional cable television for many viewers. This has caused challenges for cable systems and cable networks.

SaaS software. The advent of software-as-a-service (SaaS), which can be deployed in the cloud and reduces the need for servers, IT staff, and technology integrators, has reduced demand for on-premise software and proprietary technology hardware equipment.

Shale Oil. The exploitation of shale oil in the United States has created a low-cost, readily available source of oil and natural gas. This has put pressure on energy prices and reduced the value of offshore oil reserves.

Food companies. Consumers are eating less processed food and buying more food through the internet (with more options than they can find at a traditional grocery store). This has put pressure on traditional, center-of-the store-based food companies.

No longer is secular risk limited to small companies representing a diminutive amount of the S&P 500's market capitalization and profit pool. Big companies are now being impacted as well. All signs point to more companies, not fewer, becoming affected by secular risk.

One of the important questions I am often asked when I speak on this topic is whether it is possible to escape or eliminate secular risk.

Apple is the best example of a company escaping secular risk.

Apple's revenues declined from $11 billion in 1995 to $5.9 billion in 1998. Over this same period, its shareholder equity declined from $2.9 billion to $1.6 billion and its long-term debt more than tripled. Apple lost money in both 1996 and 1997. In fact, the situation was so dire that a portion of Apple's long-term debt was rated CCC by S&P. This is the lowest rating a nonbankrupt company can receive from a credit rating agency. Apple was viewed as a declining niche business in a personal computer market dominated by Microsoft Windows–based operating systems. Two decades later, Apple would have more than a $2 trillion market capitalization driven primarily by the phenomenal success of the iPhone.

Microsoft was once viewed as having secular risk as well. Between fiscal years 2011 and 2015, Microsoft's EPS declined. Microsoft's CEO was so worried about the rise of smartphones and their potential impact on the personal computer market that he made the expensive, ill-fated acquisition of Nokia's phone business (see Chapter 20). In mid-2021, Microsoft had a $1.9 trillion market capitalization, with its stock up almost 7-fold since the Nokia announcement as it built a highly competitive cloud computing platform and turned its legacy software application business (Word, Excel, PowerPoint) into a software-as-a-service available on numerous devices including Apple's.

But Apple and Microsoft are exceptions to the rule; it is hard to defeat secular risk. What is interesting about the transformations of Apple and Microsoft is that both companies were able to outrun secular risk by introducing new products and services for consumers and businesses.

In contrast, as with Kodak and with Microsoft's acquisition of Nokia's phone business, the success rate in using capital deployment to "fix" or "reposition" a company is very low. I cannot think of a company that has escaped the grasp of secular risk through capital allocation, but I can easily name dozens of companies that have tried and failed.

HOW NOT TO ADDRESS SECULAR RISK

Before considering what actions a company facing secular risk should take, let's first discuss what a company should not do.

Hail Mary Acquisitions. A Hail Mary deal, in which a firm overpays for a strategic repositioning acquisition is not the path to shareholder value creation. Combining a secularly challenged business with an overpriced one does not create shareholder value, but rather diminishes it. These Hail Mary deals typically fall into one of two categories: growth and diversification.

- **Growth business.** A firm with a decelerating or declining core business will buy a growth business to improve the growth profile of the combined entity. However, these deals are usually done at expensive valuations and produce low returns. Acquisitions such as Altria's minority interest of JUUL, IBM's acquisition of Red Hat, and Dr. Pepper's acquisition of Bai all fall into this category.

  Initial returns are usually low and, these acquisitions often fail to deliver on rosy expectations for multiple reasons. First, the entrepreneurs and management teams who built these companies are unlikely to stay following the acquisition. The sale process may result in a big payday for the management team, which turns its attention to the next startup opportunity. Second, the entrepreneurial culture of the acquired growth company is often lost inside of a large organization. Third, for those employees who stay, equity compensation is now in the form of stock in a decelerating or declining business. And their formerly robust, independent business, now a division in the faltering parent company, has minimal impact on the fundamentals and stock price of the new parent. In the vast majority of these acquisitions, the growth business becomes less valuable inside the new company than it was before it was acquired.

- **Diversification.** A company with emerging secular challenges will often attempt to diversify its business mix by expanding into a near-adjacent business. Comcast's acquisition of Sky Broadcasting, Kodak's graphic communications acquisitions, and AT&T's acquisitions of DirectTV and Time Warner all fit into this category. These are typically not growth businesses, but they tend to diversify and expand the company's cash flows. While the returns typically are not as bad as when a company buys a growth asset, they often produce lower returns than simply returning capital to shareholders. These deals often add significant leverage to the acquiring firm's balance sheet, reduce financial flexibility, and cause dividends to be cut.

In Table 25.2, the acquisition of a growth asset (for a premium) does not alter the economics of the core business. In addition, it results in a more leveraged balance sheet and decline in underlying shareholder value.

One could argue that I am being too conservative in valuing the growth asset at its market value pre-deal, as Company A will likely generate synergies from the growth asset and increase its underlying value. While that may be true, however, given the different growth trajectories of the two companies it is likely that they are not in the same business and thus will see limited synergies. Indeed, the growth asset will probably become less valuable following the acquisition, as the existing management is unlikely to remain with the business for the long term.

TABLE 25.2

Growth Asset Acquisition Destroys Shareholder Value

Company A Pre-Deal	
Cash Flows Declining 3% per Year	
Net Present Value of Future Cash Flows (ex/ Int. Exp.)	$2,000
Company Has $300 Million in Debt	($300)
Underlying Value of Company A	$1,700
Company A Makes Repositioning Strategic Deal	
Underlying Value of Company A Pre-deal	$1,700
Public Market Value of Growth Asset Pre-deal	$200
Value of Two Businesses Ex/New Debt Incurred	$1,900
Subtract	
New Debt Incurred (assumes paid 50% premium to market value)	($300)
Underlying Value of NewCo	$1,600
Value Destruction for Company A Shareholders	($100)
Percentage Decline for Company A Shareholders	−5.9%

This sum-of-parts analysis also ignores the heightened financial risk associated with incremental leverage. If the market correctly perceives that the management team of Company A is making poor capital allocation choices, it will award the firm a lower valuation multiple. In reality, the level of value destruction is likely to be materially greater than the 6% I assumed in Table 25.2.

Share repurchase. Buying back stock of a business with decelerating or, especially, declining cash flow is often a mistake. While buying back stock may produce good returns in the early years, the returns in the out years are often very poor.

Figure 25.1 presents two companies: Company A with cash flows growing 5% per year trading and trading at 20x FCF, and Company B with cash flows declining 3% per year and trading at 12x FCF. While the cash-on-cash returns from buying back stock are higher in the early years for Company B than Company A, by year 7, Company B is earning higher cash returns, and by year 10, Company B is generating 2% higher returns.

FIGURE 25.1

Return on Capital from Share Repurchase in Subsequent Years

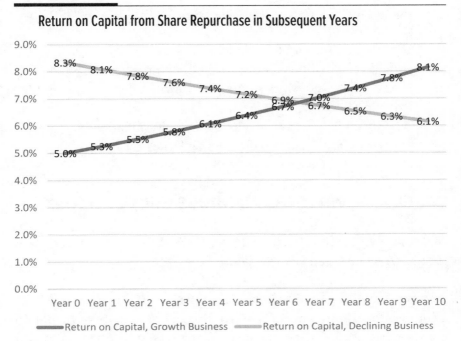

Return on Capital, Growth Business — Return on Capital, Declining Business

There is nothing wrong with a company with declining cash flows as long as those cash flows are paid out to shareholders in the form of dividends or regular special dividends to maximize the present value of those future cash flows. Share repurchase defers the return to existing shareholders and for many businesses with declining cash flows, destroys shareholder value.

As with Kodak, companies facing secular risk can create a very negative flywheel that accelerates their ultimate demise:

- Revenues and cash flows decline.
- Stock market awards the company a lower valuation multiple reflecting its secular risks.
- Given the company's low valuation, it can no longer use its stock as "currency" to make acquisitions.
- Company increases restructuring activity to lower costs.
- Restructuring spending reduces cash flows.
- Company makes strategic, low return "repositioning" acquisitions.
- Debt increases and cost of debt rises.
- Financial flexibility is diminished, company is forced to pay down debt, and its debt may be downgraded to non–investment grade.
- Company is forced to sell assets for low valuations.
- In worst-case scenario, the company files for bankruptcy.

EFFECTIVE WAYS TO ADDRESS SECULAR RISK

Now that I've outlined what not to do, I will address what a company should do when faced with secular risk.

Accept that the core business is secularly challenged and that capital allocation is unlikely to fix this. This in no way should be construed as advice that companies facing secular challenges should just give up and accept their fates. Microsoft and Apple prospered because they developed new products that their customers valued and in doing so, achieved escape velocity from secular risk.

Firms facing secular risk should create new products and services that expand their revenue potential into more sustainable profit streams. Best Buy accomplished this by growing its service business with Geek Squad; this helped it avoid the fate of Circuit City. If a distribution channel for a firm's products is under secular pressure (like traditional grocery stores or shopping malls), it can expand into new, emerging channels of distribution. Moreover, firms can still make acquisitions as long as intermediate-term returns are greater than those from returning capital to shareholders, using reasonable underlying assumptions.

The key here is the need for management and the board to accept that capital allocation can rarely, if ever, overcome secular challenges in the core business. Once a board and management team accept this, they are far less likely to fall into the negative cycle so many companies undergoing secular challenges find themselves in.

Manage debt conservatively. With cash flows under pressure, companies too often turn to their balance sheet to make strategic repositioning acquisitions. These acquisitions increase debt, elevate interest costs, and reduce financial flexibility. Ultimately, they fail to achieve the underlying strategic rationale for the deals. In many cases, these deals accelerate the demise of the company and limit the cash flows that could be returned to shareholders.

Divest. For a company that has part of its business facing secular challenges but another part still healthy, divesting the challenged business can be an option. While it is unlikely to receive a high valuation, a buyer with a competing business may be able to generate synergies by combining the businesses and pay a higher price as result.

In addition, if 20% of a company faces secular risk and requires constant restructuring programs and significant management time, it is probable that this division's challenges are hurting the performance of the other 80%, that is, the "good" business. The "good" business may not be receiving the time and attention from management that it needs to reach its full potential. In this case, a divestiture not only increases the growth rate of the company and reduces its secular risk, but it also allows management (and its investors) to refocus on the "good" business.

Create a GrowthCo and a ValueCo. For a company with some businesses that have secular challenges and others that don't, one of the best ways to maximize shareholder wealth is to create two publicly traded companies.

GrowthCo would hold the assets without secular risk. This company can support a higher level of debt and will likely focus its capital allocation on acquisitions, share repurchase, and moderate dividends.

ValueCo will hold the businesses undergoing secular challenges. Its focus should be on maximizing cash returns to shareholders through dividends and regular special dividends while continuing to invest in innovative products and services. ValueCo can also be used as a consolidation vehicle for similarly challenged businesses.

Pay a regular special dividend. Companies undergoing secular challenges should maximize cash returns to shareholders. Companies should pay out a modest regular dividend, as most investors view the payment of a regular dividend as a promise and react very negatively to a cut. At the end of the year, firms should commit to paying out all cash flows above a certain debt threshold or all cash flows after coverage of the regular dividend, growth capital spending, and acquisitions.

For multiple reasons, this is the optimal capital allocation strategy for a company that is undergoing secular challenges.

First, it reduces the risk of a cut in the regular dividend. Second, it gives the company financial flexibility. If an attractive acquisition opportunity presents itself, or a high-return, large capital spending program is developed during the course of the year, it allows the firm to pursue those investments. While these situations are likely to be rare for a company undergoing secular risk, they can occur. Third, investors will appreciate that the company will pay a regular special dividend based on excess cash flows the company generates during the year. Fourth, in a world in which very low interest rates and modest dividend yields mean investors need higher cash yields on their investments to retire, the combined yield (regular dividend + regular special dividend) from these companies can be very appealing. Fifth, and most important, the regular special dividend brings forward cash flows to maximize their present value.

Don't ignore pensioners. This focus on paying out the majority of FCF to shareholders through dividends and regular special dividends should not come at the expense of pensioners. A firm undergoing secular challenges that faces bankruptcy 5, 10, or 15 years down the road still has a moral obligation to retirees to maintain adequate funding of its pension plans.

Institutional bond holders understand the risks of buying debt in a company that is going through secular challenges and are compensated for this risk with a higher yield. Pensioners are not adequately compensated for this risk and have no alternatives. Paying out dividends and regular special dividends is the correct strategy to maximize value for long-term shareholders, but it should not come at the expense of the firm's pensioners.

CHAPTER 26

Best Board Practices: The 14-Point Strategic Plan

An engaged board with a long-term focus that creates a sustainable, comprehensive process around capital allocation, shareholder engagement, business improvement, and management incentives is very likely to maximize shareholder value. This chapter will detail the eight key strategic actions and six required mindsets boards must implement and embrace in order to achieve a strong, repeatable process with regard to these crucial factors.

THE EIGHT STRATEGIC ACTIONS

Strategy 1: Compare Returns of All Alternatives Before Deploying Capital

Every capital deployment decision should be subject to a comprehensive analysis of its expected returns over the intermediate term, followed by a comparison to the returns from alternative forms of capital deployment. In addition, it is essential to consider how the decision will impact the firm's return on invested capital, its FCF per share growth, its cyclicality, and its organic growth rate relative to all the various alternatives, including taking no action. This practice should be standard operating procedure as it will increase the odds that the firm deploys capital at the highest returns.

Strategy 2: Focus on Return on Invested Capital (ROIC) Instead of Discounted Cash Flow (DCF) or Internal Rate of Return (IRR)

With rare exceptions, an ROIC approach is the best way to judge the attractiveness of an investment over the intermediate term. It is simple but effective, and more difficult to manipulate. A DCF or IRR analysis that uses a terminal value multiple or terminal growth rate is much easier to manipulate. Can't generate high enough returns? Just change the terminal multiple from 10x to 12x or the terminal growth rate from 3% to 4% and *voila*! The acquisition looks attractive.

Also, remember to use after-tax cash flows and post-capital-spending FCF in the numerator. Unfortunately, taxes are a fact of life, and a firm that does not spend anything on capital expenditures to maintain its business will grind to a halt. These are ongoing costs and should be subtracted when determining the FCF of a business or investment.

Last, in an acquisition, the denominator should include not only the purchase price, but also the cash costs to achieve synergies, investment banking fees, costs associated with retention packages for employees, and the embedded option liability associated with a breakup fee.

Strategy 3: Monitor the Returns from Capital Deployment

Any executive who brings an acquisition or large capital spending program to the board for approval is more likely to bring attractive capital deployment programs underwritten by reasonable assumptions if he understands that he will be held accountable for the returns from the capital deployment in the future.

However, the importance of monitoring returns goes much deeper than simply holding management accountable. It is an opportunity to learn from success and failure. What are the characteristics of prior capital deployments that delivered higher or lower than expected returns? How can that knowledge shape future capital deployment to deliver better results? A board that is willing to examine past decisions critically and learn from them is far more likely to improve over time and avoid repeating mistakes.

Strategy 4: Identify a List of Potential Acquisitions

Management and the board should identify a series of acquisition targets that would fit well with their portfolio regardless of whether the businesses are for sale. They should proactively identify situations in which the owners of these businesses might be willing to sell due to:

- A change in direction that makes the business less strategic to its current owner
- Temporarily elevated leverage at the company, which might make it more amenable to a sale
- Age of CEO
- Financial distress

In addition, the board should encourage the management team to engage in ongoing dialogue with the owners of private companies, even if they are not for sale. While this does not eliminate the risk of an auction, it makes it more likely that the owners will at least consider a one-on-one negotiation when they choose to sell.

Strategy 5: Create Appropriate Incentives for Management

The bulk of management compensation should be based on intermediate-term rather than short-term performance. Metrics that are most likely to produce long-term shareholder value and lead to a higher valuation by investors should be emphasized above all else. These metrics include ROIC, organic revenue growth, organic margin expansion, and FCF per share growth combined with dividends.

FCF per share growth combined with dividends is critically important. It takes into account both ways in which a firm can create value for shareholders—through income (dividends) and capital appreciation (FCF growth per share as proxy)—and allows management to find the right balance between the two.

Metrics such as EPS or revenue growth are flawed in isolation and should be avoided. Short-term EPS growth can be easily manufactured in a world of low interest rates, but often at the cost of substandard returns on capital. Moreover, earnings are not the same thing as FCF. Earnings cannot be redeployed to create shareholder value, but FCF can. Earnings can be manipulated by altering depreciation schedules, changing book tax rates, or releasing reserves. Earnings growth that requires large investments in working capital to support it is far less attractive. For all of these reasons, boards and management teams are much better served using FCF rather than earnings as an effective measurement.

Total shareholder return (TSR) metrics that encompass both price appreciation of the underlying stock as well as the dividends (income) investors receive are also preferable when measuring the relative success of a management team. However, these objectives should be intermediate term as opposed to short term in nature. This will incentivize management to make the right decisions over the intermediate term and ultimately create long-term shareholder value—rather than making ill-advised, short-term decisions to prop up the stock price.

Strategy 6: Develop a Long-Term Strategic Plan to Make Each Business Better

What are the strategies, investments, acquisitions, restructuring actions, and divestitures necessary to improve each business's growth rate, increase aftermarket/service/consumables exposure, take market share, and expand its addressable market? If a business is growing at 2%, how do we improve it to 3% or even 4%? Is it through geographic expansion? Does the business need additional R&D and sales force to attack an adjacent market with a redesigned set of products? Is there a commoditized business line that should be discontinued or sold, thereby enabling internal resources to be directed elsewhere? This plan should be monitored at least annually to ensure that the investments made are delivering on their objectives.

Strategy 7: Conduct an Annual Review of Strategic Alternatives

Once a year, the board should take a dispassionate view of various strategic alternatives including, but not limited to, the sale of the company, spinning off one or more business units, and the sale of non-core businesses.

Strategy 8: Engage with Shareholders

Board members are the elected representatives of the owners of the firm, the shareholders. Yet board members have very limited direct contact with shareholders. This is a mistake, and more accurately, a missed opportunity. Every board should have at least one representative who reaches out to the largest shareholders at least once a year. This board member should elicit shareholders' perspectives on the company, its capital allocation, industry dynamics, and important strategic issues by asking the following questions:

- What can the company do better?

- What do you think is the right mix of share repurchase and dividends?
- How should management be compensated?
- What actions are other firms taking that we could learn from or copy?
- What did you think about the last acquisition we made?
- How is the industry evolving, and how can we take advantage of that change?
- What is your opinion of the CEO and CFO?
- If you could change one or two things about the company, what would they be?

Now clearly, not every conversation will prove to be enlightening. Some investors may advocate for an action that could increase the share price in the short term but destroy shareholder value in the long run, such as taking on too much debt or engaging in a risky acquisition. Moreover, investors may have very different perspectives on many of these questions.

Nevertheless, it is quite likely that valuable insights would emerge from these conversations. While there might be disagreement among investors in one area, there could be broad agreement in another. Investors who look at dozens, if not hundreds of companies might provide actionable insights and highlight innovative strategies that other companies are exploiting to create shareholder value.

I can think of no downside to engaging with large shareholders, and I see multiple positives, including:

- A board that understands the perspectives of its shareholders is less likely to be surprised by the reaction of its stock to a capital allocation or strategic decision.
- The act of engagement by itself breeds goodwill and builds relationships that could be useful, especially if the company is the target of an activist or hostile takeover in the future.
- If an activist emerges and demands a series of steps be taken to create shareholder value, the board will be in a better position

to respond if it has already engaged with shareholders on many of these issues. Frequently, an activist will emerge and inform the board that its largest shareholders are supportive of the activist's policies. A board that has proactively engaged with its shareholders is better positioned to resist this.

- Shareholders can provide insight into the quality of the management team.
- These conversations will highlight topics on which investors have strong, unified opinions. This does not mean the board needs to act in accordance with them, but it should be aware of them and, more important, the reasoning behind them.

CRITICALLY IMPORTANT MINDSETS BOARDS MUST EMBRACE

Mindset 1: Challenge Assumptions

Numbers in a spreadsheet conjuring up an attractive return for an acquisition, share repurchase program, or large capital spending do not make the big payoff a reality. In the case of an acquisition, the five-year forward FCF projections should be at the fiftieth percentile outcome. In other words, there should be an equal chance that the acquisition outperforms or underperforms the projections. Overly optimistic projections will lead companies down a path of disappointing returns, and overly pessimistic projections will lead companies to forgo attractive investments.

Projections for growth should be based on historical trends, external industry analyses, sell-side analyst projections, and a healthy dose of the outside view, especially if growth rates are elevated and expected to remain high.

Boards should also look at best-, base-, and bad-case outcomes for returns (seventy-fifth, fiftieth, and twenty-fifth percentiles). If the bad outcome's returns are still better than the other alternatives, it is a powerful signal of a very positively skewed risk-adjusted return.

Mindset 2: Be Willing to Say No

I have never served on a board of directors and don't pretend to fully appreciate the dynamics between executives and board members. However, over my 23-year career, I have often asked executives how many times they have brought an acquisition to the board for their approval and seen it rejected. I have been surprised by the consistency of their responses, which point to this being a rare occurrence.

In some of the worst acquisitions of all time, such as Hewlett-Packard's acquisition of Autonomy, it is clear that the board had serious reservations but still approved the transaction. If a board is well versed in capital allocation, as this book seeks to achieve, systematically looks at acquisitions versus capital allocation alternatives, and focuses on returns on capital as opposed to more manipulable metrics (DCF, IRR), it should have an easier time saying no to an acquisition, share repurchase program, or large capital spending program.

Mindset 3: Take Everything Investment Bankers Say with a Grain of Salt

Investment bankers provide necessary services for firms engaging in M&A including:

- Facilitating debt and equity capital raising
- Maximizing the takeover price in a sale process by making sure every firm that might be interested is able to bid
- Defending against a hostile bid
- Providing advice

However, investment bankers are highly incentivized toward action and the consummation of M&A. In their insightful paper "Why Merger and Acquisition (M&A) Waves Reoccur: The Vicious Circle from Pressure to Failure," Christopher Kummer and Ulrich Steger partially blame investment bankers and other promoters for the large percentage of M&A that fails to generate a return above firms' cost of capital.[1]

A board should consider its investment bankers' advice as one of many inputs informing M&A decisions, but be fully conscious that bankers get paid for doing deals. If I pick up daughter up from ballet practice and she informs me that mom says we need to buy ice cream on the way home, I will treat that information in the same way most boards should treat the advice of investment bankers. It may be true, but I would never make a decision based solely on that advice or input.

Mindset 4: Practice Patience

With regard to M&A especially, a board should practice patience and not pressure a management team to make acquisitions. There should be no M&A budget. There should be no long-term revenue objective inclusive of acquisitions. Hitting a revenue objective is often not difficult if enough capital is deployed, but size in isolation rarely corresponds to value creation for shareholders.

A board's objectives should be rooted in returns as opposed to empire building. If a firm goes down a path to acquire a business, but in the end the price becomes too high to generate attractive returns relative to other alternatives, the board should have the patience to consider it thoroughly and the discipline to say no. As I said earlier, some of the best "deals" are the ones management teams and boards have the discipline to say no to.

Mindset 5: Make Capital Deployment Independent of What Is Happening in the Core Business

A firm should not alter its capital allocation framework or objectives simply because the growth rate of the business is undergoing a change. The firm should not undertake acquisitions, share repurchase, or a large capital spending program to cover up a potential EPS miss or top-line air pocket. Deploying capital from a position of weakness or letting returns become subservient to some broader strategic objective is likely to destroy shareholder value. It also frequently fails to achieve the strategic objective underlying the poor capital allocation decision.

Mindset 6: Prioritize Shareholders over Executives

Situations exist in which shareholder objectives and executives' incentives become misaligned, especially with M&A. The average S&P 500 CEO earned $14.5 million in 2018. Many CEOs and other top executives have worked their entire careers to become a CEO or CFO, and many are unwilling to surrender that coveted role. What happens when a company is approached with an offer to be acquired for a large premium, but the CEO is only in his mid-fifties? It is quite possible that the priorities of the CEO and shareholders might diverge here. Moreover, if a CEO is close to retirement, he may be too open to selling the firm to collect the change of control package (in many cases, 2–4x his annual compensation).

Boards need to be aware of this inherent conflict and act in the best interests of their shareholders, even if that means accepting the compelling offer and relieving the CEO and other executives of their positions. It may also mean rejecting a less compelling offer when the CEO is in his mid-sixties.

Furthermore, a board should insist that any incoming calls about the sale of the company or a business are shared in real time with the entire board of directors.

Last, a board should never require or allow its CEO to insist, as a precondition for entering merger talks, that he become the CEO of the combined firm. This demand could preclude compelling offers for the firm and reduce the number of potential bidders. The latter could tilt the supply/demand dynamic in favor of the buyer and reduce the ultimate purchase price shareholders receive.

CHAPTER 27

Capital Allocation: Establishing a Long-Term Focus and Good Corporate Citizenship

Contrary to conventional wisdom, the deployment of excess capital to benefit long-term shareholders can and should be consistent with being a good corporate citizen and treating employees as partners. In many ways, these two objectives can become interlinked and, if executed well, can strengthen the firm.

Throughout this book, I have spoken about the importance of focusing on return on invested capital, optimizing the balance sheet, making dividend payments sustainable, utilizing share repurchases as an attractive capital deployment option, and creating the right incentives for an executive team. In this chapter, I connect the dots to demonstrate how these ideas and strategies can improve a firm and empower its employee base over the long term.

IMPORTANCE OF LONG-TERM FOCUS

Unfortunately, not every firm or investor is focused on the long term. Firms that cut R&D, engage in frequent restructuring, assume an adversarial relationship with their employees, and prioritize a short-term horizon are, in fact, doing all of their stakeholders a disservice. Maximizing profits in the short term can impair a firm's competitiveness and culture and, over the long term, lead to shareholder wealth impairment. I reject these policies and strategies not only as a human being, but also as an investor. While many companies have adopted these strategies at one time or another, few, if any, have created long-term shareholder wealth in the process.

Publicly traded companies today face a number of pressures that can push them to make short-term decisions around profit maximization. The performance of activist investors and hedge funds is often judged on a monthly, quarterly, or annual basis. These activists and hedge funds often pressure management teams to deliver strong results over the time period that corresponds to the investor's evaluation cycle. Many (but not all) activist investors look to make a quick buck by pressuring companies to cut costs to the bone, load up on debt, divest businesses, or sell.

There are multiple ways for firms to minimize these pressures, many of which have been discussed in previous chapters.

Focus on ROIC. Activists typically target companies with poor ROIC and a history of poor capital allocation. The easiest way to avoid activist pressure is to deploy capital wisely, with a focus on generating the highest risk-adjusted returns. This is by far the best activist repellant out there.

Engage with shareholders. A management team and board of directors that engage with their shareholders, especially long-term shareholders, are likely to have an investor base that understands the firm's strategy, believes its voice is being heard, and is less likely to pressure management to take short-term actions.

Maintain a long-term track record on value creation. A firm that has consistently created wealth through intelligent deployment of capital and an optimized balance sheet is far less likely to feel pressure to maximize profits in the short term or become an activist's prey.

Create appropriate incentives. The mix of executive compensation should be heavily skewed to the intermediate as opposed to short term. Total relative shareholder returns, FCF per share growth plus dividends, ROIC, and organic growth are the best metrics to encourage a focus on the intermediate term. While this will not eliminate the short-term market pressures a management team feels, it can partially offset them. Conversely, when compensation is heavily linked to annual metrics, these pressures are reinforced.

Focus on intermediate-term returns. When evaluating capital deployment alternatives, a firm should always choose the best risk-adjusted returns over an intermediate as opposed to short-term period. In most cases, the alternative with the best returns in the short term also has the best returns over the intermediate term, but not always. Looking beyond the short term will maximize FCF per share growth and returns on capital over the long term.

DEAR SEC: PLEASE STOP REQUIRING FIRMS TO REPORT QUARTERLY EARNINGS

I would also suggest that if we truly want to encourage a longer-term focus by management teams, boards, and shareholders, we should move away from the burdensome practice of reporting earnings quarterly. In 1970, the SEC mandated that all public companies report and file detailed financial statements every three months.

While I am generally in favor of more disclosure, this practice goes too far. It is costly for companies, especially small companies, to comply with, it takes management time away from running the business, and it encourages short-term decision-making to minimize the risk of missing quarterly earnings expectations. Today, many European companies report detailed financial statements only twice a year.

The only legitimate argument I have ever heard against this is that during the Great Financial Crisis (GFC), it was imperative for regulators and investors to know just how bad the situation was for banks, investment banks, and insurance companies. However, forcing all companies to report full financial statements on a quarterly basis seems like overkill.

It would be easy to establish rules that would require companies that are losing money, in financial distress, or are systemically important financial institutions to continue to file detailed quarterly financial disclosures. Other companies would not need to go through the unnecessary and counterproductive process of filing financial statements and hosting conference calls to discuss results every three months.

To encourage more long-term thinking and focus from management teams, boards, and investors, I recommend changing the frequency with which most public companies are required to file financial disclosures from four times per year to two times per year.

EMPLOYEES AS PARTNERS

As investors, we often value a firm based on the sum of its parts or the sum of its productive capacity. While both are important, in many respects the true underlying value of a firm is the sum of its employees. It can be difficult to gauge this underlying value from an external perspective, but a lack of visibility does not make it any less important.

A firm with an engaged, motivated, and well-compensated employee base is far more likely to develop innovative products, increase market share, and retain and attract talent. These are all critical factors in creating long-term shareholder wealth. Here are important actions leadership can take to develop a top-performing and loyal workforce.

Avoid Frequent Restructurings

A company that is constantly laying off staff will have employees who are far more worried about losing their jobs than excelling at them. Why would a talented employee choose to join or remain at a firm if she is worried about job security?

Choose Share Repurchase over Synergy-Driven Acquisitions

Critics of share repurchase fail to grasp multiple facts. The most important is that limiting share repurchase will inevitably lead to more capital deployed to acquisitions.

Acquisitions frequently involve synergies, and people are one of the largest sources of synergies. If employees are worried about losing their jobs after their firm announces or is targeted in an acquisition, their focus is no longer on serving the customer, developing new products, or gaining market share. Instead, they are worried about what is going to happen to them and their families.

When a firm announces a share repurchase program, not only is it more likely to generate attractive returns for shareholders, but it is also far less likely to negatively impact employees.

Compensate Employees More Than Peers

A firm that pays its employees more than its peers is likely to attract greater talent, experience less turnover, and have a well-motivated and engaged employee base. Employee turnover has a tangible underappreciated impact on the business. If an engineer, computer programmer, or scientist is working on a new product and then leaves the organization, how long will the product be delayed? Similarly, sales force turnover impairs sales funnels and customer intimacy.

A perfect example of this is Amazon. Amazon needs to attract tens of thousands of new employees every year to facilitate its growth. Amazon made a strategic decision to create a minimum starting wage of $15 per hour with attractive benefits. This is a substantially higher wage with better benefits than the vast majority of retail companies that it is disrupting. In many cases, Amazon's *starting wage* is higher than many of its competitors' *average wage* level. I firmly believe some of Amazon's success in recent years has been due to this investment in its workforce. In addition, in 2021, at a time in which many employers of lower-skill jobs are struggling to find enough workers as demand improves post-pandemic, Amazon does not appear to be facing the same issues, at least as of May of 2021, as it is able to attract and retain talent in part due its superior compensation.

Paying more need not hurt the bottom line. Firms should make every effort to minimize non-employee, non-value-added costs. Instead of dropping those savings right to the bottom line, they should share some of the savings with employees in the form of higher compensation.

In addition, a firm that is growing faster than the competition will also have more resources to devote to employee compensation. A firm with $1 billion in sales that is growing 3% per year with employee compensation at 30% of revenue can increase employee compensation at $9 million per year without impacting margins. If the firm can accelerate its organic growth to 5% through market share gains and new product introductions, it can increase employee compensation by $15 million per year without impacting margins.

If this same firm can also reduce low-value general and administrative costs, travel and entertainment costs, and consultancy costs from 5% to 4% of sales and share 50% of the savings with employees, it would free up another $5 million for increased employee compensation.

Compensate Management on Employee Job Satisfaction

Ten or twenty years ago, it was challenging for potential employees to truly understand the culture of a prospective firm. They might have known a couple of employees who worked at the firm and perhaps learned something about its culture during the interview process. When I graduated from college in 1998, I was so desperate to become an investment analyst that had I been offered a tobacco analyst role at an investment firm run by the devil, I would probably have said yes.

Today, Google, Facebook, and websites like Glassdoor make it much easier for a potential employee to understand the culture and working environment of a firm prior to interviewing. Firms that lack a strong culture or positive working environment will increasingly find that they have trouble attracting talent.

The best way to improve this is to compensate management teams based on a variety of absolute and relative employee metrics including:

- Job satisfaction
- Compensation satisfaction
- Quality of working environment
- Attractiveness of culture
- Likelihood of recommending a friend join the firm
- Expected period of time to remain at the firm
- Respect for firm leadership

A management team that is compensated on these metrics will focus on improving them.

Manage Downturns

How should a firm react to an economic or industry-specific downturn? Should it lay off staff aggressively to reduce the cost structure for temporarily lower demand level? While downturns in demand vary greatly across industries in both severity and duration, as a rule it is often counterproductive to lay off staff aggressively if the decline is temporary.

Cutting employees results in cash severance payments that depress FCF and limit the near-term benefits of restructuring. Moreover, reducing staff has an impact on morale and job satisfaction.

A far better strategy is to limit hires during a downturn and allow natural attrition to reduce the employee base. Not only is this less disruptive to employees, but it does not require large cash severance payments.

Instead non-employee expenses such as travel, entertainment, and other discretionary expenditures should be curtailed first. Bonus payments can and should be reduced. When demand reverts to normal in the future, the firm will not have to go through the process of finding new employees and retraining them.

A firm that protects its employees in a downturn, especially when its peers don't, is far more likely to retain and attract talented employees who will remember and revere an employer for these actions for years to come.

Being a good corporate citizen, partnering with employees, and following a long-term-oriented capital allocation strategy can also pay dividends for retail investors and retirees.

Optimize the Capital Structure

A firm that creates an optimal capital structure and annually stress tests its balance sheet is far less likely to run into balance sheet problems or bankruptcy down the road. Bankruptcy can be very painful for a firm's employees, who likely own a disproportionate amount of the company stock. In addition, pension claims for retirees become unsecured claims that are often curtailed as part of the bankruptcy process.

Don't Cut the Dividend

Setting the regular dividend at a sustainable level has advantages for retirees and retail investors in particular. These investors are much less likely than sophisticated institutional investors to be able to determine the sustainability of a dividend. They are far more likely to be negatively affected when a dividend is cut. Retirees increasingly need dividend payments to support themselves because government bond yields have collapsed across most of the developed world. Setting the dividend at a sustainable level reduces the risk that retirees and retail investors will find that the dividend that they were counting on is suddenly gone.

Allow Employees to Thrive

Throughout my career, I have experienced the benefits of working at a firm that does not engage in frequent restructurings, does not pursue large, synergy-focused acquisitions, and has continued to invest through multiple stock market downturns. The end result is an environment in which investors are singularly focused on creating value for the client with a minimal number of distractions. It is an environment that results in low voluntary and involuntary turnover, and attracts talent in strong and weak market environments. Ideally, every firm would strive to create a similar environment in which its employees can thrive.

CHAPTER 28

Conclusions

I n the opening chapter, I cautioned you that there are no easy answers when it comes to the deployment of capital. There is simply no cookie-cutter approach that applies to every company.

The implementation of a share repurchase program might be quite logical for a company with certain characteristics, while it would be highly value destructive for a company with different attributes. Increasing the dividend payout ratio to 60% might be a great long-term decision for a company with limited cyclicality trading at a high valuation. However, a 40% or 50% payout ratio for a company with more volatile cash flows that will need to cut its dividend in the next downturn would be a mistake. Two companies might bid on an acquisition with the potential to earn 8% returns on capital by year 5. Based on the returns they could achieve on other capital allocation alternatives, it might be a good decision for one company and a poor decision for the other.

Academic research and the historical record indicate that the average company deploys capital suboptimally. The data show that companies spent significant capital buying back stock in 2006–2007, only to pull back aggressively in 2009–2010 when their share prices were quite attractive. The same trend can be seen in the level of capital spent on acquisitions over a similar time period. Firms also tend to increase capital spending in the mid-to-late part of economic expansions—right before demand for their goods declines. Academic evidence on the efficacy of share repurchase has become less positive in recent years, and academic evidence on acquisitions and elevated levels of capital spending indicates that their returns remain quite poor.[1]

However, the fact that the average company deploys capital suboptimally does not predestine every firm to do so. **Not only is it possible to beat the odds, it is becoming increasingly imperative to do so.** With structurally slower nominal economic growth across most of the developed world, there is simply more excess capital that needs to be redeployed each year. The returns on the deployment of this excess capital are becoming a larger and larger driver of long-term shareholder returns (see Chapters 1 and 2).

It is my sincere hope that everyone who reads this book comes away with a deeper appreciation of the power of good capital allocation to create substantial value for long-term shareholders. I have provided examples of differentiated capital allocation *processes* that can be implemented to create shareholder value. Companies such as Roper Technologies, Thermo Fisher Scientific, Danaher, Fiserv, Marsh & McLennan, AutoZone, Texas Instruments, and many others have delivered exceptional returns for their shareholders. None of these firms delivered organic revenue growth substantially faster than nominal GDP for an any extended period of time. While all of these companies outgrew their peers organically and took market share over long periods of time, the underlying growth rates of the markets they served limited how much value they could create through organic growth alone. All of these firms delivered superior long-term shareholder returns because they excelled at capital deployment. It is essential to focus on the processes that underlie their decisions and the inefficiencies that these companies exploited, not the outcomes.

The tragedy of General Electric, while multifaceted, also highlights the danger of consistently poor capital allocation. General

Electric's board and management team destroyed enormous shareholder wealth, including in its large retail and retiree shareholder base, by deploying the vast majority of its excess capital at low or negative cash-on-cash returns. The real tragedy of the General Electric story is that the management team and board repeated the same process mistakes over and over and never learned from them.

Given the increasing importance of capital allocation, it is a topic that every executive and board member should study. A board and management team that are conversant in capital allocation are far less likely to make process errors when deploying excess capital.

By providing examples of superior capital allocation processes, along with relevant academic evidence, rules, and guideposts, this book seeks to facilitate further study and discussion of capital allocation theory. It is my sincere hope that these insights will ultimately result in capital allocation decisions that benefit all long-term shareholders and stakeholders.

BEST BOARD PRACTICES:
THE 14 POINT STRATEGIC PLAN CHECKLIST

Strategic Actions:

1. Compare Returns of All Alternatives Before Deploying Capital
2. Focus on Return on Invested Capital (ROIC) Instead of Discounted Cash Flow (DCF) or Internal Rate of Return (IRR)
3. Monitor the Returns from Capital Deployment
4. Identify a List of Potential Acquisitions
5. Create Appropriate Incentives for Management
6. Develop a Long-Term Strategic Plan to Make Each Business Better
7. Conduct an Annual Review of Strategic Alternatives
8. Engage with Shareholders

Critically Important Mindsets Boards Must Embrace:

1. Challenge Assumptions
2. Be Willing to Say No
3. Take Everything Investment Bankers Say with a Grain of Salt
4. Practice Patience
5. Make Capital Deployment Independent of What Is Happening in the Core Business
6. Prioritize Shareholders over Executives

LIST OF ABBREVIATIONS

CAGR: Compound Annual Growth Rate

CapEx: Capital Expenditures

CAPX Signal: Change in Capital Expenditure relative to change in Industry Capital Expenditure

CPI: Consumer Price Index

D&A: Depreciation and Amortization

DCF: Discounted Cash Flow

EBITDA: Earnings before Interest, Taxes, Depreciation, and Amortization

EBITDAR: Earnings before Interest, Taxes, Depreciation, Amortization, and Rent Costs

EPS: Earnings per Share

EV: Enterprise Value

FCF: Free Cash Flow

G&A: General and Administrative

GAAP: Generally Accepted Accounting Principles

GDP: Gross Domestic Product

IPO: Initial Public Offering

IRR: Internal Rate of Return

NPV: Net Present Value

OCF: Operating Cash Flow

OI: Operating Income
PP&E: Property, Plant, and Equipment
R&D: Research and Development
ROIC: Return on Invested Capital
ROTS: Return on Time Spent
TSR: Total Shareholder Return
WACC: Weighted Average Cost of Capital
W/C: Working Capital

REFERENCES

CHAPTER 1

Fernald, John, and Huiyu Li. "Is Slow Still the New Normal for GDP Growth?" Federal Reserve Bank of San Francisco Economic Letter, June 24, 2019.

Kliesen, Kevin L. "As Boomers Slow Down, So Might the Economy." Federal Reserve Bank of St. Louis, July 1, 2007.

Toosi, Mitra, and Teresa L. Morisi. "Women in the Workforce Before, During, and After the Great Recession." US Bureau of Labor Statistics, July 2017

US Bureau of Economic Analysis. Gross Domestic Product. Raw data accessed September 30, 202 via BEA.gov.

US Bureau of Economic Analysis. Real Gross Domestic Product, Quantity Indexes. Raw data accessed September 30, 2020, via BEA.gov.

CHAPTER 2

Carleton, Russell A. "Baseball Therapy: Does Postseason Experience Really Matter?" *Baseball Prospectus*, October 14, 2013.

Norris, Floyd. "Loving Your Stock Only When It's High." *New York Times*, September 18, 2009.

Waggoner, John. "Investing: Why Care About Stock Buybacks?" *USA Today*, January 31, 2013.

CHAPTER 3

Baker, Malcolm, Brendan Bradley, and Ryan Taliaferro. "The Low-Risk Anomaly: A Decomposition into Micro and Macro Effects." *Financial Analysts Journal* 70, no. 2 (2014): 43–58.

Credit Spreads 2001–2018. Barclays Live. January 22, 2019.

CHAPTER 5

Abarbanell, Jeffrey S., and Brian J. Bushee. "Abnormal Returns to a Fundamental Analysis Strategy." *The Accounting Review* 73, no. 1 (January 1998): 19–45.

Anderson, Christopher W., and Luis Garcia-Felijoo. "Empirical Evidence on Capital Investment, Growth Options, and Security Returns." *The Journal of Finance* 61, no.1 (February 2006): 171–94.

Chan, Louis K.C., Jason Karceski, Josef Lakonishok, and Theodore Sougiannis. "Balance Sheet Growth and the Predictability of Returns." Working Paper, 2008.

The Hershey Company. 2005–2007 Annual Reports.

The Hershey Company. Presentation, Consumer Analyst Group of New York Annual Conference, Boca Raton, February 19, 2014.

Li, Donglin. "The Implications of Capital Investment for Future Profitability and Stock Returns: An Overinvestment Perspective." PhD diss., University of California, Berkeley, January 2004.

Titman, Sheridan, K.C. John Wei, and Feixue Xie. "Capital Investments and Stock Returns." *Journal of Finance and Quantitative Analytics* 39, no. 4 (December 2004): 677–700.

CHAPTER 6

Allen, Franklin, Antonio E. Bernando, and Ivo Welch. "A Theory of Dividends Based on Tax Clienteles." *Journal of Finance* 55, no. 6 (December 2000): 2499–2536.

Arnott, Robert D., and Clifford S. Asness, "Surprise! Higher Dividends = Higher Earnings Growth," *Financial Analysts Journal* 59, no. 1 (2003): 70–87.

Fracassi, Cesare. "Stock Price Sensitivity to Dividend Changes." Working paper. Department of Finance—UCLA Anderson School of Management, July 2008.

Grullon, Gustavo, Roni Michaely, and Bhaskaran Swaminathan. "Are Dividend Changes a Sign of Firm Maturity?" *Journal of Business* 75, no. 3 (July 2002): 387–424.

Hart, Clare, and Mariana Connolly, *Dividends for the Long Term.* J.P. Morgan Asset Management LLC. April 2013.

The High Dividend Yield Return Advantage: An Examination of Empirical Data Associating Investment in High Dividend Yield Securities with Attractive Returns Over Long Measurement Periods. Tweedy, Browne Company LLC, 2014.

Jensen, Michael C. "Agency Costs of Free Cash Flow, Corporate Finance and Takeovers." *The American Economic Review* 76, no. 2 (May 1986): 323–29.

Jiang, Bing, and Tim Koller, "Paying Back Your Shareholders." McKinsey & Company, May 1, 2011.

Schwartz, Jeremy. "The Dividends of a Dividend Approach." WisdomTree Investments, Inc. 2018.

Zhou, Ping, and William Ruland. "Dividend Payout and Future Earnings Growth." *Financial Analysts Journal* 62, no. 3 (May–June 2006): 58–69.

CHAPTER 7

Brady, Kevin, Inga Chira, and Jeff Madura. "Special Dividend Distributions, Firm Characteristics, and Economic Conditions." *Journal of Applied Finance* 24, no. 1 (January 2014): 58–72.

Chou, De-Wai, Yi Liu, and Zaher Zantout. "Long-Term Stock Performance following Extraordinary and Special Cash Dividends." *The Quarterly Review of Economics and Finance* 49, no. 1 (2009): 54–73.

CME Group. "Dividend Payments." CME Group website.

CME Group. Q4 2011 Earnings Conference Call. February 2, 2012. Transcript accessed via Factiva.

DeAngelo, Harry, Linda DeAngelo, and Douglas J. Skinner. "Special Dividends and the Evolution of Dividend Signaling." *Journal of Financial Economics* 57, no. 3 (2000): 309–54.

CHAPTER 8

Bolten, Joshua, and Ken Bertsch. "Restricting Stock Buybacks Will Hurt the Economy." *New York Times*, March 4, 2019.

Buffett, Warren to "The Shareholders of Berkshire Hathaway Inc." February 25, 2017.

Dittmar, Amy, and Laura Casares Field. "Can Managers Time the Market? Evidence Using Repurchase Price Data." *Journal of Finance Economics* 115, no. 2 (January 2014): 261–82.

Edmans, Alex. "The Case for Stock Buybacks." *Harvard Business Review*, September 15, 2017.

Foote, Caleb, and Robert Atkinson. "Federal Support for R&D Continues its Ignominious Slide." Information Technology & Innovation Foundation, August 12, 2019.

Fu, Fangjian, and Sheng Huang. "The Persistence of Long-Run Abnormal Returns Following Share Repurchases and Offerings." *Management Science* 6, no. 4 (April 2016): 964–84.

Gibson, Kate. "S&P Buybacks Skidded to New Lows in Second Quarter." *MarketWatch*, September 15, 2009.

Gruber Joseph W., and Steven B. Kamin. "Corporate Buybacks and Capital Investment: An International Perspective." IFDP Notes. Washington, DC: Board of Governors of the Federal Reserve System, April 11, 2017.

Jensen, Michael C. "Agency Costs of Free Cash Flow, Corporate Finance and Takeovers." *American Economic Review* 76, no. 2 (May 1986): 323–29.

Kostin, David, Ben Snider, Arjun Menon, Ryan Hammond, Cole Hunter, and Nicholas Mulford. "Misperceptions Surrounding Corporate Cash Spending Priorities and the Economics of Share Repurchase," *US Equity Views*. New York: Goldman Sachs, March 7, 2019.

Larcker, David F., and Brian Tayan. "CEO Compensation: Data Spotlight." *CGRI Quick Guide Series*. Stanford Graduate School of Business, Corporate Governance Research Institute, 2019.

Lazonick, William. "The Curse of Stock Buybacks." *American Prospect*, June 25, 2018.

Lowrey, Annie. "Are Stock Buybacks Starving the Economy?" *Atlantic*, July 31, 2018.

Manconi, Alberto, Urs Peyer, and Theo Vermaelen. "Are Buybacks Good for Long-Term Shareholder Value? Evidence from Buybacks Around the World." *Journal of Financial and Quantitative Analysis* 54, no. 5 (October 2019): 1899–1935.

McGrath, Rita. "The Case for Banning Stock Buybacks." CNN, February 26, 2019.

Nathan, Allison and David Groman, eds. "Buyback Realities." *Top of Mind*, no. 77. New York: Goldman Sachs, April 11, 2019.

National Science Board. "Research and Development: US Trends and International Comparisons." *Science and Engineering Indicators 2020*. Alexandria, VA: National Science Foundation, 2020.

Peyer, Urs, and Theo Vermaelen. "The Nature and Persistence of Buyback Anomalies." *Review of Financial Studies* 22, no. 4 (April 2009): 1693–1745.

"R&D Expenditure." *Eurostat: Statistics Explained*, September 2019.
"Returning Capital to Shareholders." *Audit Committee Leadership Network in North America: ViewPoints*. Waltham: Tapestry Networks, Inc., October 27, 2016.
US Senator Tammy Baldwin. "U.S. Senator Tammy Baldwin Introduces Legislation to Rein in Stock Buybacks and Give Workers a Seat at the Table." Press Release, March 22, 2018.
Yardeni, Edward, Joe Abbott, and Mali Quintana. *Corporate Finance Briefing: S&P 500 Buybacks and Dividends*. Yardeni Research, Inc., December 13, 2019.
Zeng, Liyu, and Priscilla Luk. *Examining Share Repurchasing and the S&P Buyback Indices in the U.S. Market*. S&P Dow Jones Indices, March 2020.

CHAPTER 10

AutoZone. 1999–2019 Annual Reports.

CHAPTER 11

Bruner, Robert F. "Does M&A Pay? A Survey of Evidence for the Decision Maker." *Journal of Applied Finance* 12, no. 1 (2002): 48–68.
Christensen, Clayton M., Richard Alton, Curtis Rising, and Andrew Waldeck. "The New M&A Playbook." *Harvard Business Review* 89, no. 3 (March 2011): 48–57.
Christofferson, Scott A., Robert S. McNish, and Diane L. Sias. "Where Mergers Go Wrong." *McKinsey Quarterly*, no. 2 (June 2004): 92–99.
D'Angelo, Alex. "State of the M&A Deal in 2019." Cohen & Company, August 7, 2019.
Jenter, Dirk, and Katharina Lewellen. "CEO Preferences and Acquisitions." *Journal of Finance* 70, no. 6 (December 2015): 2813–52.
Kahneman, Daniel. *Thinking, Fast and Slow*. New York: Farrar, Straus and Giroux, 2011.
Koi-Akrofi, Godfred Yaw. "Mergers and Acquisitions Failure Rates and Perspectives on Why They Fail." *International Journal of Innovation and Applied Studies* 17, no. 1 (July 2016): 150–58.
Offenberg, David, and Christo Pirinsky. "How Do Acquirers Choose Between Offers and Tender Offers?" *Journal of Financial Economics* 116, no. 2 (May 2015): 331–48.
Renneboog, Luc, and Cara Vansteenkiste. "What Goes Wrong in M&As? On the Long-Run Success Factors in M&A." Working Paper, ECGI-Finance, December 2018.
Revenue Synergies in Acquisitions: In Search of the Holy Grail. Deloitte: M&A Institute, 2017.

CHAPTER 12

DuPont and Trian Partners. "A Referendum on Performance and Accountability." Trian Fund Management, L.P., February 17, 2015.
GlaxoSmithKline, "Why Our Transaction with Novartis Is Different." News release, February 27, 2015.

Gordon, James D., Richard Vosser, and Diana Na, *GlaxoSmithKline PLC: Novartis Business Swap and Divestment Offers Mid-High Single Digit Accretion Medium Term*. JP Morgan Cazenove Research, April 17, 2014. Accessed via FactSet.

Guyon-Gellin, Nicolas, Vincent Meunier, Amy Walker, Chris Eccles. *GlaxoSmithKline PLC: OTC/Vaccine Shift Key to Change in Growth Profile*. Morgan Stanley Research, May 14, 2014. Accessed via FactSet.

Hauber-Schuele, Alexandra. Novartis Business Update Call. April 22, 2014. Accessed via FactSet.

Honeywell. 2000–2004 Annual Reports.

Honeywell. Q4 2004 Conference Call Transcript. January 28, 2005.

"Honeywell Completes Acquisition of Novar PLC; Final Clearance from European Commission Confirmed." *Business Wire*, March 31, 2005.

Novar PLC. Interim Results Statement. July 27, 2004.

Witty, Andrew. GlaxoSmithKline PLC Business Update Call. April 22, 2014. Accessed via FactSet.

CHAPTER 13

Cornell, Robert T. *2Q Inline, RF Acq Provides Upside to '11*. New York: Barclays Capital, July 27, 2010.

Darling, Terry. *Strong Balance Sheet Optionality in Action, Maintain Buy*. Goldman Sachs, November 8, 2009.

Dray, Deane. *Upbeat Guidance and Accretive CBORD Deal Spark 5% Relief Rally*. Goldman Sachs, February 24, 2008.

Eastman, Richard. *FCF Steps up with PowerPlan*. Milwaukee: Robert W. Baird Research, May 21, 2018.

Eastman, Richard. *Q3 Shows Sluggish Trends, Accretive Acquisition Added*. Milwaukee: Robert W. Baird Research, July 1, 2016.

Eastman, Richard. *Upping CY 11/12 EPS Forecast for Northern Digital Acquisition*. Milwaukee: Robert W. Baird Research, June 7, 2011.

Giordano, Joseph, and Tristan Margot. *Roper Technologies Initiation: A Deep Stable of Businesses—All with Cash on the Brain*. New York: Cowen and Company. October 12, 2015.

O' Callaghan, Shannon. *Aderant Adds Another Strong Growth, Margin, and Cash Flow Software Business*. Zürich: UBS, October, 9 2015.

Roper Industries. 2001 and 2018 Annual Reports.

Roper Industries. "Roper Industries Announces Agreement to Acquire Neptune Technology Group Holdings Inc." News release, October 21, 2003.

Roper Industries. "Roper Industries Completes Acquisition of Northern Digital, Inc." News release, June 6, 2011.

Roper Industries. "Roper Industries to Acquire MHA." News release, April 17, 2013.

Roper Industries. "Roper Industries to Acquire Sunquest Information Systems." News release, July 30, 2012.

Roper Industries. "Roper Technologies to Acquire Aderant, Leading Software Solutions Provider to the Legal Profession." News release, October 8, 2015.

Roper Industries. "Roper Technologies to Acquire ConstructConnect, Leading Provider of SaaS Solutions for the Commercial Construction Industry." News release, October 31, 2016.

Roper Industries. "Roper Technologies to Acquire PowerPlan, Leading Provider of Software and Solutions for Financial and Compliance Management." News release, May 21, 2018.

"Roper Industries Agrees to Acquire Transcore Holdings." *Parking Network*, October 7, 2004.

Smith, David. *ROP: MEDTEC Acquisition Bolsters Healthcare Position*. Citigroup Smith Barney, December 12, 2005.

Smith, David. *ROP:CIVCO Deal to Be Additive in 2006, Represents New Leg*. Citigroup Smith Barney, June 20, 2005.

Tusa Jr., C. Stephen. *Our Take on Deltek Acquisition*. J.P. Morgan, December 8, 2016.

CHAPTER 14

DeWitt, Sarah, and Keith Cornelius. "Brown & Brown: Initiating Coverage at Underweight: Pure Play Insurance Broker with High Exposure to Softening P&C Prices." JP Morgan, June 28, 2016.

Fuller, Kathleen, Jeffrey Netter, and Mike Stegemoller. "What Do Returns to Acquiring Firms Tell Us? Evidence from Firms That Make Many Acquisitions." *Journal of Finance* 57, no. 4 (August 2002): 1763–93.

Glaser, Daniel. Marsh & McLennan Companies, Inc. Bank of America Merrill Lynch Insurance Conference Presentation. February 14, 2013. Accessed via FactSet: CallStreet, LLC.

Glaser, Daniel. Marsh & McLennan Companies, Inc. Investor Day Presentation. September 30, 2010,

Glaser, Daniel. Marsh & McLennan Companies, Inc. Investor Day Presentation, March 11, 2014. Accessed via FactSet: CallStreet, LLC.

Glaser, Daniel. Marsh & McLennan Companies, Inc. Q1 2018 Earnings Conference Call. April 26, 2018. Accessed via FactSet: CallStreet, LLC.

Hughes, Mark, and Michael Ramirez. Brown & Brown. "Q3 19 Follow Up, Reiterate Buy, Sun Trust Robinson Humphrey." October 28, 2019.

Kinar, Yaron, Charles Sebaski, and Joshua Shanker. "Willis Group: Initiating Coverage with a Hold Rating." Deutsche Bank, June 15, 2011.

Marsh & McClennan Companies, Inc. Deutsche Bank Financial Services Conference Presentation. May 31, 2016,

Marsh & McLennan Companies, Inc. Investor Presentation Handout. June 2019.

PerkinElmer, Inc. "Acquisition of EUROIMMUN Medical Laboratory Diagnostics AG by PerkinElmer, Inc." Call, June 19, 2017. Accessed via FactSet: CallStreet LLC.

Rehm, Werner, Robert Uhlander, and Andy West. "Taking a Longer-Term Look at M&A Value Creation." *McKinsey & Company*, January 1, 2012.

Stöcker, Winfried. "Transfer of EUROIMMUN to PerkinElmer." *Prof. Dr. Winfried Stöcker* (blog). June 21, 2017.

Vander Ark, Jon. Republic Services, Inc. Q2 2019 Conference Call, July 25, 2019. Accessed via FactSet: CallStreet, LLC.

CHAPTER 15
Bowen, David. "For a Fat Cat, He's Fast on His Feet." *Independent*, August 31, 1996.
Brummer, Alex, and Roger Crowe. *Weinstock: The Life and Times of Britain's Premier Industrialist.* New York: HarperCollins, 1999.
Davies, Ian. "Obituary: Simon Weinstock." *Independent*, May 20, 1996
CompanyHistories.com, s.v. "Marconi plc."
Danaher Corporation, "Danaher Corporation Announces Signing a Definitive Agreement to Acquire Marconi Commerce Systems." News release. December 12, 2001.
Danaher Corporation. "Danaher Corporation Announces Signing a Definitive Agreement to Acquire Marconi Data Systems." News release. January 10, 2002.
Danaher Corporation. *Form 10-K December 31, 2001.*
Encyclopedia.com, s.v. "The General Electric Company, PLC."
FundingUniverse, s.v. "Marconi plc History."
Grace's Guide to British Industrial History. s.v. "GEC."
Harrison, Michael. "Corporate Profile: The Man Spending GEC's Pounds 6bn." *Independent,* May 4, 1999.
Heller, Robert. "A Legacy Turned into Tragedy." *Guardian*, August 18, 2002.
"Lord Weinstock Great Industrialist Who Led GEC Successfully Until His Retirement." *Herald Scotland*, July 24, 2002.
Sabbagh, Dan, and Sean O'Neill. "Marconi: From Boom to Bust in a Year." *Telegraph*, September 7, 2001.
Science Museum Group. s.v. "General Electric Company plc."
Shaoul, Jean. "Lord Weinstock and the Near Terminal Decline of British Industry." World Socialist Website, July 27, 2002
"The £11bn Wreckers." *This Is Money*, July 16, 2001.
"UK: Arnold's Heir Unapparent- Simon Weinstock Will Not Succeed His Father at GEC." *Management Today*, November 1, 1991.

CHAPTER 16
Canadian Natural Resources Ltd. "Acquisition of Working Interest in the Athabasca Oil Sands Project and Other Oil Sands Assets by Can." March 9, 2017. Accessed via FactSet.
Royal Dutch Shell. Q4 2014 Earnings Release. January 29, 2015.
Royal Dutch Shell. Q1 2015 Earnings Release. April 30, 2015.
Royal Dutch Shell. Q4 2015 Earnings Release. February 4, 2016.
Royal Dutch Shell. Q1 2016 Earnings Release. May 4, 2016.
Royal Dutch Shell. Q4 2016 Earnings Release. February 2, 2017.

CHAPTER 17
First Data Corporation. Q4 2017 Earnings Release. February 21, 2018.
First Data Corporation. Q4 2018 Earnings Release. February 27, 2019.
First Data Corporation, *Schedule 14A, March 14, 2019.*
Fiserv, Inc. "Acquisition of First Data Corporation by Fiserv, Inc. Call." January 16, 2019. Accessed via FactSet: CallStreet, LLC.

Groberg, Jonathan, and Travis Steed. *Thermo Fisher Scientific: TMO + LIFE = A Life Sciences Staple.* Macquarie Group Equities Research, April 16, 2013.

Koning, David J., Robert W. Bamberger, and Partrick Schulz. *First Data Corporation (FDC): Nice Q4 Results/2019 Guidance; Raising FDC Estimates.* Robert W. Baird Equity Research, February 6, 2019.

Koning, David J., Robert W. Bamberger, and Patrick A. Schulz. *Fiserv, Inc. (FISV): Details on Q4 Results.* Robert W. Baird Equity Research, February 7, 2019.

Life Technologies Corporation. *Schedule 14A: Proxy Statement July 22, 2013.*

Muken, Ross, Michael Cherney, Vijay Kumar, and Elizabeth Anderson. *Thermo Fisher Scientific (TMO): One Lambda Makes TMO More "Special."* International Strategy & Investment Group LLC, July 16, 2012.

Schenkel, Doug, Chris Lin, Ryan Blicker, and Adam Wieschhaus. *DHR to Acquire GE Biopharma: Strategic and Financial Benefits Appear Attractive.* Cowen, February 25, 2019.

Thermo Fisher Scientific, Inc. Acquisition of Life Technologies Corporation by Thermo Fisher Scientific Inc Call. April 15, 2013.

Thermo Fisher Scientific, Inc. Analyst Meeting, May 22, 2019. Accessed via FactSet: CallStreet, LLC.

US Congressional Research Service, *National Institutes Health (NIH) Funding: FY1994–FY2020.* Washington, DC: Congressional Research Service, April 4, 2019.

CHAPTER 18

Al-Muslim, Aisha. "GE to Sell Part of Healthcare Business to Veritas Capital for $1.05 Billion." *Wall Street Journal,* April 2, 2018.

Ausick, Paul. "Why GE's Alstom Acquisition Was Misguided." *24/7 Wall St.,* June 7, 2019.

"Amphenol Corporation to Acquire the Advanced Sensors Business of GE." *Business Wire,* November 15, 2013.

Baker Hughes Company. 2008–2015 Annual Reports.

Baker, Liana B. "GE to Sell Rest of NBC Stake to Comcast for $16.7 Billion." Reuters, February 12, 2013.

Banerjee, Arunima. "Emerson Electric to Buy GE's 'Intelligent Platforms Division." Reuters, October 2, 2018.

Bergin, Tom. "GE to Buy UK Oil Pipemaker Wellstream for $1.3 Billion." Reuters, December 13, 2010.

Bowker, John. "General Electric to Buy UK's Sondex for $583 Mln." Reuters, September 3, 2007.

"Broadening GE's Security Business, Complementary Technologies and Channels to Market Will Create Significant New Growth Opportunities." *Buildings: Smarter Facility Management,* November 15, 2004.

Brumpton, Harry, and Rachit Vats, "GE to Merge Transportation Unit with Wabtec in $11.1 Billion Deal." Reuters, May 21, 2018.

"CareFusion to Acquire Vital Signs Division of GE Healthcare For $500 Million." *PR Newswire,* November 18, 2013.

Clarke, Peter. "Radstone Recommends GE Fanuc Offer to Shareholders." *EE Times*, September 18, 2006.

Coe, Nigel, Bhupender Bohra, and Cristian Ramos. *General Electric: Upcoming WAB and Healthcare Disposals Should Be Game Changers*. New York: Wolfe Research, 2018.

Crooks, Ed. "GE's $23bn Writedown Is A Case of Goodwill Gone Bad." *Financial Times*, October 4, 2018.

Dornbrook, James. "GE Sells Air Filtration Business for $265M." *Kansas City Business Journal*, November 5, 2013.

Gara, Antoine. "How Comcast 'Stole' NBCUniversal from General Electric." *Forbes*, February 13, 2013.

"G.E. to Buy Enron Wind-Turbine Assets." *New York Times*, April 12, 2002.

"GE Accelerates Growth in Mining with Planned Acquisitions of Equipment Makers Industrea Ltd. and Fairchild International." *Business Wire*, May 15, 2012.

"GE Acquires Instrumentarium for $2.4B." *Forbes*, October 9, 2003.

"GE Buys UK Aerospace Sensor Firm for £229m." *Electronics Weekly*, May 15, 2002.

"GE Buys Water Treatment Software Operations." *New York Times*, February 13, 2002.

"GE CEO: NBC Overpaid for iVillage." *MediaPost*, November 3, 2006.

"GE Completes $3 Billion Acquisition of Dresser, Inc.: Move Marks Latest Expansion of GE's Global Energy Infrastructure Business." *Business Wire*, February 1, 2011.

"GE Completes Acquisition of Cameron's Reciprocating Compression Division." *Business Wire*, June 3, 2014.

"GE Energy Completes Acquisition of BHA Group Holdings, Inc.; Transaction Expands GE's Environmental Services Capabilities." *Business Wire*, September 1, 2004.

"GE Fanuc Acquires SBS Technologies." *Vision Systems Design*, March 23, 2006.

"GE Healthcare to Acquire Biacore for $390M." *GenomeWeb*, June 20, 2006.

"GE Healthcare to Acquire Whatman for $713M." *GenomeWeb*, February 4, 2008.

"GE Healthcare to Take over Clarient in $580M Deal." *GEN: Genetic Engineering & Biotechnology News*, October 22, 2010.

"GE Industrial Systems to Acquire NovaSensor." *GE Reports*, August 2, 2002.

"GE Oil & Gas Buys Hydril From Tenaris for US$1.115B." *Hart Energy*, August 26, 2008.

"GE Reaches Deal with Comcast for NBC." NBC News.com, December 3, 2009.

"GE Specialty Materials Completes Acquisition of OSi Specialties." *Business Wire*, July 31, 2003.

"GE Takes Full Control of GELcore, Teams with Nichia." *LEDs Magazine*, August 31, 2006.

"GE to Acquire Lineage Power for $520 Million." *CNBC*, January 13, 2011.

"GE to Acquire Lufkin Industries." *Business Wire*, April 8, 2013.

"GE to Acquire Vetco Gray, Accelerating Growth across Oil & Gas Sector." *Business Wire*, January 8, 2007.

"GE to Buy Wood Group Division for $2.8B." *Rigzone*, February 14, 2011.

"GE to Expand in Life Sciences with Acquisition of Strategic Assets from Thermo Fisher Scientific." *Business Wire*, January 6, 2014.

"GE to Sell Advanced Materials Business Unit for $3.8B." *Reliable Plant*, September 2006.

"GE Unit Agrees to Buy Interlogix for $777 Million in Cash, Stock." *Wall Street Journal*, December 18, 2001.

"General Electric Agrees to Acquire Edwards Systems Technology." *Buildings: Smarter Facility Management*, November 15, 2004.

"General Electric Agrees to Acquire InVision; Combines Explosive Detection Technologies, Advancing GE Position in Infrastructure Security Industry; GE Updates First Half Outlook." *Business Wire*, March 15, 2015.

"General Electric Agrees to Acquire ZENON Environmental; Expands GE's Water & Process Technologies Platform with the Addition of Best-In-Class Ultrafiltration Membrane Technologies." *Business Wire*, May 14, 2006.

General Electric Aviation, "GE to Acquire Smiths Aerospace, Extending Aviation Offerings; Plans JV with Smiths Group to Build Global Detection Business." News release, January 15, 2007.

General Electric Aviation. "General Electric Company to Purchase Airfoil Technologies International-Singapore." News release, March 2, 2009.

General Electric. 1980 Annual Report.

General Electric. 2000–2019 Annual Reports.

General Electric. *Form 10-K February 24, 2017.*

General Electric. *Form 10-K February 26, 2019.*

General Electric. 2019 Fourth Quarter Performance Report. January 29, 2020.

General Electric. All M&A Deals via FactSet.

General Electric. *Form 10-K February 23, 2018.*

Gryta, Thomas, Joann S. Lublin, and David Benoit. " 'Success Theater' Masked Rot at GE: Under Immelt, Disdain for Bad News Led to Overoptimistic Forecasts, Botched Strategies." *Wall Street Journal*, February 22, 2018.

Hipple, Kathy, Tom Sanzillo, and Tim Buckley. *GE's $7.4 Billion Loss, Write-off on Baker Hughes: Another Bad Bet on Fossil Fuels.* Cleveland: Institute for Energy Economics, October 2019.

James, Meg. "NBC to Acquire Telemundo Network for $1.98 Billion." *Los Angeles Times*, October 12, 2001.

Keller, John. "GE Intelligent Platforms to be Renamed Abaco Systems; Acquisition Set to Close Monday." *Millitary and Aerospace Electronics*, November 17, 2015.

Kellner, Tomas. "Bladerunners: GE's Wind Business to Buy Danish Blade Maker for $1.65 Billion." *GE Reports*, October 11, 2016.

Kellner, Tomas. "GE Buys $500 Million Machine Analytics Firm." *GE Reports*, September 14, 2016.

Kellner, Tomas. "GE to Sell its BioPharma Unit For $21.4 Billion to Danaher." *GE Reports*, February 25, 2019.

Kranhold, Kathryn. "GE to Pay $1.1 Billion for Ionics." *Wall Street Journal*, November 26, 2004.

Kratz, E. F. "Get Me a CEO from GE!" *Fortune* 151, no. 8 (2005): 147–152.

Lehmberg, Derek, W. Glenn Rowe, Roderick E. White, and John R. Phillips. "The GE Paradox: Competitive Advantage Through Fungible Non-Firm-Specific Investment." *Journal of Management* 35, no. 5 (2009): 1129–1153.

Malone, Scott. "GE Sells Security Arm to United Tech for $1.82 Billion." Reuters, November 12, 2009.

Malone, Scott. "GE to Acquire Vital Signs for $860 Million Cash." Reuters, July 24, 2008.

Masoni, Danilo. "GE to Buy Aviation Unit of Italy's Avio for $4.3 Billion." Reuters, December 22, 2012.

Michel, Robert. "GE Healthcare Will Acquire IDX Systems for $1.2 Billion." *The Dark Intelligence Group*, October 3, 2005.

"NBCU to Buy 26% Stake in NDTV for $150 Million." *Financial Express*, January 23, 2008.

"NeoGenomics Buys Clarient from GE Healthcare for Up to $275M." *GEN: Genetic Engineering & Biotechnology News*, October 21, 2015.

Panettieri, Joe. "GE Sells ServiceMax to Silver Lake; Spins off GE Digital and Predix." *Channele2e,* December 13, 2018.

Prodhan, Georgina. "GE Buys Germany's Concept Laser after SLM Bid Fails." Reuters, October 27, 2016.

ServiceMax. "GE Digital Acquires ServiceMax to Extend Predix and Analytics Across Field Service Processes." News release, n.d.

Silverman, Rachel Emma. "GE to Purchase Osmonics in $248 Million Transaction." *Wall Street Journal*, November 5, 2002.

Skapinker, Michael. "Resilience and Flair Triumph: This Year's Global Survey of the Most Respected Companies and Business Leaders Reflects the Staying Power of Established Corporations and the Rise of the New Economy." *Financial Times*, December 15, 2000.

"Spirent Sells Its Sensors to GE." *The Engineer*, September 10, 2001.

Sprague, Jeffrey T. and Jason B. Bazinet. *General Electric Co (GE) NBCU Exits Stage Right.* Citibank Global Research, December 4, 2009.

Stein, Nicholas. "The World's Most Admired Companies." *Fortune* 142, no. 7 (October 2, 2000): 182–90.

Sullivan, Laurie. "GE Supply to Buy Assets of Questron for $89 Million." *EE Times*, April 17, 2002.

"The Big Get Bigger: Rexel Inc. to Acquire GE Supply." *Electrical Wholesaling*, July 14, 2006.

Thomasch, Paul. "UPDATE 3-NBC Universal to Buy Oxygen Media for $925 Million." Reuters, October 9, 2007.

Tweed, Katherine, and Michael Kanellos, "General Electric Buys Converteam for $3.2B." *Greentech Media*, March 29, 2011.

"Wabtec Sells Locomotive After-Market Assets to GE." *Progressive Railroading*, July 26, 2001.

Wilkerson, David B. "NBC Buys San Francisco TV Station." *MarketWatch*, December 17, 2001.

Winoker, Steven E. and Yidong Xiang, *GE: Exit the Peacock (for a Fair Price) but What will Follow?* New York: Bernstein Research, February 13, 2013.

Winoker, Steven, Peter Lennox-King, and Damian Karas. *General Electric Co: Peak Uncertainty? Upgrading GE to Buy on Upside/Downside Skew Following Recent Sell-Off.* New York: UBS Global Research, 2018.

CHAPTER 19

Comcast Corporation. "A Superior Cash Proposal for Sky" Presentation. February 17, 2018.

Comcast Corporation. "Comcast Corp. and Sky Plc Acquisition Proposal Call—UK." February 27, 2018. Accessed via FactSet.

Comcast Corporation. Q3 2017 Earnings Conference Call, October 26, 2017. Accessed via FactSet: CallStreet, LLC.

Hodulik, John C., Charlie Costanzo, Ryan Gravett, Batya Levi, and Christopher School, *UBS TV Ratings Guide: Insight into Ad Estimates*, New York: UBS Research, June 11, 2019.

Mitchelson, Douglas, Brian Russo, Meghan Durkin, and Grant Joslin. *Comcast "Wins" Sky*. Credit Suisse, September 24, 2018. Accessed via FactSet.

Williams, Gregory, Colby Synesael, Jonathan Charbon, and Michael Elias, *Industry Update: Video and Broadband Study: The Satellite Implosion and OTT Tyranny of Choice*, Cowen Research, March 6, 2019.

CHAPTER 20

"Full Text: Nokia CEO Stephen Elop's 'Burning Platform' Memo." *Wall Street Journal*, February 9, 2011.

Merriam-Webster Online, s.v. "Strategic."

CHAPTER 21

Belsey, Mark. *Sanofi Looks to Acquire Medivation for $52.50/Share, We Estimate 8% EPS Accretion by '20E*. New York: UBS Global Research, April 28, 2016.

Huang, Ying, Atsushi Seki, Catherine Hu, Dimiter V. Tassev, and Ryo Taguichi. *Medivation: Xtandi Posts $127mn in Q4 US Sales vs. Consensus of $121mn.* Barclays Equity Research, February 2, 2014.

IQVIA. "Proportion of Branded Versus Generic Drug Prescriptions Dispensed in the United States from 2005 to 2019." Chart, August 7, 2020. Accessed via Statista.

Liang, Howard, Richard Gross, and Gena Wang. *Medivation, Inc.: Strong 4Q a Good Start to Pre-Chemo Launch; Guidance Firm but Seems Beatable.* Leerink Partners, February 26, 2015.

Medivation. *Schedule 14-D9, August 20, 2016.*

Newman, John. *Medivation: Xtandi Beat in Q2 for US, EU and Japan, Positive Sign into Pre-Chemo Approval.* Canaccord Genuity, Inc., August 1, 2014.

Nierengarten, David M., Dipil Joseph, and Robert Driscoll. *Medivation (MDVN): Xtandi Sales Come in Light, Lowering Top and Bottom Lines, Xtandi Still Has Attractive Franchise, Reducing PT to $47 and Maintaining OP.* Wedbush Securities Equities Research, January 29, 2016.

Nierengarten, David M., Gregory R. Wade, and Christopher N. Marai. *Medivation (MDVN): Q4:12 Xtandi Sales Come in at $57M, Ahead of Expectations, Raising Price Target to $70, Reiterate Outperform.* Wedbush PacGrow Lifesciences, February 1, 2013.

Nierengarten, David M., Gregory R. Wade, and Christopher N. Marai. *Medivation (MDVN): Q1:13 EPS, Xtandi Launch on Track and Beating Street, Reiterate Outperform.* Wedbush PacGrow Lifesciences, May 9, 2013.

Nierengarten, David M., Gregory R. Wade, and Christopher N. Marai. *Medivation (MDVN): Raising Price Target to $62: Astellas Reports $14 million in Xtandi Q3:12 Sales, Guides to $100M Through Q1:13, Ahead of Expectations, Reiterate Outperform.* Wedbush PacGrow Lifesciences, November 1, 2012.

Nierengarten, David M., Gregory R. Wade, and Christopher N. Marai. *Medivation (MDVN): Partner Astellas Reports Q3:13 US Xtandi Sales of ~$108M, Beating Consensus and Our Estimate, Reiterate Outperform.* Wedbush PacGrow Lifesciences, November 1, 2013.

Porges, Geoffrey C., Raluca Pancratov, and Wes Shi. *MDVN: 1Q14 Showed Strong Post-Chemo Demand for Xtandi, Expense Discipline, and Ambition Beyond CRPC; MP, PT $82.* Bernstein Research, May 9, 2014.

Rama, Anupam, and Eric Joseph. *Medivation: Questions on Xtandi Patient Growth Will Persist; Read-Through from Astellas Earnings—ALERT.* JP Morgan North American Equity Research, October 30, 2015.

Rawla, Prashanth. "Epidemiology of Prostate Cancer. " *World Journal of Oncology* 10, no. 2 (2019): 63–89.

Roden, Matthew, Jeffrey Hung, Bradley Canino. *Medivation: Despite Fears, 2Q Xtandi Beats Big, Increases Confidence.* New York: UBS Global Research, July 31, 2015.

Schmidt, Eric, and Cristina Ghenoiu. *Medivation: Caution Ahead: All Signs Point to a Xtandi Slowdown.* Cowen and Company, July 29, 2015, 7.

Schmidt, Eric, and Cristina Ghenoiu. *Medivation: Don't Hold Your Breath for an Inflection in Xtandi Sales.* Cowen and Company, May 8, 2015.

Schmidt, Eric, and Cristina Ghenoiu. *Medivation: Q1 Subpar; Medivation Argues Its Future Is Far Brighter.* Cowen and Company, May 5, 2016.

Singh, Navdeep, Terence Flynn, Lisa Zhang, and Uya Chuluunbaatar. *Medivation, Inc. (MDVN): Xtandi on a Steady Trajectory but PREVAIL Remains Key Driver.* Goldman Sachs Equity Research, August 8, 2013.

Werber, Yaron, and Kennen MacKay, *Medivation, Inc. (MDVN): Alert: Xtandi Posts Solid Growth: MDVN—Strong Launch in Japan.* Citi Research, October 31, 2014.

Xu, Y. Katherine, Joe Aronovsky, and Audrey Le. *Medivation, Inc.: Second-Quarter Earnings as Expected; Continue Pushing Xtandi Growth while Advancing Pipeline; Maintain Outperform.* William Blair & Co., August 10, 2016.

Xu, Y. Katherine, Joe Aronovsky, and Audrey Le. *Medivation, Inc.: Third Quarter Preview: Xtandi Sales in Line; Continues as Market Leader.* William Blair & Co., October 30, 2015.

CHAPTER 22

Chiang, Timothy, and Allison Kelley. *Perrigo plc: Update on 10K Filing: Preliminary 1Q Figures Meet Our Estimates: CY17 Segment Guidance Unchanged.* BTIG Equity Research, April 25, 2017.

Goodman, Marc, Ami Fadia, and Zidong Zhang. *Perrigo: Preliminary 1Q and FY Sales Outlook Is Reassuring.* UBS Global Research, April 25, 2017.

Gregg, Gilbert, Esther Rajavelu, and Greg Fraser. *Perrigo: Quick Thoughts on PRGO News.* Deutsche Bank Research, April 25, 2017.

Papa, Joseph C. Credit Suisse Health Care Conference Presentation, November 10, 2015. Accessed via FactSet: CallStreet, LLC.

Perrigo Company plc. *Form 10-K May 22, 2017*. Accessed via FactSet.

Perrigo Company plc. "Perrigo Company plc Reports Record Third Quarter Highlighted by 10% Organic Net Sales Growth." News release. October 22, 2015.

Perrigo Company plc. "Perrigo Company plc Reports Record Fourth Quarter & Calendar Year Net Sales and Adjusted Net Income." News release. February 18, 2016.

CHAPTER 23

Patel, Pankaj N., Souheang Yao, Ryan Carlson, Abhra Banerji, and Joseph Handleman. *Quantitative Research: Do Spin-Offs Create or Destroy Value*. Credit Suisse Equity Research, September 6, 2012.

Yum! Brands. 2012 Annual Report.

Yum China. "Yum! Brands Announces Intention to Separate into Two Publicly Traded Companies China Division to Become Independent Company Focused on Growth in Mainland China Yum! Brands to Become Global 'Pure Play' Franchisor with Three Iconic Brands." News release. October 20, 2015.

CHAPTER 24

General Electric. Q4 2018 Earnings Call. January 31, 2019. Accessed via FactSet: CallStreet, LLC.

CHAPTER 25

Eastman Kodak. 2001–2005 Annual Reports.

O'Donnell, Carl, and Greg Roumeliotis. "Exclusive: Onex Explores Breaking up Carestream Health in Sale—Sources." Reuters, May 18, 2016.

Waters, Richard. "Slimmed-Down Kodak Emerges from Bankruptcy." *Financial Times*, August 20, 2013.

CHAPTER 26

Jenter, Dirk, and Katharina Lewellen. "CEO Preferences and Acquisitions." *Journal of Finance* 70, no. 6 (December 2015): 2813–52.

Kummer, Christopher, and Ulrich Steger. "Why Merger and Acquisition (M&A) Waves Reoccur: The Vicious Circle from Pressure to Failure." *Strategic Management Review* 2, no. 1, (January 2008): 44–63.

NOTES

CHAPTER 1

1. Kevin L. Kliesen, "As Boomers Slow Down, So Might the Economy," Federal Reserve Bank of St. Louis, July 1, 2007; Mitra Toosi and Teresa L. Morisi, "Women in the Workforce Before, During, and After the Great Recession," U.S. Bureau of Labor Statistics, July 2017; John Fernald and Huiyu Li, "Is Slow Still the New Normal for GDP Growth," Federal Reserve Bank of San Francisco Economic Letter, June 24, 2019.
2. US Bureau of Economic Analysis, Gross Domestic Product, raw data accessed September 30, 2020, via BEA.gov; US Bureau of Economic Analysis, Real Gross Domestic Product, Quantity Indexes, raw data accessed September 30, 2020, via BEA.gov.
3. 2018 proxy filings for the 25 largest US publicly traded companies. *Schedule 14-A 2018* for the following 25 companies: AT&T, Inc.; The Home Depot, Inc.; Wells Fargo and Company; UnitedHealth Group, Inc.; Facebook, Inc.; Berkshire Hathaway, Inc.; Pfizer, Inc.; Johnson & Johnson; Amazon.com, Inc.; JP Morgan Chase & Co.; Bank of America Corporation; Visa, Inc.; Oracle Corporation; Cisco Systems, Inc.; Verizon Communications, Inc.; Intel Corporation; The Boeing Company; The Procter & Gamble Company; Mastercard, Inc.; Chevron Corporation; Walmart, Inc.; Exxon Mobil Corporation; Alphabet, Inc.; Microsoft, Inc.; Apple, Inc.

CHAPTER 2

1. Russell A. Carleton, "Baseball Therapy: Does Postseason Experience Really Matter?," *Baseball Prospectus*, October 14, 2013.
2. Floyd Norris, "Loving Your Stock Only When It's High," *New York Times*, September 18, 2009.
3. John Waggoner, "Investing: Why Care About Stock Buybacks?" *USA Today*, January 31, 2013.
4. Michael J. Lee and Judy Liu, *Gilead Sciences: Is It Like 2011 Again Yet? Well Here's What's Going On*, RBC Capital Markets, February 2, 2016, 7.

CHAPTER 3

1. Malcolm Baker, Brendan Bradley, and Ryan Taliaferro, "The Low-Risk Anomaly: A Decomposition into Micro and Macro Effects," *Financial Analysts Journal* 70, no. 2 (2014): 43–58; Wai Mun Fong, *The Lottery Mindset: Investors, Gambling and the Stock Market* (London: Palgrave Macmillan, 2014).
2. Barclays Live Analytics, *Credit Spreads 2001–2018*, Barclays Live, January 22, 2019.

CHAPTER 5

1. The Hershey Company, Presentation, Consumer Analyst Group of New York Annual Conference, Boca Raton, February 19, 2014.
2. Jeffrey S. Abarbanell and Brian J. Bushee, "Abnormal Returns to a Fundamental Analysis Strategy," *The Accounting Review* 73, no. 1 (January 1998): 25.
3. Sheridan Titman, K.C. John Wei, and Feixue Xie, "Capital Investments and Stock Returns," *Journal of Finance and Quantitative Analytics* 39, no. 4 (December 2004): 678.
4. Louis K.C. Chan, Jason Karceski, Josef Lakonishok, and Theodore Sougiannis, "Balance Sheet Growth and the Predictability of Returns," Working Paper, 2008, 1, 18.
5. Donglin Li, "The Implications of Capital Investment for Future Profitability and Stock Returns: An Overinvestment Perspective," (PhD diss., University of California, Berkeley, January 2004), 5, 44.

CHAPTER 6

1. Bing Jiang and Tim Koller, "Paying Back Your Shareholders," McKinsey & Company, May 1, 2011.
2. Jeremy Schwartz, "The Dividends of a Dividend Approach," WisdomTree Investments, Inc., 2018, 5; Clare Hart and Mariana Connolly, *Dividends for the Long Term*, J.P. Morgan Asset Management, LLC, April 2013, 3; *The High Dividend Yield Return Advantage: An Examination of Empirical Data Associating Investment in High Dividend Yield Securities with Attractive Returns Over Long Measurement Periods*, Tweedy, Browne Company, LLC, 2014, 7.
3. Savita Subramanian, "Quantitative Primer" Bank of America Securities, New York, June 1, 2020.
4. Michael C. Jensen, "Agency Costs of Free Cash Flow, Corporate Finance and Takeovers," *The American Economic Review* 76, no. 2 (May 1986): 323.
5. Robert D. Arnott and Clifford S. Asness, "Surprise! Higher Dividends = Higher Earnings Growth," *Financial Analysts Journal* 59, no. 1 (2003): 70–87; Franklin Allen, Antonio E. Bernando, and Ivo Welch, "A Theory of Dividends Based on Tax Clienteles," *Journal of Finance* 55, no. 6 (December 2000): 2499–2536; Ping Zhou and William Ruland, "Dividend Payout and Future Earnings Growth," *Financial Analysts Journal* 62, no. 3 (May–June 2006): 58–69.
6. Gustavo Grullon, Roni Michaely, and Bhaskaran Swaminathan, "Are Dividend Changes a Sign of Firm Maturity?" *Journal of Business* 75, no. 3 (July 2002): 387–424.

7. Cesare Fracassi, "Stock Price Sensitivity to Dividend Changes," working paper, Department of Finance–UCLA Anderson School of Management, July 2008.

CHAPTER 7
1. CME Group, Q4 2011 Earnings Conference Call, February 2, 2012. Transcript accessed via *Factiva*.
2. CME Group, "Dividend Payments," CME Group website.
3. Harry DeAngelo, Linda DeAngelo, and Douglas J. Skinner, "Special Dividends and the Evolution of Dividend Signaling," *Journal of Financial Economics* 57, no. 3 (2000): 309–354.
4. DeAngelo et al., "Special Dividends."
5. Kevin Brady, Inga Chira, and Jeff Madura, "Special Dividend Distributions, Firm Characteristics, and Economic Conditions," *Journal of Applied Finance* 24, no. 1 (January 2014): 58–2.
6. De-Wai Chou, Yi Liu, and Zaher Zantout, "Long-Term Stock Performance Following Extraordinary and Special Cash Dividends," *The Quarterly Review of Economics and Finance* 49, no. 1 (2009): 1.
7. Brady et al., "Special Dividend Distribution."

CHAPTER 8
1. William Lazonick, "The Curse of Stock Buybacks," *The American Prospect*, June 25, 2018.
2. Annie Lowrey. "Are Stock Buybacks Starving the Economy?" *The Atlantic*, July 31, 2018.
3. US Senator Tammy Baldwin, "U.S. Senator Tammy Baldwin Introduces Legislation to Rein in Stock Buybacks and Give Workers a Seat at the Table," Press release, March 22, 2018.
4. Rita McGrath. "The Case for Banning Stock Buybacks," *CNN*, February 26, 2019.
5. Quoted in Alex Edmans, "The Case for Stock Buybacks," *Harvard Business Review*, September 15, 2017.
6. Kate Gibson, "S&P Buybacks Skidded to New Lows in Second Quarter," *MarketWatch*, September 15, 2009; Liyu Zeng and Priscilla Luk, *Examining Share Repurchasing and the S&P Buyback Indices in the U.S. Market*, S&P Dow Jones Indices, March 10, 2020.
7. Michael C. Jensen, "Agency Costs of Free Cash Flow, Corporate Finance and Takeovers," *The American Economic Review* 76, no. 2 (May 1986): 323–29.
8. Fangjian Fu and Sheng Huang, "The Persistence of Long-Run Abnormal Returns Following Share Repurchases and Offerings," *Management Science* 6, no. 4 (April 2016): 964–84.
9. Urs Peyer and Theo Vermaelen, "The Nature and Persistence of Buyback Anomalies," *Review of Financial Studies* 22, no. 4 (April 2009): 1693–1745; Amy Dittmar and Laura Casares Field, "Can Managers Time the Market? Evidence Using Repurchase Price Data," *Journal of Finance Economics* 115, no. 2 (January 2014): 261–82; Alberto Manconi, Urs Peyer, and Theo Vermaelen, "Are Buybacks Good for Long-Term Shareholder Value? Evidence from Buybacks around the

World," *Journal of Financial and Quantitative Analysis* 54, no. 5 (October 2019): 1899–1935.

10. "Top of Mind: Buyback Realities," *Goldman Sachs Global Macro Research* 77, April 11, 2019, page 6.
11. "R&D Expenditure," *Eurostat: Statistics Explained*, September 2019.
12. Joshua Bolten and Ken Bertsch, "Restricting Stock Buybacks Will Hurt the Economy," *New York Times*, March 4, 2019.
13. Joseph W. Gruber and Steven B. Kamin, "Corporate Buybacks and Capital Investment: An International Perspective," (IFDP notes, Washington: Board of Governors of the Federal Reserve System, April 11, 2017).
14. "Returning Capital to Shareholders," *Audit Committee Leadership Network in North America: ViewPoints* (Waltham: Tapestry Networks, Inc., October 27, 2016): 1, 4.
15. Warren Buffett to "The Shareholders of Berkshire Hathaway Inc.," February 25, 2017, 8.
16. David Kostin, Ben Snider, Arjun Menon, Ryan Hammond, Cole Hunter, and Nicholas Mulford, "Misperceptions Surrounding Corporate Cash Spending Priorities and the Economics of Share Repurchase," *US Equity Views* (New York: Goldman Sachs, March 7, 2019).
17. David F. Larcker and Brian Tayan, "CEO Compensation: Data Spotlight," *CGRI Quick Guide Series*, Stanford Graduate School of Business, Corporate Governance Research Institute, January 2019.

CHAPTER 9

1. AutoZone, 2000–2018 Annual Reports.
2. AutoZone, 1999–2019 Annual Reports.
3. AutoZone, 2000–2018 Annual Reports.

CHAPTER 11

1. Robert F. Bruner, "Does M&A Pay? A Survey of Evidence for the Decision Maker," *Journal of Applied Finance* 12, no. 1 (2002): 48.
2. Scott A. Christofferson, Robert S. McNish, and Diane L. Sias, "Where Mergers Go Wrong," *McKinsey Quarterly*, no. 2 (June 2004): 92–93.
3. Clayton M. Christensen, Richard Alton, Curtis Rising, and Andrew Waldeck, "The New M&A Playbook," *Harvard Business Review* 89, no. 3 (March 2011): 49.
4. Godfred Yaw Koi-Akrofi, "Mergers and Acquisitions Failure Rates and Perspectives on Why They Fail," *International Journal of Innovation and Applied Studies* 17, no. 1 (July 2016): 154.
5. Alex D'Angelo, "State of the M&A Deal in 2019," *Cohen & Company*, August 7, 2019.
6. Christensen et al., "The New M&A Playbook."
7. *Revenue Synergies in Acquisitions: In Search of the Holy Grail* (Deloitte: M&A Institute, 2017).
8. Daniel Kahneman, *Thinking, Fast and Slow* (New York: Farrar, Straus and Giroux, 2011).

9. Kahneman, *Thinking*, 247.
10. David Offenberg and Christo Pirinsky, "How Do Acquirers Choose Between Offers and Tender Offers?" *Journal of Financial Economics* 116, no. 2 (May 2015): 331–48.
11. Dirk Jenter and Katharina Lewellen, "CEO Preferences and Acquisitions," *Journal of Finance* 70, no. 6 (December 2015): 2814.
12. Luc Renneboog and Cara Vansteenkiste, "What Goes Wrong in M&As? On the Long-Run Success Factors in M&A," (working paper, ECGI-Finance, December 2018).

CHAPTER 12

1. GlaxoSmithKline, "Why Our Transaction with Novartis Is Different," News release, February 27, 2015.
2. Andrew Witty, GlaxoSmithKline PLC Business Update Call, April 22, 2014, 3, accessed via FactSet.
3. Alexandra Hauber-Schuele, Novartis Business Update Call, April 22, 2014, 11, accessed via FactSet.
4. Nicolas Guyon-Gellin, Vincent Meunier, Amy Walker, Chris Eccles, *GlaxoSmithKline PLC: OTC/Vaccine Shift Key to Change in Growth Profile*, Morgan Stanley Research, May 14, 2014, accessed via FactSet; James D. Gordon, Richard Vosser, and Diana Na, *GlaxoSmithKline PLC: Novartis Business Swap and Divestment Offers Mid-High Single Digit Accretion Medium Term*, JP Morgan Cazenove Research, April 17, 2014, accessed via FactSet.
5. Ibid.
6. Honeywell, 2000–2004 Annual Reports; Honeywell, Q4 2004 Conference Call Transcript, January 28, 2005; "Honeywell Completes Acquisition of Novar PLC: Final Clearance from European Commission Confirmed," *Business Wire*, March 31, 2005; Novar PLC, Interim Results Statement, July 27, 2004.
7. DuPont and Trian Partners, "A Referendum on Performance and Accountability," Trian Fund Management, L.P., February 17, 2015, 13.

CHAPTER 13

1. Roper Industries, 2001 Annual Report, 24–25; Roper Industries, 2018 Annual Report, 19, 30–31, 33.
2. Joseph Giordano and Tristan Margot, *Roper Technologies Initiation: A Deep Stable of Businesses—All with Cash on the Brain*, New York: Cowen and Company, LLC, October 12, 2015, 6.
3. Roper Industries, "Roper Industries Announces Agreement to Acquire Neptune Technology Group Holdings Inc.," News release, October 21, 2003; "Roper Industries Agrees to Acquire TransCore Holdings," *Parking Network*, October 7, 2004; David Smith, *ROP:CIVCO Deal to Be Additive in 2006, Represents New Leg*, Citigroup Smith Barney, June 20, 2005; David Smith, *ROP: MEDTEC Acquisition Bolsters Healthcare Position*, Citigroup Smith Barney, December 12, 2005; Deane Dray, *Upbeat Guidance and Accretive CBORD Deal Spark 5% Relief Rally*, Goldman Sachs, February 24, 2008; Terry Darling, *Strong Balance*

Sheet Optionality in Action, Maintain Buy, Goldman Sachs, November 8, 2009; Robert T. Cornell, *2Q Inline, RF Acq Provides Upside to '11,* New York: Barclays Capital, July 27, 2010; Richard Eastman, *Upping CY 11/12 EPS Forecast for Northern Digital Acquisition,* Milwaukee: Robert W. Baird Research, June 7, 2011; Shannon O' Callaghan, *Aderant Adds Another Strong Growth, Margin, and Cash Flow Software Business,* Zürich: UBS, October, 9, 2015; Richard Eastman, *Q3 Shows Sluggish Trends, Accretive Acquisition Added,* Milwaukee: Robert W. Baird Research, July 1, 2016; C. Stephen Tusa Jr., *Our Take on Deltek Acquisition,* J.P. Morgan, December 8, 2016; Richard Eastman, *FCF Steps up with PowerPlan,* Milwaukee: Robert W. Baird Research, May 21, 2018; Roper Industries, "Roper Industries Completes Acquisition of Northern Digital, Inc," News release, June 6, 2011; Roper Industries, "Roper Industries to Acquire Sunquest Information Systems," News release, July 30, 2012; Roper Industries, "Roper Industries to Acquire MHA," News release, April 17, 2013; Roper Industries, "Roper Technologies to Acquire Aderant, Leading Software Solutions Provider to the Legal Profession," News release, October 8, 2015; Roper Industries, "Roper Technologies to Acquire ConstructConnect, Leading Provider of SaaS Solutions for the Commercial Construction Industry," News release, October 31, 2016; Roper Industries, "Roper Technologies to Acquire PowerPlan, Leading Provider of Software and Solutions for Financial and Compliance Management," News release, May 21, 2018.

CHAPTER 14

1. Kathleen Fuller, Jeffrey Netter, and Mike Stegemoller, "What Do Returns to Acquiring Firms Tell Us? Evidence from Firms That Make Many Acquisitions," *Journal of Finance* 57, no. 4 (August 2002): 1763–93.

2. Werner Rehm, Robert Uhlander, and Andy West, "Taking a Longer-Term Look at M&A Value Creation," McKinsey & Company, January 1, 2012.

3. Jon Vander Ark, Republic Services, Inc., Q2 2019 Conference Call, July 25, 2019, 20, Accessed via FactSet: CallStreet, LLC.

4. Yaron Kinar, Charles Sebaski, and Joshua Shanker, "Willis Group: Initiating Coverage with a Hold Rating," Deutsche Bank, June 15, 2011, 17.

5. Daniel Glaser, Marsh & McLennan Companies, Inc., Investor Day Presentation, September 30, 2010, 40.

6. Marsh & McLennan Companies, Inc., Investor Presentation Handout, June 2019.

7. Daniel Glaser, Marsh & McLennan Companies, Inc., Bank of America Merrill Lynch Insurance Conference Presentation, February 14, 2013, 7, accessed via FactSet: CallStreet, LLC; Marsh & McClennan Companies, Inc., Deutsche Bank Financial Services Conference Presentation, May 31, 2016, 18.

8. Sarah DeWitt and Keith Cornelius, "Brown & Brown: Initiating Coverage at Underweight: Pure Play Insurance Broker with High Exposure to Softening P&C Prices," JP Morgan, June 28, 2016; Mark Hughes and Michael Ramirez, Brown & Brown, "Q3 19 Follow Up, Reiterate Buy, Sun Trust Robinson Humphrey," October 28, 2019.

9. Daniel Glaser, Marsh & McLennan Companies, Inc., Investor Day Presentation, March 11, 2014, 8, accessed via FactSet: CallStreet, LLC.

10. Daniel Glaser, Marsh & McLennan Companies, Inc., Q1 2018 Earnings Conference Call, April 26, 2018, 15, accessed via FactSet: CallStreet, LLC.
11. PerkinElmer, Inc., "Acquisition of EUROIMMUN Medical Laboratory Diagnostics AG by PerkinElmer, Inc.," Call, June 19, 2017, accessed via FactSet: CallStreet LLC.
12. Winfried Stöcker, "Transfer of EUROIMMUN to PerkinElmer," *Prof. Dr. Winfried Stöcker* (blog), June 21, 2017.

CHAPTER 15

1. Alex Brummer and Roger Crowe, *Weinstock: The Life and Times of Britain's Premier Industrialist* (New York: HarperCollins, 1999), 77.
2. Quoted in Dan Sabbagh and Sean O'Neill, "Marconi: From Boom to Bust in a Year," *The Telegraph*, September 7, 2001.
3. Michael Harrison, "Corporate Profile: The Man Spending GEC's Pounds 6bn." *Independent*, May 4, 1999.
4. For further reading on the history of GEC, as well as Lord Weinstock's life and leadership, see: Encyclopedia.com, s.v. "The General Electric Company, PLC"; FundingUniverse, s.v. "Marconi plc History"; CompanyHistories.com, s.v. "Marconi plc."; David Bowen, "For a Fat Cat, He's Fast on His Feet," *Independent*, August 31, 1996; *Grace's Guide to British Industrial History*, s.v. "GEC"; Ian Davies, "Obituary: Simon Weinstock," *Independent*, May 20, 1996; Jean Shaoul, "Lord Weinstock and the Near Terminal Decline of British Industry," *World Socialist Website*, July 27, 2002; "Lord Weinstock Great Industrialist Who Led GEC Successfully Until His Retirement," *The Herald Scotland*, July 24, 2002; Robert Heller, "A Legacy Turned into Tragedy," *The Guardian*, August 18, 2002; *Science Museum Group*, s.v. "General Electric Company plc."; "The £11bn Wreckers," *This Is Money*, July 16, 2001; "UK: Arnold's Heir Unapparent—Simon Weinstock Will Not Succeed His Father at GEC," *Management Today*, November 1, 1991.
5. Sabbagh and O'Neil, "Marconi."
6. Danaher Corporation, *Form 10-K December 31, 2001*, Accessed via FactSet; Danaher Corporation, "Danaher Corporation Announces Signing a Definitive Agreement to Acquire Marconi Commerce Systems," News release, December 12, 2001; Danaher Corporation, "Danaher Corporation Announces Signing a Definitive Agreement to Acquire Marconi Data Systems," News release, January 10, 2002.

CHAPTER 16

1. Canadian Natural Resources Ltd., "Acquisition of Working Interest in the Athabasca Oil Sands Project and Other Oil Sands Assets by Can," March 9, 2017, Accessed via FactSet.
2. Ibid.
3. Royal Dutch Shell, Q1 2015 Earnings Release, April 30, 2015; Royal Dutch Shell, Q1 2016 Earnings Release, May 4, 2016; Royal Dutch Shell, Q4 2016 Earnings Release, February 2, 2017.

4. Royal Dutch Shell, Q4 2014 Earnings Release, January 29, 2015; Royal Dutch Shell, Q4 2015 Earnings Release, February 4, 2016; Royal Dutch Shell, Q4 2016 Earnings Release, February 2, 2017.

CHAPTER 17
1. Jonathan Groberg and Travis Steed, *Thermo Fisher Scientific: TMO + LIFE = A Life Sciences Staple*, Macquarie Group Equities Research, April 16, 2013.
2. Ross Muken, Michael Cherney, Vijay Kumar, and Elizabeth Anderson, *Thermo Fisher Scientific (TMO): One Lambda Makes TMO More "Special,"* International Strategy & Investment Group LLC, July 16, 2012.
3. Life Technologies Corporation, *Schedule 14A: Proxy Statement July 22, 2013*.
4. Thermo Fisher Scientific, Inc., Acquisition of Life Technologies Corporation by Thermo Fisher Scientific Inc Call, April 15, 2013, 15.
5. Thermo Fisher Scientific, Inc., Analyst Meeting, May 22, 2019, Accessed via FactSet: CallStreet, LLC.
6. US Congressional Research Service, *National Institutes Health (NIH) Funding: FY1994–FY2020* (Washington, DC: Congressional Research Service, April 4, 2019), 5.
7. Groberg and Steed, *Thermo Fisher Scientific*; Doug Schenkel, Chris Lin, Ryan Blicker, and Adam Wieschhaus, *DHR to Acquire GE Biopharma: Strategic and Financial Benefits Appear Attractive*, Cowen, February 25, 2019.
8. David J. Koning, Robert W. Bamberger, and Patrick A. Schulz, *Fiserv, Inc. (FISV): Details on Q4 Results*, Robert W. Baird Equity Research, February 7, 2019; David J. Koning, Robert W. Bamberger, and Partrick Schulz, *First Data Corporation (FDC): Nice Q4 Results/2019 Guidance; Raising FDC Estimates*, Robert W. Baird Equity Research, February 6, 2019.
9. Koning, Bamberger, and Schulz, *First Data Corporation (FDC)*.
10. First Data Corporation, Q4 2017 Earnings Release, February 21, 2018; First Data Corporation, Q4 2018 Earnings Release, February 27, 2019.
11. First Data Corporation, *Schedule 14A, March 14, 2019*; Fiserv, Inc., Acquisition of First Data Corporation by Fiserv, Inc. Call, January 16, 2019, accessed via FactSet: CallStreet, LLC.

CHAPTER 18
1. Nicholas Stein, "The World's Most Admired Companies," *Fortune* 142, no. 7 (October 2, 2000): 182–90.
2. Michael Skapinker, "Resilience and Flair Triumph: This Year's Global Survey of the Most Respected Companies and Business Leaders Reflects the Staying Power of Established Corporations and the Rise of the New Economy," *Financial Times*, December 15, 2000.
3. General Electric, 2001 Annual Report, 2.
4. General Electric, 1980 Annual Report; General Electric, 1998–2000 Annual Reports.
5. General Electric, 1980 Annual Report.
6. General Electric, 2000 Annual Report.

7. Derek Lehmberg, W. Glenn Rowe, Roderick E. White, and John R. Phillips, "The GE Paradox: Competitive Advantage Through Fungible Non-Firm-Specific Investment," *Journal of Management* 35, no. 5 (2009): 1129–1153.
8. E. F. Kratz, "Get Me a CEO from GE!" *Fortune* 151, no. 8 (2005): 147–52.
9. Nigel Coe, Bhupender Bohra, and Cristian Ramos, *General Electric: Upcoming WAB and Healthcare Disposals Should Be Game Changers* (New York: Wolfe Research, 2018); Steven Winoker, Peter Lennox-King, and Damian Karas, *General Electric Co: Peak Uncertainty? Upgrading GE to Buy on Upside/Downside Skew Following Recent Sell-Off* (New York: UBS Global Research, 2018).
10. Coe et al. *General Electric*; Winoker et al., *General Electric Co.*
11. General Electric, 2001–2018 Annual Reports.
12. **Water:** "GE Buys Water Treatment Software Operations," *New York Times*, February 13, 2002; "General Electric Agrees to Acquire ZENON Environmental: Expands GE's Water & Process Technologies Platform with the Addition of Best-In-Class Ultrafiltration Membrane Technologies," *Business Wire*, May 14, 2006; General Electric, 2003 Annual Report, 100; General Electric, 2017 Annual Report, 21; Kathryn Kranhold, "GE to Pay $1.1 Billion for Ionics," *Wall Street Journal*, November 26, 2004. Rachel Emma Silverman, "GE to Purchase Osmonics in $248 Million Transaction," *Wall Street Journal*, November 5, 2002. **NBC:** Antoine Gara, "How Comcast 'Stole' NBCUniversal From General Electric," *Forbes*, February 13, 2013; David B. Wilkerson, "NBC Buys San Francisco TV Station," *MarketWatch*, December 17, 2001; "GE CEO: NBC Overpaid for iVillage," *MediaPost*, November 3, 2006; "GE Reaches Deal with Comcast for NBC," *NBC* News.com, December 3, 2009; General Electric, 2002 Annual Report, 99; General Electric, 2004 Annual Report, 101; Jeffrey T. Sprague and Jason B. Bazinet, *General Electric Co (GE) NBCU Exits Stage Right*, Citibank Global Research, December 4, 2009; Liana B. Baker, "GE to Sell Rest of NBC Stake to Comcast for $16.7 Billion," *Reuters*, February 12, 2013; Meg James, "NBC to Acquire Telemundo Network for $1.98 Billion," *Los Angeles Times*, October 12, 2001; "NBCU to Buy 26% Stake in NDTV for $150 Million," *Financial Express*, January 23, 2008; Paul Thomasch, "UPDATE 3-NBC Universal to Buy Oxygen Media for $925 Million," *Reuters*, October 9, 2007; Steven E. Winoker and Yidong Xiang, *GE: Exit the Peacock (for a Fair Price) but What Will Follow?*, New York: Bernstein Research, February 13, 2013. **Oil & Gas:** "GE Buys UK Aerospace Sensor Firm for £229m," *Electronics Weekly*, May 15, 2002; "GE Completes $3 Billion Acquisition of Dresser, Inc.: Move Marks Latest Expansion of GE's Global Energy Infrastructure Business," *Business Wire*, February 1, 2011; "GE Completes Acquisition of Cameron's Reciprocating Compression Division," *Business Wire*, June 3, 2014; "GE Oil & Gas Buys Hydril From Tenaris for US$1.115B," *Hart Energy*, August 26, 2008; "GE to Acquire Lufkin Industries," *Business Wire*, April 8, 2013; "GE to Acquire Vetco Gray, Accelerating Growth Across Oil & Gas Sector," *Business Wire*, January 8, 2007; "GE to Buy Wood Group Division for $2.8B," *Rigzone*, February 14, 2011; General Electric, *Form 10-K February 26, 2019*, 39; John Bowker, "General Electric to Buy UK's Sondex for $583 mln," *Reuters*, September 3, 2007; Kathy Hipple, Tom Sanzillo, and Tim Buckley, *GE's $7.4 Billion Loss, Write-off on Baker Hughes: Another Bad Bet on Fossil Fuels* (Cleveland: Institute for Energy Economics, October

2019); Tom Bergin, "GE to Buy UK Oil Pipemaker Wellstream for $1.3 Billion," *Reuters*, December 13, 2010. **Security:** "GE Unit Agrees to Buy Interlogix for $777 Million in Cash, Stock," *Wall Street Journal*, December 18, 2001; "General Electric Agrees to Acquire Edwards Systems Technology," *Buildings: Smarter Facility Management*, November 15, 2004; "General Electric Agrees to Acquire InVision; Combines Explosive Detection Technologies, Advancing GE Position in Infrastructure Security Industry; GE Updates First Half Outlook," *Business Wire*, March 15, 2015; Scott Malone, "GE Sells Security Arm to United Tech for $1.82 Billion," *Reuters*, November 12, 2009. **Healthcare:** Aisha Al-Muslim, "GE to Sell Part of Healthcare Business to Veritas Capital for $1.05 Billion," *Wall Street Journal*, April 2, 2018; "CareFusion to Acquire Vital Signs Division of GE Healthcare for $500 Million," *PR Newswire*, November 18, 2013; "GE Acquires Instrumentarium for $2.4B," *Forbes*, October 9, 2003; "GE Healthcare to Take Over Clarient in $580M Deal," *GEN: Genetic Engineering & Biotechnology News*, October 22, 2010; "NeoGenomics Buys Clarient from GE Healthcare for Up to $275M," *GEN: Genetic Engineering & Biotechnology News*, October 21, 2015; General Electric, 2002 Annual Report, 101; Robert Michel, "GE Healthcare Will Acquire IDX Systems for $1.2 Billion," *The Dark Intelligence Group*, October 3, 2005; Scott Malone, "GE to Acquire Vital Signs for $860 Million Cash," *Reuters*, July 24, 2008. **Renewables:** "G.E. to Buy Enron Wind-Turbine Assets," *New York Times*, April 12, 2002; General Electric, 2019 Fourth Quarter Performance Report, January 29, 2020; Tomas Kellner, "Bladerunners: GE's Wind Business to Buy Danish Blade Maker for $1.65 Billion," *GE Reports*, October 11, 2016. **Power:** "GE to Acquire Lineage Power for $520 Million," *CNBC*, January 13, 2011; Katherine Tweed and Michael Kanellos, "General Electric Buys Converteam for $3.2B," *Greentech Media*, March 29, 2011; Paul Ausick, "Why GE's Alstom Acquisition Was Misguided," *24/7 Wall St.*, June 7, 2019. **Aviation:** Danilo Masoni, "GE to Buy Aviation Unit of Italy's Avio for $4.3 Billion," *Reuters*, December 22, 2012; General Electric Aviation, "General Electric Company to Purchase Airfoil Technologies International-Singapore," News release, March 2, 2009; General Electric Aviation, "GE to Acquire Smiths Aerospace, Extending Aviation Offerings; Plans JV with Smiths Group to Build Global Detection Business," News release, January 15, 2007. **Life Sciences:** General Electric, 2004 Annual Report, 101; "GE Healthcare to Acquire Biacore for $390M," *Genome Web*, June 20, 2006; "GE Healthcare to Acquire Whatman for $713M," *GenomeWeb*, February 4, 2008; "GE to Expand in Life Sciences with Acquisition of Strategic Assets from Thermo Fisher Scientific," *Business Wire*, January 6, 2014; Tomas Kellner, "GE to Sell Its BioPharma Unit for $21.4 Billion to Danaher," *GE Reports*, February 25, 2019. **GE Digital:** Joe Panettieri, "GE Sells ServiceMax to Silver Lake; Spins off GE Digital and Predix," *Channele2e*, December 13, 2018; ServiceMax, "GE Digital Acquires ServiceMax to Extend Predix and Analytics Across Field Service Processes," News release (n.d.); Tomas Kellner, "GE Buys $500 Million Machine Analytics Firm," *GE Reports*, September 14, 2016. **Other:** "Amphenol Corporation to Acquire the Advanced Sensors Business of GE," *Business Wire*, November 15, 2013; Arunima Banerjee, "Emerson Electric to Buy GE's Intelligent Platforms Division," *Reuters*, October 2, 2018; "GE Accelerates Growth in Mining with Planned Acquisitions of

Equipment Makers Industrea Ltd. and Fairchild International," *Business Wire*, May 15, 2012; "GE Energy Completes Acquisition of BHA Group Holdings, Inc.; Transaction Expands GE's Environmental Services Capabilities," *Business Wire*, September 1, 2004; "GE Fanuc Acquires SBS Technologies," *Vision Systems Design*, March 23, 2006; "GE Industrial Systems to Acquire NovaSensor," *GE Reports*, August 2, 2002; "GE Specialty Materials Completes Acquisition of OSi Specialties," *Business Wire*, July 31, 2003; "GE Takes Full Control of GELcore, Teams with Nichia," *LEDs Magazine*, August 31, 2006; General Electric, All M&A Deals via FactSet; Georgina Prodhan, "GE Buys Germany's Concept Laser After SLM Bid Fails," *Reuters*, October 27, 2016; James Dornbrook, "GE Sells Air Filtration Business for $265M," *Kansas City Business Journal*, November 5, 2013; John Keller, "GE Intelligent Platforms to be Renamed Abaco Systems; Acquisition Set to Close Monday," *Military and Aerospace Electronics*, November 17, 2015; Laurie Sullivan, "GE Supply to Buy Assets of Questron for $89 Million," *EE Times*, April 17, 2002; Peter Clarke, "Radstone Recommends GE Fanuc Offer to Shareholders," *EE Times*, September 18, 2006; "Spirent Sells Its Sensors to GE," *The Engineer*, September 10, 2001; "The Big Get Bigger: Rexel Inc. to Acquire GE Supply," *Electrical Wholesaling*, July 14, 2006; "Wabtec Sells Locomotive After-Market Assets to GE," *Progressive Railroading*, July 26, 2001.

13. Baker Hughes Company, 2008–2015 Annual Reports.
14. Ed Crooks, "GE's $23bn Writedown Is a Case of Goodwill Gone Bad," *Financial Times*, October 4, 2018.
15. General Electric, 2003–2004 and 2006–2007 Annual Reports; General Electric, *Form 10-K February 23, 2018*, 28.
16. Scott Malone, "GE to Acquire Vital Signs for $860 Million Cash," *Reuters*, July 24, 2008.
17. General Electric, 2000–2018 Annual Reports.
18. General Electric, 2001–2018 Annual Reports; Antoine Gara, "How Comcast 'Stole' NBCUniversal from General Electric," *Forbes*, February 13, 2013; "Broadening GE's Security Business, Complementary Technologies and Channels to Market Will Create Significant New Growth Opportunities," *Buildings: Smarter Facility Management*, November 15, 2004; "GE Completes $3 Billion Acquisition of Dresser, Inc.: Move Marks Latest Expansion of GE's Global Energy Infrastructure Business," *Business Wire*, February 1, 2011; "GE Oil & Gas Buys Hydril from Tenaris for US$1.115B," *Hart Energy*, August 26, 2008; "GE Reaches Deal with Comcast for NBC," *NBC* News.com, December 3, 2009; "GE to Acquire Lufkin Industries," *Business Wire,* April 8, 2013; "GE to Buy Wood Group Division for $2.8B," *Rigzone*, February 14, 2011; "GE to Sell Advanced Materials Business Unit for $3.8B," *Reliable Plant*, September 2006; General Electric, 2001–2018 Annual Reports; General Electric, *Form 10-K February 24, 2017*, 27; Harry Brumpton and Rachit Vats, "GE to Merge Transportation Unit with Wabtec in $11.1 Billion Deal," *Reuters*, May 21, 2018; Jeffrey T. Sprague and Jason B. Bazinet, *General Electric Co (GE) NBCU Exits Stage Right*, Citibank Global Research, December 4, 2009; Kathryn Kranhold, "GE to Pay $1.1 Billion for Ionics," *Wall Street Journal*, November 26, 2004; Kathy Hipple, Tom Sanzillo, and Tim Buckley, *GE's $7.4 Billion Loss, Write-off on Baker Hughes: Another Bad Bet on Fossil Fuels*, Cleveland: Institute for

Energy Economics, October 2019; Liana B. Baker, "GE to Sell Rest of NBC Stake to Comcast for $16.7 Billion," *Reuters*, February 12, 2013; Meg James, "NBC to Acquire Telemundo Network for $1.98 Billion," *Los Angeles Times*, October 12, 2001; Paul Ausick, "Why GE's Alstom Acquisition Was Misguided," *24/7 Wall St.*, June 7, 2019; Scott Malone, "GE Sells Security Arm to United Tech for $1.82 Billion," *Reuters*, November 12, 2009; ServiceMax, "GE Digital Acquires ServiceMax to Extend Predix and Analytics Across Field Service Processes," News release (n.d.).; Steven E. Winoker and Yidong Xiang, *GE: Exit the Peacock (for a Fair Price) but What will Follow?*, New York: Bernstein Research, February 13, 2013; "The Big Get Bigger: Rexel Inc. to Acquire GE Supply," *Electrical Wholesaling*, July 14, 2006; Tom Bergin, "GE to Buy UK Oil Pipemaker Wellstream for $1.3 Billion," *Reuters*, December 13, 2010; Tomas Kellner, "GE Buys $500 Million Machine Analytics Firm," *GE Reports*, September 14, 2016; Tomas Kellner, "GE to Sell Its BioPharma Unit for $21.4 Billion to Danaher," *GE Reports*, February 25, 2019.

19. Thomas Gryta, Joann S. Lublin, and David Benoit, " 'Success Theater' Masked Rot at GE: Under Immelt, Disdain for Bad News Led to Overoptimistic Forecasts, Botched Strategies," *Wall Street Journal*, February 22, 2018.
20. General Electric, 2015–2016 Annual Reports.
21. For Jeff Immelt's own account of his years as CEO at GE, see Jeff Immelt, *Hot Seat: What I Learned Leading a Great American Company* (New York: Simon & Schuster, 2021).

CHAPTER 19

1. Comcast Corporation, Q3 2017 Earnings Conference Call, October 26, 2017, Accessed via FactSet: CallStreet, LLC, 3.
2. John C. Hodulik, Charlie Costanzo, Ryan Gravett, Batya Levi, and Christopher School, *UBS TV Ratings Guide: Insight into Ad Estimates*, New York: UBS Research, June 11, 2019, 6–7.
3. Statistics sourced from Gregory Williams, Colby Synesael, Jonathan Charbon, and Michael Elias, *Industry Update: Video and Broadband Study: The Satellite Implosion and OTT Tyranny of Choice*, Cowen Research, March 6, 2019, 4.
4. Comcast Corporation, "A Superior Cash Proposal for Sky" Presentation, February 17, 2018, 16; Comcast Corporation, "Comcast Corp. and Sky Plc Acquisition Proposal Call—UK," February 27, 2018, 2–3, accessed via FactSet.

CHAPTER 20

1. "Full Text: Nokia CEO Stephen Elop's 'Burning Platform' Memo," *Wall Street Journal*, February 9, 2011.
2. *Merriam-Webster Online*, s.v. "Strategic."

CHAPTER 21

1. Prashanth Rawla, "Epidemiology of Prostate Cancer," *World Journal of Oncology* 10, no. 2 (2019): 63–89.

2. Yaron Werber and Kennen MacKay, *Medivation, Inc. (MDVN): Alert: Xtandi Posts Solid Growth: MDVN- Strong Launch in Japan*, Citi Research, October 31, 2014; Anupam Rama and Eric Joseph, *Medivation: Questions on Xtandi Patient Growth Will Persist; Read-Through from Astellas Earnings—ALERT*, JP Morgan North American Equity Research, October 30, 2015; David M. Nierengarten, Dipil Joseph, and Robert Driscoll, *Medivation (MDVN): Xtandi Sales Come in Light, Lowering Top and Bottom Lines, Xtandi Still Has Attractive Franchise, Reducing PT to $47 and Maintaining OP*, Wedbush Securities Equities Research, January 29, 2016; Y. Katherine Xu, Joe Aronovsky, and Audrey Le, *Medivation, Inc.: Second-Quarter Earnings as Expected; Continue Pushing Xtandi Growth While Advancing Pipeline; Maintain Outperform*, William Blair & Co., August 10, 2016; David M. Nierengarten, Gregory R. Wade, and Christopher N. Marai, *Medivation (MDVN): Q4:12 Xtandi Sales Come in at $57M, Ahead of Expectations, Raising Price Target to $70, Reiterate Outperform*, Wedbush PacGrow Lifesciences, February 1, 2013; David M. Nierengarten, Gregory R. Wade, and Christopher N. Marai, *Medivation (MDVN): Q1:13 EPS, Xtandi Launch on Track and Beating Street, Reiterate Outperform*, Wedbush PacGrow Lifesciences, May 9, 2013; Ying Huang, Atsushi Seki, Catherine Hu, Dimiter V. Tassev, and Ryo Taguichi, *Medivation: Xtandi Posts $127mn in Q4 US Sales vs. Consensus of $121mn*, Barclays Equity Research, February 2, 2014; Navdeep Singh, Terence Flynn, Lisa Zhang, and Uya Chuluunbaatar, *Medivation, Inc. (MDVN): Xtandi on a Steady Trajectory but PREVAIL Remains Key Driver*, Goldman Sachs Equity Research, August 8, 2013; David M. Nierengarten, Gregory R. Wade, and Christopher N. Marai, *Medivation (MDVN): Raising Price Target to $62: Astellas Reports $14 Million in Xtandi Q3:12 Sales, Guides to $100M Through Q1:13, Ahead of Expectations, Reiterate Outperform*, Wedbush PacGrow Lifesciences, November 1, 2012; John Newman, *Medivation: Xtandi Beat in Q2 for US, EU and Japan, Positive Sign into Pre-Chemo Approval*, Canaccord Genuity, Inc., August 1, 2014; Geoffrey C. Porges, Raluca Pancratov, and Wes Shi, *MDVN: 1Q14 Showed Strong Post-Chemo Demand for Xtandi, Expense Discipline, and Ambition Beyond CRPC; MP, PT $82*, Bernstein Research, May 9, 2014; Eric Schmidt and Cristina Ghenoiu, *Medivation: Don't Hold Your Breath for an Inflection in Xtandi Sales*, Cowen and Company, May 8, 2015; Howard Liang, Richard Gross, and Gena Wang, *Medivation, Inc.: Strong 4Q a Good Start to Pre-Chemo Launch; Guidance Firm but Seems Beatable*, Leerink Partners, February 26, 2015; Matthew Roden, Jeffrey Hung, Bradley Canino, *Medivation: Despite Fears, 2Q Xtandi Beats Big, Increases Confidence*, New York: UBS Global Research, July 31, 2015; Y. Katherine Xu, Joe Aronovsky, and Audrey Le, *Medivation, Inc.: Third Quarter Preview: Xtandi Sales in Line; Continues as Market Leader*, William Blair & Co., October 30, 2015; David M. Nierengarten, Gregory R. Wade, and Christopher N. Marai, *Medivation (MDVN): Partner Astellas Reports Q3:13 US Xtandi Sales of ~$108M, Beating Consensus and Our Estimate, Reiterate Outperform*, Wedbush PacGrow Lifesciences, November 1, 2013; Eric Schmidt and Cristina Ghenoiu, *Medivation: Q1 Subpar; Medivation Argues Its Future Is Far Brighter*, Cowen and Company, May 5, 2016.
3. Ibid.
4. Medivation, *Schedule 14-D9, August 20, 2016.*

5. Mark Belsey, *Sanofi Looks to Acquire Medivation for $52.50/Share, We Estimate 8% EPS Accretion by '20E,* New York: UBS Global Research, April 28, 2016.
6. Medivation, *Schedule 14-D9, August 20, 2016.*
7. Medivation, *Schedule 14-D9, August 20, 2016.*
8. IQVIA, "Proportion of Branded Versus Generic Drug Prescriptions Dispensed in the United States from 2005 to 2019," Chart, August 7, 2020, accessed via Statista.

CHAPTER 22
1. Joseph C. Papa, Credit Suisse Health Care Conference Presentation, November 10, 2015, 5, accessed via FactSet: CallStreet, LLC.
2. Perrigo Company plc, "Perrigo Company plc Reports Record Third Quarter Highlighted by 10% Organic Net Sales Growth," News release, October 22, 2015; Perrigo Company plc, "Perrigo Company plc Reports Record Fourth Quarter & Calendar Year Net Sales and Adjusted Net Income," News release, February 18, 2016.
3. Perrigo Company plc, *Form 10-K May 22, 2017,* accessed via FactSet.

CHAPTER 23
1. Yum! Brands, 2012 Annual Report.
2. Yum China, "Yum! Brands Announces Intention to Separate into Two Publicly Traded Companies China Division to Become Independent Company Focused on Growth in Mainland China Yum! Brands to Become Global 'Pure Play' Franchisor with Three Iconic Brands," News release, October 20, 2015.
3. Pankaj N. Patel, Souheang Yao, Ryan Carlson, Abhra Banerji, and Joseph Handleman, *Quantitative Research: Do Spin-Offs Create or Destroy Value,* Credit Suisse Equity Research, September 6, 2012.

CHAPTER 24
1. Sourced via FactSet financial data and analytics.
2. General Electric, Q4 2018 Earnings Call, January 31, 2019, accessed via FactSet: CallStreet, LLC.

CHAPTER 25
1. Eastman Kodak, 2001–2005 Annual Reports.
2. Carl O'Donnell and Greg Roumeliotis, "Exclusive: Onex Explores Breaking up Carestream Health in Sale—Sources," *Reuters,* May 18, 2016.
3. Richard Waters, "Slimmed-Down Kodak Emerges from Bankruptcy," *Financial Times,* August 20, 2013.

CHAPTER 26

1. Christopher Kummer and Ulrich Steger, "Why Merger and Acquisition (M&A) Waves Reoccur: The Vicious Circle from Pressure to Failure," *Strategic Management Review* 2, no. 1 (January 2008): 44–63.

CHAPTER 28

1. For academic research related to share repurchase, see discussion of relevant papers cited in Chapter 8. For research related to acquisitions and capital spending, see discussion of relevant papers cited in Chapters 5 and 11, as well as Fuller, Netter, and Stegemoller's 2002 paper cited in Chapter 14.

INDEX

Page references followed by *f* or *t* refer to figures and tables, respectively.

Abarbanell, Jeffery S., 72–73
Abbott Laboratories, 342
"Abnormal Returns to a Fundamental
    Analysis Strategy" (Abarbanell
    and Bushee), 72–73
Accretive acquisitions, 169–170, 253,
    314
Acquired firms:
    information asymmetry for, 159–160
    overstating underlying value of, 160
Acquiring firms:
    benefits of acquisition for, 158–159
    returns in M&A transactions for, 189
Acquisitions:
    accretive, 169–170, 253, 314
    addressing secular risk with,
        380–383
    assumptions about, 395
    of Athabasca Oil Sands by Canadian
        Natural Resources, 225–227,
        227*f*
    by AutoZone, 151
    of BG Group by Royal Dutch Shell,
        230
    dilutive, 169
    of Entocort by Perrigo, 342–347
    EPS and share repurchase *vs.*, 128,
        129*t*
    of EUROIMMUN by PerkinElmer,
        212–215
    evaluating potential acquisitions,
        166–179

of First Data by Fiserv, 247–257
in 14-point strategic plan, 391
by General Electric, 271–272, 277–
    286, 279*t*, 289
Hail Mary, 380–383
imperfect information after, 10–11
justifying, 289
by Kodak, 372–376, 381
leverage in, 58*f*, 59
of life science tool businesses, 243,
    243*f*
of Life Technologies, 237–243
Marsh & McLennan's strategy for,
    211–212
of Medivation, 323–330, 327*t*–328*t*
of Nokia by Microsoft, 306–310, 379,
    380
of Novar PLC by Honeywell, 186,
    186*t*–187*t*
partnerships with employees during,
    403
of Pharmasset Inc. by Gilead
    Science, 25–27
of public *vs.* private companies,
    206–209
of Radio and Allied Industries
    by General Electric Co. Ltd,
    218–219
by Roper Technologies, 198–201,
    198*t*
saying "no" to, 396
share repurchases *vs.*, 131–133, 141

447

Acquisitions (*continued*)
  short-term challenges and long-term
    benefits in, 235–257
  of Sky Broadcasting by Comcast,
    299–304
  by Thermo Fisher Scientific, 235–
    243, 254–257
  for value creation, 199–201, 243–247
  of Videojet and Gilbarco by Danaher,
    220–222, 221*t*
  (See also Low-return, strategic
    acquisitions; Merger and
    acquisition [M&A] transactions)
Advertising, capital spending on, 67–70
Advice, from investment bankers,
    396–397
Agency costs, 86–87
"Agency Costs of Free Cash Flow,
    Corporate Finance, and
    Takeovers" (Jensen), 87
Airlines, futures contracts for, 99
Allergan, 342, 367
Alphabet, 86
Alstom, GE's acquisition of:
  divestitures after, 287
  as enabling transaction, 289–290
  as poor decision, 280–281
  restructuring after, 365
  write-off of, 272
Alton, Richard, 156
Altria, 380
Amazon:
  as competitor of Autozone, 151
  as contributors to secular risk, 378
  employee compensation at, 404
  R&D spending at, 82
  returning excess capital at, 86
Amazon Prime, 297
American Tower, 48
Amersham, 292
Ametek, 208
Android, 306–307, 310
Annual reviews, in 14-point strategic
    plan, 393
Apple:
  iPhone launch by, 306
  secular risk for, 379, 380, 384–385

shareholder-friendly capital
    allocation strategies of, 86
  smartphone operating system of, 310
Applied Biosystems, 238
Appreciation, capital, 85
Arbitrage, in private deals, 206
Asset size, in spin-offs, 357
Asset swaps:
  for big bio and big pharma, 336–337
  as complex transactions, 181–185
Assumptions:
  board mindset about, 395
  in M&A transactions, 170–172
  in non-core asset sales, 188
Astellas, 320
AstraZeneca, 343
Athabasca Oil Sands project, 233
  at Canadian Natural Resources, 225–
    227, 227*f*
  savings with, over Horizon project,
    226–228, 227f
AT&T, 297, 381
Audit Committee Leadership Network,
    131
Auto Anything, 152
Auto business, 42
Autonomy (business), 396
AutoZone:
  returns for shareholders at, 141
  value creation at, 147–153, 148*f*, 410
Axalta, 188–189

Bai (brand), 380
Baker Hughes, 280
Balance sheet:
  capital structure and, 30
  at First Data, 249
  at GE in Welch era, 261
  at Roper, 200–201
"Balance Sheet Growth and the
    Predictability of Stock Returns"
    (Chan et al.), 73
Baldwin, Tammy, 116
Ballmer, Steve, 306–307
Bankruptcy, of Kodak, 374–376
Banks, regular-special dividends for,
    111–112

Baseline projections, for M&A
    transactions, 170–172
Best Buy, 385
Beta, 35
Betz Dearborn, 282
BG Group, 230
Big biotech (*see* Biotechnology
    industry)
Big pharma (*see* Pharmaceutical
    industry)
Binswanger, Gustav, 217
Biogen, 337
BioMarin, 320
Biosimilars, 331–332
Biotechnology industry:
    challenges for, 332–335
    response to supply–demand
        imbalance, 336–338
Bisignano, Frank, 247, 248
Black swan events, 65
Bloomberg (company), 42
Boards of directors:
    capital allocation and composition
        of, 9–10
    restructuring strategy of, 368
    roles of, 9–10
    share repurchase decisions by,
        139–145
Boeing 737 engine, 266
Bonds:
    high-yield, 48, 49*t*, 50–52
    investment-grade, 49–50, 52, 251
    10-year, 88–90, 89*t*, 90*t*, 118, 119*f*
Brandicourt, Olivier, 323
Brexit, 303
Bristol-Myers, 26, 337
Broadband business, of Comcast, 295–
    296, 301
Brown & Brown, 210
Brownfield expansion, 79
Bruner, Robert, 155
Budget Control Act (2011), 238
Buffett, Warren, 131
"Burning Platform" (Elop), 305–306
Bushee, Brian J., 72–73
Business growth:
    capital allocations and, 5–8

with low-return, strategic
    acquisitions, 314
(See also Organic growth)
Business size:
    in low-return, strategic acquisitions,
        311
    M&A transactions *vs.* reducing, 336
Buyers, in non-core divestitures, 233

CAGR (compound annual growth
    rates), in United States, 5, 5*t*
Canadian Natural Resources:
    acquisition of Athabasca Oil Sands
        by, 225–227, 227*f*
    non-core divestitures by, 225–229,
        232
Capital allocation:
    addressing secular challenges with,
        385
    board of directors and, 9–10
    definition of, 3–4
    in 14-point strategic plan, 389–390
    framework selection for, 8–9
    growth for, 5–8
    with imperfect information, 10–11
    and restructuring, 364
    in slow growth economic conditions,
        13–18
    suboptimal, 409–411
    timing of, 118
    (See also *specific companies*)
Capital appreciation, 85
Capital expenditures, on special
    dividends, 106
"Capital Investments and Stock
    Returns" (Titman et al.), 72–73
Capital spending, 67–82
    evidence on, 72–76
    free cash flow and, 6
    Hershey's returns generated from,
        67–71
    priorities for, 78–80
    questions to ask about, 77–78
    R&D spending *vs.*, 80–82
    share repurchases and, 125–126
    views of share repurchase *vs.*,
        116–117

Capital structure:
  debt in, 65
  defined, 29
  interest rate and debt in, 6–7
Capital structure optimization, 29–52
  and debt ratings, 47–52
  with leverage, 47–52, 62–63
  in partnerships with employees, 406
  qualifications for using, 29–30
  with risk adjusted returns,
      correlations, and ROTS, 43–46
  by Thermo Fisher Scientific, 236
  with WACC, 31–43
CAPX signal, 72–73
Carefusion, 283
Carleton, Russell A., 24
Carve-outs, 188–189
Cash, returning, by big pharma and big
    biotech, 336
Cash burn rate, 30
Cash cow businesses, 336, 356–358
Cash flows:
  dividends based on volatility in, 92
  present value of future, 112
  in private deals, 206–207
Cash-on-cash:
  returns, 166–167
Cash-on-cash returns, 41*t*
  in M&A transactions, 166–167
  with non-core assets, 186
Cash payments, for distressed assets,
    222
Cash return on investment (CFROI),
    195–198, 195*t*, 197*f*
Casodex, 320
Casper, Marc, 235
  on acquisition of Life Technologies,
      240
  acquisition with short-term
      challenges/long term benefits by,
      243–244
  risk-adjusted returns during tenure
      of, 256
  value creation by, 255
CBOT (Chicago Board of Trade), 97
Celgene, 334
CFROI (*see* Cash return on investment)

Chan, Louis K.C., 73
Chicago Board of Trade (CBOT), 97
Chicago Butter and Egg Board, 97
Chicago Mercantile Exchange (CME):
  and definition of futures contract,
      98–100
  origin of, 97–98
  revenue growth at, 101, 102, 104*f*
  special dividend issue by, 89, 101–
      105, 103*t*, 108
  trading volumes of, 100–101
China:
  exporting of deflation by, 7
  smartphone manufacturing in, 310
  Yum! Brands' subsidiary in, 349–352
  Yum spin-off in, 352–355
Chou, De-Wai, 107
Christensen, Clayton M., 156
Christofferson, Scott, 156
Circuit City, 385
Clarient, 282
Clover (company), 248
CME (*see* Chicago Mercantile
      Exchange)
CME Group, 100, 101
CNBC, 266
Comcast, 300*t*, 301*t*
  bidding war with Disney, 298–299
  business model of, 295–298
  sale of NBC to, 284
  Sky Broadcasting acquisition for,
      299–304, 381
Commercial paper, debt in, 64
Company culture, 363–364
Company-owned operations, 350–351,
    350*t*
Compensation:
  employee, 133–134, 403–404
  executive, 134–137, 392, 398, 405
  stock-based, 134–137, 136*t*
Competitiveness, in spin-off decision,
    358
Complex transactions, 181–189
  about, 181–184
  asset swaps, 184–185
  carve-outs, 188–189
  with non-core assets, 185–188

Compound annual growth rates (CAGR), in United States, 5, 5*t*
Conglomerates (*see* Industrial conglomerates)
Consumer JV structure, of Novartis, 184
Consumer staples firms, futures contracts for, 99
Core business:
  in capital deployment decisions, 397–398
  low-return, strategic acquisitions and, 313, 316
  in M&A decisions, 339
Corporate costs, standard, 358–359
Correlated investments, capital structure and, 45
Cost-cutting strategy, restructuring as, 369
Cost synergies:
  in First Data acquisition, 250, 251
  in Life Technologies acquisition, 246
  in Medivation acquisition, 329
Countercyclical capital deployment:
  in M&A transactions, 158–159, 172–173
  by Thermo Fisher Scientific, 237
COVID-19 pandemic, stress test rules in, 63–65
Credit ratings, 47–52, 47*t*, 379
Credit spreads, 47*t*
Credit Suisse, 355
Creed, Greg, 352–353
Creo, 373
Crestor, 330
Culp, Larry, 222, 293
Customer-facing areas, impact of restructuring on, 369
CVS Health, 325, 333
Cyclical firms:
  long-term financial targets of, 289
  regular-special dividends for, 109–111
  share repurchase for, 139–141, 150

Damadaran, Aswath, 124
Danaher:
  Amersham acquisition by, 292
  portfolio transformation at, 202

value creation at, 410
Videojet acquisition by, 220–222, 221*t*
DCF (*see* Discounted cash flow)
DeAngelo, Harry, 105
DeAngelo, Linda, 105
Debt:
  in capital structure, 6–7, 65
  in COVID-19 pandemic, 64–65
  at First Data, 248
  incremental debt capacity, 17–18, 17*t*–18*t*
  non-core divestitures to reduce, 230–231, 231*f*
  sales of distressed assets to reduce, 223
  and secular risk, 385
  in spin-off decision, 357
Debt financing, for M&A transactions, 177–179
Decision-making:
  about capital deployment, 397–398
  about share repurchases, 139–145
  about spin-offs, 358
  in M&A transactions, 174–175, 339
  process over outcomes in, 23–24
Demand:
  in complex transactions, 189
  restructuring due to decline in, 364–365
  (See also Supply–demand imbalance)
Depreciation, 6
Differentiation of firm, R&D spending for, 81–82
Dilutive acquisitions, 169
Dilutive equity, 51
DirectTV, 381
Discounted cash flow (DCF):
  DCF analysis for Medivation, 326–329, 327*f*–328*f*, 327*t*
  and 14-point strategic plan, 390
  and terminal value calculation, 167
Discounts:
  illiquidity, 199
  sum-of-parts, 355, 358
Disney, 297–299
Disruptive companies, performance of, 86

Distressed assets, 217–223
  examples of, 217–222
  taking advantage of, 222–223
Diversification:
  in Comcast's acquisition of Sky
    Broadcasting, 303
  correlations of investments and, 45
  Hail Mary acquisitions for, 381
  Hershey's returns generated from, 68
  share repurchase *vs.*, 142–145
Divestitures:
  by General Electric, 271–272,
    284–286
  reducing secular risk with, 385–386
  by Roper, 201
Dividend payout ratio, market
  performance and, 85–86
Dividends (regular dividends), 86–96
  benefits of, 88–91
  calculating returns on, 93–95, 94*t*
  demand for, 118, 119*f,* 142, 152
  at Kodak, 376
  minimum token, 91
  in partnerships with employees, 407
  reducing, 95–96
  research on, 86–88
  setting, 91–93
  share repurchases *vs.,* 116–117, 122–
    123, 131–132, 140
  special dividends *vs.,* 106
  at Thermo Fisher Scientific, 236–237
  and value creation, 255
Dividend yield(s):
  and risk-adjusted return, 85
  10-year bond yields *vs.,* 88–90, 89*t,* 90*t*
Dot-com bubble, 117
Dow Jones Industrial Average, 267
Downturns:
  dividend cuts in, 96
  financial flexibility in, 54–55
  partnerships with employees in,
    405–406
  restructuring in, 364–365
Dr. Pepper, 380
DuPont, 188–189, 359
Duration, of investment-grade bonds,
  49–50

Earnings:
  free cash flow *vs.,* 392
  for GE, in Welch era, 260–261, 261*t*
  quarterly reporting of, 401–402
  and valuation of GE, 269
Earnings before interest, taxes,
  depreciation, and amortization
  (EBITDA), valuation based on,
  195–197, 196*t*
Earnings per share (EPS):
  impact of capital allocation on,
    18–19, 19*t*
  at Newell Brands, 361–363, 362*f*
  share repurchases and growth in,
    126–130, 134–137
  at Yum China, 352
Eastman, George, 374
Eastman Kodak:
  acquisitions by, 372–376, 381
  bankruptcy of, 374–376
  flywheel of value destruction at, 384
  graphic communications segment of,
    373, 375–376
  healthcare imaging segment,
    373–375
  special dividends at, 105
  strategic repositioning by, 371–374
EBITDA, valuation based on, 195–197,
  196*t*
Edwards (company), 282
Efficiency, restructuring to improve,
  366
Elan Pharmaceuticals, 341
Electric Apparatus Company Limited,
  217
Electric Appliance Company, 217
Electronification, of CME, 100–101
Eli Lilly, 182, 334
Elop, Stephen, 305–306
Employees:
  compensation for, 133–134, 403–404
  as partners, 402–407
End-market risk, 45
Energy companies, regular-special
  dividends for, 110–111, 111*t*
Entocort, 342–347
EPS (*see* Earnings per share)

Equity capital:
  economic cost of, 38t
  opportunity cost of, 40–41
  true cost of, 32–38, 36t
Eslick, David, 211
ESPN, 297
EUROIMMUN, 212–215
Europe, biosimilar regulation in, 332
Event spread risk, 48t
Excel, Microsoft, 312
Excess capital, 83–88
  about, 83–86
  at declining firms, 376
  employee compensation and, 133
  research on, 86–88
  returns on, 19–23, 19t–20t, 21f–22f,
    273t
Exchange, Microsoft, 312
Execution risk, 44
Executive compensation:
  in 14-point strategic plan, 392, 398
  and partnerships with employees,
    405
  and share repurchases, 134–137

Facebook, 405
Failure rate, for M&A transactions, 156
Fallen angels, 50
Farmers, futures contracts for, 99
FCF (*see* Free cash flow)
Federal Reserve, 112, 125
FEI Company, 237
Financial covenants, 51–52
Financial flexibility, in downturns,
    54–55
Financing, for M&A transactions,
    177–179
Firm differentiation, R&D spending
    for, 81–82
First Data:
  Fiserv's acquisition of, 247–255
  organic growth rates for, 251t–253t
  risk-adjusted returns for, 256
Fiserv:
  First Data acquisition by, 247–255
  lessons about acquisitions from,
    254–257

organic growth rates for, 251t
share repurchases at, 153, 153t
value creation at, 410
Flexibility:
  financial, in downturns, 54–55
  of regular-special dividends, 109
Food companies, secular risk for, 379
FORE Systems, 219–220
Fortive, 359
14-point strategic plan, 389–398
  annual reviews in, 393
  challenging assumptions in, 395
  checklist for, 413
  comparing returns in, 389–390
  core business independence in,
    397–398
  identifying acquisition targets in, 391
  and investment bankers' advice,
    396–397
  long-term plan development in, 393
  management incentives in, 392
  mindset, 395–398
  monitoring returns in, 391
  and patience, 397
  prioritizing shareholders in, 398
  ROIC focus in, 390
  and saying "no" to transactions, 396
  stakeholder engagement in, 393–395
  strategic actions, 389–395
Fox, 298–299
Foxconn, 310
Fracassi, Cesare, 92
Franchise model of operations, 350–
    351, 350f, 354
Free cash flow (FCF):
  adjustments to, 267–277
  and cash return on investment, 197f
  definition of, 6
  and dividends, 91
  earnings *vs.*, 392
  at First Data, 249
  at General Electric, 262, 262f, 267–
    277, 274f
  importance of, 19, 19t
  at industrial conglomerates, 192
  and interest rates, 60–61
  at Kodak, 371–372, 372t, 374

Free cash flow (FCF) (*continued*)
leverage and growth of, 57*f*–58*f,* 59*t,* 60
in low-return, strategic acquisitions, 311
at Newell Brands, 362*f*
with non-core divestitures, 230–231, 231*f*
at "Peaker" firms, 119–120
and restructuring, 362*f,* 363
at Royal Dutch Shell, 231f
and weighted average cost of capital, 32–38
at YUM China spin-off, 353
Free cash flow (FCF) conversion rate, returns on, 19–23, 19*t*–20*t,* 21*f*–22*f*
Friel, Robert, 214
Friendly takeovers, 173–175 (*See also* Shareholder engagement)
Fu, Fangjian, 121
Fuller, Kathleen, 205–206
Futures contracts, 98–100

GE (*see* General Electric Corporation)
GE Aviation, 266, 287
GE Biopharma, 292
GE Capital, 259
intracompany contributions to/from, 275, 276, 277*f,* 291–292
involvement of, in decline of GE, 269–271, 289–291
in Welch era, 265
GEC (General Electric Co. Ltd), 217–220
Geek Squad, 385
GE Gas Power, 365
GE Healthcare, 266, 282–283
GE Industrial:
balance sheet for, 261
free cash flow for, 262, 262*t,* 272–277, 274*f*
market capitalization for, 286–288
portfolio transformation for, 263, 264*t*
returns on equity for, 263
General Electric Co. Ltd (GEC), 217–220

General Electric Corporation (GE), 259–293
in 2018, 267–268
capital allocation at, 192, 271–288, 288*t*
as executive training ground, 192
expectations for, in 2000, 266–269
fall of, 269–271
free cash flow of, 267–268
in Great Financial Crisis, 25
imperfect information in acquisitions by, 11
lessons from the fall of, 289–292
operational execution at, 286–288
rise of, 260–265
suboptimal capital allocation at, 410–411
Welch era of, 259–266
(*See also entries beginning* GE)
General Electric Credit Corporation, 259
Generic pharmaceutical industry, 338, 345–346
Geographic risk, 44
GE Oil and Gas, 280, 281*f,* 290
"The GE Paradox" (Lehmberg et al.), 264–265
GE Power, 270–271, 275, 280
GE Water, 282, 283*f*
Gilbarco, 220–222, 221*t*
Gilead Science, 25–28
Glaser, Dan, 210–212
Glassdoor, 405
GlaxoSmithKline:
asset swaps of, 181–184
supply–demand imbalances at, 334
Globex system, 97
Google:
R&D spending by, 82
returning excess capital at, 86
smartphone operating systems of, 306, 310
work environment at, 405
Gropper, Allan, 374
Graphic communications segment, at Kodak, 373, 375–376

Great Financial Crisis:
   capital spending/share repurchases
      in, 125–126
   as default stress test, 54, 63–64
   GE Capital in, 270, 276, 291–292
   and Kodak's bankruptcy, 374
   media on outcomes in, 24–25
   quarterly earnings reports in, 402
   regulations after, 30
Greenfield expansion, 79
Growth businesses:
   for big bio and big pharma, 336
   GE's acquisitions of, 282–283
   Hail Mary acquisitions of, 380–383,
      382*t*
   spinning off, 356, 386
Growth stocks, 86, 121
Gruber, Joseph, 125

Hail Mary acquisitions, 380–383
Harrison, Michael, 220
Head-count reductions, 176
Healthcare imaging segment, at Kodak,
      373–375
Hermance, Frank, 208
Hershey Company:
   capital spending at, 67–71, 69*f*–70*f*
   flywheel for value creation at, 71
   Mondelez's proposed acquisition of,
      314–315
   playbook of, 78–79
   restructuring at, 368
   supply chain initiative at, 71
Heseltine, Michael, 219
Hewlett-Packard, 396
High-yield bonds, 48, 49*t*, 50–52
Hilb Rogal & Hobbs Company, 210
Hindsight bias, 25–26
Hirst, Hugo, 217
HMD, 310
Home Depot, 24–25
Honeywell, 185–188
   acquisition of Novar PLC by, 186,
      186*t*–187*t*
   GE's attempted acquisition of, 267,
      269
Horizon, 226–228, 233

Hostile takeovers:
   as catalysts for restructuring,
      366–367
   distressed assets in, 223
   friendly *vs.*, 173–175
   setting targets in, 348
   and supply–demand imbalances,
      323–330, 334–335, 335*t*
Huang, Sheng, 121
Hung, David, 323
Hurn, Roger, 220

IBM, 380
IBS (Intelligent Building Systems), 186
Illiquidity discount, 199
Illumina, 241
Immelt, Jeff, 266, 273, 277, 282, 290
Imperfect information, 10–11
"The Implications of Capital
      Investments for Future
      Profitability and Stock Returns:
      An Overinvestment Perspective"
      (Li), 73
Incentives:
   in 14-point strategic plan, 392
   with long-term focus, 401
Income statement:
   R&D spending on, 81
   share repurchases and, 126–127
Incremental debt capacity, 17–18,
      17*t*–18*t*
Industrial conglomerates:
   corporate costs of, 359
   free cash flow for, 262
   value creation by, 191–192, 202–203
   (See also *specific companies*)
Industry:
   low-return, strategic acquisitions due
      to economics of, 316–317
   share repurchase trends in, 140
Inferior businesses with higher
      valuations, 295–304 (*See also*
      Value destruction)
Ingersoll-Rand, 192, 193
Inhibitex, 26
Initial public offering (IPO), of First
      Data, 248

Intelligent Building Systems (IBS), 186
Interest rates:
 and debt, 7–8
 and FCF, 60–61
Interlogix, 282
Intermediate-term returns, long-term
 focus and, 401
Internal investments in firm:
 at AutoZone, 152–153
 capital spending for, 72–73
 and EPS, 127, 128t
 at Life Technologies, 240–241
 prioritizing, 87–88
 return of excess capital vs., 83–84
 share purchases vs., 131
Internal rate of return (IRR), 167, 390
Investment banks and bankers:
 advice from, 396–397
 promotion of M&A transactions by,
  156
Investment-grade bonds, 49–50, 52,
 251
Investments:
 capital spending on, 73, 76
 as catalyst for restructuring, 367–368
 in non-core divestitures, 233
Investors:
 capital allocation success for, 2
 yield-oriented, 88–90, 108, 109
Invitrogen, 238
Ionics, 282
iPhone, 306
IPO (initial public offering), of First
 Data, 248
Ireland, Sky Broadcasting in, 301
IRR (internal rate of return), 167, 390
Ishrak, Omar, 282, 283

Jarden, 363
Jellison, Brian, 192–195, 200–204
Jensen, Michael, 87–88
Jenter, Dirk, 175
Job satisfaction, employee, 405
Johnson & Johnson, 320, 359
JP Morgan, 323
Juno Therapeutics, 334
JUUL brand, 380

Kahneman, Daniel, 170–171
Kamin, Steven, 125
Karceski, Jason, 73
KFC, 349, 351–352
Kit Kat, 315
KKR (equity firm), 247–251, 256
Knowledge risk, 44–45
Kodak (see Eastman Kodak)
Kodak Polychrome, 373
Koi-Akrofi, Godfred Yaw, 156
Korn Ferry, 48
Kratz, E. F., 265
Kroger, 207
Kummer, Christopher, 396–397

Lakonishok, Josef, 73
Lazonick, William, 115
Lean manufacturing, 6–7
Lehmberg, Derek, 264
Lenny, Richard, 67–68
Leverage, 47t
 in capital structure optimization,
  62–63
 capital structure optimization with,
  47–52
 dividend cuts due to, 95–96
 and returns, 54
 in stress tests, 55–63
 in Yum China spin-off, 353
Lewellen, Katharina, 175
Li, Donglin, 73
Liberty Global, 301
Life science and diagnostics sector,
 acquisitions in, 214, 243, 243f
Life Technologies, acquisition of:
 acquisition of First Data vs., 255
 discounted stock price prior to, 238,
  239f
 financial projections for, 244t–245t
 short-term challenges and long term
  benefits of, 237–247
Lines of credit, 64
Lipitor, 330
Liu, Yi, 107
London School of Economics, 218
Long-term focus, 399–407
 and employees as partners, 402–407

importance of, 400–401
and reporting quarterly earnings,
    401–402
Long-term strategic plans, 393
Low-growth assets, spinning off,
    356–357
Low-return, strategic acquisitions,
    305–317
    and collapse of Nokia, 305–310
    factors to consider in, 316–317
    of Nokia, by Microsoft, 306–310, 312
    problems with, 311–315
Lowrey, Annie, 115
Loxo Oncology, 334
Lucky, 372

Maintenance capital spending, 79–80
Maintenance covenants, 64
Management consultancies, M&A
    promotion by, 156
Management teams:
    of GE, in Welch era, 264–265
    restructuring to change, 366
    returns on time spent by, 46
    share repurchases and, 139–145
    of spin-off, 358
Manufacturers, futures contracts for,
    100
Maration Oil, 225
Marconi PLC, 219–220, 230
Market capitalization, in low-return,
    strategic acquisitions, 311
Market presence, 314–315
Market prices, 160–164, 161t–163t
Market share, for First Data, 248–249
Market value, of GE, 275–276, 276f,
    286–288
MarketWatch, 307
Marsh Brokerage, 209–212
Marsh & McLennan Agency, 209–212
Marsh & McLennan (MMC), 209–212,
    410
M&A transactions (see Merger and
    acquisition transactions)
Mature firms:
    excess capital returned by, 84
    share repurchases for, 141, 151

McGrath, Rita, 116
McKinsey & Company, 84, 206
McNish, Robert, 156
Media, on capital allocations, 1
Medivation:
    acquisition of, 323–330
    supply–demand imbalance at,
        319–323
Merck, 336
Merger and acquisition (M&A)
        transactions, 155–180
    about, 156–157
    challenges with, 157–166
    evaluating potential, 166–179
    investment bankers' advice on,
        396–397
    involving oncology assets, 333–336
    mindset for, 347
    patience in, 397
    (See also Acquisitions)
Microsoft:
    acquisition of Nokia by, 306–310
    capital spending of, 82
    returning excess capital at, 86
    secular risk for, 379, 380, 384–385
Microsoft Bing, 307–308
Millipore, 236
Minimum token dividend, 91
MMC (Marsh & McLennan), 209–212,
    410
Mobile operating systems, 307–308
Mondelez, 314–315
Murdoch, Rupert, 298
Mylan:
    attempted hostile takeover by,
        341–343
    Pfizer's spin-off of, 336

National Institutes of Health (NIH),
    238, 240, 241, 242f
NBC Universal, 266, 284–285, 304
Near-term visibility, in M&A
    transactions, 173
Negotiations, in complex transactions,
    189
Netflix, 297, 378
Netter, Jeffrey, 205–206

Net working capital, 149
Newell Brands, 361–364
New store growth, for YUM China, 354
NextPress, 373
NIH (*see* National Institutes of Health)
"No," being willing to say, 174–175, 236, 396
Nokia:
    collapse of, 305–310
    Microsoft's acquisition of, 306–310, 379, 380
Non-branded pharmaceutical businesses (*see* Generic pharmaceutical industry)
Non-core assets, 185–188
Non-core divestitures, 225–234
    by Canadian Natural Resources, 225–229, 232
    due to supply–demand imbalances, 337
    by Royal Dutch Shell, 229–232
    value creation with, 232–234
Norris, Floyd, 24–25
Novar PLC, 185–188, 186*t*–187*t*
Novartis, 181–184
Nuttall, Scott, 249–250

Oil and gas industry:
    futures contracts for, 99
    traditional drilling in, 228
Omega, 344
Oncology franchise, of Novartis, 183
O'Neill, Sean, 220
One Lambda, 235
Operational execution, at General Electric, 286–288
Opportunity costs, of equity capital, 40–41
Optimization:
    in private deals, 207–208
    restructuring for, 365
    (See also Capital structure optimization)
Organic growth:
    for acquisition-driven companies, 200

at First Data, 249, 251–252, 251*t*–253*t*
    generating returns without, 257
    at Life Technologies, 244–247, 244*t*–246*t*
Osmonics, 282

Pall, 236
Papa, Joseph, 343–344
Parisi, James, 102
Partnerships, with employees, 402–407
Patents, 241
Patheon, 237
Patience, 397
PBMs (pharmacy benefit managers), 331
Peaker firms, share repurchase for, 119–120
Pension plans, 268, 387
PepsiCo, 349
PerkinElmer, 212–215
Perrigo:
    returns on capital for, 344–345, 345*f*
    short-term plug deals by, 341–348
"The Persistence of Long-Run Abnormal Returns Following Stock Repurchases and Offerings" (Fu and Huang), 121
Petrotech, 201
Pfizer:
    Allergan attempted acquisition by, 342
    Medivation acquisition by, 323–326, 326*f*
    Mylan spin-off for, 336
    non-core divestitures by, 337
    revenue streams of, 338
    supply–demand imbalances at, 329–330
Pharmaceutical industry:
    challenges for, 332–335
    generic, 338, 345–346
    supply–demand imbalance of, 330–338
Pharmacy benefit managers (PBMs), 331
Pharmasset Inc., 25–28

Philips, John R., 264
Pidilizumab, 320
Pizza Hut, 349, 353
Portfolio managers, futures contracts for, 99
PowerPoint, Microsoft, 312
Practice Works, 373
Present value of future cash flows, 112
Pricing power, in pharmaceutical industry, 332–333
Private deals, 205–215
    arbitrage in, 199, 235
    at Marsh & McLennan Agency, 209–212
    PerkinElmer's acquisition of Euroimmun as, 212–215
    public *vs.*, 205–207
    returns from public acquisitions *vs.*, 205–209
Private equity firms:
    high-yield bonds for, 50–51
    interest of, in Life Technologies, 238–239
Productivity, capital spending and, 75–76
Profitability:
    capital spending and, 73
    of generic drugs, 346
Profit mix, in Welch era, at GE, 263, 264*t*
Public companies:
    performance of acquisitions by, 10–11
    returns from acquisitions of private companies *vs.*, 205–209
Purchasing behaviors, low-return, strategic acquisitions due to, 316

Qiagen, 236
Quarterly earnings reports, 401–402

Radio and Allied Industries, 218–219
R&D spending (*see* Research and development spending)
Redfern, David, 181
Red Hat, 380
Regular dividends (*see* Dividends)

Regular-special dividends:
    about, 108–109
    firms benefiting from, 109–113
    reducing secular risk with, 386–387
Regulated financial companies, 30
Regulated utility companies, 30
Reinvestment, after acquisition, 250–251
Reltec, 219
Repeatable processes, in slow growth conditions, 27–28
Republic Services, 208
Research and development (R&D) spending:
    capital spending *vs.*, 80–82
    in pharmaceutical industry, 330–331
    share repurchases and, 125–126
Restructuring, 361–369
    best practices for, 368–369
    and capital allocation, 364
    catalysts for, 366–368
    circumstances for, 364–366
    at Newell Brands, 361–364, 362*f*
    and partnerships with employees, 403
    at Perrigo, 342
Retrospective analyses, with imperfect information, 11
Return on invested capital (ROIC):
    in Fiserv acquisition of First Data, 253, 254*t*
    in 14-point strategic plan, 390
    for long-term focus, 400
Return on time spent (ROTS), 46
Returns:
    capital allocation to maximize, 4, 41*t*, 389–391
    on capital spending, 67–71, 69*f*–70*f*, 80
    in carve-out transactions, 189
    cash-on-cash, 41*t*, 166–167
    on dividends, calculating, 93–95, 94*t*
    impact of economic growth on, 14–18, 14*t*–16*t*
    leverage and, 54, 58*f*, 59
    with long-term focus, 401

Returns (*continued*)
  in low-return, strategic acquisitions,
    313–314
  in M&A transactions, 168–170, 168t,
    176–177
  from private *vs.* public deals,
    206–209
  research on, 155
  from restructuring, 363
  and risk, 39
  risk-adjusted, 44–45, 184, 256–257
  in short-term plug deals, 347
  in slow growth economic conditions,
    18–23
  on special dividends, 130, 130t
  willingness to accept low, 4
Returns-focused management, 347,
    367–368
Returns on equity, for GE, in Welch
    era, 263
Returns on excess capital:
  and FCF conversion rate, 19–23,
    19t–20t, 21f–22f
  for General Electric, 272, 273t
Revenue:
  restructuring and drivers of, 369
  supply–demand imbalances and
    focusing on, 338
Revenue growth, at CME, 101, 102,
    104f
Revenue synergies:
  evaluating, 166
  in low-return, strategic acquisitions,
    313
  in M&A transactions, 164–166
  for Thermo Fisher Scientific, 237,
    242
Reverse Morris transactions, 357–358
Revolving lines of credit, 51, 64
Rising, Curtis, 156
Risk:
  dividends and, 91
  end-market, 45
  event spread, 48t
  execution, 44
  geographic, 44
  knowledge, 44–45

  and returns, 39
  secular, 377–387
  with share repurchases, 122–137
Risk-adjusted returns:
  capital allocation based on, 256–257
  capital structure optimization for,
    44–45
  and dividend yield, 85
  for share repurchases, 140
Risk-weighted breakup fee, 168–169,
    169t
Roberts, Brian L., 295, 296, 302, 303
ROIC (*see* Return on invested capital)
Roper Technologies, 410
  capital allocation at, 192
  cash return on investment for,
    195–198
  portfolio transformation at, 192–194,
    194t
  value creation at, 192–202, 203t
ROTS (return on time spent), 46
Rover and Lucas, 219
Rowe, W. Glenn, 264
Royal Dutch Shell:
  acquisition of BG Group by, 230
  distressed assets of, 230, 231f, 234
  non-core divestitures by, 229–232
Royalty income, 241

SaaS (software-as-a-service), 378
Sabbagh, Dan, 220
Sales force, in spin-offs, 358
Sanofi, 323–324
Scale, asset swaps to generate, 184–185
Scitex Digital Printing, 373
SEC (Securities and Exchange
    Commission), 290–291, 401–402
Secular challenges, 371–387
  accepting, 384–385
  acquisitions with, 256
  and Kodak's bankruptcy, 375–376
  and Kodak's strategic repositioning,
    371–375
  regular-special dividends for firms
    facing, 112–113
  share repurchases for firms facing,
    120, 139, 141, 151

Secular risk:
  about, 377–380
  facing, 380–387
Securities and Exchange Commission
    (SEC), 290–291, 401–402
Sellers, in non-core divestitures,
    233–234
Shale oil, 378
Shareholder engagement:
  in 14-point strategic plan, 393–395
  for long-term focus, 400–401
Shareholder needs:
  prioritizing, 398
  setting dividends based on, 92
  share repurchases and, 140
Share repurchases:
  academic research on, 120–121
  addressing secular risk with, 383–
    384, 383*f*
  alternatives to, 131–133
  at AutoZone, 147–153
  concerns with, 117–122
  conflicts in, 115–138
  controversy over, 72, 115–117
  factors in decision-making about,
    137–142
  at General Electric, 287, 287*f*
  at Kodak, 375
  management teams, boards and,
    139–145
  and partnerships with employees,
    403
  preventing takeovers with, 342
  prioritization of, 87–88
  restaurant case example, 142–145
  risks associated with, 122–137
  special dividends *vs.,* 106
  at Thermo Fisher Scientific, 236
  value creation with, 148–153
Short-term plug deals, 341–348
  Entocort's acquisition in, 343–347
  lessons from, 347–348
  and mindset for M&A, 347
  Perrigo's use of, 341–348
Sias, Diane, 156
Simpson, George, 219–220
Skinner, Douglas J., 105

Sky Broadcasting, Comcast's
  acquisition of, 381
  costs of, 299–304
  Disney and Comcast's bids prior to,
    299*f*
  value destruction in, 300*t,* 301*t*
Slow growth economic conditions,
    13–28
  Gilead's acquisition of Pharmasset
    in, 25–28
  importance of capital allocation in,
    13–18
  process over outcomes in, 23–25
  returns in, 18–23
  sustainable, repeatable processes in,
    27–28
Software-as-a-service (SaaS), 378
Sougiannis, Theodore, 73
S&P 500 companies:
  executive compensation at, 134
  secular risk for, 377–379
S&P 500 Index:
  return on divided as FCF yield of,
    93–94, 94*t*
  yields on 10-year bonds *vs.,* 118, 119*f*
S&P 1500 companies, share
    repurchases by, 117
Special dividends:
  calculating returns on, 94–95, 94*t*
  from CME, 89, 101–105, 103*t,* 108
  EPS and, 129–130, 130*t*
  history of, 105–108
  views of share repurchase *vs.,* 116–117
Spending:
  capital (*see* Capital spending)
  of capital from share repurchases,
    124
  research and development, 80–82,
    125–126, 330–331
Spin-offs, 349–360
  considerations with, 355–359
  non-core divestitures *vs.,* 233
  reducing secular risk with, 386
  as response to supply–demand
    imbalances, 336, 338
  split-offs *vs.,* 360
  of Yum! Brands, 349–355

Split-offs:
  as response to supply–demand
    imbalances, 337–338
  spin-offs *vs.*, 360
  for value creation, 339
S&P Packaged Foods Index, 67, 68, 70
Spreads, credit, 47*t*
Stegemoller, Mike, 205–206
Steger, Ulrich, 396–397
Stevenson, Mark, 240
Stock-based compensation, 134–137,
  136*t*
Stöcker, Winifred, 214–215
Stock price:
  as catalyst for restructuring, 366
  as consideration in spin-offs, 355
Stock prices:
  undervalued, 141, 151–152
Stock repurchase (*see* Share
  repurchase)
Stranded corporate costs, 358–359
Strategic acquisitions:
  characteristics of, 311–312
  definition of, 311
  low-return, 305–317
Strategic repositioning, by Kodak,
  371–374
Stress test rules, 53–65
  about, 53–55
  in COVID-19 pandemic, 63–65
  leverage and, 55–63
Suez Environmental, 282
Sum-of-parts discounts, 355, 358
Sunquest, 200
Superior businesses at lower valuations,
  201–204 (*See also* Value creation)
Supply, in complex transactions, 189
Supply chain optimization, 365
Supply–demand imbalance:
  in biotechnology industry, 336–338
  lessons on, 339
  at Medivation, 319–330, 327*t*–328*t*
  in pharmaceutical industry, 330–338
  and private deals, 207
  Roper's acquisitions due to, 199–200
  in value-accretive M&As, 314

Sustainable dividends, 91–92
Sustainable processes, in slow growth
  conditions, 27–28
Symbian (operating system), 307
Synergies:
  in carve-out transactions, 189
  in complex transactions, 184–185
  cost, 246, 250, 251, 329
  definition of, 160
  in Fiserv acquisition of First Data,
    252
  minimizing disruptive impact of, 176
  premiums in M&A transactions for,
    160–164, 161*t*–163*t*
  revenue, 164–166, 237, 242, 313
Synergy-driven acquisitions, 403

T. Rowe Price, 377
T. Rowe Price Capital Appreciation
  Fund, 203
Taco Bell, 349
Talazoparib, 320
Talent cultivation, at GE, in Welch era,
  264–265
Tangential businesses, expansion into,
  373, 375–376
Taxation, as consideration in spin-offs,
  357
Teleflex, 202
10-year bonds:
  yields on dividend *vs.*, 88–90, 89*t*,
    90*t*
  yields on S&P 500 *vs.*, 118, 119*f*
Terminal value, 167
Tesaro, 334
Tesla, 42
Teva Pharmaceuticals, 342
Texas Instruments, 153, 153*t*, 410
Thermo Fisher Scientific, acquisitions
  by, 235–247
  benefits of, 243–247
  during Casper's tenure, 235–237
  financial projections for, 244*t*–245*t*
  lessons learned from, 254–257
  target conditions prior to, 237–242
  value creation with, 410

Thinking, Fast and Slow (Kahneman), 170–171
Thrive, allowing employees to, 407
Time Warner, 297, 381
Timing:
  of capital spending, 74–75
  of M&A transactions, 157–158
  of non-core divestitures, 232
  of share repurchases, 117–118
Titman, Sheridan, 72–73
Trading volumes, CME, 100–101
Trane, 193
Trian Partners, 188
Tylenol, 338

Uber, 307
Undervalued stock prices:
  at AutoZone, 151–152
  share repurchases for firms with, 141
United Kingdom, Sky Broadcasting in, 301
United States:
  compound annual growth rates in, 5, 5*t*
  R&D spending in, 125
United Technologies, 284

Vaccine business, GSK, 183
Valeant Pharmaceuticals, 341, 344, 367
Valuation:
  for General Electric, 269
  of growth assets, 282–283
  in non-core divestitures, 232–233
  in private deals, 206
  returning excess capital and, 83
Value businesses, 386
Value creation, 191–204
  in asset swaps, 184
  by industrial conglomerates, 191–192
  and long-term focus, 401
  in M&A transactions, 156, 199–201, 243–247
  methods, 201–202
  in non-core divestitures, 232–234
  at Roper Technologies, 192–201, 203*t*

  with share repurchases, 148–153
  in short-term plug deals, 347–348
  with special dividends, 107–108
  in spin-offs, 354
  with superior businesses at lower valuations, 201–204
  supply–demand imbalances and, 339
Value destruction:
  in bidding war with Disney, 298–299
  at Comcast, 295–304
  at General Electric, 284–287, 285*f*, 286*f*
  with growth asset acquisition, 381–383, 382*t*
  by inferior businesses with higher valuations, 295–304
  at Kodak, 384
  in Sky Broadcasting acquisition, 299–304
  and stress test rules, 53
Value stocks, 121
Vander Ark, Jon, 208
Vetco, 280
Videojet, 220–222, 221*t*
Video subscription business, Comcast, 296–298
Vital Signs, 282, 283
Volatility:
  cash flow, 92
  dividends for reduction of, 90
  of investment-grade bonds, 49

WACC (*see* Weighted average cost of capital)
Waggoner, John, 24–25
Waldeck, Andrew, 156
Warren, Elizabeth, 116
Weather Channel, 307
Wei, K.C John, 72–73
Weighted average cost of capital (WACC):
  calculation of, 31
  capital structure optimization with, 31–43
  and cost of equity capital, 32–38
  and demand for higher returns, 39

Weighted average cost of capital
(WACC) (*continued*)
importance of optimizing, 31–32
and opportunity cost of capital,
40–41
at Tesla, 42
Weinstock, Arnold, 218–219
Welch, Jack, 259–267
West, Dale, 71
White, Roderick E., 264
"Why Merger and Acquisition (M&A)
Waves Reoccur" (Kummer and
Steger), 396–397
Willis Group, 210
Word, Microsoft, 312
World Journal of Oncology, 319

Xie, Feixue, 72–73
Xtandi:
CVS Health's exclusion of, 325, 333

and Medivation's stock price, 319–
321, 322*f*
sales of, 321, 322*f,* 324–327
Zytiga *vs.,* 321

Yabuki, Jeff, 250, 254–256
Yield-oriented investors, 88–90, 108,
109
YouTube, 297
Yum! Brands:
Chinese subsidiary of, 349–351
performance of Yum China *vs.,* 353–
354, 354*t*
Yum China spin-off from, 352–355
Yum China, 352–355, 354*t*

Zantout, Zaher, 107
Zenon Membrane Systems, 282
Zoetis, 338
Zytiga, 320, 321

ABOUT THE AUTHOR

David Giroux is Chief Investment Officer for Equities and Multi-Asset at T. Rowe Price. He also serves as Head of Investment Strategy and Portfolio Manager for the Capital Appreciation Fund, which has been ranked in the top one percentile in both Morningstar and Lipper peer rankings. A Chartered Financial Analyst, Giroux is a two-time winner and five-time nominee for Morningstar Manager of the Year, and a 15-time winner of Lipper's Best Fund in Category award. In 2005, he was named Best of the Buy Side Capital Goods/Industrials winner by *Institutional Investor.*